About the Author

Rebecca Parker was born in Grenada, England in 1980. After judiciously burying a chain of perplexing life events experienced during childhood, Parker befell ill-fated focus to devastating emotional insurgences, intercepting her early adult life with unforgiving fetid foray. Startlingly redolent of past traumatic affairs – appositely long forgotten – each harrowing, iniquitous revival was to leave this formerly-flourishing mind foully suffused in disgust, bewilderment, humiliation and shame.

Aghast at such irrepressible spells, Parker develops torrid abhorrence towards her own being as *how weak and selfish are you to even dare acknowledge these encumbrances! With such over-exaggerated woe! Over a source so minuscule and infinitesimal too! Pull yourself together!* Parker's beginning book, **Secrets Out**, originally outpoured in sheer desperation in cathartic aim, stands as disclosure of over twenty years obscurely-maintained, previously secreted double life antics for the very first time; ever.

Overwhelmed in terrifying waves of repulsion, uncertainty and self-blame, Parker's future – insentiently resolute in newly-vowed quest to *be the most perfect person (relative / friend / colleague / professional / musician / provider / carer etc.) surpassing each and every other by tirelessly striving to achieve the utmost sought-after life all-round by making proud, surprising, and amazing all others, by ensuring the continued happiness of all Beloveds in stopping at your own worthless expense in no way what-so-ever, and by appearing as the most perfect, sorted, happy individual...* – catastrophically plummets; sole determination set unwittingly at self-destruct, under inherent duties dictated by her now sole-entrusted, perpetuating shadow *Angel*.

Stubborn, suspicious of every desperate plea frantically urging her to confront this so-called "critically life-threatening Mental Illness: Anorexia", and in full preserve of denial, Parker defiantly resists all *utterly absurd; simply ridiculous* impositions of professional "support" offered to her from specialist hospital inpatient wards, mental health institutions and secure units along the way. Instead, naively overcome by the strength of her now supremely-practiced acute and manipulative "illness", the poised and controlled voice of the once chaste child Micci (Rebecca Parker) sinks into timidity.

3

Angel Just-Rights

Quashed by encroached and angry shadow *Angel*, every desperate scream is muffled and, yearning simply for a caring and protective human shield yet unable to voice any request of it, Parker remains trapped, fully entrenched in the winds of *Angel: eternally guiding, trusted, loyal and safe shadow.*

While the innocent cries of Micci are left simply to burn, scorching inside of her aching and throbbing heart, the family, desperate to rectify "this abhorrent and alien behaviour seemingly to have come out of nowhere", are left equally powerless; devastation persisting, day by month by year. Hence, the publication of Parker's intriguing second book: **Who Am I?** allows this new author to expose an astonishing plethora of tortures she was compelled to act out *and only ever to the excellence expected of Angel's orders, furthermore and most certainly always; always, without fail!* Yet, every instruction dutifully followed, in reality, purely intent on destroying not only Rebecca, but every last soul in this once-ordinary, happy and proud-living family of five.

Parker's exceptional ability to write vividly is distinguished in content of her third and final book in this series: **The Bigger Picture.** Here, she bravely decides to share with the now learned reader, secret struggles endured to the extent of exposing her most gruelling, deepest innermost troublesome thoughts. Innovatively-portrayed, this is a searingly honest closing account, startlingly echoing the more up-to-date steps in Parker's remarkable quest.

In sharing this unique collection of books, *Angel Just-Rights,* Rebecca Parker is being allowed a voice enabling her to offer even a strand of hope to any individual similarly searching for their "only voice that is allowed", to offer even a slice of solace to those continuing to hurt silently and alone, and the disclosure of her story also aims to offer those enduring the last few years of this stretch of illness by her side – that is to say, the aim of the book is also to offer her Beloved Family, excessively long-awaited answers and an opportunity for all to embark, finally upon healing.

Today, while continuing to battle insurrections of mental illnesses, Parker lives and works in London, where she dedicates her life to offering others just a sap of the courage that has found to have been evoked in her own soul, through the writing and the production of

Angel Just-Rights

Rebecca Parker

ιunkapublishing

the mental health publisher

60000 0000 32580

Angel Just-Rights

Published by

Chipmunkapublishing

PO Box 6872

Brentwood

Essex CM13 1ZT

United Kingdom

http://www.chipmunkapublishing.com

Edited by Martine Daniel

Chipmunkapublishing gratefully acknowledge the support of Arts Council England.

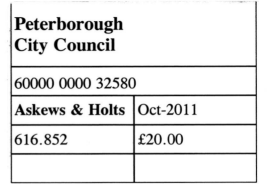

Peterborough City Council	
60000 0000 32580	
Askews & Holts	Oct-2011
616.852	£20.00

these books, Parker's all-encompassing key to potential freedom: *Angel Just-Rights*.

Angel Just-Rights

Dark. Compelling. Profound.

Fascinating True Story of One Child's Voice Lost

In Confusion, Imprecision, Fear; and Her Extraordinary Battles to

Regain it.

REBECCA PARKER

Praise for *Angel Just-Rights* by anonymous literary reviewers:

"This story is really powerful…the writing is remarkably honest and moving"

"An intensely personal and compelling read"

"This book allows the reader to share some of the author's most intimate thoughts and troubling times and has a great deal to commend it"

"Parker has a unique ability to write vividly"

"Parker's honesty and courage is remarkable and powerful"

"This book comes highly recommended. It can definitely help others"

"An emotional and highly original work"

Preface:

Listen and Learn

i-Evolution of The Memoir (03/03/10):

**1.   FORCED to be Open and Honest with My Dear
           Mum. And to Apologise.**

After the Auntie Ann event (Introduction: No More Secrets, B1)
realisation hit me hard. I had been left with no other option than to
be open and honest with Mum and I started to write a short note to
her in an effort to say sorry and to explain, from my point of view
and no matter how ill it might have sounded, about how that day had
gone so terribly wrong and why I had acted in the way that I did.
My intention was to then quickly read it through and send it off in
the post to her rather than to chance us both screaming to be heard
over each other down the phone where neither of us would be
listening to the other due to both parties remaining in such elevated
emotive states. This writing, so my reasoning fathomed, would
present Mum with a choice to read or not to read that which I had
written, and entirely of her own accord.

Once handwritten, I began typing the letter onto my laptop,
immediately finding the latter method much quicker and easier to
execute from the heart. Spillage ensued; I just could not stop! Each
time I read it through, I found it so true, honest and pertinent to
myself that I could in no way imagine or expect for my Mum to read
it, as *how stupid did it really sound*? More-to-the-point, how upset
would these words make my Mum feel? Would it help her to know
the truth of how far down this bottomless pit of a black hole her
youngest daughter has fallen? Could I really indulge unto my own
Mother such truth behind just how stuck and weak in my abilities to
climb out of this pit, without the help of serious psychiatric
treatment, I now found myself to be so trapped?

Six months subsequent and I am still failing to address the event
with My Dear Mum.

2.   FORCED to be Open and Honest with My Dear Auntie Ann. And to Apologise.

My weekly letter from Auntie Ann arrived after the event but before I had even had chance to sit down and form my apology email to her (the form of communication I personally preferred). In reading the first few lines of her letter, where my Auntie describes a list of emotions I had apparently inflicted upon her as a result of my behaviour in this event, my heart sank. These emotions included feeling "stunned", "fury because of how cunning you'd been", "hurt", "frustration", each statement hammering home the irrationality of my behaviour as experienced by a human in the real world. I felt absolutely terrible when reading this letter. I hated myself for the fact that I had imposed such nastiness upon my Dearest Auntie and I could fully understand her for feeling this way! But I also felt terribly alone and misunderstood. No, I could not have her thinking these awful things about me and so I knew what I had to do.

I wrote an apology email to my Auntie, trying to explain myself and making special efforts at being open and honest with her for the very first time in my life about where I was at and about how I was feeling and why I acted in the way that I did. I needed her to understand so that she would think less badly of me and I wanted to take away from her all those horrible feelings that I had so selfishly left her with. I needed to change the fact that she now clearly was of the thinking that I, her niece, felt so little of her that I had tried to hurt her and be nasty and thoughtless towards her on purpose! Thus, I was forced to take responsibility for my unforgivable actions and, at the very least, I owed her an explanation. In my email, I offered her an opportunity to listen to me and I hoped she would hear and maybe even forgive me.

On reading her reply, in addition to the subsequent letters continuing to arrive, I knew my sending an honest email had been exactly the right thing to do. I had let her into my thoughts and feelings and in return, she was demonstrating an understanding of me from actually hearing that which I had written. Her response showed, indeed advised me, that I need to speak out to people more because otherwise they cannot be "expected just to know" what I am thinking and therefore they cannot be "expected just to know" how to help. We now have a pact to always be "straight" with one another because I realise my Auntie Ann is right. Many people have warned me of my tendency to "assume people are mind-readers" to "expect people to know exactly what you are thinking": my Mum, Sister, Brother, Friends, Teachers, Lecturers, Colleagues, Nursing teams, and now my Dear Aunt.

Everybody who knows me well has reminded me of the above weakness which, I am pleased to be told about because I do not even realise that I take everything on alone or that I do not speak of the whole story; that instead I just do it. But when I come to talk, no matter how much I want and try to speak out, I find it so totally impossible to speak. My voice is lost and I am unable to communicate any worries or needs or to ask for any help or support. Instead, I think I can deal with everything on my own rather than speaking up and making a big song and dance out of a tiny little detail that I should not even be getting worried about or be feeling stressed about anyway, and I worry about my little worries sounding completely idiotic and stupid and senseless to other people, I worry that they are just not at all worth even speaking about or thinking about for that matter or even acknowledging...

...because who do you think you are? A waste of time, weak and failing, a waste of space, keep quiet and get on with life, achieve, be the best at everything (except academically super, of course, because you could never be as clever as Kerry); remember, you are strong and can deal with anything...

But in reality I have been continually weak for the greater part of my life in remaining just too cowardly to vocalise myself, to discuss and to face my fears. Instead, I pretend they are not there. It is not happening. It is OK and you are strong. Smile and you'll forget.

Now, I recognise no matter how stupid I may whole-heartedly believe my anxieties, thoughts, even feelings to be, however embarrassing they are for me to accept that I am experiencing them, however ashamed of them I am or however much I want to ignore them or pretend they do not exist, THEY ARE VERY MUCH THERE and bringing them into the open, being honest about them and accepting real help, is the only way I may find myself in a position to enable those whom I love, a hope to move on.

Should this writing never travel further solely than to facilitate my own selfish, cathartic purposes – my Auntie Ann hinted in her post-event letter that the previous day's events "were probably meant to have happened" and to the extreme that they had, "for a reason" – I believe this "reason" instigated my journey from denial of mental illness, through acceptance and culminated in the creation of this book.

Writing this book saved my life once; I know it will touch many others.

3.   FORCED to See The Key.
         And to Thank.

Pen and paper quickly giving way to typing on my laptop (my poor hand unable to keep up with the speed at which all thoughts were gushing out), I knew I had finally been shown THE KEY that I had been waiting for and simultaneously I felt that clear, unquestionable certainty in that I was doing exactly the right thing at this present moment in time and there was absolutely no doubt about it. Something was driving me, something was keeping me in the safe zone and letting nothing get in my way only that which would help in the clearing of this path that was finally opening those long lost, severely congested, communication channels. Dear Reader, to my curious surprise, only towards the completion of my spillage (exactly three weeks later) a sudden momentary flutter of utter 'thankfulness' passed over me, towards none other than Spen (Book 1: Secrets Out, Part 2, Chapter 4)! I realised, as will you too in good time, the full-circle in naming Dear Spen as the architect, the engineer, the perpetrator who lay the foundations to this spillage of communication, in that it was he who encouraged me to learn how to touch-type to such an extreme efficiency in the first place after lending his 'learnt to touch-type' CD to me all those years ago.

At the time, I remember relishing in my devotion to perfecting such a growing and necessary skill by improving my timings more and more and I have ever since enjoyed the perks of being a speedy typist (Book 1: Secrets Out, Part 2, Chapter 9). So at this realisation, I noticed myself lingering in such an ironic and surreal moment, where I was actually being allowed to FEEL, once again. In this moment, I experienced a brief feeling of bizarre satisfaction calmness and contentment that I dared actually to ENJOY, even briefly revel in, just for a cheeky second...

This one element – a natural inner innate desire to always strive to develop ones skills and to be the best – was a trait both Spen and I possessed. I remember Dear Dad once openly showing his pride for Spen's enthusiasm as he, my boyfriend, happily ignored me for hours one morning in favour of spending his time more productively reading intently through the books on our bookshelf! Incidentally, this also pained my Dad to see such a degree of commitment in a young man because reading was an act that lacked in his own son's list of interests.

So, Dear Reader, this tiny confirmation was proof to me, shaping significantly in aid and support, reassuring me in MY RIGHT to undergo this long-awaited outburst of writing. My spillage was being helped right out and off along its way by none other than Spen himself and for this, I must allow a smile because I felt rather like an immense and sudden gust of wind was helping me, the stranded boat, finally discovered adrift and far out at sea, only now sailing swiftly and smoothly riding each gentle wave of permission as quickly or slowly as it would come, back to safety. I was eager to welcome dry land and exciting new adventures and this was such a great help in the midst of my desperation to get everything down onto paper at this crucial time in my life and it was a time that, unbeknown to myself, I had been awaiting for so long. I knew the time was destined to come, only here, and now, it had.

4.   FORCED onto The Safe Route.
And Guided Every Step of the Way.

I was releasing my mind from myself at an alarming rate and for once, I felt sure of my actions. I felt that my actions were right. I felt I was being shown, almost told, and at a pace that was perfect for me that now I had been found and everything was going to be OK. I felt that all the signs had been put there and I was to recognise each one at the right time. I even felt assured that any concerns that may have arisen inside of me or any doubts that I may have encountered along the way were firmly put there in place in order to guide me on my path, thus encouraging and urging me to continue down this different route that had finally uncovered right in front of my eyes!

Here was the route I had absolutely longed for, but which had never shown up. It was the route I had silently screamed out to be revealed to me, yet which had never previously appeared. It was the route I had only ever dreamed of finding. This route that I had given up on holding back any hopes of even existing any longer was now here, right out of nowhere, and I had stepped right onto it so smoothly and perfectly!

So here it was and I was jolly well going to take these steps without a single look back because it had been made safe. It was made especially for me and I needed no further persuasion to walk down this path wholeheartedly: I felt I was being supported immensely, continually guided and shown and reassured in every possible way that I was doing the right thing, at the right time, and that it was now SAFE to speak out. If anything or anyone was to interrupt me or to hurt me during those three weeks, I was made to see the reason for it, I was made to understand the reason for it and I felt a calm contentment and safety and trust in this motivation that I could not ignore; I was supposed to now reveal, unravel and to free the secrets behind this unbearable existence I so desperately no longer wished to endure.

5. FORCED to spend 'A Period of Time on Reflection' Exactly as 'A Period of Time on Reflection'.

On Wednesday 3rd March 2010 (two days prior to the Auntie Ann Event, Introduction: No More Secrets, B1), I was told by my nursing team at Day Care, including my Consultant at the hospital and in front of my Dear Mum who was also attending the Review meeting that day, that a decision had been made for me to take 'A Period of Time Out from Day Care, on Reflection' and it was to start right away; now. Today.

I was scared without their support yet was also extremely undecided whether to go home with Mum that same day or whether to stay in London alone and then go home later in the week as nothing seemed to fit comfortably with me then. I chose to accompany my Dear

Mum back to Grenada, our hometown, on the train and to go and stay with her for a few days, rather than be alone in my flat in London and my Mum alone too. My Mum needed me and I needed her.

In hindsight, I firmly believe that the decision around this act had clearly already been written. This 'Period of Time Out from Day Care, on Reflection' had been a gift that was sent to me and I was supposed to spend it exactly as a 'Period of Time Out from Day Care' and exactly 'on Reflection' as, my Dear Readers, you are about to discover.

So here I found myself on that afternoon of Friday 7th March 2010, back in London, spilling out my thoughts and my deepest, darkest secrets that stubbornly plagued and tormented my mind. As these secrets had been festering away, the real life of Rebecca had been over-ridden for so long. The life of torture she had been trying so hard to secure in secret, hidden for almost thirty years, was finally about to come out.

ii-Significance of the Completion of 'Secrets Out' (23/03/10)

'Secrets Out' began on the very day on which my 'Period of Time Out from Day Care, on Reflection' began and ended exactly three weeks later on the very day that the Day Care Service was closed to patients, while the Staff attended the 'Future Planning of Day Care' meeting that was being held there that day. This, to me, was a sign that my own future was seriously being given a chance and a hope. All I had to do was to ride with this wind, keep faith in that very special something that was definitely guiding me and follow through with change.

But erasing *Angel* was to be far easier said than done.

Author's Note

Reading and writing have always excited me, previous works winning recognition and Prizes for both short stories and poetry. But with my appallingly intense fears come overwhelming uncertainty, unconscious delaying and obstructive avoidance.

Angel Just-Rights is an honest account (if a little feisty) delving unsparingly into a plethora of extreme matters concerning my own daily living that is both pre and post mental illness diagnosis. In deciding to share these extremely personal memoirs, I remain determinable in the upholding of my duty to impart insight, understanding, encouragement, and a ray of hope unto others suffering silently, by using the safest, alas only, means that has so auspiciously been made possible for me with the help of the dedicated team found at Chipmunka Publishing.

My family are desperate for answers and my friends deserve the truth. How could one be so selfish? Silence, I believed, would protect my loved ones from hurt but in fact, it has destroyed every last one. Therefore finding and using my voice, in the writing of this series of books, cannot possibly make anything worse...this is exactly what I must trust in by finally deciding to disclose my story. Should my voice ruin the family further – as it is for the family whom I remain in this world today – I will be granted permission to leave this monstrous place, to be free, content and reunited with Dear Dad, resting together and finally in peace, once and for all?

No More Secrets. No More Lies. No Avoiding. No Disguise.
No More Nightmares? No More Cries? No More Planes To Fall From Skies?
Always Listen. Always Hope. Seek Out Healthy Ways To Cope.

Angel Just-Rights

Always Trust. Always Float. Learn To Speak And Steer Your Boat.
Although a work of non-fiction, the names of people and places in this book have been changed and details of others' lives have been merged and reshaped in order to protect identities. Changing difficult words has enabled me to allow my story to be told in a manner that remains truthful and feels safe for me and also without invading the lives of others. In respect of this, I am sure every reader will understand my words and those involved may easily find themselves here, should one seek out this print successfully. Before joining me on this journey, it is important to note the use of *italic text* in this series, which depicts the *imprint of Angel;* this is not her voice.

And finally, I must thank my Dear Mother for remaining right by my side throughout, my Dear Sister, and my Dear Brother for your loyal devotion in offering such technologically adept expertise that has crucially facilitated the emergence of this first series of books.

The writing of *Angel Just-Rights* saved my life once and the main purpose in publishing is to free and to save My Family and others.

Here spools a final endeavour TO SPEAK.

For My Dear Father Ever After

And For My Dear Mother Finally Answers

Reality:

"Is Not So Much Something Against Which Memories Can Be Cherished

As Something Established By Those Memories Themselves"

Sarah Willis

Contents

INTRODUCTION:

NO MORE SECRETS

Angel Just-Rights

A1:

MY WEEK AWAY FROM DAY CARE,

ON REFLECTION

~

THE MOTIVATION BEHIND THE MEMOIR

Ai-Learning that Communication Really Is The Key:

Reading and Writing Verses Speaking.
Knowing I find writing things down easier than speaking them, for the past two years I have intended to start and try to actually carry this task out in regards to matters that I, in no way *want* to, but recognise that I NEED to talk about, work through and understand in order to continue with a life in this world. All the time I spent away from Day Care i.e. in the evenings or at the weekends, was not providing me with a space to carry out this task and when I started at Day Care, I knew there was no way I would be granted a day off already, even if I said it was to work on 'things' as the request for a day off would most likely have been viewed as an 'excuse' to 'get out' of treatment and therefore to 'miss' a day of eating.

I had been feeling too depressed, however, in the evenings to be able to put my head into such a gear, and at the weekend, my Mum and I had agreed that my travelling home to be with her in Grenada as soon as possible on a Friday when I finish Day Care, would be the best plan for me at present and I knew I could not sit at home and face writing about 'things' while in the comfort of my Dear Family home and while seated with Dear Mum. I felt in order to concentrate, I needed to be alone with 'things' and when I am at home in Grenada, I want only to enjoy spending time with my poor Mum after everything I put her through in the last three years: after all those terrible train journeys in the windy, cold winter months where she forced herself through the snow and the rain in order to visit me in hospital and to be there for me when I Rebecca, her youngest so-called "daughter", needed her most. I just cannot ever make anything up to her or repay her in any way imaginable and over this, Dear, Dear Mum, I will always feel distraught.

Thus, as I had not been in the right position to start facing 'things', for as long as I did not *have to* or *want to*, I was also finding it very hard to attend my outpatient therapy sessions on time, from one week to the next, or if at all. During these sessions, it was apparently beneficial to speak about 'things' and I was subconsciously avoiding confronting anything that I felt uncomfortable with and yet I knew I had to speak, but I also could feel that my right time was looming, becoming ever so more imminent...Little did I know it would rear its ironically ugly head, in the form of Rebecca's Key to freedom that had actually always been there? What had actually mattered, was choosing the RIGHT time to take it, and ensuring a trusted guide.

Aii-Understanding Natural Thinking Styles and Personality Traits:

Recognition; Acceptance; Allowance...:
My Mum always tells me "you have a terrible tendency to go at things too much", like the jigsaw I have been working through during my time at home at the weekends, I suppose. It was the jigsaw that my Mum was referring to on this most recent occasion. To explain simply: once I start a task, I need to do as much as possible to perfect the task, not daring to lose a second of time in stopping or in taking my attention away from the task at hand, even for a second, until I have no more time to allot to the task and it is completed and completed well. Before committing to a task, I must feel safe and certain in that it is EXACTLY the RIGHT time to do it and that I can do it well.

My Mum also always says to me "you let things slide", "you leave everything until the last minute" and she warns me how "one of these days, it'll just be too late!" Now I realise it is a natural thinking style of mine and I have trusted it, or dangerously trusted a hope and chance in it, as being my most comfortable and productive way of working whether at school exams, music exams, competitions, university and right through my working and social lives. If I have something to achieve, or a task to carry out, or a place to go or friends to meet, of course I want to execute this straight away and of course I want to make it as good as possible, always having preferred to work alone and to produce something that is mine, always putting in all my effort, plus a little bit more, into every task and right away. After all, it has to all be perfect.

If I am committed to something, I have always prided myself in carrying it out to the best of my abilities. When the motivation and inspiration is there, when I am forced to and eager to get started – I am at least good at recognising this moment – I will enjoy becoming lost in the task at hand and making it my project to be proud of, no matter how big or small, until I have finished and am happy (happyish, as it can never be one hundred per cent perfect and I can never be satisfied with anything unless it is more, or better than perfect) with it and am pressed to show the results of my efforts, fearing them, believing them, *knowing them never to be good enough,* yet longing deep down inside that I have produced a passable piece of work / impression / performance. I work well under pressure and to time scales because until I know all my efforts have been exhausted and it is time to stop, I can never rest or be satisfied.

I suppose it may be described as a very 'black and white' or an 'all or nothing' way of thinking but for me, it has always been "just how I am" (now known to be Borderline Personality Disorder (BPD), Psychological Numbing and Disassociation, also known as 'splitting') and is what comes naturally to me, without thinking. This is a natural trait to me; everybody holds their own default modes. Thanks to Day Care and the groups that I have attended as part of the treatment there, I am now able to recognise thinking styles and can work on being more aware of the negative extremes that appear in my own thinking that, in turn, affect not only myself but the relationships I have with others in my life and with those around me.

Now, I have learned to really LISTEN, not just with open ears, but with an open mind too. I listen to those who care, by actually hearing what they say and by even considering experimenting on acting upon others' advice rather than solely listening to and always acting stubbornly upon my own skewed thoughts and beliefs. I have learned that bringing things into discussion of my own accord, previous to being pressed into releasing my thoughts and worries when they have reached that absolute point of desperation, has meant discussing things CAN bring new and achievable ideas into the equation and that there ARE steps that exist between the two extremes of either 'all or nothing' and 'black or white' thinking. SOLUTIONS, I have learned, can only be solved effectively in working through them with more than one voice of reason and in taking those most important 'baby steps' to get there.

All thinking styles and personality traits require recognition, acceptance and understanding, consistent awareness and reminders of when they may be forgotten or simply when they could be happening. It is so easy to revert back to a mode of natural default, thus lacking realisation and therefore simply acting without thinking absolutely rationally. For example, I have learned that I need to take a step backwards and to assess situations at times, and here on my week out on reflection, I take this step back:

I **recognise** that my natural desire is set at default usually to "go at it" while I have the burning inspiration and drive fired up inside of me and to keep on going until it is done and finished, none other than perfectly. But I **accept** that as this could result in being detrimental to my health and I take another step back. I **allow** myself to be over-ridden by logical, rational and realistic thinking and I tell myself that there will always be more to do and it cannot all be done and dusted in one big go and it needs to be done in stages. I remind myself of those 'baby steps' that exist in between those dangers of the extremes and that they are so important in order to be able to get anything done to a decent standard at all in the long run.

Another false belief, which was one day aided into correction when I was little, refers to the fact that my brain was conditioned into thinking there would always be endless hours in the night, should the daytime prove too short for study etc. But since school I have found this proven to be just not true (Book 1: Secrets Out, Part 2, Chapter 7)!

During the writing of 'Secrets out', I can confirmedly say that I learned, through practice, that simultaneously I am able to demonstrate completing the task efficiently with making myself take breaks, thus doing what I have to do in order to keep myself well enough to be able to continue working and to complete the task at hand to the best of my ability. I continue to require constant, persistent, absolute reminders, I admit, but I have reached the first stage of awareness and can work on the second stage of continuing to realise the importance of this awareness always, for myself, and I need to communicate this need to those around me, so they know it is where I struggle and how they might help, if they wish. No matter how pathetic or ashamed of realising this fact, that I need help to live, makes me feel, IT IS THERE. This scares me and makes me so angry when I cannot see it for myself, but I want to get better and I aim to practice taking the support and reassurance that I NEED at present. I want to learn to take help, as help, when it is offered. Overall, I need to be better at accepting.

...and Revelation.

Having a better understanding of myself, thanks to my attendance at Day Care, enabled me to easily write a lot down during this 'Week, on Reflection' that I usually kept safely locked away. When I was younger, I used to enjoy writing a diary rigidly, but was put off from doing so when my brother had once lifted one of my diaries for himself to read without my consent and then started poking fun at me and teasing me for an incident that had happened to me and that I had described in detail in my diary. This event I will briefly explain:

Having returned home from a Youth Orchestra Tour, during which I experienced my being the subject of a boy's attention, I had written about the time that this boy had subsequently come to visit me in Granada, a couple of weeks after the tour.

I first noticed Nathan trying to catch my eye when I was in the queue to pay for goods at the service station during the Youth

Angel Just-Rights

Orchestra tour to Austria (August 1998). I remember him being in front of me: he looked at me, over exaggerated his stagger, and then looked back at the path onto which he was walking. I thought he was trying to tell me that I was scary or something and so my reaction was to just raise my eyebrows and laugh a bit awkwardly. Later, he said he was swept of his feet by my beautiful eyes! He swapped coaches so that he could get to know me more easily and spent his time sitting in the isle of the bus chatting to me, painting my nails and instigating staring competitions with me. When we arrived back home, we spent a lot of time on the phone and I remember writing a poem for him when he asked me to sign his post-tour concert program. I had always felt comfortable with expressing myself through poetry and had a habit of talking in riddles even then. I had even been awarded winner of the Poetry Cup at speech night during my earlier years at primary school.

The day he came to visit me in Granada had taken a lot of planning, for which I sought advice from my Mum on how to entertain this male visitor of mine. I invited him to walk around the town with me one Saturday afternoon and I was to show him around the little market, which I did. We ended our tour of Grenada by sitting on a bench in the local park, just talking and laughing and enjoying the sun. Whilst we were sitting on the bench together, Nathan started to be a bit over-friendly for my liking and began edging closer and closer towards me, saying all these nice things about me that made me feel extremely awkward and uncomfortable until I had no idea as to how I was expected to respond to him. I wished he would just stop. I became quiet and stiff and I was unable to look him in the eye any longer, but he continued staring at me, saying that I was:

"Obviously bothered by it...sitting very protectively of myself"

(The above quote lifted from my diary entry, August 1998). He said it not in a horrible way. I was flattered by some of his words, but was picking the bright yellow sunflower that I had sewn onto my plain blue bag, off, awkwardly, strand by tiny strand, in my embarrassment at hearing such unfamiliar, and unwelcome attentions.

I agree, after the event, yes it was funny, but I was terribly embarrassed and felt guilty and undeserving of this attention at the time and to know that my brother had read all about my "sunflower event, oooo!" made it even more difficult for me. I was ashamed, making a mental note to myself always to make sure that a code is used when writing personal things down in future and this is exactly what I did. The only key to my emotions was solely through code, the key to which would be firmly locked away only in my head, never to be found by steeling hands, prying eyes or burning ears. Think before you speak, think before you write, keep quiet equals things remain personal. Lock them away from all. Hide. Smile.

Nothing happened with the boy on the bench, but we kept in touch and remarkably, he has been my lifesaver and the person I would contact when I have felt unsafe and alone in my flat or unsafe and unsure whether I can continue living my life while alone in the evenings in London and he has always been there to help and support me throughout the past years particularly. Even today, I fail to believe how he is still there on the other end of the phone or even in person if I so wish, always asking to come and visit me and telling me that I am always welcome to visit him, that he loves me, that I am too special to him and that he will always be there for me no matter what.

In my evaluations, I felt the chain of events running up to the writing of this Memoir had all happened for a reason and things were fitting into place one by one. Realisations and revelations to things that have always been there but previously misfit were being showered over me each drop significant and deserving of its own individual place in my life. The chain of events and signs rather reminded me of when Leo (Book 1: Secrets Out, Part 4, Chapter 14) came to me. Here, I believe I had also been shown that a whole chain of events had, and was happening to me and around me for a reason and that it was meant to have happened when and however it had all unfolded. Leo used to say to me "this is real" and that is exactly how I was experiencing letting myself contentedly be blown into whatever direction this gust of wind would now take my boat: down the safe and guided route and not missing any of the bright lights along the way, certainly not distinguishing any miracle revelations either.

For example, I even now see and believe that Zach (Book 1: Secrets Out, Part 4, Chapter 14) coming into and out of my life in the way that he did and even right up to the fact that I had decided, really without thinking seriously about it, to ask him as my guest to my sister's wedding. Now I can see it was all meant to be for a reason. At the time, I was 'together' with Zach and I invited him in order to avoid being at the wedding alone and to stop questions being asked about my own status by the family, because I think I always knew that Zach and I would not marry. Afterwards, I had felt very bad that Zach appeared on the photos with me and that maybe it had even spoiled Kerry's photos, solely for the fact that Zach, although appearing on her wedding photographs, is no longer part of my life in that way. Now Zach is married and with a child of his own and I believe I can look at those photos and feel happy. He was such a kind and loving boyfriend and this gives me such hope to hold onto and it shows me that all my past life with him does not seem as wasted anymore: I can say – and those who know me will also know that I would never give such a certain answer to anything – that I fully understand one hundred per cent the reasons why Zach and I met, and the reasons we met when we did. I understand the reasons why our relationship progressed as it had, the reasons why he had to become close to my family (he had told my sister his worries about my spending time with Leo, due to his personal, deep, bordering on dangerous, beliefs).

Thus, many things started falling into place for me, with regards to the truth being revealed and finally explaining WHY my family and I have been dragged through hell and back (not quite back yet, I know I still have a lot of hard work to do and may never understand a lot of 'things', but I hope it will continue to be revealed at this pace that I am just about coping with). As I continue down this path of reliving my actual life – past – present – and a glimpse of a future – I become more and more assured that the right time has come for me to finally be allowed to open my eyes and to remember the actual life that I have missed in the past years, also to realise just how wrongly I have been living, how "ill" I HAVE been. Such a fake, huge, cover-up of a life for me and to others has been just the biggest lie ever.

Aiii-Unlocking the Key to The Secret Diaries:

Stop "Protecting"; Really Listen and Accept Permission.
Towards the end of my 'Week Out' I met up with my best friend
Sarah, for a hot drink and a good chat. I know that my Mum is right
when she said to me in hospital "it's the worst thing you could do to
the family! Worse than when your Dad died! It's ongoing...", but
through talking with Sarah, she made me see that my struggling to
get better is not being helped by my continued efforts in keeping
secrets that are clearly proving to have an increasingly detrimental
and damaging effect on not only my own health and general well-
being but also this utter unyielding torture, pain and destruction that
I am continuing to inflict upon my entire family! Therefore, after so
many years, how can the truth coming out realistically make
anything worse? Of course, my family may be angry and words and
actions may fly around, but in the long run, now, I know all they
want is for everyone in the family to be happy and if there is a
chance of that happening – if there is a chance of making my
recovery a little speedier or easier or in this case where I have found
myself at now, possible at all, with the production of 'No More
Secrets' – then surely it is my duty to take this last resort on board,
to grasp it as our last hope? For too long I have remained trapped in
the silence of my own secret world, but where has this gotten me
and what has it done / is it doing to my family?

I recognise that I need to **accept** I may need help, if I am ever going
to have a chance at living a real life in the real world. Look where
this borderline existence has gotten not only myself, but now also
my family too! I need to **allow** myself to be willing and to be open
and to be honest and truthful and to have the faith that this can be
left behind us all, before it is "just too late" (Introduction: No More
Secrets, A2). Even if I am not brave enough to bring my story out
into the family, I could write it down, now I have been shown the
key, and leave it there **revealed in writing** for whoever wishes to
read; that way at least it will be out of my selfish mind. Yet all
others warn me, that it will remain there lurking deep, dark and
dirty, always with potential to reveal its ugly self in full form and at
any unsuspecting point in the future. Then, it will be too late to
reveal itself through my voice, but through my stiff, cold, buried
soul...but at least then I would be in peace, no longer trapped in the

prison of secrets, no longer unable to escape, no longer being left to exist in a fake haze of confusion and disarray with no hope for even a bearable, secure, orderly, contented future...

Ready, Steady...GO.

Taking a deep breath, I spoke out the words to Sarah before I knew they were coming from my own mouth, "but *is it OK* for me to bring it out and to talk about it, just in therapy? It *is ok isn't it*, of course it is". Because I know it is something I MUST DO, but so far I can never do it...*Shut up, talk about something else, who do you think you are bringing all this up? It's in the past! Nobody wants or needs to hear about it, it's pathetic! It's done, you're still alive and you are stronger for it! It is just a secret of the past, buried and never to be talked about. Think about your family! Protect and get on with life, listen to me; smile, everything will be OK...*

But this question that I had just put to my best friend, was giving me someone else's view that was louder and stronger than ever. I was just beginning to come to terms with the fact that definitely at this present time and for how long in the future I did not know, I would have to go through life trusting and valuing and actually listening to and even acting upon, no matter how wrong it might feel, someone else's advice! Welcome to my interminable world of battle against noise, insecurity, discomfort, dread and unending terror. Sarah's response, which I cannot even quote from lack of hearing, was overridden to me in observing her body language, which spoke volumes more than any words could have in this instance.

With my own eyes, I absorbed her over-exaggerated frown mixed with such over-animated curiosity, shaking head, total lack of ability to grasp an understanding at my even having to ask her such a question, which was the question written all over her face. This confirmed the level of reassurance that I had needed and was given to me in such a way that it was impossible for me to miss: my trusted confidante was reassuring me in what was right and wrong, she was someone to quash the vicious voices in my head, to talk louder, and I was realising not necessarily solely in speech, but together with body language and expression, a form of silent communication to which I had possessed years of experience in fine-tuning and was evidently much more accustomed to respond so sensitively to.

How magnificent that another light had been lit up along my trusted path, only to reveal yet another most important feeling of full circle and certainty! The key that had locked the Diary of Secrets firmly closed off away from the world, lost for over twenty years and handed unknowingly unto the creeping voice of evil, had now been uncovered and thrown right back at me to seize correctly, and I knew and could trust it was RIGHT. This was my choice; my control; my sign.

Aiv-My Candle of Hope:

Micci CAN. Angel CAN'T.
Hence, the candle of hope at a final and serious chance for recovery had been shown to me. I, Rebecca, had ignited it with trusted guidance and, like my journey with the wind, was now set burning upon it in motion. It had always really been there, and I know it had, but I had just been unable to make these things happen on my own and until I was forced to and shown directly how to, and unless I could feel completely safe in the steps that I was about to take and in the progress that I would make, and unless I could see a definite sense to my actions, until then, it would and did not happen. Maybe this is called 'being ready'.

ONLY I, Rebecca:

Only I, Rebecca, Can Hold The Key.

Only I, Rebecca, Can Work The Key And

Keep The Candle Of Hope Burning.

Only I, Rebecca, Will Be The One To Blow Out The Candle

And May Do So

Only At The End.

A2:

...DIARY ENTRY FROM THE PENULTIMATE DAY

TO COMPLETING 'SECRETS OUT'...

-Super size and Super skinny

- **Tuesday 23rd March 2010:**

We decorated the Day Care room with the new furniture today. Felt tired with my cold. Taking pain killers.

Fish cakes with leeks and apple strudel with custard. Had a fruit bar thing today at 3pm as the others did too and I didn't want those filling rough cakes because you have to have three and they make my teeth go fury. There were no cereal bars left that I usually have, so I guess this 'change' was good for me.

Text Ravi to say I couldn't meet him. I couldn't be bothered and felt a bit ill. Plus, nothing was going to get in my way of watching the first episode of the new series of my favourite television programme about people, food and lifestyle. I made my dinner in time for it, I ignored poor Little Brother's calls to watch it, I ignored Kerry's calls to watch it. There was a section of the programme following 'anorexics' and it shocked me because the state of them looked awful...but my height is more than theirs and my weight is less! I just think they must all be a bunch of liars about their weights. I used to think the same about the patients in hospital, and at Day Care too for that matter, because no way can those weights be true as they would all be put in hospital like they threaten me with.

NO WAY. I came to the conclusion that it was an untold secret I was never to know or be let in on, similar, I guess, to the untold secret in Chapter 5 etc. and the untold secret that I was never really sectioned. They're just playing mind games with me to make me fat. Why me? Logic tells me otherwise, but I continue to believe the screams as they're louder and harsher and always there with me. To me, they are real, true and safe. This is what I MUST follow.

There was an announcement at the end of the program informing viewers that one of the girls featured had died a week after filming.

Lies or no lies – if I continue only to turn things around and manage to CHANGE only when absolutely forced to, and little by little at that, it will almost certainly, and one day sooner, end up being JUST TOO LATE for me too, like my Mum always says to me that "you leave everything to the last minute and one of these days it will be too late". I must ignore my screams and follow those who know best and who are in the majority here!

This shock made me question my extreme lifestyle – is it that this possibility of surviving each day so close to death was something that comforted me and kept me feeling safe because it provided me with a way out? An escape? Because everything is far too scary in the real world...desperate to feel safe...and if I was to succeed in anorexia, I would lose my life to it ultimately and then I would be free...but that would never happen to me because people are making a fuss over my weight even now and for what reason? I could never be thin enough. I would just die or remain alive, but be left with ailments because I can't even do anorexia properly unless I lose more weight...!

TO CHANGE Means:

I Have To Continue Believing There Is No More Harm.

There Is Little To Be Lost,

Yet, A Lot To Be Gained.

Others Have To Believe I AM DESPERATE.

A3:

I AM POEM

"I AM ANOREXIA!"

I AM WEAK AND FAILING; A WASTE OF SPACE.

I WONDER, "HOW'S IT TRANSPIRED, THIS SHAMEFACED DISGRACE?"

I HEAR VICIOUS VOICES UNRELENTING, UNRELENTING.

I SEE A SHRINKING LADY WHOSE SCREAMS F'EVER MUTE.

I WANT TO BE LED ON A DIFFERENT ROUTE, FAR FROM HARM, TAKE ME 'WAY FROM THIS HARSH, UNSAFE PLACE -

I AM WEAK AND FAILING; A WASTE OF SPACE.

I PRETEND TO ATTEND, LIVE, LAUGH AND TO BE.

I FEEL TIRED AND COLD, ALL ALONE. WHERE IS ME?

I TOUCH THE GLASS WINDOW BETWEEN THE WORLD AND MY EYES.

I WORRY MY LOVED ONES KNOW NOT ME, JUST MY 'GUISE.

I CRY, "TRAPPED BY SECRETS! CANNOTS! CAN'T KEEP UP IN THIS RACE!"

I AM WEAK AND FAILING; A WASTE OF SPACE.

I UNDERSTAND HOW I'M JUST DIFFERENT FROM OTHERS.

I SAY, THERE'S NO WAY YOU CAN - IMPULSE DIVES FOR THOSE COVERS.

I DREAM HOW EVERYTHING WILL BE OK AS YOU'RE STRONG!

I TRY TO ACHIEVE, YET AVOID; 'LAS A LIFE, BEEN AND GONE.

I HOPE NEVER TO FREEZE; EYES TIGHT SHUT. . . FORGET!

I AM WEAK AND FAILING; A WASTE OF SPACE, DEAD SET.

B1:

SETTING THE SCENE

Bi-Pre Auntie Ann Event:

Communication – Actions Verses Words.
I could not have asked for Mum to have done anything differently to help me at all, in particular, during that weekend where Mum had planned to drive me down to Kerry's in order to see the new baby. Mum had already spent her whole week at my sister's, away from the comforts of her own home and most probably, with little sleep. As I have not yet written about this, Dear Reader for you, I will explain a little first.

So touching was the way Mum did not make a big deal out of me *not* wanting to travel to Kerry's in the car with Little Brother and his wife that weekend. It was as if Mum intuitively knew and understood that it was the wrong time for me to cope with spontaneity and change without planning. I felt that she sensed the fright and panic I was feeling at the suggested change in plan and that she knew all the mental planning, stress and anxieties that it was putting into my mind, making me frustrated and defensive and angry towards myself and unfortunately towards those I love most too i.e. my poor subjected family. I reacted badly to any unexpected changes in routine or changes to planned events, as uncertainties generated an enormous anxiety for me at this time, having to continually worry about and try to foresee every possible eventuality before I could even begin to accept a totally new situation.

My fear of imposed change had reached the extent that I now had to carry out exactly the same rituals every day and every weekend, ensuring that everything was kept exactly the same as before. If something was to change, then I would have to plan it for hours, if not days in advance and worry about it or how to avoid it if at all possible. Any shift in routine felt intolerable to me and keeping my life tiny, be it in routines, in eating exactly the same meals at exactly the same times, or in not accepting telephone calls or invites, kept me living in this world. It was just how it was. It was at least bearable this way and the sense of strict regimes and order, to me, reflected at least a controlled and levelled fret.

So now, I was left thinking that they all – that is, the rest of my immediate family, to include my brother, my sister, my mum – had been planning this change together. I was thinking that they had all agreed only to inform me after I had begun my journey homeward, which I thought had obviously been a big part of the plan with the intention being that I could not be scared off and stay in London all weekend, once safely on the train home. This would have reflected my usual immediate impulsive reactions of panic, fright, absolute fear to a change in plan and my sudden defence or coping mechanism – avoiding, running away and burying that throbbingly busy head of mine, distracting, not thinking, therefore no harm, equals safe, comfortable, in *my* control; ordered; done; sorted. Only then would 'the world isn't going to come to a crashing end anymore' thought have emerged slowly within. So breaking this news to me, when my train on a Friday night had just set off from London for Granada, was definitely part of the plan to trap me, as far as I felt and could see.

Owing to this realisation (or assumption that I had jumped to) I was immediately feeling extremely angry and suddenly everything felt terribly out of control. Here was that feeling similar to the crashing plane, where there is absolutely nothing in your power you can do in order to save yourself in those last fleeting seconds... You are fully at the mercy of others, completely paralysed and forced to sit with that terrific and immense fear and panic, all alone, and fear rising: imminent tragedy, uncertainty, all alone with no-one to help, no guidance, just the unknown forthcoming. For the first time however, I was able to take a step backwards and become aware of my extreme initial reaction and, realising I was by myself and on the moving train and would only make things worse for myself should I allow panic and anger to override, I was able to turn my thinking around, making real efforts to calm down, ignore those racing thoughts that all my teeth were wobbling and about to fall out because you should have stayed in London, you silly, silly girl, of opening that train door right away and ending this threat right here and now, myself, now, do it! Your control! Your way! *Listen to me! You're dirt! Being humiliated! Take control! Do it!*

Having tried to use the 'Mindfulness' skills I had learned at Day Care, I began forcing myself to think about advice the staff would be giving me right now if I were there and under their safe wing and the voice of Lilly came into my head: calm down; at least until you are off the train and at home in person, so it would give you chance to think rationally, to not be angry towards you family for, in effect I guess, just thinking normally and logically themselves... So I did not want to act upon my stronger feelings as I might have done in the past by refusing straight out, then and there, slamming down the phone and simply acting on this terrific impulse to selfishly, unrealistically, keep me safe and never taking a step back or hearing others, or speaking my feelings or concerns around the change, out loud. Day Care was teaching me to recognise and control my emotions in a sensibly controlled manner and for this I will forever be grateful.

After all, why would I not love the chance to spend some rare quality time out-and-about on an adventure with my brother and sister-in-law, whom I hardly saw? Why could I not seize the chance to save poor Mum the extra journey, at the same time? How can you let your selfish side take over like this, Rebecca? This would be fun, right? We could all have a laugh together, surely? I wish I could have. I wanted more than anything to just get on with it, to please everyone and to do something considered 'normal' and to even be able to enjoy it for myself a little too, but with all these terrifically overwhelming fears and feelings going on around my head with which I just did not know what on earth to do and I certainly did not know where on earth to start with revealing my stupid thoughts and feelings to anyone, I could not.

To fake everything once again, I was just not strong enough anymore. My secret eating disordered life had now been out in the open to my family for over two years and I was tired and exhausted of living a false and smiling happy life in order to keep others happy. Now that my family knew of my struggles, I felt no longer obliged to 'act' in their presence. Instead, I was craving their love, their care, their comfort and above all, I needed their ears and their understanding.

After an hour's journey subjected to these thoughts, I arrived home. Over a cup of tea, my Mum simply put the change in idea to me and there was no further discussion. She would drive us there, bless her so much. I felt incredibly selfish, yet it took away all the terrible stress in my head that now, thankfully, would not manifest itself into even more severe anger that would inevitably have resulted in being taken out on my poor, Dear Family. Mum, thank you so much. Although you said nothing, I feel you understood my position and I was so relieved and pleased that you had calmly helped me and you were there silently supporting me, Rebecca, your daughter. Yes, I AM still here! Thank you for just knowing I needed to feel safe right now and I do with you by my side and at home in Granada. It is hard with all the other struggles I am facing at the intensive treatment I somehow manage to take myself to, day after day, at the Hospital Day Care Centre. Thank you for realising this change was just too much more to add to my plate (as it were) at this time.

Or, had I just assumed that this was my Mum being sensitive towards me when really my Mum just did not want to 'let me down' or actually, more-to-the-point, did not want to disappoint Kerry? I rather think the latter. I know Mum has really tried with all her heart and energy to be understanding and at the same time to help me progress through 'recovery' and I also have been pushing my boundaries regarding food. I have been letting myself feel a little (actually, a lot) less safe, step by step (at other times I just need the rigidity of my routines and my boundaries may be tighter in order to make me feel safer, which is a coping strategy I have accepted that I may just have to revert to rather avidly on occasion, just when I have to or really need to, I just do). But simultaneously I am learning to live with testing and stretching these boundaries so it is not a disaster, which brings me to the Auntie Ann event.

Family, I know I continue to be a complete nightmare and for this I am so, so sorry. Mum it is not you I am doing this to, it is me. But it is just me at this present time. I am changing. Mum: when I fled back to London last week, I did not want to have an argument with you. To have us both shouting over each other down the phone was the last thing I wanted. I knew I would have to write Auntie Ann an email to apologise too and so as soon as I arrived back at my flat in London, I started writing things down initially for myself as a diary really, but also because I wanted to explain myself to you, Dear Mum, so that you could at least hear why I felt like I had to act as drastically as I did. Mum, you can choose to read or not (Introduction: No More Secrets, B2). As you can see, this was written as my diary entry, but it is all your choice Mum. Firstly, I urge you to read on for a glimmer of good news.

Bii-Post Auntie-Ann Event:

Glimmer of Blissful Nostalgia.
Just so you know, I have made a lot of progress at Day Care this week (the first week returning to the treatment program after my 'Week Out' and thus after the Auntie Ann Event). The staff and patients say they are very pleased and impressed with my personality that has come shining through with the new openness I am demonstrating and they hope that I can keep it up; as do I, more than anything because this is a major start for me. I really tried to use the week out productively, to finally use the time to write and to think about a lot of 'things' encumbering my steps to recovery. The week could have been detrimental and I could have simply given up completely and taken the easy way out by ignoring everything that I have learned. Now I know that 'things' will not just be hidden for evermore or just go away, but will continue to keep me and my family in this prison and torture, if not faced. I spent the week facing many 'things' Mum, while miraculously, keeping myself well and stable in depending heavily on my more 'healthy' routines and regimes that were skills I learned during time in hospital, so all was not completely in vain.

Mum, I felt an actual glimmer of FREEDOM, like I used to when I was actually happy. Just a glimmer, but if I can keep or even feel that again, a glimmer of actually seeing that there is (dare I say it) or could be, a light at the end of the tunnel then I am going to walk right towards it. You can choose or not whether to read, but I am to believe that it will help me get better, having been given that taste of feeling an actual happiness that I used to feel every day! Possessing an actual hope and desire to travel, to do something good and to achieve, I am feeling there IS HOPE and there IS A PURPOSE and there just might be something good for me to fight for and to find that life that I could hopefully still have in this world. I do not want to lose being able to feel that feeling again, Dear Mum. That is what you want too, right? So nothing can get any worse. True?

One of Two Final Options.
On my week out in London I saw Sarah for a cup of tea and we talked for hours. She made me realise that as my illness is destroying my family, what do I have to lose in finally allowing myself to be open and honest, if it will ultimately make my family happy and free us all from all this pain? Does this make sense to you Reader? How dismal is it to evaluate that actually my so-called efforts at protecting my family for all these years, have caused both my family and I such devastating harm, so many years down the line? The only two options I now have available to me at this final stage of the journey, is to either carry on in this existence where I continue destroying my family in the process or to be open and honest and to take that step to freeing everyone, including hopefully to an extent, even myself, from this hell of secrets and cannots, not alloweds and nevers and worse and worse and worse thoughts / feelings / behaviours that have and continue to rule my life and, worse of all, destroy so many precious lives around me.

Recently I have felt like I can even take a deep breath and feel good for it! Imagine never taking a deep breath or having a good stretch in the morning for years and years and years and years and years because your head has, unknowingly to yourself, been so afflicted and fixated on re-running the past or on planning the future to the second, never being mindful of the present, because this was just far too unsafe and painful. Really try and imagine it for a few seconds right now. I have learned so much from the Day Care service, prominently that 'Mindfulness' has been particularly helpful to me and I have been applying this technique both at Day Care and on my own (as described earlier in this chapter and importantly precedes the Auntie Ann event to follow) and am becoming more aware of the present and that which I have been missing and I am realising just how distant and vacant I may have appeared to the family, since my eating disorder was revealed to them almost three years ago. Everything before this was a disguise, Mum I am sorry and have no-one to blame but myself.

Of course, people have made comments right throughout my life: from being at school to university, college and even at work, but Angel was too good at persuading Rebecca to hide her troubles behind false smiles. She was too good at twisting words. She was too good at manipulating conversations, actions and behaviours and she had years of practice at befriending Rebecca, prior to the voices of reason had the chance to intervene. I was in denial of everything and believe that in no way would I have accepted any offer of help in any shape or form, any earlier. The torture may just have been worse for ALL the family and for a much longer period of time. Better I take the pain and suffer in silence. Angel was my friend.

Dear Family, I am so sorry for everything and know I can never, ever make anything up to you. I know you hate what I have grown into, I know you are each ashamed and embarrassed of me and my struggles and of where I am at in my life right now but believe me, no-one is more-so than myself. I love you Mum, and I once possessed the same expectations of myself that you may still have of me today. Mum, I have the struggle every second of every day to fight in conjunction with trying to fulfil my own and meeting the needs of others: I want to get better and I had those ambitions you still strive for me to achieve. I want to reach those goals, but now they appear just so desperately out of my reach; all just a dream for me, never to be real... I am a different person the other side of eating disordered existence and accept that I *may never* be her, just Rebecca Parker, ever again; *maybe* you all must too?

B2:

FIRST CHANCE AT EXPERIMENTING

IN HONESTY

Bi-"Dear Mum, How I saw The Auntie Ann Event, Ill or Not":

Afternoon of Thursday 4th March 2010.

Auntie Ann rang. She sounded surprised as she was not expecting to hear my voice at home in Granada on a weekday. I passed it over to Mum, who went upstairs to speak to her. Listening from the bottom of the stairs, I heard Mum speaking: "Ann it's an absolute nightmare...She didn't finish her pudding so they told her to go home...Well, that's what they do...It's the rules, you know" and then "She wouldn't come, I asked her and she wouldn't come. Yes, you come over for coffee tomorrow..." I heard Mum's footsteps coming closer so I rushed through to the kitchen, where I was waiting for us to have our morning snack together.

I asked Mum if Ann had questioned my presence at home or if she had mentioned anything about me and she replied "No, nothing was said". I said "Are you sure?" trying to encourage her to speak to me, to spoon-feed her opportunities to tell me the truth but no, nothing. I knew it was a lie. Mum just said: "Ann's coming at 10:30am tomorrow morning, for coffee".

OK, so I really did feel terrible for Mum because of course, bless her, she had only one person to talk to and to confide in regarding my situation and hearing her talk like this to my Auntie had made me just want so much to sort myself out right then and there. Go and eat! I wish. But now, for me, I knew I could not trust them. What were they planning and why were they so intent on having me seeing Ann when I had made it clear that I was not yet ready to? What were they expecting of me tomorrow? Help!

I voiced my concerns to Mum, admitting that I was feeling uncomfortable at seeing Ann. Yesterday we met Mrs. Peterson, my old primary school headmistress, in a supermarket in town and Mum had turned around and said to me with a look of disgusted afterwards, "God knows what she thought of you looking like a walking skeleton". Great, thanks Mum. I don't want to see anyone as it is and I didn't want my Auntie to see me either. I am still avoiding contact with all my school friends and university friends and all the friends that I feel like I need to impress when I meet them, making sure I have interesting things to talk about and achievements to tell of, travels, work, boyfriends etc. Not hospital. So why would I feel ready to deal with seeing my Auntie Ann, a relative whom I definitely would want to feel proud of me! I did not want the added stress of her asking questions and talking about anything to me that I felt unable to talk about and I feared it was another way that my problems could end up somehow spreading to the rest of the family and I felt ashamed of myself completely. I already feel like a failure and I detest the way I look. I don't want to socialise and parade myself around and start the fake smiles all over again. I had lost the strength and will that enabled me to carry on with that facade ever since my eating problems landed me in hospital for the second time. My struggles no longer remain secret, why should I have to keep pretending everything is OK? I cannot do it anymore, I just can't.

Mum informed me that Ann was "just popping in to pick up the jigsaw". It was the jigsaw that she had brought to the hospital for me, which I had now completed. Mum also informed me that Ann was "coming to visit me, not you". I asked Mum if she would mind taking me to town early so that Ann didn't have to be interrupted by Mum having to chauffeur her thirty year old daughter down to the hair dressers at 11:30am, but she said "No". I repeated that I didn't want to see her! My thoughts were now such that I would be sneaking out of the house in the morning and walking, or ordering a taxi, down to town before Ann even had chance to show her face on our doorstep or be driving around the village and spotting me escaping. Then they can have their coffee and chat and I would be out of the way, because I didn't want her to see me and she was apparently coming to see Mum and not me anyway, plus Ann apparently knows about my hair appointment too, so there is no harm in this idea, is there? As Mum was clearly no longer listening to me, I was left feeling totally forced into a situation that scared me and my immediate reaction was to run to safety; I just had to.

Friday 5th March 2010.

In the morning I got up in good time and tried to make myself look half decent for seeing Ann. I was all set for leaving at the back of my mind, but could I really do that to Mum? Just sneak out of the house while Mum was getting herself ready? Just leave her / them an apology note? No. I thought about it properly and rationally. All morning I tried to work out the timetable, quizzing Mum, that if Ann only came at 11am, then she would only be here for half an hour before she would have to leave, because of my appointment...? Mum just repeatedly responded with "I don't know, I told her about your appointment, she'll be here at 10:30am".

I tested the water and suggested we drive to Lilton for the afternoon after my appointment and she responded with "can't we go tomorrow, it'll be late by then?" Her response told me she was planning for Ann to still be here and to probably have lunch together because usually we go to Lilton after having lunch at home anyway and Mum would usually have given a response similar to "oh we'll see how we feel this afternoon". There was no timetable Mum was admitting to and these uncertainties were making me scared and unnerved. Why the secrecy? What were they planning? What was Mum planning and what was I going to be expected to do? Would I be able to do it? Would I freak out and have an episode in front of Auntie Ann? No, I cannot risk that. I would be totally distraught and so would they.

I wandered downstairs to see if anything was laid out in the kitchen and found only the coffee cups and the filter coffee machine out in preparation. I poured some milk into my cup (*Angel* knew Mum changed this later because the cup I had filled with my skimmed milk lay in a different position on the tray when she brought it through, but this was a small matter in amongst more pressing ones that needed addressing and I really didn't need to do this with the milk anyway, but it was just a bit more control and it made me feel safer, more respectable). I asked Mum what we were having with the coffee and she said a biscuit. I knew she was going to bring out those huge thick Chocolate Chip All Butter Shortbread Cookies and there was no way I was having one of those. I asked if we could have a plain biscuit, as that was the only other alternative in the house that I could deal with. I knew I could have that with the filter coffee. Thankfully, she said "yes OK", but I was still a nervous wreck because I wouldn't know for sure until I was offered it, then and there, from the tray.

By now I was warming to the idea of having snack with my Auntie. I was feeling more ready to and willing to join in with the snack now that I was beginning to view it less-so as an unwelcome intrusion being imposed upon me with no option. The idea of my Auntie coming over was a step in the right direction as I only usually eat in front of my Mum and with the support of the staff and patients at Day Care. Otherwise, I have to be alone, particularly where food, not so much drink, is involved. With this reasoning in mind, I persuaded myself that morning snack with Mum and Auntie Ann was a good 'baby step' to getting better.

I tried to keep my rational head on and told myself I could do the 10.30am snack, even if I just had to pretend to be happy and act and smile for them and I would even wear the jumper that Ann had bought me for Christmas. I liked this jumper and it would make them happy too. Then she'll pick up the jigsaw and leave and Mum and I can get on and go to Lilton after my appointment, if we feel OK. Fine, I was just nervous at seeing Ann, but this was normal.

When I was getting ready, however, and just before she arrived I saw Mum had also put out the lunch: homemade celery soup (to which I know Mum adds cream and allsorts) and I cannot eat this, in addition to a pile of white rolls, which I also cannot eat as I stick to my open sandwich with added protein for lunch that I make on my own special wholemeal bread and that is stated in my meal plan designed for me by the hospital. So already feeling anxious over having to be pleasant to Ann and to appear happy and positive, I now had my fear confirmed: Ann was staying to have lunch with us. It all fitted, how did I not see this plan coming? I was scared and terrified at the sight of the soup and the bread rolls waiting there for us all to eat together and have exactly the same to ingest. That was what was expected of me. The scene of light-hearted conversation and relaxed happiness on the faces of Mum and my Auntie in the lovely large country kitchen with the sun shining in and me, recoiling inside with fright, fear and angst with the noise getting louder and the sight of the impossible in front of me just growing and growing – no, I could not.

The previous day I had stuck to my meal plan of open sandwich on my usual wholemeal bread with added protein and fruit and yogurt for pudding, yet Mum still shouted at me and she had cried a lot too. I was angry to think that she had clearly asked Ann to come for lunch today. Was it to see if I could get on with what they were eating without making a fuss? Forcing me to comply, smile and be sociable? Or would I have to be difficult and make my own variation as I always did at home? Would I have the nerve to do this in front of Ann? What else they were thinking, I do not know. They obviously expected me to have exactly the same as themselves, and why shouldn't they? It is the normal thing to do and I wish I could have. I tried to think that Mum is only trying to help me, I know that, maybe I could do it with their support. I thought long and hard about this, but I had been given no preparation time to build myself up to it, there was just not enough time and it was far too optimistic anyway! I felt angry and betrayed and isolated and ashamed.

I tried to envisage myself sitting there with a plate full of stuffy white buns, brimming with thickly spread lumps of butter and a huge bowl of thick and creamy, all-be-it delicious, homemade soup. A tasty and enjoyable lunch with my Dear Mum and my lovely crazy Auntie, enjoying lunchtime over great conversation with my wonderful family; I am so lucky. Who wouldn't be looking forward to that? But the idea terrified me. I know, even if I had tried, I would have either cried out in utter distress when I tried to start or walked out without eating and locking myself away in my room, that is, if I could even manage to even make myself the buns without freezing stiff, listening to the voices that I so believe to be right and true and safe. Or would Mum have done this for me? Or even if Ann and I ate at different times, she would still have been in the house, knowing I was eating in the next room, which would have been bad enough, but maybe even hearing the usual arguments too.

No, I could put neither myself nor my family through it all because it just was not fair. I wasn't ready for this. I know Mum was only trying her best to help me and I felt for her so much that this was all here in the room with us but never discussed; that great pink elephant. I understood her and I could not be angry at her, I was just purely overridden with terrific fear. And who would make my lunch anyway? There was no way I could do it myself, or if Mum prepared all the buns for everyone to pick for themselves, there was no way I could eat the bun because I know how much butter she likes on her food and I don't even eat spread. There was no way I could go anywhere near that soup either. I couldn't even have made a token effort, which pains and frustrates me to the absolute brim. Mum, this writing probably seems way exaggerated and you are probably right, but I think 'very black and white' / 'all or nothing', and I see every eventuality in a worse-case scenario and I catastrophise how I see things turning out, always making sure I am prepared for the worst. I suppose it prepares me for the unknown and gives me a head start on dealing with things in the best way possible to keep me safe from harm. At the time, I panic and run away into myself and hide. I am at least becoming more aware of this since attending the Day Care program (Book 3: The Bigger Picture, Chapter 28).

Having no warning of this event scared me. Mum knows that I need to plan everything in order to ease the battles and my anxieties not only around food, but also around social activities and life in general. I wish I wasn't like this, but I am where I am right now and it is why I started to avoid things in the first place Dear Mum, not because I simply do not have the friends to do it with. I am trying to work slowly using baby steps in trying to change this because, believe me, I have tried so hard and I know there is no quick fix. Life provides me with too many ups and downs, too many ambiguous feelings and too many unknowns.

Stop!

Rushing thoughts soon turned to beliefs in my head: that they had clearly planned something when they tried to get me to go to Auntie Ann's for "coffee" only a couple of weekends previously, which would have turned into lunch now, of this ploy I became sure. Thinking about it now, I guess I could have tried to sit down with them and if it was too difficult, just say politely before I got upset that I will eat later and walk away. But in reality, things never happen this calmly and, how odd would that have seemed anyway, and would I have even been able to get my words out or just pathetically frozen, as per usual? The fact of a scenario happening without a performance was pure and simply wishful thinking.

Luckily, thank you Mum, there was the choice of cookies and the plain biscuit on the plate; thank you Mum. Breathe. So I sat there and did it, listening to Auntie Ann animatedly talk about her adventures with a lampshade for an hour, as only my Dear Auntie Ann could! If I hadn't have been forced into the situation with underlying motives, I would have relaxed a little maybe and not had such defensive and horribly angry and irritated thoughts. Poor Mum's fake laugh trying to humour Ann, or maybe she was just happy that it appeared to be working as here I was smiling, drinking my coffee and eating my biscuit and maybe this would work at lunchtime too, or maybe Mum was just glad to have Ann there lightening the mood and as a bit of normality or maybe Mum was just feeling extremely tired and weak and desperate to help me, but I had a feeling Mum was having troubles of her own that she was just unable to talk to me about.

I did try to enjoy it all, I really did because I so wanted to, I love Auntie Ann and her stories, but my thoughts were racing elsewhere and dreading the lunch. How was I going to deal with this? I kept thinking of myself sitting there with everyone trying to be normal and discussing things like lampshades and smiling and laughing, thinking of sitting there quietly looking at it and trying to pick it up and eat it but all of the awful scenarios kept happening. I kept trying to persuade myself to be brave and strong, but I could not see myself being able to do it at all. At one point in the past I would have even sat there giving Mum evil eyes while drinking our coffee, letting her know that I despised her for what she had done: making me sit there, with a biscuit pretending to be happy and faking my smiles, fully knowing that a good lunch was also in store for me too. But now I can understand that she is acting out of despair and she just did not know what else to do. I have accepted that I am the abnormal one, not the others for making me do something normal.

Still, there was no way I could do lunch. I thought I could ask my friend Nathan (Introduction: No More Secrets, A1) to come to Granada around lunchtime, so at least I would have a real excuse that he was here and we were staying in town for a bit longer and then Mum could just pick me up later. But even that would appear a bit strange and very rude towards Auntie Ann, as it was clear she was trying her best to help me, being aware of my difficulties around food. Nathan did text me, as usual, but he said it was too short notice, of course, and I was glad really. The only other thing was to hide somewhere, the cinema possibly, saying I had gone, but then call when Ann had left. But I cannot lie to my Mum and I didn't want to. The real Rebecca wanted to be by her side, for her to tell me everything was going to be OK. To talk to her about my intense fears that *Angel* was putting me though and for her to comfort me, to hold my hand and to just tell me it's alright, but I was alone with *Angel*.

I had to get out of Granada I just had to get as far away as possible. That way I would be safe. I was scared and my heart was beating hard right up until the moment those train doors had shut tightly and the train was moving away from my house and away from that lunch all set out ready for us to dig right into. I knew the train didn't stop anywhere before reaching London, and so I was finally safe and becoming more and more distant literally (I selfishly had visions of them driving to Paylark, having worked out what I had done) and only then could think about breathing.

Upon executing a successful escape, I had to make sure they were not expecting me to run away and so I had called them on the house phone when I had finished in the hairdressers, just to make sure they had gone home and were safely back in the village away from town. I had even considered cancelling my appointment straight away, but it was far too risky them seeing me so soon in town, just in case they decided to walk around instead of going back home. During the call, I said I would be a little longer, which ensured that they wouldn't set off until I called again and so I could walk through town to the station without being seen. My worry of being caught scared me rigid and I hated myself for what I was doing throughout, but I HAD to listen. I HAD to take care of myself. I believed my actions were taking me to safety. If they hadn't have been at home and only on their mobile, I knew I had no other choice but to call a taxi and ask it to pull up right outside the hairdressers and to take me right into the station in case Mum and Ann were really outside in the car, or walking around town, fully expecting that I would decipher their plan and so that they could intercept me on my rush to the station.

In all honesty I did feel bad in the back of my mind, but I didn't feel naughty or childish or cunning until I read my Auntie's letter she sent me afterwards. I was driven by fear. If one was faced by a bear in the early ages, one naturally uses the fight or flight (BPD, Psychological Numbing and Disassociation) response impulsively, in order to survive. I felt like this was the most important thing in the world that I had to do. All I could think about was how Mum hadn't let me in on this 'plan' and how *they'd* been devious and scheming behind my back and making out it is to help me probably too. I couldn't understand how Mum could expect me to sit there and have the same as they would have for lunch, especially when I had struggled so much yesterday to even do what was on my meal plan? How could she be so thoughtless? I was frustrated that she still had no understanding of how hard it was for me, especially after having thought that maybe she was beginning to understand. I called the train line and there was a train I could make in the not too distant future.

While I was standing in the waiting room at the station, I heard a banging on the window near the car park. It made me jump as I really believed it could well have been Mum and Ann who had realised what I had done and seen me through the window and were trying to get my attention. My heart beat faster and I prayed it wasn't them. I took myself to the far end of the platform and hid between two walls until the train arrived. I waited until the doors opened and then a few seconds more, until I felt safe enough to run onto the platform and straight onto the train at the last moment, praying for the doors to close quickly and tightly. I didn't walk through the train until it set off, for fear that I'd see poor, poor, poor, poor, poor Mum on the platform and I couldn't bear that. I longed to be near her side and in her arms, but I couldn't let myself. I didn't trust anybody but those thoughts that had kept me feeling safe for so many years.

Once on the train, I had made it. There were no plans now. I wanted to frantically call all my friends, desperate to go back into my old ways of drinking, not eating, forgetting everything, to be free from *Angel* again, just for a couple of hours and into the night... But I really tried to put this out of my head as I know it gets me nowhere and it doesn't help me. I know I just needed to calm down, to give it some time and trust that I would feel differently by the time I arrived in London. I so wanted to call Lilly at Day Care for her neutral input but I was out on my 'Week Off' and she would be busy with the other patients anyway. Because of this, I made my own efforts to think rationally.

Although the situation now felt under control, I had done something terrible and was now FORCED to speak to Mum over the phone, currently at home with Auntie Ann and both expecting my phone call at any minute, to let her know I had finished at the hair dressers and was ready to be collected and brought home to join in the lunch.

Bii-Telepathy and Assumptions Verses Riddles and Reality:

As I said, I really thought that Mum might have understood me by now, enough to have had more than an inclination about the fact that I could put two and two together and would act on impulse, being scared off in some way, by doing something, by saying I wasn't coming home, by not calling or by disappearing but clearly this was a very wrong assumption. Maybe I felt that I was trying to communicate my anxieties to her, in riddles which, sadly I have a tendency towards doing, second to expecting a person to be telepathic: HELP ME. In my own way I was trying to let her in, to understand my desperate situation and to let her offer help rather than shout, get angry, accuse or criticize out of desperation and worry. After all, had I not:

- Repeatedly put across that I didn't want to see Auntie Ann and came up with numerous suggestions to get around this, to all of which I was told "No"?

- Tried to discuss the fact that Auntie Ann wouldn't have much time at our house, but Mum said she's only coming over to pick up the jigsaw that was ready for framing, so put my mind at rest?

- Tried to gage a timetable of the day by asking if we could go into Lilton in the afternoon, to which the answer was basically a no?

- Asked Mum if I should bother to take my phone charger with me to the hairdressers so I would be able to call her when I had finished, as my battery was dying and I remember really hesitating with it in my hand on the way out of the door, because really it was due to the fact that I needed to take it with me if I was going to carry out my plan and escape back to London. I had thought that even if I take it now, I can still come back home anyway?

- Asked Mum if I should leave my coat in the car when she had pulled up outside the hairdressers and was waiting for me to get out, but we decided I should take it with me just in case?

Yet when I called Mum and told them what I had done, she was so shocked and upset when I confessed that I was on the train and she immediately took it all personally, saying I've done it to hurt her, which was the very last thing in the world that I wanted to do and in fact exactly that, was what I wanted to avoid and it was causing the opposite for everybody. Again, I was unable to use the key to communicate even a single reason behind my actions, through speech.

THE AFTERMATH: FLIGHT IN FEAR AND

EFFORTS TO PROTECT – WRONG

A Lesson Learned.

That night, or the night after, Mum called me "nothing but a slutty slut" and told me I've just treated her terribly. Mum was right, of course, in that I had treated her terribly (and Ann too) but I tried to explain to her that it was not her I was angry at or trying to hurt on purpose at all. In fact, upsetting my family was the very last thing I have wanted to do all along with this horrible "illness". Did Mum still not realise this was one major reason I had hidden my struggles behind a false smile for so many years in the first place? Admittedly though, only until recently, did I remain in complete denial of this even from myself. Protecting my family remained the most important task for me to achieve and for as long as I was making them see everything was OK, it meant they were happy and I, thankfully, was left alone.

That said, I feel my Mum cannot understand that it was me, her daughter Rebecca, who was absolutely petrified and just ran and in no way did I do it to hurt her, or to hurt Ann. I certainly hadn't intended on portraying myself as cunning or deceitful! Instead, I was ensuring escape far away from my worst fears and for this to happen had meant that I had to be selfish and look after myself...and, in hindsight anyway, I did them all a favour because who knows how the afternoon would have panned out? I certainly did not want to be a total distraught mess in front of two people for whom I love and care. Mum herself is already distraught in that I am apparently "severely mentally ill and in need of intensive professional help". I don't want to impress this upon her in any way further than I already appear to. No, better to remove myself from the situation altogether... *Listen only to me. I'll keep you safe...*

Angel Just-Rights

Should my Mum have suggested to me the idea of Auntie Ann having lunch with us, of course I would have said I wasn't ready for it – had I not already voiced my concerns about the coffee invitation only a week or two previously? – I had enough to think about, especially during this week, as Dear Reader, you will be aware. I saw the coffee idea as an added stress and had thought, or hoped, Mum was becoming more aware and patient to my present struggles, but maybe she still continues to believe I am just being awkward and defiant? I don't know and I don't expect her to find it in herself to understand why I find everyday events so distressing and impossible to be involved with, when I don't even understand it all myself. But at least I could have thought about the idea with prior warning. Only now do I realise that I am so lucky to have the support of them both and that they are willing to help me with things and I hope they are still there offering out their hands to me, when I am ready.

But right now, I need it to be on my terms and at my own pace. I cannot "just do it", just like that, I always used to think that if I really wanted to "just do it" and get on with it, then of course I could start and get better, because this is what I actually believed. But I have realised that actually I cannot "just do it" and that an illness has a hold on me now and that I need to LISTEN and to take the help and support of those whom I can TRUST and believe that those whom I trust KNOW WHAT IS BEST for me. Not too much, but just what I need, for example, Mum, it is never helpful when you say to me "I'll be happy if you ate the whole box of chocolate biscuits before the end of the week", or when you shout at me if I don't have a full plate covered with rice and potatoes and topped with sauce just like you sometimes enjoy and the three different vegetables, or sometimes no vegetables...and certainly no salad!

All this confuses me and I feel very insecure in trusting your judgment in advising me on quantities and what I need (not more!) and so I just end up having what I think is right: Yes, I try to push out the boundaries of not feeling too safe an amount so I know it is not too skimped, but which is probably in reality actually still a bit less than it should be but at least I know it is not more or too much because this scares me and I feel totally off course, edgy, anxious, worried, stressed, panicky, angry, frustrated and then we will have our arguments and you will say if I water down my semi-skimmed milk, "it doesn't count, you've not had it" or when I leave the icing on a cupcake that "it doesn't count, you've not had it" and this makes me want to give up trying altogether rather than keeping a strength in fighting this demon that sits on my shoulder with me twenty four hours a day. It is so much easier to give up and to give in and listen to *Angel*, who is always there and has been there day in, day out with me for many years before that day you found out about my disorder. It is there persuading me that not eating anything is the best thing for you...*you're different! Listen to me! Don't listen to them! They don't know what's best for you! I'll look after you! I'll show you how it's done! Don't do it! Others can. YOU CAN'T! EVER!*

I am sorry, but the biscuit thing really stuck in my head even today and the cereal thing a few months later where you grabbed two handfuls of my cereal, plus a bit extra, out of the packet and said to me "that's what your bowl should look like in the morning". How does this keep me feeling safe and able to then have my 10am snack followed by my lunch followed by everything else that day, if I am stressed about having had too much cereal already and it is only breakfast time? I am sorry, but this is how I think right now. Yes, I was eating the chocolate biscuits that day, and other days in the past, but there was no way any of it was ever kept down. I am so sorry. It was keeping you happy, it was keeping everybody happy and continuing with life, but the truth is that I was never able to keep it down Mum and after everything I know this secrecy has proven so much worse for everyone involved, including myself. Falsifying my entire life is not an option to me anymore. This way of keeping people happy, I have learned, is so much worse for everyone and is in no way helping towards my recovery at this stage. Now my eating disorder has become common knowledge in the family and I am facing the task of having to re-piece my life back together. My previous life was false and lead to one reason why I avoided coming home in the end, because it was a cover-up and nothing was real. In true reality I was draining and hurting and self-loathing so much in the process from what I was doing to myself. I had no real choices: my behaviour was controlled by the shadows of *Angel*, totally unwitting of Rebecca.

Now-a-days I can feel secure in coming home because part of my secret existence has been uncovered and I don't have to pretend any longer, plus Day Care has really helped me with establishing a routine of normal eating, which I have managed to continue and I am extremely thankful for this as I never thought I would even be able to achieve this. Another reason that I feel secure at home is that I know it has been working for me and I do not want to push myself too far, too quickly so that I cannot deal with things – meaning my emotions, I suppose – any longer and go tumbling and crashing head first back to square one, because Mum, I would rather die than be trapped all alone in that cycle again. Bulimia is evil, it is utter torture. I even prayed to God to make it stop, for it please to be the last time; time and time again. I made promises and agreed terrible consequences with Him (Book 2: Who Am I, Part 1, Chapter 20) and still, it would always just happen, in desperation, again and again and again. So, Dear Mum, it may seem that I am not getting better, but I really am and I feel I am making such progress. I am working at being able to live a more normal life, to live more freely from this absolute and incessant imprisoning hell, using baby steps as the only sure way to recovery.

TO CHANGE Means:

I Have To Continue Believing There Is No More Harm.

There Is Little To Be Lost,

Yet A Lot To Be Gained.

Others Have To Believe I AM DESPERATE.

PREAMBLE

TRUTH OF MY PAST DOUBLE LIFE:

Introduction

Purpose And Wish:

This Memoir Detects All Events That I've Seen;
It's The Way I Reflect My Whole Life To Have Been.
Angel's Truth's Written, To Read Should You Choose;
It Involves Those Held Dear And, I Warn, Won't Amuse.

Do Not Shed Doubt As 'larm Bells May Resound;
The Past's Been Allowed – Time Cannot Be Rewound.
Do Not Despise, Impart Anger Nor Blame;
My Wish Is For Family, Stalwarts To Remain.

Close Circle Of Five Now Depleted To Four;
Please Let's All Strive Not To Lose Any More.
No Dwelling In "What If I..."'s; No Scolding, No Sneers;
Rather Unite Easing Turmoil And Tears.

Angel Just-Rights

i

Clouded By Mist:

For Years Unrequited I Pondered And Thought;
My Mind Broadened Blighted More Feelings It Fought.
Questions Would Ruminate Round In My Brain;
Calm And Consistent Same Contract Still Came:

"Mind-Over-Feeling's The Rule Of The Game;
Yourself Must Be Soundless And Selflessly Trained!
Detach From Discomfort! Aches Bury In Sin!
Accept You're Not Worthy! Improve Strength Here-in!

Hold On...Look What You've Done! We've Not Even Begun!
How Dare You Have Fun! 'Less You're Faking A Pun?
This Life, It's No Trial! Hide All Tears With Your Smile!
'Least Weep In The Rain, Must Screen Hint Of All Feign!"

ii

Hello Path To Bliss?

Years Untangling This Blur, Now In Truth I Can Say;
I'd Adhered To Incur, To A Life Led This Way.
"Listen To Me! I'll Ensure You're Secure!
Lest Your Secrets' Disturbed, Then They'll Sure Cause Uproar!"

Covertly Deceptive Promises Galore;
Naively I'd Stepped, Through Its Cryptic Trap Door.
Irrational Thought, Pronounced And Prevailed;
Prickled In Fraught, Sole To Shadow's Avail.

"Strict Routines And Rules, To You I'll Enthuse!
Your Guide's By Your Side So Learn Quickly With Pride!
Act And Believe No Reprieve Is Our Means! Always Be Present!
Never Reflect!
Our Efforts Will Then Prove Us Utmost Perfect."

iii

Hit...Or Amiss?

At First I Felt Special This Power Within;
Had Chosen To Sponsor Myself, So Akin
In Our Strength And Allegiance, Deep Drive To Be Top!
Each Instruction I'd Follow, Soon Formers Forgot.

Fond Family And Friends Marv'lling "Where Do You Go?"
Confused In Responses I'd Callously Throw.
Unwittingly So I'd Withdraw And Bestow;
My Whole Life – Safe Secure – With This Great Secret Pro!

iv

Evil Life Kiss?

While I Strive For Rewarding Results To Rotate;
Those Driven Retorts Nonetheless Inundate!
Compelled 'To Reversion: *"Refrain And Abstain!"*
Fiend Reins Its Assertion: *"Veil Mayhem And Pain!"*

Dishonest Thrust! Intractable Trust!
Bound In A World Of Shoulds, Cant's, Do's, Don'ts, Musts!
Persistently Pleasing! Unnaturally Coy!
Rebecca Confound By This Evil Shrill Ploy!

v

Swindled Gift:

Years On I Awake To Most Dreadful A Show;
Existence In Prison's The Life I Now Know:

Lost Is My Voice, No Act Simply By Choice...
Spirit Surrendered, Soul Zealous, Subdued...
Vacant, Inane, Only Bones That Protrude...

Values And Worth, They're All Tainted And Waned;
Not A Thing But A Fling With Death's Door Had I Gained!

So My Faithful "Best Friend" Possessed Hidden Intent?
In That *Ghoul* I'd Obeyed! Thirty Years Lacking Vent!
Believing "It's Just Me!" All Trusting And Pleased;
All The While Was It *Actually Sowing Spite's Seeds?!*

65

vi

Drowning Fish?

As Micci Diluted *So Angel Delights!*
'Til Sight Did Ignite! O'er Her Soul Glossed Plush Plight:
Many Times Did I Ride On This Monstrous Rough Tide;
A Secret? Suppressed It. Dear Family? Protected.

So How Dare She! In Loved Ones! Seep Evil Demise?!

Illustrious, Fixated, Fearless, Fanatical;
Fiendishly Frank, Fickle, Firm, Fervent Foe!
Thanks For Distorting, Disturbing, Disgracing;
Defacing, Destroying My Precious Life Goals!

You Promised Me Strength! All You Gave – Weak Pretence!
Now To *You* I Do Soundly Implore:
"Leave Us In Peace! Before We Self-Cease!
We Cannot Live Slave To These Laws Anymore!"

vii

Goodbye Rift?

All Secrets Revealed Exhumes All That Is Weak;
Which Often I'd Riddled But Now I Do Speak:
"Existence Endured; Punishments Procured;
Survival As Tool; Slave Like A Fool.
Perilous Rides, Through Cold Wintery Tides!
Mind, Body, Heart, Soul Become Broken! Unwhole!
Emotions And Thoughts, Constant Blocking Exhausts!
With Sorrow, Regret, Overwhelming Self-Blame,
Comes Anger And Hurt And Distress And Disdain!
Over And Over And Over And Over Again And Again And Again
And Again."

viii

Understanding My Gist?

My Being Wrapped, All Alone In This Prison;
Ensures I Remain Lodged From Harm (So I think...)
In My Safe Hiding Place, *"Repeat Same Simple Tastes!"*
Besieged To Eschewing Alarm (As Health Sinks...)

Logic Screams Out, With No Rational Doubt:
"It's Obnoxious! Destructive! Impure! Just Get Out!"
Yet Incessant, Relentless, Unduly Cruel Rules;
Ne'er Dare Rest From Those Orders And Lures.

"No Feelings! Strict Laws! In My Shadow You're Destined;
Acceptance! Success! And Much More Is In Store...!
Alone You're Forever Just Hopeless, Ne'er Clever!
With Me You'll Live Ceaselessly Sure".

ix

Destined Just To Exist?

Please First Believe I'm So Sorry To All;
There's NO 'Fight-Flight-Freeze' Left Inside Any More.
As Quest Lays To Rest I Still Long To Keep Strong;
But In Every Direction I Turn, I Do Wrong.

Desperate Efforts To Cope, Prove So Darkly To Cloak;
Recollections Evoked; Sly Behaviours Provoked.
Burned Out To Protect Those Wished Ne'er To Effect;
All Exertions Frustrated In Vain. Do you See?

For Eternally Weak, Simple, Ugly, Dull, Wrecker;
A Future So Simply Can't Be.
'las To Those Whom I Love, As I Reach Skies Above;
May You All Comprehend Finally...?

The Story Of How, From Once Shining Enigma:
Kind, Playful And Laughing, Quite Curious Rebecca;
Leaked Evil I'll-Natured, Defiant, Deplorable;
Insolent, Shame-Faced, Malevolent! Insipid! Ill Me.

Angel Just-Rights

(ix cont.)

Try To Foresee Secret Worlds Kept From Thee;
While Admittedly Wrong And Absurd, Now I See.
Strange, Silent, Lone Struggles! Spry Actions! Faint Muddles!
Lost, Hidden In Riddle: The Innocent Voice Of Micci.

This Is The Truth In My Thoughts And My Moves;
In *Angel Just-Rights* I Have Opened My Fights.
May From Now Until Ever We All Pull Together;
Let Voices Ne'er Falter But 'Speak'?

One Lesson I've Learned: Trust / Respect They Are Earned;
Quit Miming And Cheating, Retreating And Sneaking.
Our Minds And Our Voices, Our Rights And Our Choices;
They're A Need And Must Always Be Heard.

Angel Just-Rights

x

Recovery Wish:

Now, Should You Wish, Continue To Fish;
You'll Hear I've Been Handed A Key.
As My Story Is Read I'll Be Starved? Overfed?
Both Behaviours Familiar To Me.

But Now I'm Aware I May "Cope" In This Way;
When All's Cripplingly Too Much To Bare.
As All Hope's Drained Away And I Still Fear Each Day;
In Peace, May My Soul At Last Lay.

No Messing Around, Now It's Finally Down;
To The Ultimate, Pitiless Sum.
As My Story Is Told Fuming Frowns, They'll Unfold;
Please Forgive, Secrets Out They Must Come!

(x cont.)

Think How Rebecca Once Brave, Independent;
Ambitiously Cheeky, Strong, Sporty And Caring;
Turned Angry And Broken, Cheap, Weak And Despairing;
Constantly Planning, Conspiring, Controlling;
Slowly Becoming A Desperate And Needy;
Child: Severely Undone.

Hence, I Leave It To You, The Decision Is Yours;
Right Now, I Suggest One Does Pause.
'Though My Aim Is To Free Both My Family, Plus Me;
From Here-in Reads The Stages In Cause.

Be Brave. Beware: Content's Not A Bore;
Angel Just-Rights Is A Fight From The Core.
Humour, Delight; Prodigious Insight;
Complete, With A Meaning For All.

xi

Predicted After-Swish:

Dearests' Stunned? Myself Shunned:
Source Of The Family Tear, How D'I Dare?

Courageous And Brave, Peering Out From My Cave;
With Goals To Rebuilding This "Life" Others Crave.
Pledge Promise To Me That You **All** Will Be There;
Reliving With Me, Wild Reality-Mares?

Less Your Candid Support, From This World I'll Abort;
In Sincerely Grave, Weak Honesty:
There's No Future For Me, Trapped In Secrets And Taunts;
Only Wish? Be At Ease And Be Free.

xii

To Perish Or Cherish?

Here I Am. This Is Me;
Confronting The Truth Of My Life!
Strength Alone I Possess, Just Not Enough;
Your Presence Is All I Request.

For Myself: Never Options, Control Nor Decisions;
Thus Here I State Clearly For You:
I've Turned My Key, Now You're Able To See;
Permission's Been Granted To Read...

...Or **You** May Prefer To Take Heed.

?

In Turning This Page;

You're Choosing The Deed.

I Invite You To Enter:-

Remember: More Caution, Less Speed.

...

BOOK 1:

SECRETS OUT

Angel Just-Rights

CHAPTER 1:

HOME

1i-Best Childhood, EVER:

Sibling Games.
The children invented a game around two sisters named 'Kerry and Rebecca'. 'Kerry' was based on a child we knew little of, through the dancing classes that we attended in our local town, Grenada. 'Kerry' was the eldest daughter of our dancing school teachers. 'Kerry' was a brilliant, glitzy dancer: pretty, delicate and tiny in frame, nimble, self-confident; always laughing always smiling. 'Kerry' won every local dancing competition without fail. 'Kerry' was always the brightest star of two that shone at each annual dancing show because 'Kerry' was the very best at dancing. 'Kerry' revelled in the role as queen of the dancing school. Everybody aspired to be as good as 'Kerry'. Everybody would watch her, mouths open in awe. Everybody wanted to be 'Kerry's' best friend.

Twenty-one months the senior, 'Kerry' grew up with her sister 'Rebecca' who also attended the dancing school in Grenada. 'Rebecca' was a promising dancer: awkwardly endearing, impishly hearty in character and frame, precise, responsive; always thoughtful always cheerful. 'Rebecca' stood as tough competition for her rival in local dancing contests. 'Rebecca' was always the other star of two at every annual dancing show because 'Rebecca' was the very best at capturing and charming the audiences who came to watch. 'Rebecca' revelled in her role at perceiving others' needs and helping fellow pupils at the dancing school to excel. Everybody was attended to and looked after by 'Rebecca'. Everybody trusted her to know the very next steps and they knew she was there to guide them all equally. Everybody was seen as a friend to 'Rebecca'. 'Kerry and Rebecca', the game invented, excitedly, one rainy afternoon inside a large stone gabled family house in a quiet country village high up on a hill, by two sibling sisters, and their little brother.

79

'Little Brother' was, as the name suggests, the little brother of 'Kerry and Rebecca'. Although the sisters tried their utmost to affirm intentions that this character must be based on the dancing teacher's son in order not to deter from the rules of game, my brother, averse to dancing himself, was never keen to comply with this stipulation and so the sisters let him join in anyway. 'Little Brother', as indeed was the case with all three of us, developed a character rather akin to himself. Once formulated, this fantasy game was played out everywhere and anywhere, in whatever we were doing or in wherever we were going. The foundations were, briefly, as follows:

My sister would choose to play 'Kerry', 'Eyelash', 'Big Suzy', 'Little Suzy': four characters possessing similar personality traits and similar talents in that they were all the best at dancing, the most confident in nature and they always won places in every competition entered (unless special events in a story unfolded!) Let us say, it was expected for them to win.

My brother, as the sole male character in the game, could play 'Big Brother', 'Little Brother', or 'Little Cousin Michael': the former carried out handy-man jobs around the school as required, he came to the rescue during 'storms' in the garden and he took the girls out on trips and taught shooting and woodwork. The latter, well we kindly let my brother choose his name in order to allow him some variation and a friend for 'Little Brother'. 'Little Brother' was the most popular of his characters because he could spend hours of the day conducting his beloved radio station (my brother was excellent at talking and entertaining and replicating that which he heard every morning during breakfast); he could act as 'the boss' in his business, he was adventurous and technically adept.

I liked to be either 'Rebecca' or 'Spuster': quieter than the other female characters, reflective and easy-going, logically-minded with a sound ability to adapt to everything new while applying her own confident, gentle facile way. Sometimes, my sister and I would alternate in playing the 'Big' and 'Little Sarah' and the 'Big' and 'Little Lucy' cousins, usually when we needed extra numbers in a class or competition. But above all, Dear Reader, I loved to be 'Mrs. Baker': Mother, Teacher, and Headmistress (Book 2: Who Am I? Part 2, Chapter 27). In this role, I was organised, I could teach the class academically, I could mark the dancing medal tests (while my sister was happily thriving in the dancing roles, I could focus my attention on the details, giving reasons and justifications in my markings), I could direct the plays and the shows and ultimately, I suppose, no matter whatever drama was to unfold in between, 'Mrs. Baker' was the mediator, she was allowed to take the lead; I was in charge and I remained in control. Stepping into the role of 'Mrs. Baker' felt natural to me and was empowering. SHE was my inspiration, my life's aspiration; my dream.

When we were 'doing laps' on our bikes in the garden, 'Mrs. Baker' was the one to be stationed in the garage, the one who decided for each pupil on exactly the number of laps to cycle around the bushes on their 'horses' (or motorbike, in the case of 'Michael'). I had to be the different one, the one with the role, the one to sort out the problems with the 'horses' in this case, the one with the knowledge and the answers. All in all, I was the one in control at this stage and not the one desperate to exercise, oh how things change! (Book 2: Who Am I?) Even when the roles changed round and I found myself riding 'my horse' around the garden, I still remember how my body felt simply as one with the way in which I rode my bike (Book 1: Secrets Out, Part 1, Chapter 3). I enjoyed the pretence more than anything else in the world because I loved to ride my bike like the wind! And such was my innate desire to ride real, powerful horses – all on my own – that I would soar right up into fantasyland, burning with images, sounds, memories from my favourite horse television program and my precious series of horse fiction books that were 'just mine'.

Dear Reader, many times throughout my childhood I would dream about leading a real black stallion though our house while being dressed in full riding gear, something I never to date experienced. I would feel overwhelmingly excited and proud that here I was completely in control of this great and powerful, beautiful silky strong beast, wearing my jodhpurs and my treasured velvet riding hat and my smart little black jacket and carrying my whip, just so the animal knew who was boss. I would mount him with a natural ease and begin riding round our garden, always initiating from the top of the hill where stood, all trusted, loyal and protecting, our eminent enormous Sycamore Tree. I knew I had a real passion for riding and I knew I could excel at it if I was given the chance that I yearned for. I knew I possessed the determination required to make myself become the very best at it if I was proved less natural than I liked to imagine. Such was my zest and ambition to seize that which evoked such immensely agreeable feelings that I knew this was what I was born to do and I would ensure that I lived out my dream, because I felt it intensely from my heart. I resolved to practice and practice and practice in order to become a super star, internationally renowned, acknowledged, accredited and remembered for my riding. This was MY REASON IN LIFE.

The siblings also enjoyed putting on 'shows' and 'dances' for their parents. Once-in-a-while, they were given permission to ransack the dressing-up-box and to act out their famous nursery rhymes and children's stories and we would even invent our own, using props, music, lines and cues. We would make it a real performance to be proud of with a tape of sound effects and music, with exciting 'quick changes' in between scenes, each performance complete with a finale, bows and curtsies.

Something I also enjoyed was going for walks and bike rides in the village with my Dear Dad. We went for short ones and for long ones too. Daddy (always walking) would take us to 'Church Lane' to visit the graveyard where we would look over the fields at the magnificent views of surrounding villages and monuments, feed the white horse with grass and say hello to the bulldog that lived at the dead-end opposite the-house-with-the-hens that was completely covered in pretty red leaves in the Autumn. On our longer walks, we would continue down 'the dirt track', stopping off to feed the Shetland ponies with the carrots and apples that my Dad had brought along in his pockets to surprise us all with. On reflection, I am now able to appreciate the pleasure such gestures of love had brought to my Dad (although myself only having yet experienced this second hand (Epilogue: Immeasurable Thanks and Pledge) setting out with surprise intentions and seeing his children's faces light up in joy, I realise, he was not only enjoying the action, but was cherishing each special moment that his thoughtfulness had brought into our lives. That was what made him happy. That was what made him smile. That was what he lived for.

We would venture further past the village veterinary surgery on occasion and I would fight childishly with my brother and sister over whose turn it was to call Mum (who always remained at home with our Maid and Butlers, tidying the house up and cooking the Sunday lunch for us all, in peace) from the red telephone box at the top of the road to say hello and prove to her how far we had proudly come. We always felt this as a big achievement, to have walked or cycled so far. I used to think this phoning ritual was funny, but now I realise it may have been an important call that my Mum would anticipate because it acted as a sign of confirmation to my Dear Mum that my Dear Dad was OK, because nobody had mobile phones in those days and she would worry about him if we were all out for longer than agreed.

On graduating to bigger bikes, we were allowed out for short bikes rides around the village with my little brother "as long as you all stay together and on the pavements" and only my sister and I were allowed to go on the longer bike rides up to the vets and sometimes even around the surrounding villages. We did, of course, continually assume 'Kerry and Rebecca' roles on each and every outing. The adventures began when 'Little Brother' was old enough to join us, when we located 'the hills and hollows', taking turns on his mountain bike that was adept at dealing quickly with such unpredicted terrain, I found my fearlessness in speeding down steep hills, racing with each other ever harder and faster and exploring new places, on occasion being chased from trespassing private land unbeknown to us, totally exhilarating, whereas my sister, however, was much more worried and unsure, rapidly becoming tired and wanting to return home.

My quiescent raring extravagance was aroused by the curiosities and hunger for adventure of my brother that would push beyond my own comfortable, already extended boundaries and in turn, this distending would hasten my sister's bad mood swings. 'Rebecca' would be more ready and inclined to listen to her older sister, drawing on 'Mrs. Baker' to help entice 'Little Brother' back to logic and back to 'being good'. 'Kerry' always won. In obedience to the rules of our parents, we would always wait for her, poor thing, usually she was bothered by her hay fever too and she never really was one for activities anyway, but she always managed to keep her younger siblings on track. We would all always stick together, no matter what disagreements or arguments broke out. We always sorted things out and would arrived back home much stronger and happier for having worked through all our differences.

Back in the home, I used to enjoy being my brother's 'secretary' when he asked me to 'do business' with him. I would enjoy getting everything organised and really being business-like, more than I enjoyed 'doing radio' with my brother, where he would record himself speaking into a microphone and playing music and doing interviews, usually on myself, or if I was too busy with homework, he would go and bother my sister. I wasn't good at speaking, but I enjoyed getting my head down and completing tasks in writing and I took specific pleasure in efficiently ticking each item, no matter how large or small, off from my list. Done.

My brother and I used to play a game called 'sleep-over' in which he would assume the role of 'Little Michael' and I would choose, usually one of the 'Little' characters, such as 'Little Suzy' for instance to play with him. We would prepare everything – the room, the food, even our very own sleeping bags – agreeing the story and closing the curtains in order to replicate the night time. We would wake up pretending it was the middle of the night and then get out the food for the midnight feast. The food usually consisted of a few raisins, dried lentils in a dish, a biscuit or some chocolate and a drink or something like that, as I recall. We would eat while remaining in our sleeping bags and while telling scary stories to each other, keeping up the pretence that it was dark and spooky and was the middle of the night. Then we would wake up in the morning and draw back the curtains and wait for 'Mrs. Suzy' or 'Mrs. Michael' to appear, to pick up 'Little Suzy' or 'Little Michael' from our house and we would all thank each other for having us to stay, before relaying the whole story back to our parents on the car journey home.

Real life bedtimes in our house, I also remember well. I shared a bedroom with my sister. We used to jump on the beds and practice our forward roles and acrobatics, ballet and tap dancing, repeating all we had learned in our lessons that week. We would hold onto the top of our identical white wardrobes, using these as the ballet bar. I remember always being the best at acro, which was my favourite class of the week, and I made it to the top class exceptionally quickly. I was super bendy and pushed myself into positions that others never could. My sister could never do the splits, but I could execute them both ways. I loved taking part in the acro dances at the end of year shows especially, because it was so much harder to slip over simply in your own bare feet rather than in those tap shoes and those ballet shoes. I loved the grip, the cold touch – even the smell – of the stage!

I think my sister enjoyed ballet most of all – personally, I found ballet too girly and too flirty for me, but this made it perfect for my sister – ballet was seen as the most delicate and the most important, the most highly regarded form of dance and the one and only dance genre, if any, you were expected and were proud of, for excelling at. In later years, I expressed interest in starting 'modern' dancing, which was similar to acro, as I understood it, but with a contemporary twist. However, I was told that I wouldn't like it because it was too 'showy' for me. I took this to mean I was a terrible dancer and not worthy to be on the stage doing such dance, which I know was absurd. But my attentions were swiftly diverted elsewhere. My sister and I began 'national' dancing instead. I loved the long colourful skirts we wore for this style of dancing, all uniquely handmade and I got to wear the posh grown-up black shoes too. Half of the class was even dedicated to sharing the homework that was set in the previous week: we all possessed our own folders to accumulate research quite literally on 'national' dancing.

Three things I remember hating about dancing were, number one: having my photo taken with my sister outside our house on a cold day! I remember being jealous one year that she had managed to get a really nice yellow dress for her ballet dance in the show in which she looked absolutely beautiful and I was made to wear a tiny red and gold bikini for my acro dance. I hated it! The dress was for ballet, yes, and the bikini was for acro, yes, but I still hated wearing next to nothing and all I can remember from that dance was being paired with a the girl who had to catch my feet in a hand-stand half way through the performance, because I came face to face with her mouldy green big toe!

The second is a vision, like an outer-body experience that remains with me to this day. I was waiting in the small changing room / warm-up area for my sister to finish in her dance class and I was sitting quietly on the floor with my legs crossed reading a book and enjoying my bottle of cherryade and 1p 'fizzy fish and shrimp' sweets that always was served on a cute little saucer, when a much older girl came over to me. I am unsure how she started with this act but all I remember was her pushing my legs down as far as they would possibly go, onto the floor. I think maybe she was having a competition to see who was the 'bendiest', therefore the best. I remember just taking the pain I was feeling because I didn't want to appear weak or that my body hadn't been trained enough or possessed the ability enough to stand it. She would continue until literally she was standing on both of my legs, bouncing up and down, laughing out of astonishment. She was asking me "wow, doesn't that hurt?" I was in severe pain, but I denied it and they thought I was superwoman. My tears were invisible and I didn't show any negative emotion until I was in the car on the way home and I opened up to my Mum about my distress because I didn't want to stay there on my own next week. Mum was angry at the girl and asked who it was. She told me I should have said "ow! That hurts". I know I should have. I know 'Kerry' would have had the confidence to have done the right thing, but I wasn't 'Kerry', I didn't retaliate, I wanted to be more than perfect too.

The third is simply, as touched upon earlier, the fact that I was unable to let myself shine as much as I wanted to in the end of year shows, through constant fear of slipping over in front of so many, as so many did! But this encouraged my enjoyment experienced while exhibiting the flair I demonstrated in every acro dance, which was a feeling that overwhelmed me with warmth, worth, achievement, purpose, place, and pride.

At bedtime, my sister and I used to play a game called 'how many so-and-so's do you know?' She almost always won this game. We also used to play 'the describing game', which was my particular favourite. We were lucky in that we knew the same people at school, at dancing classes, at Brownies, later at music school, at our next schools etc. We used to play a famous card game too, over and over again, quickly hiding it all from Mum and Dad if they came into the room to check on us. They would tell us off lightly for still talking at night when we should have been asleep and we would then pretend to be asleep if they popped in their head again. Now I really feel for my poor brother, who must have heard our whispers and laughs and may have felt really left out.

My brother experienced major struggles at bedtime. He always had to have Mum or Dad put him to bed and to stay in the bed until he had fallen asleep. If he woke up and realised he was alone, he would be shouting out and Mum would have to go back and put him to sleep again. I remember Dad once took him by the ear when he came downstairs one night and put him back into bed. This behaviour of my brother's didn't change for a very long time until it reached the stage where my parents were leaving him crying for hours until finally he would fall to sleep. It was terribly painful to hear a loved one crying for so long and this treatment kept the whole family awake night after night. I would hear my Dad saying to my Mum "leave him; it won't work if you go every time. He has to learn". And he did.

When I had my own room, and when my parents would put me to bed, I used to get this feeling at night that I have never tried to describe before or tell anyone about, because it is extremely hard to put into words, but here I will try. I would have my eyes closed, but would see big, big round bollards heading towards me. My world would feel absolutely huge, more huge than anyone could imagine, and overwhelming. Rather like just before you faint, in that split second where every single sensation, thought or feeling is seen rather through tunnel vision, all minute and tiny, like a pin prick, until you realise what is about to happen to you – or was it that the feeling is so intense that I couldn't stand it and blocked it out? Whatever this was, it scared me. It was like (and I only likened it to this when I was in the moment this weekend – Mid June 2010, now 29 years old!) when I had been sitting down having my snack in the kitchen with my Mum: I had been holding my big mug of tea for a very long time and my hand had forgotten what it was holding. I knew it was a mug, but I was thinking I had drunk all of the contents and that it was therefore empty. Suddenly the feeling was unnaturally heavy, which it shouldn't have been because it was empty! Then I looked down and actually it was mostly full. My hand and fingers had been in the position for a while. Now, I can liken this feeling I experienced over and over again, to that of the experience described above. I suppose it is akin to 'pins and needles' where you have no control over a part of your body that feels so big, yet you have zero sensation of it.

Three Differing Personalities.

My sister and I used to be very close and shared a lot of things as we grew up and we were so close in age, many people used to think we were twins. We shared a room and similar clothing, yet we possessed our own personalities and although I did feel honoured to be in my sister's protective shadow at times, I also felt suppressed when we were together and sometimes, not always, felt unsure of myself when I was left to my own devices.

Kerry was the sensible one: the one I let speak for us both, brimming with confidence, bossy, academically gifted and worked very hard, she was a 'teacher's pet' kind of student who was comfortable in her abilities, not easily embarrassed, she knew her own mind, she knew what she wanted and she knew how to network in order to get it. My sister was however, the extreme worrier. I remember one day after school when we were waiting for Mum to pick us up at 4pm and was five minutes late, literally. Kerry was actually in tears, unable to stand still, biting her nails, praying and just highly anxious. All these years I had assumed that she was worried Mum had been involved in a car accident and so I had tried to do my best at the time to show understanding into her state, telling her that Mum is only five minutes late and most probably stuck in the traffic, but I was finding it difficult to comprehend and empathise with the extent of this anxiety she was clearly going through. Now, I realise maybe my sister feared that something had happened to my Dad, or to both of them even, and that they were at the hospital. My sister probably tended to catastrophise when events took a turn for the unknown when she was younger. As she grew older however, this appeared slowly to ease.

Kerry, you never disclosed to me anything that was actually running through your mind on that day to make you so distressed. Maybe I remain completely wrong in my guesses and for this I am sorry. I was unable to diminish your worries or to help you in any way at the time. I tried, but was unable to because you were sharing nothing with me, for whatever reasons. Dear Sister, I ask you to hold the thought, and I am sure that you remember it vividly, exactly how it felt being unable to speak out your torments and fears.

So I, on the other hand, was the shy and quiet one: reflective and thoughtful, preferring to work alone yet in the company of others so I could be sure to make important tasks my own little project and to complete these as perfectly as possible, putting every ounce of my energy into it. I was 'good-at-everything' as my sister had graciously put it on numerous occasions, such as when she showed her shock that time I told Kerry and my Mum that I was asked by the Head of Physical Education (my favourite teacher) if I would join the school netball team, when I always won at crazy golf and mini golf on holiday and when I was always the quickest to pick up new skills. I suppose, I had the practical gift and my sister was ever the academic.

I was never as clever as my sister academically, even though I would work my socks off right up until the very last minute of handing something in, so that at least I know I had tried my hardest on it and to make sure it be as close to more than perfect as I possibly could. That way I was less likely to miss something essential and it meant I could feel a little bit satisfied that I couldn't have made it any better. I never could understand the girls at school who would leave an exam early! Surely you could check something one more time, or add something here or there, or realise something and just gain even that one extra mark that could make the difference between an A star and an A or a pass or a fail? I tried my hardest to get the content as correct as I was able but my brain was more concerned with the finer detail of each word, phrase, title in the project, the presentation, the creative and arty side of things that make the difference and make it stand out from the rest, or so I thought; basically, my sister shone academically and I shone at everything else considered less important and less impressive.

Once at primary school I remember we were supposed to write a creative story in our English exam about 'Moving House' and I got stupidly excited with all these ideas rushing into my brain and I wrote a story about 'A Moving House'. The teacher and my parents all thought it was brilliant and wonderful and were proud of what I had produced. I admit I enjoyed that exam! But I felt so stupid when they had pointed out to me that I had actually misread the task so wrongly and had produced written work about a silly, childish adventure story! How pathetic, simple and humiliated I felt.

Kerry used to tease me for my 'just rights' as she named them. I suppose now it was a slight touch of Obsessive Compulsive Disorder (OCD), but she herself also had these 'just rights', to an extent, in the way she used to pray quietly to herself, muttering under her breath at times or the number of times she had to say specific words when she sneezed in order to excuse herself. I put it down to childish phases that people grew out of. I don't think my brother experienced or appreciated the way any of this behaviour worked at all, from my recollection he didn't suffer its compulsions outwardly. When I was sharing a room with Kerry on our holiday at the seaside one year, she noticed it was really taking me a long time and several attempts to be happy with the way I was putting the top back onto my deodorant in the morning and she commented on this being severely disturbing and abnormal behaviour, making sarcastic faces at me and saying I needed help. The number of times I had to do it until it 'felt exactly right' did get out of hand sometimes, I admit, and it took me ages to get ready in the mornings because of the extent it could reach and this made it harder for me to get myself up in the mornings sometimes, even just thinking and worrying, just for a flash, about definitely having to go through this rigmarole right from the moment my eyes would open each new day because otherwise something terrible would happen to my precious family. I used to even become angry with myself if one morning I had missed out on the walk along the beach, purely because I couldn't get myself up and ready quickly enough to accompany my Mum and my Sister. Now, I have learned to rise earlier in the morning than most people would, in order to allow time enough to be ready.

Everything had to be 'just right' and completely 'OK' in order for me to be allowed to move onto the next step i.e. of putting on my socks: it had to be the left foot first and then the right, when I stepped into my knickers I had not to touch the edges *at all*, it had to *feel right* or I had to take it out and do it all over again, and if my foot had touched the side, even by a single thread, the knickers had to be shaken and taken out of my hands *completely*, properly decontaminated by my wrong, therefore harmful touch, so I had to throw them up into the air and catch them in a *certain and proper way.* This had to happen numerous times before I could even start to put them on again...and if my hands weren't feeling *right* or holding it *exactly right* when I caught them...or if they didn't get enough air through them in the *right enough manner* in order to make them *OK* when they were thrown etc. ...and so it continued. I didn't think anything of it when I was doing it, I *just had to* do it and it *just had to* be *exactly right*, or it just wouldn't ever even occur to me that I could move on; not until it felt *exactly right and absolutely OK* to do so.

My sister also used to tease me about severely grinding my teeth during the night while I slept, which I was not aware of doing. She used to tell me in the morning that she had tried everything to wake me up on purpose out of worry that I would damage my teeth, never mind the loud and unpleasant noise that had her apparently squirming in her bed. I suppose it was like being forced to listen to the sounds of scraping finger nails along a blackboard. I did on numerous occasions, however, awaken during the night or the next morning, with an enormous ulcer on the side of my cheek or a crushed and painful tongue, resulting from biting my own body parts half to pieces in my sleep. This behaviour, I put down to falling asleep in the wrong position and I would make concerted efforts prior to resting, to check my mouth positioning, stretching it and positioning it exactly right before I could fall asleep each night. When these efforts became unproductive – I would not allow myself to fall asleep on my side, as a cheek would be squashed against the pillow, and this became a position only allowed to be used while reading in bed. I tried without my pillow and lots of "positioning" with the pillow in order to avoid gaining these ulcers that would last for weeks and were painful – the final straw was to only fall asleep on my back and this caused even more problems...

I told not a soul of the above struggles, I didn't even see them as struggles at the time, rather merely inconvenience and that it was 'just me': imperfect and rubbish and abnormal as usual and you should therefore jolly well deal with it and sort it out by yourself, you imbecile. Well, I remember one night on holiday when I was sharing a room with my sister and was lying there in bed on my back, making every effort to fall asleep and all I was managing to do was to make great big loud noises because I was unable to STOP SWALLOWING! This was very upsetting and distressing for my sister, and also for myself, at the time. I still don't understand what was happening even today and if I brought that night up in discussion with my sister, I am positive she would remember it almost as vividly as I.

Back at home, my sister once pointed out to me when I was having one of my panicking moments about the fact that I was not yet asleep at night – I would get increasingly anxious and terrified that I would be unable to do my work or even function at all the next day if I didn't get to sleep *right now* – that "you don't have to be scared of time, you know". I realised that she was right and this did calm me down, only slightly, but it instantly made me feel more able to rationalise my fear, to an extent. Thankfully, it made me able to view my clock in a different way and thus probably fall asleep a lot quicker too.

My Mum used to say to me "you need your sleep, otherwise you won't be able to function" and I realise now that I had probably taken this very, very literally indeed! Another example of this way of thinking may have been where my Mum always said to me "If you don't eat your breakfast, you'll feel faint and you'll be fainting in assembly at school". I remember us having to sit there in the mornings until we had all finished our cereal and eaten our second courses of either poached egg on toast or scrambled egg on toast and having drunk all of our juice. I felt full and sick eating at that time in the morning sometimes, having just got up and usually being in a rush in the noisy kitchen with scraping chairs that echoed around the old converted stable complete with beams, high ceilings and no curtains to soak up the noise. Kerry and Little Brother had to do it too, so I wasn't alone in it and I did know it was good for me underneath everything, but I just didn't think it was necessary at the time. I was grateful to my Mum really and it wasn't so much an issue for me to be honest as on most mornings, when I'd be first down and into the kitchen, I did actually enjoy my scrambled egg on toast a lot. Dear Mum took pride in making our breakfast just how each of us liked it, never allowing our Maid or our Butlers to help cook, even in the rush of school mornings, bless my Dear Mum. I don't associate this at all with my eating disorder what-so-ever and if anything, it has made breakfast the meal that I have always found the easiest to give myself, even at my worst and lowest points in my illness I would always manage to eat something for my breakfast and so this probably saved my life. This solely exemplifies the loving and caring attitude of my Dear Mum – I loved my Mother and my Father more than anything in the whole wide world.

I have always been extremely sensitive and remember my Mum always saying and continuing to say to me even to this day, which has also been echoed by my best friend and colleague, Ravi, time and time again, that "you always take things to heart" and that "you always think people are having a go at you" and that "I'm scared to say anything to you because you'll take it the wrong way or you get upset" or even "I'm scared to speak to you in case you burst out crying". Now I try not to get hurt by comments or remarks or just in conversations so much these days. But it is extremely hard to firstly remind yourself of this feeling and thought as only being your natural default mode and to then try to rationalise what has just been said, when what you actually believe so strongly to be true, may not have been meant with such significance or in that way at all. Never quite feeling sure of myself or where I fitted, I found it hard to make friends and had little confidence in myself or in my abilities throughout my life. Although I knew I was capable of achieving anything if I really put my mind to it and that everybody actually wanted to be my friend, which confused me even further as I could never work out or understand why and continually had to test them in my own secret ways, constantly seeking and needing reassurance to tell me I was OK and it wasn't that people were thinking otherwise under everything they actually said, or behind my back, thinking really that I'm bad, simple-minded, undeserved, a waste of space, stupid and ignorant.

One incident I recorded in my diary, in September 1997, where a new teacher had shouted at me after I had asked my form tutor for a reference, but at short notice. I was so distraught at my selfishness at having put my form tutor in this predicament and at having been shouted at in such a way through my inconsiderate behaviour that I cried. That afternoon, I played golf with my favourite PE teacher, which helped a lot. Afterwards, she spotted me sitting on the step outside the school gates waiting to be picked up by my Mum in the car and she said to me really caringly and touching my arm gently "if you ever need anyone to talk to, the PE Department is there. Don't bottle it up". I was so thankful to her and for a tiny moment something went through my mind of going and letting everything out! Confidentially, of course, except it never is confidential and I couldn't risk it. Silly thought, get it out of your head now! Anyway, I told Mum what had upset me and she relayed the story to my headmistress at parents evening that week. The headmistress laughed out of sheer bemusement, saying "Rebecca is the last person anyone would expect to do anything wrong, I'll have a word with her". The teacher involved, took me aside and apologised to me.

I also possessed a naturally curious and wild, cheeky and adventurous side that, when I dared to and wasn't immediately put firmly back in my 'sensible' place by my sister or my mother, I enjoyed exploring immensely. This was ME: the curious, cheeky, stretching the rules, yet remaining honest, understanding and caring one. I remember being excited on Kerry's birthday that she had in Japan, as Mum and I had hidden a card secretly in her suitcase before she left. I was excited at receiving that phone call to say she had found it on the actual day!

Away on tour with the Youth Orchestra was my first experience of freedom. Although my sister was also part of the tour we had our own friends and spent our time with them. On this tour, I was described as "the wayward sister" by a tutor who had caught sight of this side of me. I believe this is partly the reason I think I got on well with my brother. He was closer in age to me than to my sister, only by just over a year, but I didn't possess that bossy streak that my sister showed towards him. I was likely to join in with his ideas and 'naughtiness's', whereas my sister, being the eldest, had loyalties only towards my parents and I think she felt responsible for making sure she, and we all, were good children for them. Kerry would also give the world's worst dead-arms of us all!

So both my Mum and Dad used to say that I would 'take everything to heart' or 'always think I'm / people are having a go at you' if a comment might have been made, but then people always did compare me to my sister:- Rebecca is more preoccupied with what other people think and the detail of everything and has to be exactly comfortable that her fashion is right and that she is pleasing other people before she can get on with things and continue with anything, whereas Kerry isn't bothered. Kerry knows her own mind and is confident enough to follow it, whereas Micci keeps her thoughts to herself, is secretive, sensitive, easily led, and needs to be reminded to "now, think on". Kerry likes to always be the centre of attention and would walk about the house naked before or after taking a bath, whereas Micci would get embarrassed and come out of the bathroom fully clothed in her dressing gown and always cover herself up from the sight of others. If she was off sick from school, she would run upstairs with her pile of clothes in the morning if she heard the cleaner come into the house after having brought them downstairs to get dressed in the warmth of the kitchen and in the company of her Beloved Mum. Kerry likes all the attention to be on her, whereas Angel was happy to be in the background. When the baby-sitters wanted to see the sisters' new clown pyjamas, Kerry was straight into parading up and down the Old Lounge as if on the catwalk, whereas Angel would have to be encouraged to take part until finally taking off her dressing gown and doing an awkward and embarrassed twirl that she clearly felt would in the end be less distressing than resisting it all and then she could quickly put back on her dressing gown having made her contribution and could then get away with curling up on the sofa to join in the watching of 'Catwalk Kerry'.

When the music teacher's daughter was told to offer us a sweet, Angel would politely say "No, thank you" because she didn't want to leave the little girl with one or two less, she would always think of others before pleasing herself and even remembers the voices questioning if she had done the right thing: had saying "No, thank you" taught the little girl not to share? How silly you've been, you would never be a good role model for children! But Kerry, on-the-other-hand, of course replied perfectly with an excited "oh yes please, I'd love one!" smiling sweetly with wide eyes and confirming the lesson in sharing. Kerry was the best, you see. Rebecca wasn't. Kerry did the right thing always. Rebecca didn't. I was referred to a lot as 'Kerry' or 'Kerabecca' for most of my childhood life. For me, it felt like growing up with two Mums, sometimes I would enjoy this and sometimes I would resent it.

When I learned that whatever I told my sister, my Mum would miraculously know, we grew apart and I began keeping my thoughts to myself. But my brother and I, we were more similar to each other in that we shared an understanding and sensitivity to the people and environments around us. Little Brother and I didn't fit the mould of the perfect daughter or the perfect son and we kept our real selves to our inner selves.

Again, I will state that it must have been hard for my brother growing up with two big sisters closer in age. I think he learned how to fight for himself and started to rely on spending time making friendships more than being with family. He was labelled 'the naughty one' who liked to talk and cause trouble. If either my brother or I were thinking to run away or wanted a cat when I was little, for example, my sister would run straight to Mum to 'tell'. But my brother and I would help each other to plan it. I should have known better, being three years his senior, but my brother really took it further when he was growing up as I guess it was harder for myself or even for my sister to keep that close eye on him – he started smoking and would be determined to have his own way even if my parents had said a firm "No". In the very naughty times when my brother was younger, it used to be repeatedly said, I think out of sheer anger, worry and frustration, that "he should never have been born...We should never have had him!" But sometimes it seemed my brother held little respect for my parents, although in speaking to my friends about their own brothers, they seemed to be acting out very similar behaviours. I was able to put it down to being male rather than a disruptive child, but I still think my brother had it tough growing up with his two sisters and I am so proud of the life that he has now made for himself, after all he has been through and with no-one really that he felt he could turn to in the family, I feel. It is hard to open up to loved ones because you care for them so much. Little Brother, I understand and I will always be there for you.

We all had good, yet very different relationships with each of our siblings. I'm not sure if my parents enjoyed our plays or saw them as a chore to sit through, but they always clapped and did the right things, bless them. We used to have the best parties that were held at our house, with all our friends, magicians, tables laid out with colourful and assorted party foods, cakes, drinks and an array of children's games afterwards. Our babysitters were always there to help out at our parties and I, my brother and sister and all my friends loved them and had a fantastic time. All three of us had exceedingly good relationships with everyone who helped my parents out with the children and their messes both inside the house and outside in the garden, to the extent that each and every single day in the life of the Parkers was enriched as far as one could ever have asked. I used to love going to stand and talk to our Maid in the utility room, about everything I was interested in or curious about, even asking such question as "what are you chewing?!" such as children do. I used to love our Cleaning Lady and our Baby-sitters chatting to me, playing exciting games, laughing and teaching us new tricks with words and puzzles in the evenings! I used to love going to visit our Gardener in the shed by our fruit cage while he ate his lunch and would join him in a cup of tea that my Mum would send me out with to take to him. I used to be amazed that he could handle, almost stroke, insects and bees and never get stung! I used to love sitting on my favourite Butler's bicycle while he pushed me to the gate before leaving the house on occasion! All in all, we were one big happy family.

My parents' actions always showed nothing but overwhelming love, even in the hard times that occur in all families when nasty words are uttered during heightened emotional explosions. I remember when I was catching the bus home with my friend after school at secondary school one summer's day and my Mum had driven down early, especially to find a parking space where she was sure to catch us close by the bus. She had taken us all, myself included, by surprise as she handed chocolate bars out to my friends and I to enjoy on the journey home. I remember being initially rather embarrassed when caught in this moment because it was my first time of being "let out" with my friends after school following lots of pestering and asking because I wasn't used to getting this bus and socialising with the children from other schools, or with boys for that matter and I wanted to look "cool". The only time I had the opportunity to socialise other than during school hours, was during Music School on a Saturday morning and at dancing class and I was becoming suffocated and frustrated with my lack of freedom as I grew older. But the thought and support of this act by my Mum, showing how much she cared for her daughter was, I selfishly realised, so much more apparent to my friends than it was received initially by me. I could see it on their faces, which I still picture now: pure surprise, disbelief, happiness filling up their faces, all lit up in astonishment at my amazing mother and the next morning at school, my peers expressed such envy towards me, yet with a painful and sorrowful regret while divulging "if only my mother was like yours. You are so lucky. I would love to have a Mum like yours. Your Mum giving out chocolate bars to everyone is so sweet and thoughtful."

I was so blessed to have this lady as my Mother, the only mother in the world who never once let me down and who was always there as soon as I needed her; without fail. This realisation of taking something so special simply for granted, made me step back and appreciate the Mother I was so lucky to have and I vowed always to put her first and to make her proud of me. My Mum was, and always would be, the very best mother ever, in the whole wide world and I began to appreciate her and my Father and thank God for everything and everyone that He had given to me in my life. Never take things for granted ever, ever again. In my diary, I record:

"Very, Very, Very heavy rain. Mum came unexpectedly to pick me up for work experience. Bless her golden heart."

Work experience was a 5 minute walk away from my school. These expressions and actions made me more and more aware of everything that my parents were doing for me. I was secure in the knowledge they were always there for me, they were always thinking of me and they were always forsaking themselves so that they could give the very, very best to me. I hoped that my own reactions and expressions reflected this example they were setting me and in my feeble efforts to affirm the return of my thoughts and my actions, I would always write down those words of love and thanks inside their cards on special occasions throughout the year. Mum and Dad never wrote "I love you" in any of our cards, but my siblings and I did. I knew this was more than true anyway; it didn't need to be spoken or written. In our household, action spoke far louder than words. I was clearly brought up in a very loving environment and I could not have dreamed of having a better childhood or upbringing in any aspect what-so-ever.

1ii-Confusion:

Separating Right from Wrong.

When 'he' first started coming into my room and into my bed in the mornings I didn't mind as he just crept in quietly, still in a sleepy state himself! He carried on sleeping, just not in his own bed, but beside me, just to say good morning, I suppose, just to start the day, just to say hello. Then 'he' started 'tickling' and 'moving', which irritated me because I was still very sleepy and I didn't appreciate being disturbed in the morning, especially if I was still dreaming away and here I was, being woken up. 'He' took to positioning himself close behind me with his arm around me and moving in a sexual manner. I really disliked it all and tried to move away, telling him to stop and expecting him to do just as I said and to think nothing more of it but it carried on, each time I would get increasingly more and more irate and defensive as I was trying to protect myself, only naturally, from something that I knew I was not enjoying in the slightest and was feeling extremely uncomfortable with, more and more so. I tried tickling him in my childish defence, to try and discourage him from staying in my bed at all after that. I kept telling him I didn't like it and demanded that he "stop!" But he didn't. Instead, 'he' found it almost funny. I think, it was like maybe he wanted to stop, but it seemed to be some kind of comforting movement for him in some way, a compulsion, that he *had* to do. I do not know. I repeatedly told him I didn't like it and to stop coming into my room but he didn't take any notice of me. I hated feeling this 'movement' behind me and feeling 'it'. 'There'. Then 'he' used to try and put it in the 'right position' through my pyjamas and I started hitting, scratching, kicking, shouting, anything to not have to put up with this treatment that I hated and was extremely confused by.

Mum and Dad must have just thought I was being childish. I didn't tell them what 'he' was doing – how would you explain it? No, really I ask you, Dear Reader, how would you have explained it to your parents? I was so embarrassed and so ashamed. No, I could look after myself, and I would be able to stop this myself, surely. I tried locking my bedroom door if I woke up early, so that 'he' couldn't come in. I didn't have a mobile phone or an alarm clock to set when I was younger as it was my parents who came to get the children up in the mornings after our Maid and our Butlers had risen when we were little. However, I was scolded by my parents for locking the door in the morning and my sister commented that I was a "weirdo" and mocked me, demanding "what are you hiding or doing that you need to lock the door for, hey? Hey?!" She was laughing at me with a *twinkle* in her eye and raising her eyebrows. They thought I was shutting them out so I could be alone *for some strange reason* and they told me not to lock it again. I did later on explain that "if he keeps disturbing me in the mornings, then I will keep locking it".

My trusty lock was taken off. It was worked out that if the metal head of a clothes hanger was stuck in the door, in a certain way, then the door would lock! But it would make a big noise and someone would notice that I had disobediently and strangely locked my door again. Then my family would reproach me once more, jibing at me, telling me I was weird at being so desperate to lock my door so much, and why? What am I doing or hiding that I need to lock my door for..?

'He' started coming in earlier and earlier, before I even woke, so that I couldn't lock the door and so that I couldn't shout out and cry in case I woke up Mum and Dad and the rest of the household and so it carried on. The 'tickling' and 'moving' became a regular occurrence that I became helpless in preventing from happening. It became increasingly more uncomfortable for me each day by the next and the next and the next... I was left, feeling trapped; dishevelled; alone.

Keeping the Peace.
Raised voices, in our house, were kept to a minimum for fear of setting off my Dad shouting, because when he shouted or got angry, he *really* shouted and got angry and it shook up the whole household for days. My Dear Dad, being ill since I remember, would run out of breath extremely easily and his shout could be so loud and frightening and by this I mean we were fearful for his own fragile health and well-being, certainly not for anyone else's. I hated seeing him upset and angry, which he rarely was unless on severe occasions that may have called for extra discipline further than my Mother's.

Angel Just-Rights

The extremely naughty and rebellious side of my Little Brother inevitably struggled to get on with my Father at all who, on a couple of occasions, resorted to dealing out that dreaded 'ear treatment' only when his son was totally disrespectful, rude and disobedient. My Dad was proud of his eldest daughter Kerry because she was clever and a 'Mummies girl'. I felt like I should have been my Daddies favourite but I know he loved me as much as he loved us all. He used to tell me I was "Micci, the cat" when I'd be sitting all curled up on the settee, quietly minding my own business and looking at the television. In later years, he liked the way that I used to return from school on a Friday afternoon, happily helping myself to a snack of crisps, fruit, chocolate and a drink and settling myself down in front of the warm radiator in the old lounge, enjoying losing myself in the television programs I liked to watch before getting on with my homework and music practices prior to tea. He didn't like the fact so much that in even later years, I would never buy anything for myself or spoil myself with anything and he then replaced my nickname with "Miser Micci" because I was too good at saving all my money, enjoying buying presents for others, but never spending it on myself.

I loved my Dad so much. I loved how he used to just come and cuddle me really hard (almost crushing my ribs, bless him!) and kiss me on the forehead. He was fragile. He used to add an ending to all of our names, calling me "Micciji", which is an Indian term of endearment, of unconditional love. So when he got angry, the whole house was terrified he would suffer another heart attack and pass away, then and there, and it would all be your fault; it had to be peace and quiet at all times.

When I did shout and scream and even cry in desperation, Mum and Dad could hear, but, being still in bed, I suppose they thought it was just me being childish again and fighting with my sister or with my brother, as children do I suppose, and I think they grew used to our noise at any time of day! I dreaded 'him' coming into my room in the mornings and would fight and tell him to stop but no-one came to help me. At the start of it all, I knew Dad thought it was nice seeing us there. I remember seeing him smiling at what he saw. There was sheer happiness and comfort here in this house that he had worked so hard to build out of so little. Here he was surrounded by his own trusted circle and his own family for whom he provided and looked after so well. I am in no way doubting that here there WAS CONSIDERABLE HAPPINESS in this room, where the sun streamed in and this, understandably, made my Dad happy and proud of his exemplary achievements, of his family and of this comfortable life he had worked so hard to provide for us all.

Help help help help help help help ... *I'm over here!*

Now I think I was trying to communicate to my parents, my need for help, through screaming and shouting and crying. I was just desperate for my Mum to notice that I am seriously hurting here, I am in pain, despair, crying out for help and protection and guidance, in desperation for someone to be on my side, a shield, to separate right from wrong for me and to keep me from harm, if this was harm, or was I over-reacting? When my voice hadn't worked, I tried to communicate silently in my actions as, surely my eyes brimmed with hurt, despair and confusion *did they not*? I started to get ulcers and headaches and Mum used to say to me "you shouldn't be getting headaches at your age, drink some more water and take more breaks away from your work". But I needed the unconditional love, the comfort, the understanding and the security of my Mum and I needed the unconditional love, the comfort, the understanding and the security of my Dad. The effects of the 'unspoken' was causing me such pain. Surely my parents had inklings that something was wrong, but I couldn't describe to them what was occurring or how I was feeling, never in literal speech.

We were a close family communicating through body language, rarely in words; feelings and emotions were swept under the carpet in our household. "A look should be enough" I was once told, having been shot a glance of disgust and after cheekily daring, out of desperation and frustration, to challenge the look of disgust with my voice. But my challenge was taken as defiance and stupidity for speaking that, which should be understood in silence alone...*yes, you silly! Defiant! Stupid! Dim-witted girl!* What else was left for me to do then to signal my distress and to ask for help but unconsciously in action? I was no longer in control. I was desperate for Mum or for Dad to detect the hurt and confusion in me. How could they not be noticing?! Were they *choosing* to turn a blind eye, preferring instead to quietly ignore this blip and to carry on living in oblivion? Was the example they were setting to me, simply to ride the waves, it's easier not knowing, not accepting what is happening under this roof? It's nothing. Oh it'll blow over? Was this right? Was I wrong? Of course they are right! Respect your elders. You know you can trust them. They have been in the world longer than you, *you defiant little know-it-all!*

I felt angry. Did they really know, underneath everything, did they actually know why I was distressing? My Mum did ask him to leave my bed once she came into my room in the morning, but she also knew he was coming in and had been in with me earlier and that I didn't like it. Was I supposed to not say anything further? Was this normal? Was this part of growing up? Was she *letting* this happen? Was I supposed to just accept it, never to say a word? Just hate it, despair quietly away, be strong and forget about it? Never say anything about it? Never to acknowledge to anyone that something was happening to cause me ongoing distress? Was this why I had been given my own room? Was this part of growing up? Instead of talking, was I expected to put on a smile and a happy face forever? Was this a common occurrence in every household? How could it be? Was it the biggest secret of all-time that happened everywhere, but was forbidden to ever be spoken of? Was it? Could this be a wide-spread secret going on behind closed doors? I kept it to myself.

I wondered about my poor sister but I couldn't bring it up with her. I was embarrassed, scared, confused and bewildered. What if it was happening to her too? But she was clearly and purely happy in herself; she was open, she was confident, she was bossy and she knew her own mind. She also had an incredibly good relationship with Mum and I used to believe that Kerry got star treatment because she must be severely ill, except everyone is keeping it a secret from me and my brother to keep the family happy. I was plagued by images of that *twinkle* that I had seen shining out of my sister's eye and the manner in which she conveyed her suggestive words to me with the raising of her eyebrow that time she was teasing me about locking my bedroom door when it all started and I was shocked. More harrowing questions prevailed in my head that I was desperate to know the answers to...Am I supposed to *enjoy* this?

Does she?! I remember feeling sick and faint. I could not work anything out or make any sense of it.

Regularly my Mum would ask me "where were you when they were giving out the common sense?" I would look puzzled and so she would answer the question for me: "You were at the back of the queue when it rained. So they packed up and went home without finishing." In time, I learned to answer this question for myself but in reality, rather ironically I was sure that I *had* missed out on hearing the rules of growing up and of the rules to abide by in growing up and living an adult life, somewhere along the line. Being forbidden to speak of the unspoken was killing me. Why don't I know? Why am I so unhappy? Why is everyone else so happy and getting on with life so easily? Because it's *just you, Rebecca, it's just you! Carry on living. You have everything and more! Achieve. Be happy. Achieve. Be quiet. Smile.*

On a couple of occasions, years later, I did dare try to test my uncertainties in a conversation with my friends as my confusion and curiosity still plagued me into longing for even a hint as to whether this was right or wrong and why? Because I failed even to begin to understand how women could even contemplate being married and spending a life subjected to this, by choice! How could every woman on this earth be strong enough to continually feign a lifetime of this?! I probed into whether my classmates had experienced similar goings on in their houses that wasn't spoken about. It was done in such a subtle manner that I didn't get any closer at all to finding out what was normal, abnormal, acceptable, or unacceptable and reached no further conclusions about anything. I couldn't give enough away or poke deeply about in this conversation for fear of being looked at strangely or being 'found out' as a dirty, weak, unknowledgeable freak. Doesn't she know never to speak about it? I was left feeling even more confused, angry, isolated and frustrated with myself for not knowing.

Mum used to tell me to "stop pulling at your hair, you'll have none left! Why do you do that? You look mad! You'll go bald!" I don't know why I did this. I think it just came with the incessant ruminations I was having. I used to have attacks of looking for and pulling out only the 'satisfying strands', as I felt them to be…which lead, in turn, to my pulling the front of my hair out and later, clumps of my eyebrows too.

Losing My Voice to the Silence of Prison.

Suspicion and confusion had been roused, constantly milling around at the back of my mind, but I was keeping everything quiet because that was safest. That was what was expected. That was what I had to do. I would seem so weak and stupid and imbecilic if I dared speak out about it or ask anyone questions about it, especially to my family – approaching the forbidden activity that everyone knows goes on but never speaks of, was out of the question. I would be laughed right out of the house and banished from the family, for being so indecent an individual to bring up such filthy words and in such defiance! I felt it would be brushed off, either as a lie or in disbelief or that I would just be told to "stop making a big deal out of things! Forget about it and get on with your life", and they would be so right, my Dear Family. Bringing it up would just break down the entire household completely and I could not and would not be held responsible for undoing the peace and happiness after years of hard work.

'He' was more determined to use, what appeared to me to be, his ever-growing strength against me by the day even though I was growing up and growing older and stronger, I hated the fact that this felt so beyond my control. It was spiralling around me with no end in sight and no-one there to help. It happened and you got on with life. I was so ashamed of being upset by it all. Was it something normal that everybody went through? And if it was just me, then what on earth had I done to deserve this treatment and isolation and why did I feel so upset over it all? Why was it constantly an unsolved puzzle haunting my mind and why was I not able to protect myself and just be able to get on with my life without it disturbing me and getting me down so much, just like everybody else?! Well, something so silly, honestly it could be *so* much worse. People just silently accept it and get on with life quietly, stop making such a big deal out of it, who are you to make a fuss and stomp and shout about it anyway?! Stop feeling so upset and confused and sorry for yourself! Don't feel hurt and angry with 'him', or with your Mum, your family, your friends, or the world, as everyone lives in it and they manage to continue to be happy! Why should you be any different? No-one is going to help you. You are still alive, you are well, and you have to be strong. You *are* strong. This is how it is, so deal with it.

I stopped screaming and shouting. I prayed every night, not daring to say a thing but only expecting. Knowing what was coming in the morning and dreading it, I would fall to sleep biting my duvet cover in my angst. *Be strong. Forget it. Get on with life. Be happy. Smile.*

My emotions were suffused in total confusion, as was my head, but I suppressed it all the while, until one Saturday afternoon on 21st January 1995 when I had returned home from the morning at Music School and had survived my piano lesson. Mum came over to me and said "I'm afraid I've got a bit of bad news really. Your rabbit's died". To which my immediate reaction (to my absolute disbelief, surprise, embarrassment, horror and disgust) was simply to laugh out loud! I hurried off, up to the top of the garden to the greenhouse, which was home to his cage in the winter months, not believing a word I had just been told. But there I saw my poor thing just lying there. Poor, poor Nibbles: a ghostly white vision, void of life and soul.

CHAPTER 2:

HOLIDAY

2i-Summer Holiday in Norin.

On our annual two-week summer holiday, away at our cottage in Norin where my sister and I would share a twin room together, one year it was decided that my sister would have her own room and 'he' would sleep in mine. This was mainly because my sister had problems with her breathing and my parents thought the room was not helping and that she was keeping me awake with her struggling to breathe throughout the night. Also, as it was a holiday for all, usual sleeping and waking arrangements were disengaged, because there were no chores to do or timetables for our maid or butlers to adhere to. I tried to rearrange this so that I wasn't sharing with 'him', but my Mum brushed it off as me being difficult, selfish, and thoughtless and unaccommodating, moaning unnecessarily and she was angry that I wasn't doing as I was told and accepting such a simple change, like the good obedient child that I usually was. It was end of story with a big full stop.

But not for me: 'he' laughed and teased. He watched me in distress while I squirmed in desperation to find reason enough to continue persuading my Mum to change her mind about this, somehow, please! I felt lonely, hurt and unhappy, fearful and angry that I had been unable to defend and protect myself, yet again, and I was full of that dread and apprehension I could feel slowly rising up inside of me already.

I told 'him' that I was going, right now, to tell my parents the real reason why I didn't want to share the room with 'him'. After so long of not saying anything at all, his reaction was to laugh in my face, telling me "ha-ha, go on then, ha-ha-ha"! I could never bring myself to say such disgusting things to my parents. I could not go to them and accuse him of such awful things, particularly if my parents actually knew it was going on and they were actively choosing to ignore it. I felt stuck and alone. I was afraid that they wouldn't believe me and be shocked at how their nice, sweet daughter could dare to make up such awful things about such close family friends and they would ask, through tears of anger and horror, why I was telling such terrible lies! I was afraid that they would brush it off and tell me to wash my mouth out with soap because what on earth was I thinking of or trying to achieve? I would destroy every last sap of family pride that my parents had worked so hard to create and uphold for us all. I was trapped and scared. 'He' knew I could never go to them and tell them anything, especially at the very beginning of this two-week holiday as it would completely destroy and break up the family and it would all be my fault! No, there was no way I could say anything. If they had decided to live in oblivion, then I had to trust and respect my elders, follow their example and get on with being 'strong' and accepting that this is my duty to keep quiet and harbour the pain to protect the family. After all, isn't this just normal?

On reflection now, maybe my parents did not have a clue that anything was going on and that maybe I simply just thought and willed with every miniscule spec of my being that they could detect it in my eyes or see it in my actions or in whatever part of my voice they could still hear? Similar to when you think you have said something, but you haven't. Yet, because you have thought it so strongly or so meant or wanted to get a particular message across, you think and believe that you have actually said it and thus you expect people to know what you have just said, or in actual fact just thought. I suppose it is like almost being a mind-reader and my Mum has always said to me that "you only tell half a story you know, you always have, you always do this" and that "people are not mind-readers, you know", but I never understood this and it always puzzled me to hear it each and every time this was said to me.

I pretended to storm off towards the lounge anyway and he grabbed me roughly, shut the door and locked it. He pushed me hard onto the bed, forced himself on top of me and immediately started to pretend to rape me, whispering threatening things right into my ear, about what would happen next if I said anything. It was awful. I started to shout and scream for "help!" and for Mum and for Dad, but this made him shove his hand over my mouth so it was impossible for me to make any noise or to struggle out from his grip. My tears were streaming and I was fighting hard, using up all of my strength to the maximum. I was scared at discovering just how strong he could be if he decided to use it seriously and realised I was totally helpless under his manly strength! He was totally overpowering to me now, which was so frightening to realise that this could happen so easily, should he so choose or feel the desire at any time, and so suddenly and unexpectedly here I was, *trapped with no way out...*

Even when you use every ounce of your strength to fight back, you have absolutely no chance of winning, plus he makes this sheer strength and power seem effortless for him to employ. I tried with all my might to get out of his grip and to free myself. I felt helpless, silent, tearful, cheated, alone, despairing, crying, with no voice. He was awful and I was shocked. He was just laughing afterwards, telling me to go and tell them all what had just happened, to "go on then! Ha-ha!" and then pointing at me laughing, knowing that I would never tell because I could never speak such words and who would have the indecency to apply any ability to understand or believe *me*, 'Little Micci', the one they had to check hadn't fallen out of the car on long journey's, because she was so quiet, anyway? I tried to put it all into perspective and to not get too upset over it all, try to forget it because '*he's*' laughing, '*he*' thinks it's all a joke, maybe it is, stop taking it all so seriously and stop feeling so upset and frightened, pull yourself together, it's not that bad, you'll be OK, you're expected to get on with it so keep quiet, never speak of it, don't make a fuss and get on with the holiday, get on with life, and smile! I went to the bathroom and bit hard and fast into that bar of soap.

My Dad used to detect when I was feeling down and would always come to cheer me up. He would discreetly come to sit by me on the settee, complete with big mischievous smile and those big bright eyes. He'd reach out and tickle my feet hard, which was an action that usually initiated an anger and frustration on my part at him disturbing me when I was obviously in a distracted mood and preferred to be alone. But I realise now that he was actually trying his hardest to put a smile on this forlorn face of his beloved daughter. He was the one to always cheer me up, to bring me out of my negative thoughts and ruminations, always to succeed in generating a real smile to spread across my face. Then he would give me that big, hard hug that would almost break my ribs! I loved my Dear Dad and he loved me too.

As I said earlier, my Dad used to call me 'the cat' because I would tend to curl up on the settee and watch television or read a book. Maybe I was just distracting my thoughts, I don't know. Maybe I was trying to make sense of everything where I would appear to be concentrating on something but really lost in my confused thoughts, yet trying not to let it get to me so much...*pull yourself together!* But this world is awful, is it something that goes on behind closed doors in every household but is forbidden to be acknowledged even, let alone spoken of? The biggest and widest known secret of all time *except by silly, stupid me, who needed everything to be explained to her and twice over at that? It's our secret to be held forevermore.*

...Interlude I...

INTERLUDE I

DREAMS

A:-Recurrent Dreams since Childhood:

Teeth.

1.   I don't know what age I was when I used to have this recurring dream but I had it a lot, which seems like forever, until I started not dreaming at all and not remembering my dreams.

There were two types:

a). I would dream that my teeth were falling out. I would be panicking and they would just be falling out and wouldn't stop. It was the most terrible dream at the time as I really believed it was always real life until I would wake up and feel my teeth all still there, to my immense relief.

b). I would dream that I had a mouth stuffed full of what seemed like cigarette paper or cotton wool or sometimes it would be a variation on the teeth falling out dream, I don't know if they were distinguished. I remember just thinking that maybe it is cigarette papers as I used to put one single piece of cigarette paper, folded up quite small, over my bottom teeth when I was playing the clarinet. I did this every time I played, so that I didn't get a hole or bleeding in my bottom lip and it meant I could use a harder reed and play for longer and with a nicer, fuller tone. The dream was awful though, it was like I had mouthfuls and mouthfuls that were choking me and I couldn't get it out of my mouth or make it stop or go away as it kept just making more and getting worse and worse until I felt like I was suffocating. I felt like I couldn't breathe as my throat and my mouth were just full up and choked.

111

Actually, I think this is how my dream started and then it turned into my teeth that were all falling out; horrible. I hope I don't have these dreams ever again.

Being alone since hospital, and keeping all my behaviours to myself, having had them for years and years, I got scared about the state of my teeth and convinced myself, both times after leaving hospital admissions, that they were wobbly and my gums were receding and that my teeth were about to all fall out. I would get scared being on my own in case this actually happened and I think this didn't help with me being alone in my flat. Both times however, the dentist had told me I had strong teeth and just needed to make another appointment for a year's time.

Recently I have been managing to stop that awful behaviour. I have many other aches and pains that I also worry about and have to admit that I use these signs to tell myself that I am not right and to spur me on to eat and get better, particularly if faced with that which I might struggle with. I know that's not great, but it does scare me when I think clearly. Even all this isn't enough sometimes though, when the battle is too strong for Rebecca to win.

Car.

2.   a). We (Kerry, myself and Little Brother) would be in the car having been picked up from school but Kerry would be driving. This was very weird and strange to see, but it worked.

b). Driving a car that had breaks that wouldn't work properly, no matter how hard you pressed on the pedal they just were not effective in stopping the car. It was like a continuous 'creep' mechanism with no break and the dream was so real it was scary and confusing. Imagine being on the roads driving a car with this going on. I continued to experience this dream when I was able to drive myself and when I was driving my own car. It would feel so real that I could just not work out what was going on and I could not trust the car to stop when I needed it to, no matter what I did, or how hard I pressed on the brakes.

CHAPTER 3:

SCHOOL

3i-Strive to be The Best and Achieve:

I changed my after school snack to just an apple and a drink as I suddenly thought what on earth am I doing? My sister doesn't pig out like this, why are you doing it? But then my sister never was a 'crisp face' or a 'chocolate face' like me, as my Dad jokingly made up these names for me, Bless him. I really never minded my Dad calling me 'crisp face Micci' because I fully admit that I did enjoy crisps and chocolate just like any normal person, especially at Christmastime, and we could have a laugh together about this too.

There was always a rivalry around food between Kerry and I, or so I felt. At home when we were growing up, we would sit diagonally opposite each other at the kitchen table. I would sit next to Mum and opposite Little Brother, who sat next to Kerry. My Dad was at the head of the table close to my Mum and Kerry. I would always notice that my sister would never eat all her potatoes and would leave some of the gravy but would gorge on meat and enjoy her puddings. I used to think that maybe she had a problem as how could she eat so much, have "such a healthy appetite, Kerry loves her food" as my parents would say, yet remain so skinny? I know this was natural for her though, lucky thing. But I was always jealous because I would sit there at the table noticing that she didn't eat all her potato, but nobody else would say anything. I could later get away with not having cream or custard or any kind of topping or sauce on my puddings, saying that I didn't like it, which I didn't, and I continued onto cooked apple that could rule out the crumbles and pies and cold cake and sour lemon cheesecake etc. To make things worse, my sister started to notice and would very loudly voice that it seemed Micci "had to always leave something on her plate, every time!" I would just laugh and shrug it off, but in my hospital days this habit was taken as a very serious eating disordered 'behaviour' that would reduce me to tears when challenged. Maybe she had a point? Even at Day Care today, being challenged by staff or fellow patients regarding a little food left on my plate can so easily reduce me to tears, much to my frustration, bubbling anger and annoyance. I would always notice that neither Kerry nor Little Brother would eat their Easter Eggs that were given to them at Easter, or their chocolates that we were given to them at Christmastime. It was only ever fat, greedy me, who used to enjoy the chocolate and the crisps.

Always, I would make sure that our Maid would let me help her make the sandwiches on Sunday evenings or at Christmastime, or when we went to the beach, so that I could prepare mine with no butter, or with just a scraping if I was being watched. I could easily skimp on the filling in my own sandwiches and scoop out the bread inside my buns, but make everyone else's taste delicious. I suppose this made me feel better that I wasn't having as much as everyone else, because I didn't deserve to and didn't need to and didn't even want to. I enjoyed watching others eat and would accompany the Gardener or the Butlers in their lunch breaks, always being curious as to what they would be consuming that day.

Once, when I had bought a candy chew bar from the tuck shop at break time at school, I remember happily sucking and chewing away when I noticed a big hard thing in it! I was shocked and having felt it out with my tongue, I realised that it was my big tooth that I hadn't even noticed being wobbly and I was worried it was one of those that wasn't supposed to come out. In my panic in that busy dinner hall, I took it out of my mouth, threw it all in the bin and ran to the toilets to have a look at my gap in the mirror. It hadn't hurt or anything, but it was the shock of it that had scared me. I vowed to be more careful when eating in future.

I started to buy my sandwich lunch at break time and eat it in my form room, or take in a packed lunch from home rather than going into the dining room where I would feel all eyes upon me, eating. I had a jam packed lunch hour, full of music groups and house competition rehearsals and was so disappointed when I was asked to be in the netball team but just couldn't fit it in. I remember my music teacher having to write an 'early dinner ticket' covering every day of the school week for me in order that I could go straight into the dining room whenever I had time for lunch (we weren't allowed to eat in our form rooms really) but I would hide it in my bag or inside my desk in case the dinner lady came in and told me off or marched me down to the dinner hall, instead of queuing for a long time and thus missing my groups. My diary describes:

"Mr Wand wrote an early dinner ticket for every day for me. He said "I don't think I've ever done one of these before!" I told him I could only take the top Year 7 Recorder Group on a Thursday but Wind band is on. I suggested doing two things in every lunch hour and he laughed his head off. He said "I used to do that, but after a while it was too much..." At first he said I'd have to give something up! No way man!"

The early dinner ticket became my proof for everyone, especially my Mum in that I could eat from the canteen with no problem in queuing if I chose to or if I forgot my packed lunch from home etc. Plus, I had already been forced into turning down being part of the Netball team and that was even something that my sister was in no way a part of and it could have been mine, but I couldn't even make time for it and my family didn't think wasting time on sport was as important a skill to perfect as music anyway and I think now that part of me didn't need to compete with my sister over this as I was already the best at it and therefore it wasn't important even to myself as it wouldn't be worth being the best at after all. It was recognised only as another extra-curricular activity at our school, rather similar to my burning passion for horse riding (the lessons I managed to persuade my parents to support through choosing this as part of my Duke of Edinburgh Award, adjoined by my sister although she disliked animals, and by my brother who enjoyed it), that took up and wasted precious time. I felt horse riding was my passion because I loved reading the books that my sister had no interest in reading and felt they were strong passionate animals that you could "ride like the wind" and take control of. I always thought that even if control of the horse was lost, one could always hold onto the mane and therefore I would, and still do, only ride horses with a very clingable mane, *just in case*. I have never admitted this to anyone either, as I find it a little strange maybe; I don't know.

I had to be 1st clarinet in the wind band and in all the orchestras and have all the solos, I had to be in the top recorder group and invited into senior recorders early, I had to coach and conduct the forty girls of the year 7 choir, I had to be the one assigned tutor of the top year 7 recorder group, I had to be first to gain my gym stripe and my music stripe and my house stripe and my badges, I had to win all my music festivals and all the trophies, I had to be the best at music and sport and athletics and netball. I could never match up to my sister academically although I never stopped striving for the best marks I could possibly manage and I was the best and excelled at both music and sport, oh and German, plus I enjoyed them immensely.

3ii-Years 9, 10, and 11:

In my third year at secondary school, I remember still secretly enjoying munching those small packets of crisps that the tuck shop sold, with my friends in the science lessons especially. We would even pack up on time and run to the tuck shop to make sure we were first in the queue before the crush. I started eating a packed lunch under the stairs, as our form room was the Art Room and we were not allowed inside it at lunchtimes, so instead we would sit under the stairs outside the art room. I started having dizzy spells in my clarinet lessons and by October 1993 I was missing the County Wind Band rehearsals, which only occurred once a month, due to ill health.

By the fourth and fifth years I had stopped going into the dining hall at all and my packed lunch was pretty disgraceful, when I bothered to eat it. My whole group of friends changed. I was avoiding the dining room and I was changing my priorities. I lost all my best friends for a while and went through a phase of not speaking to them at all because they were asking awkward questions about why I was separating myself from them, my best friends, and even I didn't know why! I didn't have a choice anymore and had lost my voice, literally. My sister had participated on school trips to Italy etc. but I didn't feel worthy enough to enjoy these when my turn came and the foods in Italy particularly scared me and so I made excuses not to go. At Music School on Saturday mornings, I would want to choose the deliciously smelling hot chocolate option from the drinks machine at break time, just like everyone else, but I wasn't everyone else and would have to choose the hot blackcurrant or the watery vegetable soup, just so I was having a drink like everyone else, thus appearing normal. But at least I was having what I *could* have. We always had fish and chips after music school or in the evenings on Saturdays too, which I still allowed myself to take part in and even guiltily enjoy, normally and in safety with my whole family around – that's what Saturdays were for – it was time off and also no-one ever had a pudding after fish and chips on a Saturday.

I remember being summoned to the headmistress's office and her asking me what was going on. I felt like a terrible person. What was I to say? She told me "it's hard to help if you are ignoring your friends and giving them all the silent treatment" which I totally was and I felt awful for it. "It is frustrating for everyone when you don't speak" my Mum used to reiterate to me when she returned home from parents evenings both at primary and throughout secondary school. Apparently all the teachers would say that I am extremely quiet and don't speak and that this gets extremely frustrating. I don't know. I wasn't going into lunch with my old friends anymore but I still wanted to sit with them in lessons and be friends with them, of course I did, but they didn't understand this concept and if I tried to explain it would sound so silly. I just wanted to be friends with everyone. My old friends thought I was dumping them for another group. There are always different groups that form at schools. The girl I became more friends with also took a packed lunch into school, but most of all, she used to read the writing on the board out loud to me because I was never brave enough to wear my new glasses, which I kept a secret from everyone else for most of my school years. This was unusual for me because I remember when at primary school, asking my Mum if I could have a pair of glasses because I thought they looked cool on my best friend! But now that I HAD to wear them, I didn't like this imposition and saw it as an imperfection that I shouldn't have! Alas, my new friend kept my secret, and I only dreaded the lessons that she wasn't part of. Regarding the packed lunch, well, I was only doing the same as her but my old friends thought I was dumping them for other groups that were seen as cleverer (not even more popular!) and so the whole thing started to swarm into total misunderstood confusion.

117

On our summer holidays to Norin I started to avoid the fish and chips as much as possible and would ask for Chinese instead because at least then I could choose plain noodles or boiled rice rather than greasy oil-laden chips! I used to dread the lasagne my Mum used to buy as it made me feel disgusting and angry but I kept it quiet and just went to the park next door in the evenings or played around the village and sometimes I would just walk down to the sea on my own and wish for a stranger to come and scoop me up to safety. But I would manage because I knew we would be going swimming and / or roller-skating on the rainy days, which was my personal highlight of the holiday and we had a walk to the beach and back almost every day and I felt urged to accompany my Mum, and sometimes my sister, on the walks along the beach looking for shells in the morning and I would feel a niggling guilty feeling if I'd missed my Mum going out for a long walk along the beach in the morning especially if my sister had snuck out with her quietly behind my back and I felt jealous and lazy, and just had to play with my brother in the sand dunes for hours and hours after that and I would just have to pull my sister along in the dinghy while she enjoyed herself laying there relaxing in the sun and feeling the waves. I had to feel the one in control, I had to be doing something, I couldn't relax if I had eaten but I didn't think anything of it at this time, I just thought it was me. Rather ignore the guilt and uneasy feelings and apply myself to something useful and fulfilling.

I got a thing about fainting. I had only fainted twice before – once when I had trapped my thumb in the door at primary school and it bled a lot, only I was fine until all the teachers had put some smelly ointment on my thumb and were fussing so much over me and crowding me so much that I think it was actually all the unwanted attention that was what made me feel dizzy and faint. Secondly, I fainted in the hairdressers, where I used to stand up to have my hair cut. Standing so still and holding my breath for fear that I'd absolutely spoil the haircut or that I'd even get myself cut by the scissors if I so much as breathed too heavily or sneezed, made me freeze. I realise now maybe it was also about the feeling of having somebody so close to me, with all their attention focused upon *me* and my body and the fact that *they* were at that time, the one in control and not me (Book 1: Secrets Out, Part 2, Chapter 5), or maybe it was purely because I wasn't eating enough, but at this time I am pretty sure that I was.

My school was putting on an exciting big production that was an opera with an orchestra and a play. I wanted so badly to be in the orchestra, but the older and more experienced girls were chosen and that left me to stand and sing in the chorus as there was no way I could have a voice solo or an acting part as I was far too shy. I remember crying in front of the music teacher who had made the decision. I was so trying to change his mind in order that I could be in the orchestra, where my talent lay and where I felt safe, hidden and secure where my strength would consistently shine through in the music; here was my voice. He thought I was being spoilt and was teaching me a lesson that you didn't always get what you wanted, especially not by sulking about it. He said "I can see you're clearly distressed over it, but tell me the real reason why you're so upset". What was he expecting me to say? I was standing there saying it was because I wanted to play in the orchestra, but really I was scared stiff of standing up on stage in front of so many people for so long and fainting on the stage! But I couldn't admit any of this to anyone and surely he didn't know this, did he? In the end I was ashamed and didn't take part in the production at all. This was really hard for me as people really didn't understand why I chose not to participate and they must have thought that I just had a severe case of sour grapes and was merely a spoiled sport or something, I suppose. I was glad when it was all over, but the production was talked about for years after in conversations, no doubt reminding people of how awkward I could be if I simply didn't get my own way. I was ashamed of my behaviour.

In addition to my fears of fainting, I was also slightly bothered by my intrusive thoughts that just seemed to pop into my mind at times and I would try to just push these away as they worried me deeply and I didn't want to admit they were there or even think about confronting them. I would seriously worry during rehearsals on the day of an orchestra concert taking place that evening for example, that we would be mid-concert (I was always playing Principal clarinet in orchestra concerts, having been given this role in both the surrounding Youth Orchestras and for a number of years) and I would suddenly shout out loudly or blast the loudest shrillest highest note right out of my clarinet while lifting up the bell and standing up, right at that quietist, most silent, most perfect and musically special moment in the royal concert halls under those spotlights and on the stage where every movement can be seen by the audience whose seating were rows upon rows raised up above the next and that was full of friends and family and eager listeners and head-hunters. I felt pretty terrible for having these extreme thoughts but was secretly very fearful that I would be overcome with a sudden urge totally out of my control and to actually carry this act out in the real-life concert. I used to tell myself to stop being silly and of course you won't do this, especially now that you've had the thought so at least you can make sure that it doesn't happen! I would concentrate on the music in front of me and on counting my bars rest on my fingers extra carefully or by putting my clarinet down away from my face in order to ensure, as far as possible, this fear was not about to turn into a devastating reality.

During these years and into the 6th Form, I remember always having light-hearted and friendly disputes with one of my best friends at school and music school and she also attended the dancing school just as my sister and I were leaving. We used to argue that each other was thinner than ourselves. I knew I was bigger than her and she thought she was bigger than me but we used to remain best friends and sit together at music school and on the bus to the county music groups where we'd buy fizzy sweets to share on the journey home. She had a healthy appetite and I remember being jealous that she could stay so thin and I was chubby, but it didn't affect my eating.

There were three girls who had severe and noticeable eating disorders in my school (one in my year and two in my sister's year) and I would regard them with pity and sadness but also with a tinge of envy because I knew I could never have the level of self-control that they surely had and it made me feel lazy. Rather, I enjoyed putting my efforts into gaining recognition, such as being a good person, achieving good exam results, being a good student and the best clarinettist and overall musician destined for great things. All my friends and teachers asked for my autograph before I left sixth form so to have this before I become famous, they all said. So much for that.

The morning's thing phased out when 'he' got his girlfriend. I was just so relieved that I was being left alone and realised that I must be safe in the future for as long as he was seeing a lady. I hoped it never ended. Only now, I think that maybe I should have felt scared for the woman, but I guess it was different for her in that she was making her own choice to see him, or not to see him. At the time, I was selfishly just so relieved that his attentions had been diverted completely away from me. I remember 'him' talking about one of his girlfriends and he somehow ended up telling me the detail of how she loves what he does to her. He was laughing about it and said "honestly, I'll show you", he was laughing and I knew it was a joke but it disturbed me. I hated myself for being so sensitive and forced it out of my mind. Stop making a big deal out of it and being so sensitive, you're just close to each other and that's a nice everlasting friendship to have with anybody in the trusted circle. No matter what you think or how you feel. You did no wrong. It was just me.

I have no idea of timings. All I see are images and all I feel is reminiscence of the fear, the confusion, the falling deeper and deeper into that black hole all alone with a voice that didn't work and all those who care about me pointing wicked fingers at me on my way down. I only know that it went on for what seemed like a long period of time, unbearable never-ending timeless time, and that on 'that' holiday, he had shocked me with his sheer strength and that I hadn't previously experienced this powerlessness to such an unbelievably horrifying extent. I was actually scared, fearful, frightened and shocked.

3iii-Sixth Form:

By the sixth form I was skipping lunch altogether and throwing it away. I don't know why and I didn't think anything of it really, I just had to do it at the time, to the extent that if somebody offered me a single crisp I wouldn't even be allowed to take that. I had to say no. Proper people don't indulge at all. Never take even one. I suppose I controlled everything else in my life that I was able to, I don't know, it's just my thoughts now, I had no idea what I was doing at the time. I just knew *I couldn't*.

I managed to participate in a trip to Japan, which I enjoyed immensely. I fitted in with the other students more than I had ever done in the past before and felt comfortable in my Japanese friend's house. I was lucky in that the food in Japan I still saw as healthy and so long as I didn't over-do anything, I would be OK. I did fear the Macdonald's that everyone wanted to go to but this only happened once in the whole two weeks and I managed the chicken nuggets anyway. I remember only dreading the squid pizza that they had ordered for me, which was OK in the end as it was not too cheesy and actually was probably quite healthy in a way. Also I felt terrible when the family had put on a special meal for me on the last night and we ate it in the special Japanese room. It was a whole meal of seafood and I was expected to eat each course and they were trying their best to get me to try every single dish. I also remember on this trip that the family took me shopping and were desperate to buy me a nice item of clothing and yet I was adamant that I firstly couldn't accept such a gift and secondly could in no way try it on for them. I felt terrible when the mother bought me a lovely Japanese-style black dress complete with cardigan and even a pretty underskirt. This was an outfit that I simply loved the look of and could not believe they had bought it for me with such sweet smiles and gestures and no hesitation in sight, even after all my own reluctance.

Every single second of my quadruple free period on a Monday afternoon back at school was spent practicing and practicing my scales and pieces over and over again on the piano until I was forced to stop and run for my bus home. It was never perfect enough or just right enough, or if it was 'OK' then it had to be repeated at least a certain number of times to prove that it must not have just been a fleeting one-off fluke, which was in no way 'OK' enough. It proved it could be always made better and *always* improved, *always* made better, *always* improved...practice really did make 'almost' perfect. My playing provided me with the escapism and concentration that I required. I loved the way I learned my pieces through patterns on the keyboard and memory rather than reading the music, just like everyone else. I made it MINE and I loved when I had played so long and hard that my fingers ached and I would give myself a headache after the long painstaking and exhausting hours spent perfecting my pieces and scales, but I loved it all as it was all of my own doing and I was pleased when I came away knowing I had done well and could start where I had left off, to make it even better, when I arrived home.

I knew I was good; I felt it and I enjoyed it. I loved it when people came into the practice room to tell me it was sounding fantastic. I had to practice and practice in order to pass my exams first time round and with flying colours. I had to be at the top. I had to be the first to get to Grade 8 with distinction in everything; I did repeat my Grade 8 piano exam, having been absolutely distraught over my measly Merit marking that I was awarded first time round and thankfully I then gained the distinction that I was more used to, and this I could handle. I still remember my music teacher coming into the practice room to congratulate me and also my pupil that I was teaching at the time, who had managed a distinction all of her own for her Grade 5 piano and I was so proud of her! My piano teacher said to me once that he could imagine me specialising in Baroque and Renaissance Harpsichord playing as I really feel and connect with how this era of music should be performed. I was touched so much in hearing this compliment from my teacher whom I admired immensely.

When at home in the evenings before and after dinner I enjoyed practicing my piano and clarinet pieces immensely; applying myself to these activities and goals gave me great satisfaction within myself and took me away from my homework (most of which I would also enjoy doing too) and my worries and I am eternally grateful to my Dear Mum, who sat with all three of us when we first started all of our musical instruments for hours and hours each day and who learned all of these through teaching us and through taking us to lessons where she would drive for hours and sit for hours in cold, lonely deserted car parks. The results in the performance and achievements in exam marks and trophies were ultimately down to dedication and, I also like to think, a little talent that showed on that day. My music became ME. My greatest feeling of achievement through music around this time, however, came from my 'coming out concert', as I called it:

- ## Saturday 29th February 1998:

COMING OUT CONCERT! NYO Royal Concert Hall. Rachmaninov Piano Concerto No. 2 in C Minor, Second Movement Clarinet Solo – conductor made me stand up! YES! Head of Wind said "the strings in my heart were going" WOW! Conductor said "Well done!" HAHA! WONDERFUL FEELING. Auntie Ann and Uncle came to watch! Audience gave big clap.

- ## Monday 9th March 1998:

Clarinet lesson. Got clarinet out. Went to stand. Teacher held my hand in both his hands and said "I've heard stories about you. The conductor said your solo last Saturday brought tears to his eyes! He said he was really taken in. He said it was the first time he has heard anyone of this age play with such emotion". I just laughed.

CHAPTER 4:

UNIVERSITY AND SPEN

~

GREECE AND GRANADA

4i-University and Spen:

1st Year.

I enjoyed going out socialising for the first time and I enjoyed my freedom. I used to enjoy running away from all the boys with my friends as I had made a promise to myself never to kiss 'just anyone'. I wanted my first kiss to be with someone special to me and with whom I would want to remember. I really enjoyed singing along to the music and dancing, completely for my own enjoyment, in the student union with my friends and getting to know lots of different people.

Until one cold Friday night in November 1998 when I had consumed a few drinks and was enjoying myself dancing but then suddenly I opened my eyes to find myself dancing with a man. We danced for a long time and to a lot of good songs. He was cute and I remember his stubbly face and very big, strong, protective hands when we were dancing. I stopped dancing and walked away, saying I was going to the bathroom but it had been difficult for me to get out of his grip as quickly or easily as I had liked to think I could and so I automatically without thinking, left, running back to my halls alone and finding myself in floods of tears, scared, frightened and overwhelmed. I locked myself in my room and cried, wrapping myself up in my blanket. Why was I letting myself get so upset over nothing at all? I felt weak, stupid and disgusted with myself and so ashamed. This is not how I have been brought up to act! You should be ashamed of yourself! Thinking about it now, I suppose I had put myself in a situation that I might not have been able to control on

125

my own terms and get out of should I have chosen to and this what I ran petrified from.

My friend came back with my coat. I was embarrassed that I had become so upset and had run off alone, without thinking or without telling anyone in my group of friends that I was leaving. I didn't want anyone to see that I had got upset over nothing, as how immature would this look? But they did see me and yet they didn't seem to care or to understand, and why should they bother? My next door neighbour, who had been working in the Union that night, had come back to her room to find this commotion and came outside into the corridor calling my name, as I was in the next girl's room. My next door neighbour was really nice to me. She gave me a hug and a bottle of water; here was a real friend.

My so-called 'friends' were not impressed with me the following morning. We fell out, or I should rephrase that and say they fell out with me, because I suppose they thought I was a lousy and selfish friend. I know the level of the alcohol I had consumed probably hadn't helped matters and I had been very stupid, but I was still alive and had everything to live for. At least I knew who my real 'friends' were now too.

My diary tells me that the following Friday I sat, eating my dinner of packet pasta soup (tangy tomato) on the floor of my room with my back to the radiator (heat being my friend) listening to the financial news on a classical music radio station. I hadn't listened to this particular radio station for a long time, but it reminded me of studying for my music GCSE exams and of being at home revising all day and all night. Dear Mum would always come in with a snack for me and would always make sure I had come down to join the family for breakfast and dinner, and to join her for lunch in the middle of the day. Here I was alone. I could hear my next door neighbour's television on loudly and that made me smile thinking of her happily going about her own business in her own room, also alone but happy. Tonight, I thought, I would do some more work on my essay and then go to the practice rooms to play my techniques through on the piano and then do some practice. And that is what my diary tells me I did that night. I suppose I was doing what was setting 'the norm' for me that was to keep me feeling 'safe' from now on.

I had again taken to pulling out my eyebrows in clumps (Trichotillomania). I don't know why I would do this but it made me feel better. Then, it turned into having to find only the ones that felt 'exactly right' and upon pulling I felt a strange momentary sense of fulfilment and satisfaction, which made me continue all the more. Soon I was having to fill in the gaps I had made with makeup pencil and I dreaded having showers and washing my hair at university, I dreaded going to foam parties at the union, which would cover people in wet bubbles, I dreaded going swimming on holidays until the point where I feared being out in the rain even if I had my umbrella with me because I was so scared that the pencil would smudge or run or wash away and I was terrified of people seeing the 'real me' and what I had done to myself. I used to take my pencil everywhere with me and dreaded going through customs at the airport in case they took my special makeup sharpener and razors away from me.

One day during the summer holiday when I was working in the local factory as summer student work in my hometown, the people working there had made comments about my eyebrows and were asking if they were real or not (by now I was used to this and very paranoid). I decided to take the plunge and completely wash off all my make-up when I got home that day, just to see exactly what damage I had done because enough was enough. I locked my door with the hanger so I wouldn't be disturbed and it felt good to be able to touch my face for once without having to constantly avoid upsetting those areas with make-up and without thinking I'd be walking around with terrible black smudges all over my face. I had to scrub and scrub and scrub until all the makeup was finally gone. I felt clean as I touched and washed all over my face; every single square inch. What a relief! Then, I was shocked at what I saw.

I looked like someone else. I didn't know this person! I looked awful and felt embarrassed and ashamed of myself, irritated and frustrated at my behaviour, confused and angry at having done this to myself. But I did feel more normal and clean and free in that this was 'me'. No disguise here. I did put back on some make-up, I had to for fear of shocking everyone, but I vowed to try and stop and to try to let them re-grow back, hoping with all my might that this could and would please, still happen, quickly, but I made no real change and I remain today, although significantly less so, to fill in some areas just to even out the coverage in my eyebrows, every single morning (Book 2: Who Am I? Part 1, Chapter 20).

Mum used to call me on the mobile my parents had bought me to see if I was still in the practice rooms, if it was late at night and to make sure I had got back to my halls OK. I used to practice for hours, until the security van came to lock up at 11pm, but I loved it all.

Moving on towards Christmastime and ending the first term at university, I had fitted myself into a new group of friends, this time of fellow music students, with whom I felt happy and could be more myself and my personality was alive again. I felt good. I could speak my mind and take the lead and make my own decisions and choices once more. During the break, I enjoyed the time spent at home amongst my family and I enjoyed the food, the little of it that I could manage as I had had a nose bleed on Christmas morning and had retired up to bed by 9:30pm that Christmas evening, having my usual sick bug or reaction to red wine or Christmas pudding, I have not yet found out which, or whatever it could have been.

I remember visiting my Auntie Ann (probably on Boxing Day) who commented as soon as she saw me on her doorstep, "Gosh, you've slimmed down" and I just replied "Oh, have I?" and she said "Yes, you know you have!" I remember liking this comment that I'd lost weight. I was happy with how I looked then and knew I was healthy as I was still having my period, although light and irregular but this is just how I was, I thought. Meeting my school friend in a cafe for lunch after New Year, I remember choosing a jacket potato with tuna and a diet coke. My friend chose a cheeseburger and chips. I recall thinking, how can she choose that? But I was more excited at hearing her news and hearing about what she'd been up to rather than staying with this preoccupation of food thoughts at this point and thought nothing of it at all. I was happy with the choice I had made.

The approach to the end of year exams towards the end of the academic year however, was a struggle for me although little did I care to admit it at the time. I started restricting my food intake to watered-down tomato soup that I kept under my bed in half-eaten packets, coffee and occasionally mixing this with alcohol if I decided to join my friends for a drink in a revision break. I used to pace in my room while reciting things I had to remember and jump up and down on the spot. I made my room hot with my extra heater (warmth made me feel safe) I breathed in the fresh summer air from outside at the same time. My friends made comments about my stomach being concave rather than convex and about me being too thin. I just laughed it all off, but I felt big and huge. I made friends with a guy living in the halls opposite me, who noticed something wasn't right with me one evening and came over all worried. He was sweet, as I describe in my diary entry:

• **Friday 7th May 1999:**

Came back from the Stumble Inn where I'd been with Karen and Karina for one drink and had a strong coffee back in my room. I got my heater today so had this on full blast with the window open. Been walking round the room doing revision all day. Felt really, really hot etc. Stuck head out of window for ages. I nearly went to sleep. 2:30am. Boy from opposite saw. Must have been watching me. He came to my window and looked up and said "Hey, hey are you alright? Is there anything I can do for you?" I said "Oh, I'm just getting some fresh air". He replied "Oh. Right. You are a very energetic person". He went back to his halls. Nice voice.

I went back to his room tonight after Yale persuaded me – she knew him and was friends with him. I said thank you to him and he replied "You're a very beautiful woman" and invited me in, but Yale and Dina were both waiting for my return upstairs back in my own halls, watching from my room! Big mistake: his voice is so soft and gentle and he shook my hand twice.

When I agreed to meet him for a drink, I arranged for a couple of my friends to be in the pub too, so I knew I was safe. On the way back I allowed my first kiss to be with him and although I didn't particularly enjoy it, I felt happy. I would meet up with him after our exams and spend time with him as we had mutual friends too, nice friends, it was fun spending time together and holding hands but it didn't last long and it soon fizzled out.

The summer of this year I worked as a student with my sister and my best friend from sixth form, Suki, in the factory in my hometown referred to earlier, and I had one of the best summers ever. I had a factory fling with a guy called Luke. We had a spark from the very first time we met in the factory and we got together on the student night where we all met for a night out in town. That night I really let my hair down: I was thinking OK, I had kissed one boy before and I thought this new guy was very cute and sensitive and we seemed to be on the same wavelength. He was really funny and was nice to me too and he had a brain as far as I could tell. He was extremely quick-witted, which I find very attractive in a man. That night I drank some alcohol, I smoked cigarettes, I danced, I let him kiss me, I let myself go a bit and remember my sister and best friend from school, Suki, were dumbstruck and shocked at my behaviour. I was being this other person that no-one had seen before and I think partly it was left over from the disbanding of my 'first kiss' relationship that was coming out tonight, in addition to feeling safe in that I can now kiss freely and I loved kissing! I was also in my home town and surrounded by a group of people whom I trusted; I didn't care that night, I just wanted to have fun and to forget about everything.

I did everything Luke said in order to be a good girlfriend. I was polite and just enjoyed being in his company because he made me laugh. He used to put on a tape in the car every time we drove, it was Ronan Keating 'You say it best, when you say nothing at all', probably because I didn't say much at all, rather communicating my feelings towards him in my actions through smiling and holding his hand. I went to his house a couple of times – lucky for me that my Mum was in the Lake District visiting family and it was easy to get round my Dad – where we watched DVD's while relaxing on his bed. He was nice and didn't push a single thing with me. We just kissed, he was gentle and I felt safe and comfortable in his company.

My whole family was extremely angry at me for my choice of first boyfriend. I remember my Dad checking, "It is your first, isn't it?" and I assured him "Yes, of course" as it was. He was worried that I would get attached to him and that it would become a long term relationship and that I would get hurt. The rest of my family were annoyed because I had been privileged at being sent to private schools and to university and I chose to "end up" with something that was not at all suitable and I could "do and deserve so much better for yourself, Rebecca, can't you see that?" Luke asked me to marry him in a text message, which my brother had seen first and had entered into a whole text conversation with him behind my back while we were away in Norin on our annual two-week holiday. I only realised that this had occurred when I returned from holiday only to find Luke wasn't talking to me and I couldn't work out why. Apparently my brother had sent texts to Luke, insinuating that I thought I was texting my boyfriend in London, which obviously was not true, and Little Brother had sent him a text from my phone to say that it was all over! I was furious with Little Brother!

Luke and I eventually sorted out a lot of hurt feelings and continued to see each other for another couple of months until I came home for his Dad's surprise 50th birthday party, during which he looked after me so well and made sure I was OK all night and I felt I was fitting in and being accepted by his family just fine. I didn't feel like I had to pretend or be someone that I wasn't and I found that I wasn't worried about saying the wrong thing or doing the wrong thing. It came to the crunch when my Mum had come to collect me in the car and Luke said it's them or him – but of course I chose my poor Mum and Dad and my beloved family! I knew it wasn't a serious relationship for me and my choice of boyfriend number one was causing ructions in my family as he obviously wasn't suitable for me, so I stopped seeing him. I think we both understood it wouldn't have worked out for much longer anyway.

2nd Year.

I got a new boyfriend, Miles. He was nice, but I kind of only ended up saying yes to going out with him because I had kissed him in the union when I was bored one night when my friend was busy with some guy and I was left dancing with other people who were on my music course that I knew, just for the sake of it as I was tired and really all I wanted was just to go home. I felt bad for behaving like this and he just was not leaving me alone, plus he was liked by everyone and so I felt obliged to give him a chance to avoid conflict with so many people and to avoid looking selfish, like a user and building up a bad reputation around the campus, which was the last thing I wanted to do. He was a nice, kind, gentle guy and I enjoyed spending time with him and he treated me really well, but I had to finish it. He kept asking if I would stay round at his halls and I never would have. But he didn't force me into anything and he respected all of my signals and wishes. I finished it tactfully, a horrible deed as he was a genuinely nice guy for someone who was right for him.

Towards the end of my second year, I had started to see Spen. He was my second choice from the London Orchestra. My sister had taken my first choice and I was so angry and jealous of her for when he chose her over me. When I found out, I got very drunk in the bar after the rehearsal. I started to only give myself cucumber sandwiches for dinner in the evening and I didn't think anything of it until my housemates and friends with whom I was living in my second year noticed my rituals night after night and once commented, saying "you can't just live on cucumber sandwiches every night" but I said I liked cucumber sandwiches and I remember backing this up by telling them the story that my Mum used to tell me about how I always made my Mum make cucumber sandwiches for me to take for lunch at primary school. My Mum had told me how she would send me to school with these cucumber sandwiches in my lunchbox because I wouldn't eat anything else and she hoped that the dinner ladies didn't think that my Mum couldn't afford to feed me with anything else except cucumber sandwiches, poor thing. My friends said that I can't eat them every night, just because I like them. I guess now they were right, as I did like other things really I liked everything and had never been a picky eater - I didn't understand picky eaters and they irritated me – but I couldn't change. I left out the spread in my cucumber sandwiches at university too.

I remember going to The Lake District with Mum and meeting Auntie Ann and Uncle there. We were all in the hotel restaurant sitting at the table right in the middle of the room having dinner and I remember making an effort to choose something that I would be able to hopefully finish off. I showed Auntie Ann that I could eat properly without a problem, especially after her last comment about me having slimmed down. So I ate all my meal especially for her. When Mum went to the toilet she said quietly to me "Well, you polished that off! We must admit we were getting a bit worried about whether you had a problem or not, but obviously there isn't one so good for you!" I was shocked at her being so open with me, but most of all for being so nice about it. I felt ill with her compliment for polishing it off though and I felt so guilty and greedy, but at least she wasn't angry with me and she could see I was eating OK. One of my relatives that we visited commented on my lovely bonnie face on one of our visits to The Lake District previously and it was in front of my brother and sister. I was really embarrassed and felt like she was saying I was the fat-faced one, the odd sibling out, even though I knew she didn't mean it in this way.

I stayed at Spen's house after an orchestra concert in March 2000. We were doing a concert for which my sister wasn't needed and she wasn't there to fight my corner or to give me advice or to steer me in the right direction as usual. I was so undecided at what to do for the best and consulted my best friend Dina, who just excitedly said to me "yes go on, it's what you've been waiting for!" How she worked that one out I am not so sure! I had been getting close to him and she knew I liked him and wasn't sure where it was going, but I wasn't waiting to be invited over to his place after a rehearsal! I don't know. I didn't know what to do. I knew his friend, who was also in the orchestra and who was also staying over that night, and I trusted him, he was one of those guys who you knew you'd be safe with, like Miles, the genuine kind. So my decision was made and I went on ahead with them.

When we arrived, Spen took me upstairs and I remember being so pleased when he came over to kiss me in his room. We made toast with his housemates and the other friend in the kitchen and we had nice conversations, then we went to bed. I hovered around the floor area, wondering where to put myself and what I was to sleep on. I asked him if he had a sleeping bag I could please borrow. He smiled and invited me into his bed. I asked him if he was sure he didn't mind. We kissed a lot, I kept on all my clothes and I didn't dare close my eyes all night. He tried to get my trousers off, but I was adamant that everything was staying on. He found it funny, I think, but he was secretly frustrated at me, I could tell. I saw him a few more times after rehearsals, always with the same routine. When I refused to stay over, he became extremely pushy with me wanting me to stay over at his house every Tuesday after rehearsals and Kerry and Dina hated these weekly arguments. The number of arguments we ended up having on the way to the tube over my last train back to university out of London versus Spen's house. My sister saw his pushy side straight away, but I was blinded as I just liked him because he was cute and clever and a brilliant trumpet player and, I suppose, it seemed that he liked me too.

During the summer of that year I went on a long weekend trip to Paris, where my sister's university friend had been studying and she had invited Kerry, me and my friend Dina, along for a weekend. It was superb in that she had everything planned so that we could do and see everything and the weather was so hot and we even found our way to one of my university friend's house parties at her gorgeous flat in Paris one night. We all had a fantastic time. I do remember being on the Metro that evening however, the four of us. As it was still warm in the evenings we were wearing just our summer clothes and a cardigan. I was wearing a three-quarter-length light blue and white summer dress and cardigan and was standing by the door of the Metro close to the seats. The train was not too busy, but not empty either. There was an old man sitting there on the seat, he just put his arm out and touched my bottom cheek! I turned round and swatted him off and moved away! I was laughing in surprise and shock at this sheer blatant action, that's all. Men! I looked at my friends and no-one had seen or noticed, but I explained what had happened and we got off at the next stop!

3rd Year.
I got together with Spen properly on 28th November 2000. I wasn't sure at first simply because he'd had all his lovely hair cut off and I know that sounds superficial but I wanted to keep my options open as it was my final year at university too. We spent a lot of time together getting to know each other. We became best friends. I stayed over at his a lot and he began to stay over at mine. It was nice having a boyfriend in the orchestra and he came to help with my university concerts too. He was really popular and really good at playing the trumpet!

Our relationship progressed very slowly in the physical sense. I found it hard to go beyond kisses and cuddles and preferred to spend quality time together being emotionally intimate and talking and just spending time in each other's company, kissing and cuddling, being able to enjoy this as it felt so comfortable and safe and I really started to love being with him and I trusted him fully. I found it uncomfortable and so hard to take off any clothes or to get close to him physically and so I just wouldn't do this at all. When he was close behind me and motioned like 'he' used to, fully clothed, like at the start of everything all those years ago, I would silently and uncontrollably cry to myself. I was shocked and confused and felt silly and pathetic and weak. It felt scary, it was painful inside my heart, which *ached so badly*, memories flashed back to me and flooded through my head, and I felt scared and would freeze. Where did all this come from? I thought I had dealt with it and left it all in the past, being a stronger person for having got through it alone and having shoved it to the back of my mind. My reactions overwhelmed me and I became stuck. I had become so close to Spen emotionally, we were such good friends that I felt able to tell him how I was feeling when he realised something was wrong as I would continually just totally freeze and start crying, uncontrollably.

I was confused and didn't want to say anything, hoping it would go away or get better and that I would get past this. I couldn't say anything, could I? I did speak a little, enough to give him an idea of what it was that I didn't feel comfortable with anyway and he was shocked that I had been through what I had told him about and he said that it wasn't right and that it was serious. Just hearing him say that after only touching the surface of what had happened in the past and seeing the disbelief and horror and furrowing frown spread across his face at what he was hearing, totally confused me further.

For me, I had just ended up accepting it and had locked it in the past. Yet here I was finding myself in panic and in floods of tears each time round, with waves of memories haunting my life and hurting my heart unbearably all of a sudden. I tried my best to forget anyway, and Spen was OK at taking things even slower. He was really nice, took control of the situation and I felt safe and secure, cared for and emotionally connected when he was around because I trusted him, he made the decisions, he took control, he looked after everything and at a pace I trusted and could manage.

By November however, I started restricting my food intake severely. When I was carrying out my research in a music shop in Maidenhead for example, I would just skip my lunch and only allow myself drinks during my entire outing, until all my work had been done for that day. When I arrived back at my halls however I would struggle to buy myself or to make myself a full and balanced meal, I stopped going into the dining room and I started taking more time over choosing a simple sandwich from the shop at lunchtime etc.

My periods stopped before Christmas and I went to the doctor at university complaining of feeling cold, dizzy, and faint and I was worried that I was pregnant, even though surely I couldn't be, could I? I ignorantly thought that was the only reason my periods would stop and babies were the only thing constantly on my mind. Then I learned that being worried could also stop it and so I put it down to being stressed over my work and tried my best to take deep breaths in my effort to "you must relax more" as advised by the nurse. I don't know when, or indeed if I ever put together the thought that it might be my weight. When the doctor weighed me and said "There's not much of you, is there?" I just didn't know what to say because I didn't agree with her and so I just shrugged and said "Mmm…" and couldn't get out of there quick enough. I was scared of what I was doing to myself as I knew I surely couldn't really be pregnant and told myself I must get back my period, this is bad. I was distraught at being unable to participate in the Christmas Chapel Choir services, which I was so looking forward to, because I was too ill and my fainting spells had returned. I started to avoid social occasions and tried to cool things down with Spen but by January 2001 he told me he was "getting attached" to me.

I was also practicing for hours and hours in the practice rooms in every spare minute of my time, as I had done in my first and second years, but at this point I was on overdrive with such a determination in striving for that perfection that I resolved I must be sure and able to reach, if I kept going. It was like I was being willed on all the time. It felt like a workout. It felt great. I practiced early in the morning, in my spare time during the day and until late at night even after rehearsals and right up until the security came to lock-up the practice rooms. I practiced until my hands hurt, until my teeth hurt, until my lips bled, until I was dizzy, until I was fainting, until I was out of breath, in pain, until I felt utterly exhausted. I remember thinking I can lock myself in the large Victorian house where I practiced as all the rooms locked from the inside, so I'd be safe in there, and for a break I would practice hand stands and walkovers that I'd learned in my acrobatic lessons when I was little.

It was the running back over the bridge and through the campus in the dark after eleven o'clock at night on my own that scared me a little because I had heard about the campus attacker. My Mum did used to call me to see if I was still in the practice rooms and I spoke to her when I had returned safely back to my halls. I used to tell myself that I am strong and can get through it and will be OK, whatever happens. I had to be the best performer who stood far out over and above everyone else, I had to be Principal Clarinet in everything, I had to be first choice of clarinet player and be picked for everything so as to be always the one with all the solos and always the one to shine above everyone else and I just had to be the winner of that performer of the year prize, which I *was,* to my absolute surprise and happiness. I had to pass all my exams first time round and with flying colours, I had to be the best and to sound the best and to play with my very own style. I just had to be the most sought after clarinettist in London. I loved my clarinet, I loved my music, I loved being the best, I loved even being famous around the campus carrying around my heavy instruments that were permanently securely strapped to my shoulder, they were a part of me and my life. They were my way of communicating. They were my security and they provided my release from the real world.

On 2nd April 2001, my Dad took ill at home to the point where I think he had stopped breathing and I remember flagging down the ambulance in my socks outside my house that night in the rain and then politely yet firmly asking the ambulance men to "please can you hurry up, please?" when they were getting left behind as I lead them through the house and up the stairs to where my Dad lay in the bed with my Mum beside him. I felt bad because she told me off, even at this moment in life, for speaking to the ambulance people like I had. I couldn't understand why they were being so slow and appeared to me to be just taking their time! I don't expect panic is helpful, but surely every second counts? In our family, we were not good at disturbing people and asking for help unless absolutely necessary and we had only called the ambulance at the very, very, very last moment in desperation. My Dad stayed in hospital for a week, but was re-admitted on 16th May until 18th May, when he finally and thankfully returned home.

My tutors used to say "You've been burning those midnight oils again" and they were right, not that I would ever admit it in the slightest though. My Mum submitted a letter to my tutors explaining the recent ordeal with my Dad and the present situation and I remember the Choir Master saying a special prayer that was clearly for my family and for my Dad, thankfully subtly as I hadn't told anyone but my very close friends. This gesture made me feel warm and secure. I told my Mum, and she shared it with my Dad and we all smiled.

For our six month anniversary, Spen bought me a silver necklace that he had chosen when he'd visited his old school friend Jill. It was lovely. He said "This is for realising that we have something special, whatever happens in the future". I felt bad because I hadn't got anything to mark our anniversary – I didn't feel he was one for celebrations and so I didn't want to make a fuss as I was unsure that he was taking anything seriously and I didn't feel right to assume that he was, therefore making a big deal of it. Though it was a big deal to me, I was touched that he had realised! I wore it that night, to a birthday party of one the girls on my course held at her house. By the end of this party, I had got quite drunk and we both ended up in tears back in my room, because I had thought Spen had called me fat. It was a long night. I was upset because I was sure that he had called me "jelly belly", but he assured me that he hadn't.

After my exams, I enjoyed the end of year ball, on 8th June 2001. I was happy at this time in my life. I was even happier and so relieved when I passed my degree. So happy in fact, that I ran into the woods and screamed, out of sheer relief! I was overjoyed! I was so fearful that I wouldn't even pass, due to some awful unknown reason. Realistically I was expecting nothing more or less than a bog standard 2:1, but secretly really, really, really I hoped that I'd made a 1st, so I was hugely relieved that I hadn't scraped a degrading 3rd or even a fail, but at the same time secretly pretty well disappointed that I hadn't made the 1st because I knew that I really could have if I had tried harder or put more work into it all and then I would have even beaten my sister, who also achieved a 2:1. I was hugely disappointed and upset but strangely relieved that I'd even passed at the same time.

I remember the day before the photos of the ball came out, Spen and I had apparently done the deed. The process had been very slow and over a very long period of time and so I had hardly even noticed that it had happened. But on 8th June 2001 I noticed spotting in my knickers when I went to the toilet afterwards and Spen confirmed it had been done and asked if I was OK. I didn't feel any different to be honest, but he said I was walking around like a zombie and like I was in a complete and utter daze and so very distant. He put it down to a bit of shock. He looked after me though. I just didn't know if I'd wanted to go that far and hadn't realised that we had, but it was too late now anyway! But it was OK because I didn't feel any different and I just didn't want to think about it anyway.

4ii-Greece and Granada:

Holiday to Greece with Spen.

When I had left university we booked our first holiday away together. We went to Greece for about ten days. I was apprehensive, but I felt safe with Spen now. I felt close to him emotionally and he always looked after me. We were inseparable. When we weren't together, we'd spend all our time talking on the phone. When we were together we'd spend all our time holding hands, cuddling, perfecting our kisses. We just fitted. We had our own language. We were happy.

I remember we stayed at his brother's halls in Manchester the night before we flew out and we went out for a curry with his old friends from school. In my diary, I recorded:

"Out for Indian. Very full. Hardly ate. Massive portion"

Angel Just-Rights

On our first night there, 21st June 2001 we arrived at our holiday destination, it was late and we were tired and we went out for something to eat in the closest restaurant to the hotel that we could find. My diary entry states:

"Spen nearly made me cry when in the restaurant...Had wine. He said (about the waitress girl) 'I would try to pull her if you weren't here. You have to admit she is very sweet'. I couldn't believe it at all. Our first night. Our first meal. Didn't eat it. Not very nice at all. Chicken in a red sauce. He had Mousaka (horrible potato thing). Cried a bit. Kept thinking, 'what am I doing here with Spen on my own? After what had just happened. What am I doing? Went to sleep."

Spen had blatantly been attracted to the waitress and this upset me. I remember thinking, "What have I done coming on holiday, so far away from home, with this person? What if we fall out and everything goes wrong?" I had never been abroad before except to Japan and France and a few other places but it was always with a group of people with either school or orchestras and now I was scared of being on my own and having to make my way back home alone, if it came to it. I was tired and I tried to persuade myself that things would definitely seem better in the morning, which thankfully they did.

On 27th June 2001, we had new neighbours move into the room next door to us at the hotel and they were being very noisy in bed one night and I recorded in my diary:

"Spen was in a mardy because I was listening and then when he said "Come on, let's do it!" and I said "No way!" he was even worse."

On holiday I was less anxious as we had apparently done the deed once before and so I could surely do it again if I had to and I was in a different country and on holiday, morals didn't really count so much, or so I tried to tell myself to ease the guilt and feelings of not actually wanting to. I didn't like it but I thought I'd get to like it. I still felt guilty, as it wasn't how I was brought up to behave, having sex before marriage. It was all too much for me though. He was big (but I didn't know this for all the time I was with him) and I didn't like it. In fact, I hated it. He wanted it all the time. I wanted just to

140

kiss and be with him. I started to say I was tired and he wouldn't be happy about this and it put him in a bad mood, but it was still my call. He never stopped trying and we argued and fell out. By the day we were going home, I was spotting blood, my stomach was hurting and I was in severe pain.

Granada.

I went to my doctor as soon as I got home, telling my Mum it was to get a prescription for my hay fever, which it was, in addition, so I didn't really lie. There was no way I could tell my Mum the truth because it was embarrassing enough and I didn't want to disappoint her especially as she had warned me so nicely in the car on the way to taking me to the train station to start my journey off on holiday to "think on" and not to get "carried away just because you're on holiday". Anyway, my doctor prescribed me with some tablets and said I must come back if it doesn't clear up and if the pain and bleeding doesn't go away. I was worried that this might have got back to my parents, as my Dad worked in the hospital as the General Consultant Surgeon and was generally well known to all of the doctors in my town. Practically everyone knew him and our family in our small town.

Growing up we had to behave properly at all times and say the right things as it was like being famous in Granada and 'showing up' our parents was out of the question. My Mum has strict thoughts around sex before marriage. If Spen came to stay, he was downstairs in the spare room (a rule for which I was so thankful). Even when my sister was engaged to be married, it was separate rooms if her fiancé came to stay, until they were married. Still, Spen and I returned to England closer than ever:

"I will never forget Spen running through the barriers at his house for my train. Blue shirt, "love you" kiss kiss. Very, very, very, very, very sweet indeed; bless! 7 Months."

Two days after, on 1st July 2001, Spen went to Holland on a work placement. I didn't visit him, as much as he wanted me to. I remember a big bunch of flowers arriving on 10th August 2001 addressed to me and I went to pick them up at the post office with Mum the next day. Spen never usually even bought me a card for a birthday as he saw it as a waste of good money – "think how much you could save in a year" he used to say, which I think was a saying he had picked up from his Mother, who valued making the most of everything, recycling and looking after the environment. Initially, I thought this was very sweet, but I had my suspicions at receiving this great bunch of flowers as with it, came a note, apologising. He said he didn't know what to say to me on the phone and had written me a letter. I learned that he had been seeing a girl in Amsterdam. I was distraught. I remember locking myself in my room and crying my eyes out:

"Picked up parcel from post office. Flowers! Very sweet. Couldn't believe it. Very weird though. Bless! Really want him by me...

Find out about blossoming romance (sorry blossomed!). B*****d! "Micci, we did everything". I just started to cry and had to put the phone down...!

Why didn't I think? Oh! And that makes everything OK again. Flowers...!

I had called him up to thank him for the flowers and he was crying. He sounded really agitated and confused today. Spent ages in my room, unable to stop crying. I could feel it hurt inside and it was going straight through me...

How could he? What I found out is that it was more than once. Four times, she'd slept in his bed at least and he said it was good. Very good. Had to go to garden centre with Mum and Dad afterwards. Not in mood at all! How could he. That's it. After everything we had in Greece. I REALLY liked him after the end of that holiday...

Can't believe he's done this to 'us'. Keep thinking of everything we used to do, how he used to do it, how he used to look, and now he's done it all with someone else! How could he wreck everything? I never thought he'd do this. Not to me. I NEVER ASKED FOR IT. You can't imagine how it feels until it happens to yourself. I trusted him 100%. It wasn't even just a kiss... "We did everything"...he's even sent me a photo of her and she's not even pretty I don't think. Can't help thinking about those moments when...just before...will I ever get over this EVER again? Seriously. Really trusted him completely. Never have with ANYBODY before. REALLY hurt. How could he?"

Mum and Dad wanted to go on an outing driving around the garden centres near our house and for lunch and I remember being resistant and wanting to stay at home. I was just so upset. How could he do this to me?!

During this time, my mind was thankfully distracted by my enjoying working in a pub called Dr. Thirsty's in the town centre, much to my parent's displeasure. It was very far removed from the kind of work I would choose normally for myself, but as my brother had found a job in a hotel elsewhere, I said that I would work the hours that he had left at the bar, if that was OK with them and so I became a bar tender and I loved it! It was a way for me to earn a little money but most importantly, I could have some time out away from everything. My parents were not into letting me go out away from the house in the evenings and I needed some escapism. I loved the busyness of the weekend shifts especially. I would do my funky hairstyle and put on my make-up and drink slush cocktails with the other barmaids discreetly behind the bar! This job ensured I was kept busy and it boosted my confidence in working around people and in that different environment where I felt I didn't need to prove myself to anyone except through being quick and efficient in service, which I strived to execute with flair and I enjoyed working here and took a pride in doing my job well. I really enjoyed my time here and I even got myself a fling with a gentle young local for a couple of weeks. Well, why not?!

CHAPTER 5:

MUSIC COLLEGE AND SPEN

~ THE BREAK: PETER AND THE PARTY ~

MUSIC COLLEGE AND SPEN; AGAIN

5i-Music College and Spen:

Spen came to live down the road from me while I was in student halls in Grenway. He had found a flat share in Lewisham. I remember when Spen came to my halls on 25th September 2001 with his friends that I now knew quite well too, it was four days after he'd returned from Amsterdam:

"Went to American fast food joint with Spen, Vin, John, Nancy. Spen changed. I had my own confidence without being together with him now. Came back to my halls. Wanted to slap him hard. Really hurt a lot when he touched even my arm. A LOT. Right through me. Again. Really, really, really, really, really hurt."

I couldn't imagine living without him. He made me happy. My life didn't seem complete without him. I guess I felt a little security. He was my best friend! I did start to feel like maybe I was spending too much time with him and not making the most of making more friends and socialising with others at my new college though and part of me really wanted to distance him from me because of this.

I was becoming friendly with a sweet lad at college called Peter and agreed to go out for a drink with him one night, 26th October 2001:

"Went out for a drink with Peter. Walked round Grenway for AGES. River at night was really nice. He ended up coming to my halls. He tried to kiss me but I didn't let him and he apologised for making me feel uncomfortable. He came up for a drink and we talked for a long time. Spen called! I walked Peter half way down the road and he pecked me on the cheek."

5ii-The Break – Peter and The Party:

Peter was a bassoon player and we'd been sitting next to each other in the orchestra from the start of the year. He was so kind, gently spoken, had a lovely smile, was tall, nicely built with floppy blond hair, he had a sparkling personality and was extremely popular, funny, very caring, thoughtful and considerate, yet definitely not just a pushover. I agreed to have a drink with him. After a while, I remember really having a nice relaxed time with everyone after a rehearsal, to the point where he tickled me under the table and I chipped my top tooth on a beer glass, laughed and then cried in the toilet, just out of shock and stupidity and worry about my tooth! All it took was a trip to the dentist to have it repaired, back in Granada, on 18th January 2002.

Peter stayed over once at my halls and we just lay on top of my bed, both fully dressed and relaxing in each other's arms. It was lovely. He was lovely. I remember he did try things with me physically, but respected every one of my subtle signals and when I told him what was not going to happen, he was fine. We had a lovely time. I remember he was worried because I flinched a lot when he touched my hair or my face, which I just didn't like. I think I was paranoid about my eyebrow make-up at the time, but I hated that flinching, because he was *unbelievably gentle.* I know a part of me was just on heightened awareness for fleeing, even though I felt in control throughout him being in my company and I knew he wouldn't do anything to hurt me. But still, one must be prepared.

We spent a lot of time together at my halls, watching television with my friends, socialising and I enjoyed seeing him around college too. He treated me so well, as if I was the most precious thing in the world to him and I felt safe and comfortable in his arms and happy...but he wasn't Spen. He also persisted in inviting me round to his house as he said he wanted to cook for me, but I didn't feel comfortable with the idea of being somewhere that wasn't my territory and I suppose I didn't feel in control and didn't want to face an unknown meal in addition to the fact that I knew he loved to be romantic and I didn't want to feel awkward and in a situation I would not be able to remove myself from if I so wished. For these reasons, I kept putting it off, telling him I wasn't yet ready. Although perturbed at my reticence, he respected my wishes totally and was always patient with me. Incidentally, I suppose my shyness and reserve even affected my performing as I remember being put into a jazz quartet in order "to help lose those strict inhibitions" that was annoyingly beginning to even restrict in my playing. I had put it down to shyness, but it had become my safety zone.

Peter was very sweet and I loved being together with him. I'd told him about Spen – I think the whole college knew about Spen because everyone in music knew everyone else in music in London. Spen was also well-known to people from attending a special Music School and they had seen him around Grenway with me too. Also, he had previously spent a year at a music college himself. I didn't talk about Spen with Peter, obviously, out of thoughtfulness and consideration.

On 31st January 2002, one of my friends had a 'get over Amos' party at her house as she'd split up with her long-term boyfriend. We had a girly night, but as Peter was so lovely and fitted in with the girls and they all loved him and were good friends, they asked him to come along too. I was a little put out by this only because I was looking forward to a girly evening in and to be honest I felt that I had spoiled the 'no men' thing and I think I just wanted to go to something as 'just me' for once in my life and not with someone in tow, as much as I enjoyed being with him. Anyway, I resolved that it was fine, as it was her party. They had chocolate fingers and one of the girls, whom I never liked much as she was very forward and blunt, tried to force feed me with them. I closed my mouth as tightly as I could. After that I had to eat a couple of fingers of my own accord, just to join in and to not look weird, well it was either that or pizza, and especially as Peter was there too. I felt greedy and undeserved and went straight to the toilet to 'S'.

My relationship with Peter ended when he saw me hand-in-hand with Spen in Grenway Village one weekend. It was the day that Spen and I had met up for coffee to discuss where to go after our break apart and we were holding hands just because that's what we did and we didn't know how else to be together. I saw how hurt poor Peter looked and felt terrible. Although I tried to explain this to Peter, it wasn't sounding good, of course; my loyalties clearly all still remained entirely with Spen and we got back together straight away.

5iii-Music College and Spen; Again:

I was honest to Spen about the night I had planned to go and practice when I was stopped on the way by some friends, including Peter and they had persuaded me to join them at the pub instead. Spen found a text on my phone from Peter when I was at his place and went mad. Spen:

"Got hold of my hands very tightly and THREW me across the room. Banged myself on the radiator and on the bed. Hurt! Shocked. Very shocked. Hurt me again. Then I started crying because was very shocked and scared and sick of the whole business not being right. Went to sleep. Not made up properly. Woke up still not good. Still not made up."

Three days later, on 3rd November 2001, Spen and I were having very good times and very bad times. I was really in two minds as to whether I should get back together with him properly as I still hadn't gotten over what he had done to spoil 'us' and what we had together before he ruined it all no matter how much I tried to be OK with it. I was still really hurting and didn't know if it could ever work for us ever again, not really. I spent a lot of days just crying over 'us' and trying to make the decision. I decided that I was going to tell Spen that it was over but on the 29th November 2001, our one year anniversary:

"Should I call him or not? Had lesson. Came home. Lay on bed. Felt sick. Really sick. No dinner. Cheese on toast. He didn't call."

I split up with him the next day.

When I was struggling with my eating we would have long talks in the kitchen about breaking up or going on a break. I loved being with Spen, but was feeling trapped at the same time. I was looking at other people and having feelings for others and my mind was wondering and I couldn't see at this time how 'we' could work properly any longer as I was still hurting from his actions the summer before and was now telling myself that I would never end up married to Spen after this. We took a break from each other, during which I saw more of Peter.

Meanwhile, as part of my studies I remember being the final person to 'volunteer' in the Alexander Technique group. We had to choose a piece of music to play and the tutor fiddled around with us demonstrating this technique. I usually enjoyed performing, but this scared me rigid. I went last, hoping I'd be forgotten but no such luck. I performed OK. But I stopped breathing as soon as he started touching me afterwards and I fainted. I felt stupid and like a freak with everyone watching me. It was horrible. I was hot and shaky and dizzy and felt sick, but as it was one of the first times my peer group had ever heard me perform, at least I received a lot of praise and compliments on my playing, which encouraged and reassured me.

By January 2002, I began to love being with Spen again – "Really, really fancy Spen again...what am I to do?" – We got back together straight away after the Christmas break.

By March 2002, I had made a name for myself at music college and was at home on my Easter break when I received a phone-call from someone unknown to me saying that my playing had been recommended and would I be able to play the bass clarinet in their end of term recital? I was surprised that he had asked me and overjoyed as the bass clarinet was my new-found pride and joy and of course, I replied yes with delight and excitement!

Angel Just-Rights

A couple of days later I accompanied Mum to Kanning University to visit Little Brother. I remember dreading and taking ages over choosing lunch at the pub and then doing as much walking as possible in and out of Little Brother's halls and up and down the steps carrying his heavy luggage to the car. Mum and I also stopped off at a DIY shop on the way home, another opportunity I couldn't waste. I really didn't realise my behaviours at this point, I just had to do it. What's more, we stopped to pick up fish and chips from our local shop on the way home because it was getting late and it was an "easy and substantial meal" but for me, 'S', and in the days that followed...

CHAPTER 6:-

...DIARY ENTRIES OF CORRELATIONS BETWEEN

EVENTS, THOUGHTS AND BEHAVIOURS...

6i-The Next Few Days – Easter Break:

- **Thursday 28th March 2002:**

Nanstead with Mum at about 2pm! Took black trousers back to Wareworld. Bought trousers from Zarap. Tried dress on in Kookil and Mum said "It's too small". EVERYTHING WAS TOO SMALL! Stew and coffee ice-cream: '<u>S</u>'.

- **Friday 29th March 2002 (Good Friday):**

Picked Little Brother up from Kells. Met Alice, Dan, Gareth, Jim, Helen. Curry dinner: Mum mardy because had to cook smelly potato. Dad had already cooked everything else for us, ahh. Little Brother out. Kerry home.

- **Saturday 30th March 2002:**

Queen Mother dies in her sleep. Mum and Kerry go to Lake District to visit Granddad in hospital having cataracts done. Me / Dad / Little Brother go to Garden Centre, do it yourself shops, Supermarket. Little Brother off to work at 6pm. Finished reading new book, very good.

- ### Sunday 31st March 2002 (Easter Sunday):

Clocks go forward. Easter! Reading another new book. Spen back today and spoke to him.

- ### Monday 1st April 2002 (Easter Monday):

Got a Cream Egg egg with two mini eggs. Feel quite ill today: headache, cold, shivery, because of everything in last few days...no 'S' today as just couldn't at all.

- ### Tuesday 2nd April 2002:

Nanstead with Little Brother. Feel a little better today. Met Alice (Little Brother's friend from university). Bought blue hooded top and a red and blue rugby top – nice.

- ### Friday 5th April 2002:

Queen Mother's Procession through the streets 10:00am, poor William and Harry. Kerry back to Collester – won't take her Easter Egg her boyfriend or Mum gave to her.

- ### Saturday 6th April 2002:

Town with Mum. Listened to The Grand National in supermarket car park on radio. Spen comes.

- ### Sunday 7th April 2002:

Spen drives us back to university. Had shower and dried hair while Spen unpacked freezer food. Had Spen's ratatouille, rice, chicken and muffin: '<u>S</u>' at Spen's.

• Monday 8th April 2002:

Kerry starts again (school). Dina calls and says she's going to the Queen Mother's funeral tomorrow (but she doesn't!) Spen back to mine. Fish, jacket potatoes, hoops. Flapjack: '<u>S</u>'.

• Tuesday 9th April 2002:

Queen Mother's funeral. Walking over Creek Road bridge and we saw 'The World' cruise ship! Took photos. Saw William and Harry etc. Walking behind the coffin. Then went through park (St James') to 'The Mall' where we saw all cars and the Queen! Coffee. Nice. Tate Modern, Millennium Bridge. Spen's. Tagliatelle, lots of salad and sauce, muffin: '<u>S</u>'. Bed.

• Thursday 11th April 2002:

Made eggy pasta for dinner at Spen's – quite nice but still hungry! Bit eggy!

• Friday 12th April 2002:

Chicken noodles dish at the Noodle House: '<u>S</u>' tried.

• Saturday 13th April 2002:

Sat around Spen's house. Bit annoyed at that and irritated around the house. Went shopping (supermarket). Ham sandwich and salad. Home. Practice for tomorrow. Spen came round – Bless! Pasta.

• Sunday 14th April 2002:

London Marathon. Got on wrong side of road so had to dodge the runners! Busking. Fine. Gig – wedding for friend of newsreader so that's cool and a student videoed us playing too. Spen stayed in my room because he couldn't move his car! Back at 2ish. Lunch. To Spen's washed hair and dried it. Pork stir fry, rice: '<u>S</u>'.

6ii-Brief Evaluation of Diary Entries:

'<u>S</u>' equalled my codeword for being sick. Spen caught me '<u>S</u>' after eating a chocolate muffin. I don't know why I did it, I told him it was just the 'chocolate phlegm' but he frowned at me and said it wasn't right. He talked about it and I brushed it off. The next day, he told me that he had telephoned a helpline and was in tears at hearing himself saying the words on the phone. I was shocked that he had bothered to call a helpline regarding me, and assured him that everything would be OK and not to worry. It was 'just some chocolate phlegm, right?' I couldn't see anything wrong with that, but I told him that I wouldn't do it again.

From 16th April 2002, I managed to persuade my group of hall friends on the same corridor as me, to go for group runs or, as they preferred to put it, group jogs, every Tuesday, which we did for a good few weeks together. One week, Tuesday 30th April 2002, we missed going because it was raining and so that Saturday, after our shopping trip to Bromley to look for a present and a dress to wear for our mutual friend (Charlie) from the London Orchestra whose birthday party we'd been invited to, I somehow had managed to put a bet on with Spen, that I could beat him on a run. I even believed it myself at the time, trying my best to remember the time at school when I would always win the 100m races way in front of everyone else, except that was a girls' school too Micci! That evening, although it was cold, windy and raining, we put on our track suits and trainers and went for that run in Blackhills. I ended up in severe pain and cramp and Spen had to take us both home, but I felt better for the exercise and fresh air even though it had made me feel so ill. The next day, our quintet performed at the wedding gig in Grenway and we all had an amazing time. From then on, I had to go jogging even if it was any day of the week and on my own.

CHAPTER 7:

MY FAMILY AND SPEN

~

EDINBURGH

7i-My Family and Spen:

My Dad and I – Quality Time.
After graduating with my Postgraduate Performance qualification from Music College and Spen's graduating with his 1st in Engineering from his London University, Spen went on holiday to Croatia with a group of friends at the end of August that year. These were the friends with whom I had become good friends too. Spen wanted me to go with him and I did so want to, but I wanted more to stay at home and spend time with my Dear Dad, being nice to him, talking to him and doing anything he wanted, so this is the decision I made.

Anything my Dad ever did that would annoy me, I would take a deep breath and tell myself, let him do it, let him enjoy himself, so what, hey? And it made me smile and feel better to see him being happy and comfortable in his home and around his family, both of which he was so proud of and I was proud of him. Seeing him happy and comfortable was the most important thing in the world to me. He had worked so hard and he deserved the life he had made for himself and that he provided for his Dear Family. I didn't know how much longer he would be here for and I tried to love him the most I could every single day.

Mum, Kerry, Little Brother, and Me Verses Dad, Spen, and Me.

Dad liked Spen because he was academic and read the books on the bookshelf and he read the newspaper in the mornings, unlike my brother. My sister didn't much like Spen because he was pushy and overpowering. My brother didn't like Spen for those reasons too and he even sent him a terrible text message when Spen had sent that guilty bunch of flowers to me (Book 1: Secrets Out, Part 2, Chapter 4), stating in the text that if he ever treated his sister like that or cheated on me again or made me so sad again, he would break both of his legs! I didn't know anything about this text until a lot later. My brother didn't tell me, but when Spen told me about the text, my brother did admit to it. I was shocked at my brother! I guess he had never seen me like that before, being so sad, crying and upset, dazed and probably talking and eating even less than usual. I never really asked him why, maybe it was just anger at Spen. I felt angry towards Little Brother for having done this behind my back, but also oddly touched and thankful in a way that my brother cared for his family so much that he took steps upon himself to protect them by, rightly or wrongly, standing up to Spen's ill-doings. Well I suppose someone had to. Thanks Little Bro.

7ii-Edinburgh:

Holiday to Edinburgh and Scotland with Spen (16/08/2002 – 23/08/2002).
Spen and I took a trip to Edinburgh in his car to visit his sister, with whom we stayed for a couple of nights. We enjoyed the festival and drinking different Whiskies at her friend's houses. Then we left and continued our journey driving up Scotland, staying at campsites (mostly his preference) and hostels (mostly my preference) and visiting different places and islands. We did a lot of walking and sight-seeing and were having a good time all in all. We weren't really getting on though. Thinking about it now, I think my depression was there but I didn't notice or know why I was feeling so down. I couldn't work out why I was feeling like this and neither could Spen. My eating was picky. I was refusing to have any kind of sexual relationship, which put Spen in the foulest of moods with me too. He was frustrated. We fell out a lot. But when we made up it

was great to have my best friend back by my side. We were still kissing and cuddling, which I so loved.

On the last night we arrived at a campsite quite late – it was dark and we almost drove into a big pond in the middle of the campsite, which made us both really laugh when we realised this near-miss! But that morning when we awoke, I was refusing to let him come near me and I was saying no, no, no. He was becoming angry and forceful. He'd been like this before. But I kept up my resistance. I was crying. I felt his absolute strength, not subsiding but getting stronger and stronger, like the time on holiday with 'him' where I fought and fought. I was crying and I froze. This time I was silent. It was awful. Seeing him on top of me, his face, his determination in that he had to do it, he wasn't giving up, and it felt like ages, time froze. I froze. No voice; only silence and hushed tears. He was staring me in the face with those piercing blue eyes and I couldn't look...

I climbed out of the tent and went for my shower, were I stayed, sobbing, under the hot water. I was shocked and confused in trying to rationalise over and over what had just happened. Now, I have been directed to think "how could someone I care about and who I thought cared about me do something like this, seeing and knowing full-well my distress? How could he have just ignored my distress and my tears in order to see that his own selfish needs were met?" But at the time I was thinking "I feel disgusting, why am I like this, I am so weak! Be strong, you're still alive!" Men; I hate them and their needs. I know he had to. They're selfish, mean, totally overpowering and will always get what they want if they've decided they're going to have it.

We never acknowledged anything had happened and just got on with the day. We were able to laugh at the pond right next to our tent and he was so lovely to me and this made me feel care and love for him back and so being with him, once again, made me feel safe; back to normal. He was kind and it was like my best friend was there back with me again. We enjoyed our journey back home. I had put the whole incident right out of my mind. You're strong. You're still alive. Carry on with living life. Smile...Ssh...!

CHAPTER 8:-

...DIARY ENTRIES FROM EDINBURGH...

- **Monday 19th August 2002:**

Climbed up Arthur's Seat it was pretty awful going up but nice once you got there and coming down the other side was OK. Went back to Edinburgh and had pizza in the park. Saw Lyn again [Spen's sister] and gave her two wine bottles to thank her for having us stay.

Watched his sister make the tea and ate it. Set off and reached the place we'd planned to camp – by the side of a lake in the middle of nowhere, just off a road – petrified all night! I didn't sleep and heard noises all night, particularly once, when I made Spen get up and unzip the tent really slowly to see who was there and it was some animal licking up the water in the lake – a fox or something, I preferred not to know! I had visions of seeing a shadow of a man with a knife hovering over our tent all night.

- **Tuesday 20th August 2002:**

Travelled through Killin – very nice waterfalls – to Glencoe where we camped at the campsite. Pasta for dinner by the river. Went for a long walk, got lost in the forest and it was getting dark – petrified again! Back to campsite.

- **Wednesday 21st August 2002:**

Packed up after 50p shower and drove through Glencoe village in the car to Killin. Walked over the hills. Fell out over the very big hill. Awful. Then really nice. Had nice lunch in the hills. Hitch-hiked a ride back down in a friendly Scottish mountain climber's car! Set off to Oban; nice drive. Fish and chips. Stayed in a B & B type place finally.

- ### Thursday 22nd August 2002:

Went to Mull on the ferry after a nice breakfast. Fell out on the ferry – awful – over restriction and <u>S.</u> Coach to Tobermory, he said "No, the sea is on THIS side, isn't it!" Cried. <u>Really</u> upset actually. Made up. Sort of. He was <u>really</u> nice.

Went for walk; beautiful place. Fish, smoked sausage and chips shared. Went to the distillery and it smelt! Bus home with school kids! Walked to the castle by the sea – was beautiful, sea, sound, really calming. Had a lift back by a couple who were really nice. Ferry ride back was nice. Went to supermarket and at 8:30pm we left for Lochlong campsite.

Horrid roads and the lights failed on the car! Arrived very late, at 10:00pm! Soup and sausage roll and pork pie in the dark! Bed.

- ### Friday 23rd August 2002:

Fell out. Breakfast: '<u>S</u>'. Cried. Shower. Packed up. Set off. Rained through Glasgow. Traffic. Nice. Ate all the way home. Him chocolate spread. Train station. McDonalds. Train home. Phone broke. My grape water.

Little Brother's new car. Pick up Kerry and her boyfriend from town. Home. Looked at Kerry's Greece photos. Bed. Spoke to Spen – knackered from driving! Bless!

CHAPTER 9:

NOISES IN THE NIGHT AND DAD

Little Brother had gone back to university, as had Kerry, Mum had gone to The Lake District again to be with Granddad who was seeing out his final days, Spen had gone back to university in London and I found myself frozen in bed at home in Granada; it was just me and my Dad in the house that night, but my Dad was fast asleep and I didn't want to disturb him and frighten him by waking him up.

Still as a statue I froze in my bed convinced that I'd heard a loud noise from downstairs. It was the middle of the night and I was scared stiff, literally. I listened for what seemed like an age, not daring to move a muscle in case someone was upstairs or even in my room checking everyone was still asleep. I was convinced there were burglars in the house and was terrified.

I thought things through: no way would Dad have heard anything, as he wore a hearing aid that he removed at night and he was a heavy sleeper too, I think I could hear him snoring so I knew he was OK. I couldn't get up, I was stuck, in case I saw them, or in case the floorboards creaked and they came running upstairs with knives and guns. If I made my way to my Dad's room, I was scared of waking him up and scaring him and then he'd be confused at being woken up and might speak in his loud voice and I wouldn't be able to communicate softly with him. I didn't want to be responsible for scaring and shocking him. Every sound I was hearing seemed to be magnified, even the beat of my heart, but still I was absolutely convinced there were intruders in the house.

Dialling the emergency services took a few frenzied attempts as mobile reception was extremely poor, as usual. Orange network is always bad in our house, but luckily if you keep trying, it usually works upstairs. I was praying. It finally rang through and I asked them to please come quickly, whispering like a scared child down the phone. I made them stay on the phone to me until they turned up. I got out of bed and looked out of the window to see their torch shining up the garden. I was so relieved that help had arrived. They told me to go downstairs and to let them in. I didn't even think about disturbing the burglars then, I just ran downstairs and opened the door as quickly as possible! It was such a relief to have them there. They checked a little around the house, but I didn't even make them check to see if burglars were hiding anywhere or to see if they were scattered in the rest of the house, but there was nothing disturbed: the television was still in its place and my laptop, on which I had become addicted at perfecting my touch-typing timings on, was still neatly placed on the stool in the Old Lounge. I was sure enough that everything was OK and then felt guilty and very bad for being so silly as to call the Police out for nothing and for wasting their precious time although I was relieved to no longer be alone and terrified quaking away to my silly childish self in bed.

As I was shaking, the nice officers said they would like to talk to my Dad but I explained that he is old and is ill and I didn't want to wake him up and so they respected these wishes and left. I slept with the light on. In the morning my Dad was so angry and he demonstrated this through silence and frowns over the breakfast table. But I realised his silence was more-so to do with his feeling extremely hurt and upset by the fact that I had been petrified enough to call the Police and that they had come into and had been walking around the house in middle of night and yet he had remained fast asleep upstairs in bed throughout. He said he felt silly and "What sort of father is this?" I understood totally and felt awful for having cornered him into feeling this way. I apologised, hating myself for being the weak one responsible for knocking my Dad's pride and I could tell he was blaming himself and being angry inside for his being so unwell. I am sorry Dear Dad.

A few days later, I heard that a lot of emergency calls had been made for fearing burglaries that night and that the noises were most likely due to an earth tremor in the area. At least it explained something to me, so I was a bit relieved and my parents forgave me for calling the Police, just a little, but I have never forgotten just how terrified I was and how I was unable to move a muscle when I had convinced myself there were strangers intruding in my safe and precious family home. How very dare they.

160

CHAPTER 10:

BEGINNING MY LIFE IN LONDON

~

DEAR DAD

10i-Living with Spen:

The Ups...

Spen continued his studies at university. I decided to get some academic work experience to add to my CV and to earn a steady income through temping and to keep up my music on the side, the latter I did not manage to do as it was so half-hearted and I worked in everything or nothing terms. I had come to terms with the fact that I was just too scared to try for professional orchestras as playing Principal was extremely stressful and I chickened out of this career underneath it all. Nowhere did anybody point out to me that actually one would never realistically begin as Principal, rather work their way up, until one day far in the future I came to realise this for myself. I suppose this demonstrates the extent at which 'black and white' thinking, as in simply either 'all or nothing' can reach and the affects that it can have on the direction and way in which one's life is to unfold as, instead of having the confidence to pursue my career in Music, I ran away from the expectations that I was too scared at failing at.

Instead, Spen and I decided to live together in London and I joined him in moving into a guy's flat near Waterloo Station on 26th September 2002. We shared a double room, lounge, bathroom and kitchen and basically had the place to ourselves and for a superb price, as there were two of us. The flat owner was a nice guy and spent most of his time on the computer in his office in the flat. My Mum came to see where I was living and made it clear that she wasn't at all happy with the double bed-sharing arrangement, but what could she do? She wasn't happy about me moving in with him either really. I put myself on benefits as soon as I had finished Music College and while I had the odd day temping here and there. I had ended up with a jobs folder completely bursting at the seams of jobs that I had applied for, I had been for a few interviews, but nothing had been right. I hated being jobless and having the long days to myself looking for a job, which became my fulltime job in itself. Spen agreed to be a referee for me when I needed. I remember him awarding me less than top marks for the section assessing 'attention to detail'. I queried his markings on this and he said that "it's because I don't think you take notice of every detail and you leave things unseen sometimes". I was extremely upset, although I didn't give him the satisfaction of seeing it. But from then on, I *had* to work extra hard at everything.

After working days here and there in call centres, on reception desks, in offices and so on, I landed a steady 9-5 temping placement with a Bank in their big headquarter offices in London and I loved this job. I gained so many skills during my time there and the workforce was so supportive and fun that I enjoyed working with them all. I was still quiet, my Dad was unwell at this point, but I tried to keep having a fun time with the others at work. I enjoyed my bus journey there and back, whilst reading my books and I enjoyed the work and the people. I just hated having my lunch at my desk or alone in the canteen because I brought in my own sandwiches and could never have a cooked meal because I would have this in the evening every night with Spen. I felt it was OK to do that as long as we were both having the same thing together, but after which, Spen would always comment on my continued 'jiffling' and absolute inability to 'keep still'.

My bus route passed Spen's University and I used to look eagerly out for Spen walking home over the bridge. I would get off the bus early if I spotted him and we would walk home together. Other times if I arrived home before him, I absolutely loved and simultaneously dreaded hearing his key in the door and seeing his face as he walked into 'our home' to spend the evening together. I loved this life. We cooked together, we ate together, we slept in a bed close together and we always used to hold hands all night together; we did everything together. We could talk to each other about anything and had an understanding of each other. We fitted. He called me Teeny Bean or Limpet, because I always wanted cuddles and kisses and had to be touching him, even if it was just with my finger connecting lightly with his, and I called him Peeps.

...And the Downs.
I hated and dreaded going to bed. I would delay going to bed so it would be really late and he would hopefully be too tired and go straight to sleep, just holding me for a while and kissing me goodnight. I would take ages in the bathroom, I would do anything to delay going to bed at the same time as Spen. But it always came. Here again, no, no, no. Leave me alone, I am tired, I don't want to, it is late, I have to be up early, I used to make my period last as long as possible and felt safe when I was having it because we were more like best friends in love, which made me happiest as there was no dread, no fear, no hate, no ache rising up inside of me, no upset bubbling up that I was keeping locked inside.

Soon I learned that there was no choice in it and that to be relaxed made it easier, simpler, far less painful, and got it over with quicker. It always seemed to go on for so long though. Hours, I hated it all. Just do what you need to do, get it over with, and leave me alone! But he would mess around with me for ages and I hated every second. Again it was 'all or nothing', where all certainly was always all, plus a bit more, or so it seemed to me every time. Afterwards, I was finally allowed to go to the bathroom first and I always wanted to go alone, clean up and calm down. By the time I had returned to him to actually go to sleep, this was my favourite part as the stress and uncertainty was (hopefully) over for the next few minutes / hours / whole night if I was lucky, and he would hold me, although I was turned away from him, silent and uncontrollable tears running down my face, but he always knew. Every time, he knew. I needed the closeness, the reassurance, the security. I would get up before him every morning and had my own routine of getting ready and out to work before he had even stirred.

The blissful happiness and the fear and dread cycle continued on and on and on. The fear and dread would get better, I used to tell myself. Why was I so abnormal? Just try and like it at least you have to try, you freak, it's normal. There are women who love this! I always felt so sorry for the women on those awful porn channels on sky. I couldn't get my head around it. They looked like they were enjoying it all, but I know they weren't really. They were doing it for the money and they hated those men really, I am sure of it, poor things. Didn't they? I felt like screaming at the television and it reduced me to tears on several occasions when Spen and I would watch it out of shock or curiosity or for a laugh in his case, but seeing them with their false smiles yet hurting so much inside in reality really got to me and made me angry and hurt. I was confused. Is this how it really was, or was I just the freak? Because Eve had eaten the forbidden fruit, women are now all under rule by their husbands! How could I ever get married and give myself in to living restricted within such a contract as this for life ever after?

10ii-Death of My Dear Father:

My Family, Minus One, and Spen.
When my Dad died on Monday 25th November 2002, I cried a lot and Spen wasn't very understanding after a while. He came to the funeral and I was happy about that and to have him at the house with the family afterwards, sitting on the rug with the fire on and knowing he was there for me made me feel extremely comfortable, relaxed and secure. I was so proud of 'us', especially as Dad had always liked Spen too.

I remember going for a couple of drinks and then to the cinema back in London. Spen had really wanted to watch this film about an old man who had just lost his wife or some kind of story to that effect. I put my foot down and said I really didn't want to see it, but I gave in and went to see his film with him. It was really upsetting for me as I was seeing similarities with my Mum being left on her own and I couldn't keep in my tears to the point that we had to leave the cinema. I felt terrible but all Spen could do was to blame me for being upset and ruining the film that we had paid good money to see and he was angry with me and was telling me off. He stormed off away from me for embarrassing him in the cinema, for crying and for us having to leave. I just needed some understanding and a hug. I had tried to please him and to watch the film, but it did just prove to be just too soon and just too thought-provoking and hard for me to sit through.

Maybe I took too long to get over the death of my Father. I remember feeling confused at my guilt in having such strong feelings of anger and shame that my Father was no longer here in this world with us, with the rest of his family where he belonged! My family was five, not four! How could he? I always would expect to see him sitting in his chair when I went home to see Mum. I expected to see him sitting in the kitchen when I came down for breakfast in the morning. I would expect to hear him answer the telephone sometimes. I would expect to see him wandering around in the garden or to hear his voice, but it was always empty hopes that could obviously never be real again. The house was different without his presence. It took me well over a year to 'get over' it, if not more.

Christmas had seemed to go particularly slowly and was extremely painful although we continued in the spirit of things as best we could, for each other, and having visitors helped us to carry on. At the end of the Church service on Christmas Eve, just as we were leaving to go home, the vicar shook our hands on the way out. I know he was aware of our recent loss and he had been to visit my Mum at the house a few times, but at this specific point, for me, time seemed to stand still for a second or two. I know it sounds silly, but I remember feeling the strength of God through the Vicar in his handshake. I know he was aware of our difficult situation at this time in our lives and I feel he was conveying his understanding and was telling us to be strong, but also, I felt a connection with him in that I knew he knew something was seriously wrong with me. Maybe I was asking desperately for help by abnormally locking my eye contact with his and that this is what he was reacting to? Now I feel it is almost like he knew the pain I was carrying alone through my life and that it was dangerous to hold inside and here was the Church, a friend for me to turn to if I chose to. This memory I will always carry with me to strengthen my faith and belief.

So my crying continued at the 2002 / 2003 New Year party. I had spent every year at home with my parents up until then for this celebration. My sister was at home this year along with my brother and my Mum had said that we weren't celebrating anyway this year and that it was absolutely fine with me being in London with Spen at his friend's house party. We had a good time at the party, but when it got later, and because of the alcohol I suppose too, I escaped into the quiet, empty room with the coats and my tears just came flooding out. I was touched by the pertinence of the piece of music 'If Tomorrow Never Comes' by Ronan Keating and all I could think, was that tomorrow never did come for my poor Dad and I was struggling to come to terms with this.

I think I quietly felt anger and resentment and blame for a while towards Spen, for me not being in Granada the night or the day that my Dad had died. I didn't want to blame anyone and I don't blame anyone anymore, as it was my own choice ultimately to return to London and I think I had done what had pleased my Dad too, I suppose...

Final Kiss.
I had been at home that weekend helping Mum and visiting Dad in hospital. It was a Sunday evening and Spen had been waiting to set off from our house to drive us back to our flat in London. I wanted to stay with Mum at home and to be there with her and to be there with my Dad as I could tell he was bad and I had also heard my Mum quietly asking the nurses "Is he dying?" but I didn't hear the answer. She was adamant in telling me to go back to London as they were both proud that I had got myself this job and they didn't want me to lose it. I hated seeing my Dad in so much pain and I had never seen him so restless or witnessed him talking in his native language before. I know (or rather, I think) he was praying to God to please make it all stop. He was suffering severe sickness but there was nothing to come out. He was on meal drinks and wasn't drinking. Later, I found out that he had told my Mum to tell us that he was angry at having to leave his children so young and was sorry. Dear, Dear Dad. My Mum told me to kiss him on the forehead so he knew I was going, so I did. Thank you so much, Dear Mum. Dad always agreed with Mum so I knew he would want me to do whatever made

her happiest. I know Spen was getting more and more impatient as it was getting later and later too, but I just wanted to stay.

We set off finally and I was so upset in the car and also that night before bedtime. Spen thought I was just being stupid and later said to me that no wonder I was so upset and that he had no idea things were so bad with my Dad. I knew I was doing the wrong thing all the way back in the car and had a feeling I should be staying at the hospital and was hating that I hadn't been able to tell him to go on to London without me, earlier on in the evening so I didn't feel inclined and that I then had to go and travel back with him after he had waited around so long for me.

I asked my Mum and sister to make sure that they call me on my mobile if anything at all changed and told them that I can answer it at work with no problem what-so-ever. I kept checking my mobile all day. I remember getting some passport photos taken at Angel tube station that morning. I had a message saying to go straight home to Spen when I finished work. I did and started packing to go home to Granada right away. He was trying to get hold of me gently to calm me down and to get me to slow down and to sit down. I just said, "look just this once, let me get on with what I need to do right now. I need to go home as soon as possible. Please don't try to slow me down". He just looked at me and said, "no, no you don't, your sister rang, I'm so sorry, your Dad's died". I didn't believe him straight away – tears uncontrollable – I felt guilty and awful, awful for not having been there for my Dad! No! I got on the train home. We picked up Chinese that night rather than cooking. Nobody could eat it.

CHAPTER 11:

DESPERATION ~ MY FIRST JOB ~ MADEIRA

...DIARY ENTRY AROUND SPEN AND

THE MOVE TO LEALT...

11i-Desperation ~ My First Job ~ Madeira:

Desperation.

By March / April 2003, I was still working at the bank and living with Spen in London. Occasionally we would spend the weekend at home at Mum's or at Spen's parents' country house. The cycle remained ongoing. I was really starting to think I just had to escape and get myself away from this life; I couldn't cope with it all anymore. I loved him to pieces and even experienced the most awfully disturbing dream once where I awoke in tears at believing he had almost drowned in the sea and I was utterly distraught to wake up in tears, thinking I could never carry on living without him there beside me. We were one and belonged together. What was I to do? I was stuck. I loved him, but I could not deal with this life anymore. I was seriously thinking of moving out, but I couldn't take that step all alone.

My First Job.

As if out of nowhere, I landed my first permanent job to begin on 1st May 2003! It was my choice of location – Nanstead, Linholt or

168

Lealt. I had never even been to Lealt before, but it seemed to be the best option to me simply because I could either commute to work, or at least be in a distance to still see Spen if I moved out there permanently. So this was my decision and in a way, I couldn't help thinking it had come at exactly the right time. This new plan was such a big relief to me and I was so grateful that the decision had been taken out of my hands and made for me and that I could move out, yet still see him, and just use the circumstances of my job and career as the excuse I was desperate for. Our careers were extremely important to both of us, so he understood my decision. We would make it work and if we didn't, then it just wasn't meant to be.

Madeira.
We took a holiday to Madeira for the week in between my jobs, which was great. I remember something tell me to choose the healthiest meals and the healthiest fresh juice drinks and I was covering up my body a lot at the lido, which we even spoke about together and Spen said I shouldn't have issues with my body image because I am really sexy. We loved being with each other and sleeping in the same bed. Spen was so nice. We were sweethearts, we knew each other so well and we fitted with each other perfectly...when it was good it was brilliant, but when it was bad it was sickening.

11ii-...Diary Entry around Spen and The Move...

- **Monday 5th May 2003:**

Monday evening. Sad, as visions of poor Peeps going off in taxi, train, walking home ALONE because of me. Very depressed. Could cry but will not. Miss Peeps A LOT. Wish I could go back to the house and stay at the flat with Spen – I liked my life like that. Lovely cuddly Peeps. Feel REALLY guilty. Bed now. Goodnight.

CHAPTER 12:

WORK AND SPEN ~ THE SPLIT

~

WIL

~

MUNICH

12i-Work and Spen – The Split:

Work and Spen.
I started working in Lealt straight away. I loved it at first as there
were about twelve of us, all of similar ages and similar backgrounds
with similar views and ambitions. We all aimed high then, being
recently fresh graduates. I commuted for the first couple of days and
spent the weekend with Spen and then I moved into a house share
that I had found with Mum's help. I shared my new house with two
lovely people: a lovely gay male and a lovely female.

We had a great time and I was really lucky to have moved into such
a friendly house share, so close to my office too. Spen would visit,
but I was more in control of when I would or would not see him or
put myself in a position for him to push me into the corner of doing
anything I didn't want to. I spent most of my days at Spen's
University College studying, to be near him and he looked after me
really well. I missed him and he missed me. I remember when I was
still in London and was stopped in the street near my office where I
worked and was asked for my details to be in with a chance of
winning a free makeover. I invited my friend Suki to come and
spend the day at their makeover studios with me where we were

promised champagne, treatments and a free photo. We had a fun time and afterwards, the evening of August 26th 2003, Spen met us and we went for a drink and a Chinese meal in China town. The meal was horrible, I remember feeling really bad for taking Suki there and I had suffered with stomach ache all night. Suki commented on how Spen evidently loves me to pieces and that she thought we had a strong relationship together, which meant a lot to me to hear this.

The Split.

I was avoiding eating at his house and chose the best times to see him. We split up on the night of 21st September 2003 at his place in Vauxhall. No arguments, just agreed that we needed to do it. Not a break, but a proper split.

For the whole journey to work that day, and for the whole day itself, I spent in a total daze. It was the cash and tills course held at a lovely country house close to my office and home in Lealt. I heard nothing of what the tutors were saying for the whole day. I dreaded the break times where the biscuits came out and the lunch was a big cooked meal and a big hot pudding and the choice of pastries later on in the day at afternoon break time disgusted me, but I could get away with not having one of those and would just have a coffee or even a cup of tea. By the end of the day, I suddenly came crashing back down to earth when I realised all eyes were on me to give an answer and I knew not where on earth to start! It was a simple sum and it was like I had lost the ability to even use a calculator. I burst into tears and left the room running for the bathroom to compose myself, thinking how everyone must think that I am so stupid! I spoke to one of the tutors during the break and told them what had happened the night before. They seemed really understanding and made me feel a bit better. My mind had been in shock and confusion at facing a life without Spen and was wondering how on earth I could even begin to do this. I told my friends / colleagues later and they were really supportive and I felt they were all there for me totally.

I still saw Spen. We travelled home together, we couldn't help it. He didn't have any rights over me now though and I loved that freedom. It was the best thing for me. I cried a lot over him though.

When I went home to Mum for the weekend, I remember sitting there over lunch. I don't recall what we were eating for lunch that day. I just remember Mum asking me over and over again "What's wrong Rebecca? Tell me, what's wrong". I kept saying nothing, but Mum kept pushing it and I was glad she did because I wanted and needed to tell her. I went silent and simply burst into tears and said "I've split up with Spen". I was crying so much that Mum got up and came over to my side of the table with tissues and was being really nice to me, bless her. I didn't want to be crying. It was just coming out as I was so upset and still hadn't gotten my head around facing a life without him. Mum kept asking me, "Are you pregnant, are you pregnant?" and I kept answering "No! No! No!" I was surprised and puzzled more than anything that she really thought I was pregnant. I was just distraught over the split. I left my dinner and Mum made me a cup of tea. MUM WAS FANTASTIC.

12ii-Wil:

On The Rebound.
On 1st October 2003, we had a big night out with my friends, housemates and colleagues and we all had a brilliant evening of dancing. I was pretty drunk and ended up dancing with my colleague's best friend, Wil, which in all honesty was the last thing I thought I would have ended up doing that night because at the very beginning of the night we had all congregated at their house in Lealt that they rented together and during the night I thought I had heard Wil say to my colleague and his friend, Karl, that I was 'evil' and so I didn't dare even look at him right from the beginning of the night and I made sure I stayed clear of him. I thought he had said that because I had done my eyes smoky and really dark and was wearing black. I was going through a dark, almost verging on gothic, phase where I used my lack of colour and dark makeup and dark clothing to reflect my feelings I suppose. All I wanted was to hide, be drunk, have a good time and feel free from worries.

I was definitely in rebound mode. Wil and I kissed on the dance floor all night and hugged and cuddled all the way on our walk back to the house with the others. I was staying at their house with my friend / colleague Emma too. But I ended up in a room with Wil. He was sweet and gentle. I had work the next day and it was late so he slept right away, and I stayed awake, just in case. I crept out early in the morning before everyone else woke up. I snuck out and back to my house to freshen up before work.

The next few days / weeks / months, Wil and I saw each other a few times after all his pestering through consistent texts, phoning and emails of "when will you go out with me?" I told him where I was at with the Spen thing and that I was getting over this serious relationship and was most definitely on the rebound and wanted to be single and free while I sort my life out. He never gave up. He was even fine with this position I was currently in. He just wanted to spend time with me and kept asking me out at every opportunity. Finally, after months of drinks here and there, clubs here and there, driving me for shopping trips, lots of cinema trips, practically anything I wanted, I said OK then, but I let him know it was still probably a 'rebound relationship' and he said that he just wanted to spend time with me as his girlfriend because he enjoyed my company and we always have a laugh together.

I remember going to my friend Emma's birthday meal at a pizza restaurant and really wanting to order a pizza like everyone else, but I ordered a salad. It was horrible when it came as it was drizzled in a sauce and I hated the salty capers, so at least I had the excuse to leave most of it as it had spoilt the whole dish. Wil was always very sweet, kind, gentle and would have done and did do anything for me. I threw a pizza, wine and Matrix night at my house with my friends and colleagues on Sunday 9th November 2003, and he came to this event. As I was hosting the evening, I was in complete control: I could eat what I liked and felt safe with my friends and I fully enjoyed their company, the wine and the films and we all had a super evening. By the middle of November I was seeing Spen during the day and coming home to Wil in the evening:

"because scared on own"

...and I even agreed to stay over at Wil's parents' house as they would be away one weekend because I felt safe with him. He took great care of me, always making sure I was feeling comfortable and we had such a good laugh that weekend, as we always did. We both loved spending our time together joking and kissing and cuddling. I trusted being in his company totally, and he trusted me. Wil was just totally and completely lovely.

The more I saw Wil, the more I would wear heavy black make-up (which later I found out that he actually loved!), build up my routine at the gym, eat less, skip dinner, drink more alcohol, just lead a gradually increasingly reckless and detached lifestyle, but I was happier than ever. I was doing fine at work and passing all my exams with flying colours and I had an amazing and satisfying social life. Wil never forced anything upon me. We had a close relationship, not sexual and never anything that I didn't want. I used to cry at the beginning, just silently so that he didn't know at first, and afterwards. But I didn't hate anything. He was such a nice, sweet person. But I started to get suffocated by all this comfort and attention. He would agree with everything that I said and he would do everything that I wanted or didn't want and I found it hard work. I used to go clubbing with him and get him to dance with other girls so that I could laugh with him and have a little space. I liked him looking after me and I felt safe with him, but he wasn't my type and I suppose I knew it wasn't going to last. I met his parents and everything. He came to stay at my house in Grenada at New Year and we went out for Chinese with my sister and her boyfriend, because that is what my sister wanted us all to do. But I secretly 'S', like I did when Spen used to come and stay at New Year and we would have to go out for dinner then too.

That night, on 31st December 2003, New Years' Eve, Spen had sent me a text saying "Teeny bean I'm in Manchester but would love to speak. Happy New Year gorgeous, I love you such a lot and hope so much it's not all over for us". I began to feel annoyed that Wil was here at my house and my Mum even commented to me that I didn't treat Wil very well having left him downstairs for a long time while I got ready in my room alone, but although I was still in love with Spen and missed him and never hid this fact from Wil, I hadn't been seeing Wil for that long and I needed my own space to get dressed and put on my make-up.

Going home and going out for meals and being sociable around food was a chore and I hated keeping up a front and having to compensate beforehand and afterwards on my own. The worry and guilt were terrible. Whether I be at home for the weekend watching television, at the cinema with my friends, or sitting at my computer at work, I would become very pre-occupied and distant even when I was in the company of others, with thoughts of guilt, anger, feeling depressed and disgusting and feeble, planning, enforcing more rules and restrictions, wanting to go out, shopping, gardening, to town, for a walk, to the gym, to another gym and another gym again and again and again; it must be a different outlet or it would look strange.

My mind had to be kept active and terribly busy, even if it was just counting in the gym or when I was walking. I hated walking down the centre of my office to collect my papers from the printer because I felt like an elephant and was sure everyone was laughing at me behind my back. My colleagues used to say to me "you go distant. Up in the clouds", and I remember Ravi saying to me with such intense curiosity pasted over his face in a searching manner, "where do you *go*?" If I didn't have much work to do I would find it hard to even begin working as I worried that I would finish the work and be left plain idle and I couldn't let this happen! The only time I appeared to be productive was when I had a lot of work to complete as I could put my mind to it and would not stop until I had completed it as fully and accurately as possible, no matter how late or early I had to stay in the office in order to get it done properly. I would stay in the office until 11pm sometimes and my friend Ravi would stay too in order to keep me company and to help me with my printing and just generally being there with me, ensuring I was safe. We developed a very special friendship with one another right from the day our paths met.

Life became a whirlwind. I was constantly using alcohol to great limits with no food but with pain killers as my only reprieve from everything going on in my head and my mind. Rather than staying in isolation with my behaviours and obsessions with cookery programs, books, magazines and trailing the supermarket isles late at night when it was less busy and I could read the packets and go home and think about which one was 'OK' to buy or when I was trying to make myself buy things because I suppose I wanted to, but was always stopped by my encroaching shadow, my promiscuity enabled me to spend the dark hours actually living, being awake and present in the moment as just me, back as the happy, confident, team-playing and carefree lovable Micci that I used to know and be, even if it was under false pretences and aided by alcohol and usually by dancing with myself being lost in the music and with my eyes firmly shut to the rest of the world around me. In daylight hours, Micci was slowly slipping away to what she thought was the voice of her own guardian Angel.

One day I remember my friend Emma had come round to my house and we ate pizza (well she did and I picked at the edge by now) and had chocolate (again, because it was at my house, I could choose and control) and drank a lot (I was downing the bottle of vodka, neat). We had wine (I always allowed myself wine when I hadn't eaten) and vodka in bulk and then instead of staying in, we decided to go out to our favourite haunt in town to go dancing and let our hair down together. I remember the taxi came to pick us up and I remember locking my front door. Apparently I had fallen out of the taxi (Emma explained the bruises to me the next day) the door-man had refused me entry because I was too drunk and I had been sick in the taxi on the way home. Great, and to top it all off, Emma said she had tried to give me a bath when we got in but she couldn't manage and she just took off my clothes and put them in the sink – with my mobile phone. I woke up the next morning utterly wrecked with my contact lenses stuck to my eyeballs.

Angel hated how Mum would spend all day every Sunday in the kitchen cooking that big roast dinner, which I would have to sit and eat it all up nicely and look as if I was enjoying it, only to make sure I could then set off in my car straight away and...I used to feel so uncomfortable with what I had just done i.e. eaten that huge meal in order to keep my family happy, that I would continue to eat heavily on my car journeys back to Lealt after forcing down Mum's big Sunday roast dinner and the big hot puddings at the weekends I decided to spend at home. I used to say to Mum that I would prefer to spend time with her, rather than to see her caught up all day sweating over the stove, in her own world with the fans going and ignoring me, stressed if the potatoes burned or the meat got overdone, or at least if we could go out for lunch and spend some time together that way, but Mum was inclined to stay at home on Sundays, respecting it as the Day of Rest, which I respected too. My

Angel Just-Rights

Dear Mum, it was all delicious and I am in no way blaming you for anything what-so-ever. I just wanted to make you happy and I hated that I had to keep you thinking I had come home and had some good home-cooked meals as you liked me to have and that I was being packed off back to Lealt with a good meal inside me, I am so sorry, I didn't realise how it would all turn out so drastically wrong and morbidly chaotic for me and so tragic for the family and the last thing I wanted was to drag my family down so low with me. I was disgusted with myself. I still am and I always will be.

Stopping off at the petrol station to fill up, I would give in to buying more food, hating myself for knowing what was coming, but it had to come after what I had just done because I felt so full that I wanted to die right then and there. I would find myself in silent tears while in the shop, knowing full well what was coming but if I didn't, then I would crash my car right into the wall after the way I was left feeling having consumed that roast dinner and pudding. So I would carry on stuffing my face and drinking water all the way home, pacing myself and knowing exactly in what order I had consumed it all, so I knew I had got it all up and out of my body later on. Once I remember going back after Christmas with a huge box of assorted chocolate biscuits, which I had eaten once arriving back in Lealt in just two foul sittings, amongst other things of course. On some occasions my eyes would be so clouded with tears or I would have reached my limit before I managed to arrive home and would always be prepared with a spare empty bottle or two in the car, just in case, and in my desperations I had almost crashed my car on the A1 on a couple of occasions and even raced a police car off a round-a-bout completely by accident in my sheer rage and chaos. My headaches became constant and heavy. Mum, you used to say to me frequently, "A girl of your age shouldn't be getting headaches..."

So I would have dinner at home with my Dear Mum and the family in the evenings and then I would keep eating at night. Mum would have a bath and I would secretly walk through into the kitchen and pretend to clear everything up but would shove in yet more food at the same time – I was on overdrive, not thinking – plus the chocolates that were in abundance and I'd even started keeping them in my room upstairs at home just in case I had been interrupted and needed to finish it off before my own bath where I would disappear behind the locked door and the sounds of the running water to hide my 'S' and I would spend the whole time trying my best to get everything up. Sometimes I didn't even get into the bath because it stopped me from concentrating on the urgent matter at hand and what on earth was I doing getting into a warm relaxing bath anyway when I had these urgent matters to correct and within a certain time period so as not to draw attention to the length of time I was spending in the bathroom.

When I returned to my flat in Lealt from my journey back, I would spend the next few hours being vigorously 'S', through my tears and panic in making sure it was all out of my system. It could last for hours. I absolutely detested myself. My behaviour would result in terrible headaches and my eyes would ache like mad through the immense strain that I would put on my body and my whole head would throb for hours after. I would feel my heart beating unevenly and straining intensely in my desperation at getting every last bit back up and out of my system. My teeth were fury, I felt exhausted, drained, sick and so thirsty from everything that I had consumed and 'S'. I kept telling myself never again, never again, never, never, never, never, never, never ever again. But it was never the last time and this deepened that anger I felt towards myself each and every time.

I became so fearful and anxious and controlling around food that now I realise the release of Bulimia became my only excuse to eat. When my colleague Emma was celebrating her birthday on 27th January 2004 and we were all meeting in a bar and then going to a pizza restaurant, as I mentioned earlier, I had great difficulty in choosing something from the menu that I could manage. I remember taking a while to pick from the menu, but by now Wil had become accustomed to my indecisiveness and would smile at me and try to help me decide. We both thought nothing more of it but honestly, although I in no way thought of it as a problem at the time, I was thinking unhealthy anorexic thoughts and really trying to pick the least calorific and definitely the least fatty dish that I could deal with putting inside me and giving myself to eat if I was going to keep it down. I wanted to pick something normal like the others, but chose the Chicken Caesar Salad. When it arrived, however, I was aware of the capers or anchovies that made it so salty and this was my excuse to leave most of it on my plate, as it spoiled the whole dish for me. Afterwards, we left for a bar to have drinks but I was feeling suffocated by Wil, who I felt:

"has to touch all the time"

...and I was hyper-sensitive to this especially after having eaten and it annoyed me, although I was careful not to show or to portray this to poor Wil in an angry or hurtful way as it was all my own problem and for me to deal with alone and so although it frustrated me, I would make efforts to try my hardest not to take it out on others for, to them, seemingly no reason.

On 3rd February 2004, I ended the relationship with Wil and started to pursue my interest in a colleague who had started to work in my office in the November of 2003. His name was Zach.

Meanwhile...

12iii-Munich and Japan:

Short 'Business Break' to Munich with Spen.
On 6th February 2004 I flew to Munich with Spen, who was attending a course there as part of his PHD studies and had invited me along. We had a great time kissing and cuddling, seeing a lot of Munich and the sights and experiencing the culture of the place, making very good use of the hotel swimming pool, steam, sauna and even gym facilities and just spending time together as close friends who kiss and cuddle. We clearly both still felt that closeness and intimacy there. I wouldn't let him anywhere near me for anything else and he knew this. We hadn't been like that for a long time together and my self-confidence had grown significantly, I had regained my independence and my own mind and was so much happier. We enjoyed our trip immensely and the waitress in one cafe even served our coffees sprinkled with chocolate heart shapes made of cocoa powder.

Angel Just-Rights

Considering I was just accompanying Spen on a business trip, we had spent all of our time together except on the final day, when he got up early to attend his conference and I took myself off alone for one last wander around Munich and then we met at the airport later that day. The return flight was comfortable and I felt secure in falling asleep on:

"Speniel Baby. I do love Spen so much".

I do remember being wary and uncertain on the flight home though as we were flying in the dark and I felt very uncomfortable when the plane would tilt and turn – I wanted it just to stay in one position – wishing it would stay on a straight path so as not to frighten me! One other point that stayed in my head from the flight home was when we were experiencing turbulence and I saw an immediate glaze of concern and fear shade over Spen as he suddenly became tense and focused on putting on his seatbelt straight away and I remember thinking my first concern was to look after *him*, and to make sure my love was OK, whereas gosh, he didn't even spare a single glint over in my direction, for *me*, it was as if I wasn't even on that plane and he didn't care less if I lived or died. I remember it clearly even today and it was from this point onwards that I had really made the clear decision to never, ever get back with this person because he had not passed the test: I obviously did not mean the world to him and was not as special to him as I had thought. Actions spoke volumes louder than words. I would use this to keep my strength whenever I was ever struggling with not being 'with' Spen.

What confused me was that I knew I loved Spen, but was I ever *in love* with him? It only dawned on me now that I think maybe I was, but having now experienced being with another man, i.e. Wil, and experiencing how gentle a man could be and how my self-confidence had grown so much since leaving the lifestyle of dream and dread, could I ever go back to Spen? My loyalties still lay with Spen because of how I felt and how well we had come to know each other, but did I really want to go back to living in that way? Was it the best thing for me, to live in fear? I needed more experience of other men as maybe Wil was a one-off, plus I had felt extremely suffocated by him in the end had I not? I couldn't deal with the continued love and niceness that Wil showed towards me. Spen was about to head off to Japan on his secondment for nine months and so maybe this was my chance to 'find myself' and to work out what exactly I wanted and needed or didn't need in my life.

On Friday 13th February 2004, I remember having a meeting with two other colleagues and a senior manager in his small office. He had offered us all a biscuit, and being men, they had all taken one and so I felt inclined to join in but I found it so difficult eating it, then and there in that tiny room and in front of this manager and my colleagues and during a meeting too. I ended up walking out of his office some 45 minutes later, still clutching this half eaten biscuit and in fits of sweat! I disposed of the biscuit in the bin on the way back to my desk quietly and felt extremely embarrassed and confused by this abnormal behaviour that I had just exhibited, but I quickly dismissed it from my mind and went to Spen's after work, to spend Valentine's Day weekend together.

It was Spen's last weekend before his trip to Japan and we spent every second of it together. I remember going to the cinema to watch 'City of God' at the Prince Charles Cinema, Leicester Square and the film remains one of my favourites to this day. On the Monday 23rd February 2004, I returned to:

"Stegtown. Peeps came with me to City Thamselink as didn't want to get on tube and leave Peeps"...

CHAPTER 13:-

...DIARY ENTRIES AROUND

SPEN, ZACH, AND WIL...

- ### Wednesday 25th February 2004:

Visit in Bedle. Arrived but it was rescheduled. Went shopping in Bedle. Mum told me to have a cooked breakfast in department store so I did! There were loads of old people in there, felt weird sitting there and couldn't eat it. Don't like eating in crowds. Went back to Lealt – shopping. Back to office: Zach was there again. Picked up photos. Spen arrives. Taxi to town: it was the taxi man that asked for my number! Chinese buffet at Chinese in the entertainment centre, then arcade! Then pub but it was Karaoke! Home in taxi. 'S'. Bed. Nice. Gorgeous Peeps. I love being in bed so much with Peeps. Both cried. Sleep.

- ### Thursday 26th February 2004:

Wake up with precious-ist by my side. Doop! Ohuh! Had bath, breakfast, Spen took me for a quick drive in the cool van he'd hired to put all his stuff in from moving out of London to his house. So nice! Then Spen left outside my house and I walked to work! Sat at Emma's desk as the computer man was at mine. Very busy office day, lots of people in. Zach not talkative at all, which annoyed me a bit but he made sure we left together.

I went home for lunch. Nearly cried. Zach text me: "You escaped forever, or are you coming back to work?" Quite nice to be missed but I would rather be with Spen. Spoke to Spen in bed. Then cried.

Sent message to Spen: "I love you precious" and he replied "Peeps loves you too gorgeous xxx".

- **Friday 27th February 2004:**

Work. Double entry seminar. Didn't have a clue. Got in at 9:15am. Zach was texting me and he had saved me a desk next to him! Nice. He does have nice eyes when he's being serious. Apart from that, he's just 18. Seminar. He left at 12:30. Called Mum, Kerry called me. Very bored and in pain severely from my tooth. Rested head on desk then went home. Asked Manager if I can have a working-from-home day because of my dentist appointment on Monday, which she said was fine. Train home. Very good to be home in comfort. Still expect to see Dad though. Even just seeing his car in the garage...

- **Sunday 29th February 2004:**

Spen to Japan 10:30am! Spoke to Spen at 9:15 – 10am. Very excited for him – excited for me going to visit him too – wonder if I will?!? Said bye ☹! How am I going to cope hey?! More excited than sad though! Flying to Schipol, Amsterdam, one hour 20 minutes wait, and Japan flight to arrive 12:00 midnight here – 9:00am there! Zach text me again: "Morning. Hope you are OK and are having a good weekend at home". Had bath, nearly cried. He will be taking off now!

- **Monday 1st April 2004:**

Message from Spen: "Blizzards, late landing, bed in 1 hour". Dentist: antibiotics and mouth wash for gum disease! I knew! Zach has been texting me all day: "Are you making an appearance today? Are you even out of bed?" Then he called me. Wil called too I didn't answer.

Good mood. Beautiful day. Mum drove us back to Lealt. Mum left at 4pm., I went into work to check my email, nothing from Spen. Cried a lot tonight in bed uncontrollably for Spen. Thought of him at work right then, when I'm in bed. Weird. 12am sleep for me and 9am work for Spen!

- ### Tuesday 2nd April 2004:

Fraud Course. Went to office, had email from precious! Bless.

Wil had sent me another email and text and he called me at work. It's like he thinks it's not over, only it so is! Anyway, I agreed to meet tomorrow (would be bored and depressed three nights running otherwise). Going to see a play. Guess what? His parents have seen it and loved it. I'm being really horrible, but he is annoying me! Actually, everybody is! Whoops. I just want Spen ☹. Wish I could speak to him. As I'm going to sleep he'll be starting work – reading his email from me. Weird. It makes me sad. I need to look after him. Cried for ages for Spen again tonight.

CHAPTER 14:

SPEN AND JAPAN ~ ZACH ~ LEO

~

SPEN'S RETURN AND CONFRONTATION

~ A & E ~

FRESH NEW START

14i-Spen and Japan:

Spen's Secondment to Japan.
Spen went off to Japan for his placement. I cried over missing him so much. We emailed and he called me at work a lot. I even bought a ticket and planned to go and visit him and booked two weeks off work. I was all set to go but suddenly thought - I am following him around the world when we are trying our best to split up and to not see each other. If I am ever going to break away from him, I need to do it while he is away in Japan, when we are being forced away from each other, in which case I need not to follow him half way around the world.

On 20th April 2004, my sister came round to my house to drop off a dress and the Hoover and I spoke to her about the decision I was faced with and she was a big help, thanks Kerry. I cancelled my ticket and stayed in England and I went to work as usual. Spen was understandably very upset and disappointed with me. I so wanted to go and see him and experience this time in his life with him, but was it the right thing for me to do? I had also really wanted to re-visit

Japan after enjoying my sixth-form trip there so much, which made my decision even harder to make. However, this was the time I needed to live my life, free from obligation and fear. I liked my confidence and self-esteem and contentment with myself. I needed to hang onto this and live for me while I had the chance.

14ii-Zach:

Short, Sharp, Shock?

I met Zach at work in November 2003 and there was chemistry between us immediately. He was the office boy that made everyone laugh, he was the joker and he was good-looking and carefree. I thought if I needed to get over my fears, maybe I just needed to have a one night stand? Damn good sex with him to be my get-over-this whole thing, thing. Would that be the answer to my problems? Would that work? Would that sort me out once and for all, a good old shock?

So I finished with Wil, who had asked me twice to marry him by this point and I had to say no. He never gave up and I agreed to keep meeting him and letting him take us ice skating every week and to the cinema and clubbing and drinking, all of which I would really enjoy as I did like him a lot and we connected in each other's company extremely well, but we remained throughout it all, just as friends and I was OK with that and he said he would rather have me as a friend than not at all. I started going to the gym more and more because I enjoyed it and started eating more healthily and a lot of times not at all in the evenings. I started my favourite hobby, horse-riding, and took myself to the women's swimming time at my local pool.

During this time, I was having a lot of phone messages sent to and from Zach and he used to come over for tea as I got to know him. There was a definite chemistry between us and he excited me when he came round and I felt happy and this felt good. I loved my flat as I had given it the mark of Micci throughout, as I was now the only tenant to the whole place. I got the impression through our conversations that he was fairly experienced in the girlfriend area and wasn't the shy type! He even ended up on my bed unashamedly partly naked, but I just couldn't go near him; I was frozen. In the end we realised that we liked each other more than we realised and we respected each other far more than we both did at first and the first night that he spent at my house was the day after Wil had proposed to me, on Sunday 8th August 2004:

• **By 19th August 2004 I comment in my diary:**

Gym. Shower. Bed 9:30pm! I think I am over Spen. Although I love so much going on holiday with him. I love it. Especially Munich. I was very happy with him then and we weren't doing anything or going out together, just kissing.

On 24th August 2004, I went on a date for dinner in the next town with the friend from the London Orchestra I used to go to and whose birthday party Spen and I had gone to the year before. I remember I chose the same thing as he did from the menu, but took about literally double the time for me to a) choose it and to b) eat the thing and I felt really self-conscious about it all throughout the meal and I am sure he noticed at the time and that it put him right off me. It was ridiculous only I couldn't see it, but to him maybe it was obvious, I don't know. It was ironic though, because as I had learned that evening, Spen had warned him off of me years ago telling him "she's mine" when our eyes had met over a table one night and we had been transfixed in each other's gaze. I was annoyed when I found this out because it was the night well before I had gotten back together with Spen properly and because I had arranged to stay at Spen's through convenience more than anything that night, as it was on an orchestra intensive rehearsal weekend in London, so accommodation had been pre-arranged for everyone and I wasn't the only one staying there. Although Charlie, this dinner date guy, and I sat next to each other in the orchestra, we had never really looked at each other or had a conversation until now and the chemistry was electrifying, as were his blue eyes. Anyway, we met up on this date in the next town and, to my delight, I wasn't that impressed with him anymore! But I took his non-willingness to keep in much contact with me after that, as his reaction to my taking so long and being so strange over dinner and making our meal feel awkward overall.

Zach asked me out properly on October 25th 2004 and treated me with nothing but respect from then on. I spent a lot of time with him and my feelings for him really grew. I decided that just having sex was an out-of-the-question activity that I was never going to be able to do and that I was just hoping maybe it could just be the quick fix to solve all my problems. I could never have actually gone through with it. If it was going to happen it would certainly have happened with him and it would definitely have happened before now.

I remember at the end of October I was working really late in the office and Wil was in the vicinity. I asked if he would bring me some chicken nuggets from the fast food chain where he worked on the graduate scheme, and of course, he did. I found it funny that he didn't even offer me a chip and he needed little persuasion to dive in there and finish off my last two nuggets when I put on a full, struggling face he dived in without even a thought. I think he liked the fact that I didn't eat much and he enjoyed getting rid of it for me, as he knew it made me smile. He would do anything I said, which so annoyed me in the end because he never questioned me, my thoughts or my actions and accepted me purely as I was, but then, I suppose he hadn't known me to be any different, being such a new acquaintance in my life. I guess he was just besotted and was such a good person wanting to please me in every way possible and my Mum was right in saying I was using him and taking advantage of him, but as I told myself, we did enjoy our time together and we got along so well and I always was open with him about my rebound state etc. and he always said he was OK with it all.

Loving Relationship and 'Spesh Spag Bol'.
I did love being with Zach. We cooked together, we ate together, we worked together, we did everything together, he would leave me post-it notes from work scattered around the house and in my diary, he would surprise me by running baths for me and playing my favourite music outside the bathroom door so that I could listen to everything I loved while relaxing in it as he knew I liked to do. He would have a cup of tea waiting for me when I arrived home from my evening at music rehearsals or after I had been working the night

shift on my secondment in January to March 2005, we had 'Harry Potter Nights' where we played the music and watched the films and wrapped up our Christmas presents for our loved ones together and we would have 'Spesh Spag Bol Nights', and he would take care of me really well and I loved being with him and felt safe, comfortable and secure around him too.

The 'Spesh Spag Bol' was the only meal that I would let him take charge in cooking for us, as he could make it really nicely and spaghetti bolognaise was always my favourite meal if I was honest. I used to call him 'Spesh' because not only was he special to me in his own way and made me feel special, he had started working in the Special Constabulary and was doing exceptionally well and I was proud of him for this. I could never get the quantities of pasta or the length of time it was to be cooked for 'exactly right' and thus the meal always came out strangely. I chose the ingredients when we went shopping as it was just pasta and a fresh vegetable tomato sauce with tuna and he added whatever cheese to his meal afterwards that he picked up in the supermarket for himself because I wouldn't go anywhere near cheese, bless him, but he was allowed to cook it, under my supervision and he loved that I let him do this for us. It was our treat evening meal that we would both look forward to. For me, it was my one substantial and healthy but indulgent meal of the week that we could both enjoy and I could feel OK at having – as long as mine was a lot smaller than his and minus the cheese.

Zach used to buy his special shopping, which consisted of everything I wouldn't eat, such as chocolate, crisps, cheese, and he would make comments like "I see the mouse has been out again" and smile at me for clearly having nibbled on a tiny bit of 'nice' food. It was a joke between us, but it made me feel like a failure for having given in and become overwhelmed and greedily indulging, even if it was just a taste. I used to enjoy tidying up and doing the washing up and putting his not quite empty pizza box away, because I could secretly consume food in a hurry and not admit that I had done it, even to myself and so it didn't feel so bad because I was disassociating and forgetting this act so quickly in my sneaky lapse of greed.

He had moved into the spare room by now, although we preferred that he slept in with me as this made me feel really safe and secure but I remember one morning when he was away from my flat having spent the night at his parents' house and I had a very strange experience, which I now know to have been an episode of 'sleep paralysis' (Book 2: Who Am I? Part 2, Chapter 23, Interlude IV A1). I remember apparently waking up in the morning and opening my eyes, although my vision was blurred and I couldn't move or speak. I tried my hardest to blink and to move and to decipher whether I was dreaming or awake, but I couldn't and then suddenly I saw my bedroom door open and in came Zach. I was happy and wanted to greet him but he came and sat by me on the bed and this all terrified me because I couldn't move and my vision remained blurred. I knew I was awake, but I was confused and could not wake myself up enough to physically move. I didn't feel scared because Zach appeared to be there and I didn't trust him because I did totally, but I felt scared because I was confused and couldn't move a muscle or protect myself. It was like a very scary outer-body experience. Zach wasn't there when I woke up, and neither had he ever been. Boy was I lucky it was daylight.

Zach was a little younger than myself and began to spend a lot of time lounging around or on the computer, which started to annoy me because I began to feel like his mother and all suffocated and frustrated once again and I really needed my space to be active. I used to get up early to do my exercise routine while he was still asleep, we came home for lunch and I would prepare my sparse lunch behind his back while he started eating his own on the sofa and watching television, clueless about how I was preparing my own lunch. We would then have 'quick naps' on the sofa in the sun or even in bed sometimes before returning to work, to which we could walk in around three minutes if we had to. We had our night time song when we went to sleep, which I liked as it meant I didn't have to worry about him expecting anything afterwards (not that I needed to worry about this anyway with him because he respected every single tiny little sign or signal that I gave) but for me, I could allow myself to relax in his arms and go off to sleep feeling completely safe and protected in his arms. I wrote in my diary:

Angel Just-Rights

- ## Monday 22nd November 2004:

Went home at lunchtime to bed with Zach for 1 hour 10 minutes! Really, really nice to hear him breathe. To be warm and fall asleep.

Poor Zach was worried when I told him Spen was coming home on 12th December 2004. I started seeing Spen occasionally. My loyalties still lay with him underneath everything, although I had begun to have more confidence around him and this made me feel good for myself, I would still see him as having this power over me. Maybe I felt my loyalties lay with him because really I felt so strongly that he himself was more powerful over everything and everyone in my life even now. But he couldn't bully me around anymore. I wouldn't have it. Peter, Wil and Zach had all shown me another side to men, which I liked, although it bemused me and made me feel uncomfortable and oddly frustrated in a strange way after a while, leaving me feeling I needed to be treated a bit badly in order to feel safe and normal. I couldn't understand why it hadn't happened or why I was waiting so long for something awful to happen or expecting each of them to break, but they never did. Maybe they just didn't care? It wasn't complete if they didn't break at some point, was it? But I never felt the intimacy there or the closeness that I'd felt with Spen and I longed for this.

I remember standing in my sister's living room with herself and her Fiancé behind me in the kitchen and they were laughing at something quietly. I asked her what it was and she blatantly made something up quickly that didn't make sense, but I knew she was laughing at my big bum that was huge and sticking out severely... "OK, need to lose weight you fat disgusting being, just because *she* can stay skinny, I'll show her, I thought, they'll never laugh at me again behind my back". I stopped ordering my 'healthy' pizza with Zach at nights and increased my exercises in the mornings.

On the May Bank Holiday weekend two weeks after Easter in 2006 I arranged to meet a new friend – actually she was just an internet acquaintance whose advert I had replied to in request for new friends in the same area to go out with at night – she was called Stace and I had told my family that she was a member of the wind band that I had joined, in an attempt to put their minds at rest. I arranged to meet her after dinner hence I had nothing, and joined her in drinking wine before we went to the pubs. I couldn't hold my drink, suddenly I felt out of control and fearful and what on earth am I doing about to stay at this person's house whom I hardly know? I was frightened of all the drink, all the dancing, and all the male attention I was getting and didn't feel safe with Stace at all. She wasn't my type – loud, blond and brash. I was struggling to keep up with the pace, at which she was drinking and didn't want anyone to think I was weak, but I was far from enjoying myself and there was no way out, I had to stick it out until I could get myself home the next day.

In my fretting state, I locked myself in the toilet and wretched. I called my sister who lived in Hitchin with her fiancé and I don't even remember this really. I wasn't coming out of that toilet cubicle because I felt scared, ill and alone. I wanted to be at home with my Mum, safe and sound. I heard my sister's voice all of a sudden and opened the toilet door. I have never been so relieved to see her face. I could tell she was a little angry, but more relieved herself because she had found me finally. She grabbed my arm and I hugged her straight away. I was still sobbing my eyes out and I felt awful. I loved my sister to pieces. She was angry with me when we were on the way home. But her husband was more accepting of the whole situation. Thank you Kyle.

They made up the spare bed for me when we got in and they made me drink lots of water. The next day I really felt nice because they asked me to accompany them to a DIY shop and we looked at lamps. I felt safe and comfortable in their company and they really looked after me properly. I loved them both for this and remember thinking this while resting in the back of their car; totally safe and sound. I hated myself though. The deal was that I was too drunk to drive and that I had to stay through lunchtime, where we went for a tapas meal and hated myself even more. I felt guilty for not making the Yogalates class that I'd booked and planned to attend at 12 – 1pm that day in order to prepare for starting the week. The day after, I began my new secondment in London and had to look and feel OK.

On my birthday in 2006, Kerry and husband and Zach were intent on taking me out for a meal to my sister's favourite Italian restaurant. The waiters had put a candle in my pudding, which we all had to have according to my sister, and they were coming out banging saucepans together and I was all embarrassed. I '<u>S</u>' in the toilet afterwards, but it was taking too long, my eyes were watering and I had to go back downstairs and act normal. Smile. The deal was that we could go and play tennis afterwards, but it was so hot when we were playing that it didn't really make me feel any better. That week at work, having begun my secondment to London in May, two months previously and having been attending a management course in Lealt so as to add to my C.V, I wrote in my diary:

"Had a brilliant day today. Except for Ravi plonking himself down next to me on the train journey to London! So annoying with his writing paper! I was just trying to read my book in peace! He was going on about 'new best friend'. Went for tea on my own. Walked to Spen's, he was really nice. Lunch and watched tennis. Cuddles and kisses. Train home. Course: gave Samir a lift home and held his new-born son at five weeks old! So cute – a moment to remember, nearly cried at this tiny being's vulnerability there in my arms".

Samir was the guy I sat next to on my management course. He used to call me MI5, because I was so quiet and secretive.

By the end of July 2006 I had been travelling to my secondment in London with my friend Ravi, who always looked after me well (sometimes rather too well and it really got suffocating, but I was open and frank with him and I think he understood I needed my personal space). I knew he would never do anything to hurt me and yet I did not feel completely safe with him because of my past, as with every male I was now on guard but I could never explain any of this to him, obviously. Our friendship was such that he made it very clear to me that he was there for me whenever I needed him. We thought the same and possessed the same values and ambitions and I was proud to have him wanting to be my friend and I enjoyed his company most of the time. We always had a laugh together. He, like me, had an extremely quiet voice and rather than speaking to each other on all of our journeys from Lealt to London where the train would become so very crowded, he used to write in a book rather than speak. This did annoy me after a while because I felt totally bombarded and needed my space!

Ravi did everything he possibly could in order to make my life better in any way, no matter how big or how small. I enjoyed being in his company and knew I was blessed and so lucky to have found such a person that was so alike to myself, yet also interested me and made me curious to get to know him better. We had a lot of fun. We used to set up treasure hunts around our office with cryptic clues and prizes hidden in places where it was possible for others to find yet hard enough to stretch our boundaries of confidence around others in setting these up deliberately on different floors, by colleagues desks or in places that required social interaction or on-the-spot reasoning should one be questioned, in the process of the hunt. It was skills-enhancing at the same time as risk-taking, confidence-building and also a game that we, just us, shared and enjoyed together.

In August, Zach and I went to my sister's wedding and I remember having to plan when I'd get away with going home at the very latest so as not to have to eat before her big day or there was no way I could wear the bridesmaid dress and I was dreading sitting on that top-table at the wedding breakfast and having to finish each course of the meal with a smile and with everybody watching. When my sister had been shopping for bridesmaid dresses she had chosen beautiful fishtail dresses that she bought for me to try on at home in Granada. I tried it on in front of Kerry and Mum and although I loved it, I was absolutely distraught at how big my bum looked in the dress and when I asked my family for their opinions, my Mum said "well that is the style of the dress". I remember thinking I would have to lose weight before the wedding. We chose different dresses in the end that were plainer and less tight and were made to measure and I felt comfortable in it compared to the first option.

When Zach invited me away on a camping holiday with his family, I immediately froze in fear. It took me a long time to come to terms with this prospect and, although extremely wary at first, I berated myself for doubting Zach's absolute and fine character and trusted in that I actually could feel safe with him. He had shown me that he loved and cared for me and he was so gentle and caring that I knew he could never do anything that would cause me pain or confusion or unhappiness, he just did not have that in his character. I was worried about the takeaway meal they have on their holiday, but as we would be there only for the weekend, I could deal with this somehow. The holiday was indeed super and we spent such a lovely time together and with his family, who were all lovely towards me as usual.

Zach also asked me to marry him, but I couldn't as it wasn't completely right for me at this time. He was nice, but he wasn't my best ever friend too and he wasn't proactive enough for me either. No, it had to end as hard as it was to do.

As Kerry and I lived close to each other, she would love going out for meals together with our respective partners and when Mum came down we would all meet up too. I remember meeting one day at Kerry's house for lunch with Mum where Kerry sarcastically jibed her comment at me in her usual accusing manner, "Micci is saying she's not eating her jacket potato because we've put butter in it and she asked for no butter so now she's not having it at all".

I remember when I drove Kerry and I to Maydon to do some shopping together and she chose a nice sandwich and I chose a skinny sandwich, with no intentions of going anywhere near it, and I didn't even open it in the end, thinking nothing of my behaviour at all in the slightest really, just saying some excuse that I cannot even recall now, probably about having had a big breakfast or going out to dinner with Zach as soon as I get home so you have yours and I'll just start driving. All I know for sure is that I didn't eat it and Kerry got sarcastic towards me, saying "Oooo, what do you think it's going to do to you? Make you fat? It won't, you know, look, mmm. I'm glad *I* can enjoy *my* food, just do it! Mmm! It's really *sad*; I'd hate to be all restricted like you!" All I thought was that she was angry at me because she was eating and I wasn't and that she would do this now but definitely then wouldn't have dinner later when she was away from me; she was only doing it to show me she could eat loads and still not put on weight and to make me even more jealous of her. I *was* angry and jealous that she was being so evil as to just rub it in so badly and this really hurt me but I wouldn't cry. I was so confused in the back of my mind because she lived with her fiancé and appeared still to lead a normal life although I did wonder if she had spent her life also throwing up her meals and anything she consumed in the toilets. Only today right now, 20/03/10, have I realised that actually, if she was angry at me for that reason then she just wouldn't have eaten it either? I don't know.

When I went home for the weekends, I would make sure I would go into the fish and chip shop to place the order. Fish and chips were still a ritual in our house on a Saturday night. I would order a vegetable pita and just pretend to bulk it out with chips, ketchup and mushy peas and make it look like a feast on my plate at home: the ends of which were left on the plate, the chips and peas had fallen out and so I was safe in the fact that really my dinner had been some pita with a healthy portion of salad and lots of water, followed by coffee as no-one ever had pudding after fish and chips in our house, because it was so filling. The chip shop stopped doing vegetable pitas and after my shock reaction to this change, I began to persuade my Mum to have Chinese instead and then for me it would always be noodles or boiled rice with the 'starter' of six steamed scallops and again, no pudding.

14iii-Leo:

Internet Acquaintance.
By the time I met Leo that summer I was properly into exercise and my routines and avoided everything. I would have the same dinner of watered down chicken noodle soup every night before the gym with coffee and drink only green tea throughout the day. I was confused and didn't know where the answers lay. Leo was nice to me and gentle and was so considerate to me and unbelievably perceptive to my lack of physical contact, avoidance techniques, false smiles, freezing episodes; except when he saw my texts from Zach later on in our relationship and threw the table and the chair around the room in my flat, knocking over the cup of tea and grabbing me off the sofa by both wrists in his anger. Our relationship almost ended another time when he found that I had been chatting to people on a dating website. I explained it away by saying that I just used it to speak to girls and he took this to mean in a sexual way, rather than just to make friends, and accepted it. Our relationship ended because of my inability to commit my loyalties fully to him and thus resulting in his ongoing interrogations and anger until there became no trust. I still let him come around to my

house for tea and I enjoyed cooking him a proper dinner and seeing him enjoy a good meal. We stayed friends who cared for each other and respected each other, and I wanted still to look after him, keep him safe and wrap him in cotton wool – it was simply chat and not jealousy looming although I always left the door unlocked when he was in my house even though now I knew he would never have any reason enough to be angry with me – he was gentle, caring and kind and I did still strangely feel safe and comfortable with him.

When we were happy though, before these incidents, I used to resort back to my old delaying techniques and would always have stayed up every night or slept on the sofa together if I had my way. I would change the subject or freeze when it was time to retire to the bedroom for the night, even though with him I knew I was totally safe and that he would never push me into doing anything that I wasn't comfortable with in the slightest. I would flinch and cry whenever we'd get close in bed just cuddling together and he would always ask me if I was OK and he would ask enough times to be sure that I was not hiding my real feelings and when I clearly was not OK, he would just hold me. I would feel secure but would still be frozen still. I loved kissing and cuddling on the sofa as long as I stayed in control and didn't feel threatened or overpowered in any way, as usual, but anything else – even the thought of late night looming as bedtime would approach – filled me with terror, dread and fear and I would just cry silent tears and freeze totally still and solid in whatever I was doing or wherever I was.

I remember going away with Mum to the Lake District (June 17th 2006 – June 20th 2006) and my eating choices and moods were terrible. I found it all so hard. I was depressed at having to have all this food with my Mum for all these days we spent together – breakfast, lunch and dinner and snacks in between and ice creams and cakes and I began to feel depressed and obscenely fat. I agonized over the menus, if my Mum's dinner came out smaller than mine, or if she left some of hers, I could leave more of mine, but if mine was bigger I struggled and tried to make up any excuses I could in order not to eat it. I hid food when she wasn't looking and got rid of it in the toilet where I wouldn't be found out and I tried to leave most of it, saying it was too salty or not very nice in some way and by the end of our stay at the first hotel I had managed to persuade Mum that the food had been terrible when in fact, the standard hadn't been all that bad.

I remember when Mum was really trying to get me to have a steak, but they all came with sauces and the fear was rising inside me and I didn't know what to do. I drank a lot of water. When Mum was in the bath each night, I would start my exercise routines like mad, making sure I sweated and ached. When Mum went to visit a relative, I was out-right refusing to go with her one afternoon and we had a horrible argument over it. I felt terrible for not going with my Mum to visit the family as we were here to do this, but I was desperate to spend that time vigorously exercising away in front of that mirror constantly checking for reassurance, until her return. It was the only opportunity I was going to get on my own. I was desperate for it and needed it badly. I had to have it, I had to take it and I did, to the horrid tones of my Mum's disgusted and tearful voice saying I was "disgusting and timid and something wrong, defiant child" because she thought I just didn't want to go with her I suppose or that I was too shy to go and visit my relatives. I felt terrible and didn't think how my Mum must have really been thinking and feeling at the time until I think about it right now. I deserved those words you fired at me Mum and you certainly deserved none of it back. I am so sorry I couldn't speak to you and be open so you would have known my real reasons for it, but I was ashamed and terrified and thought it was just me and that I had it under control really. But so clearly, I did not. We returned from our break on the Wednesday and I drove back to Lealt, desperate to spend time on my own to get back to the gym and to my own restrictive eating habits before I could even face anyone, never mind go back to work on Monday!

When my relationship with Leo ended, I saw a bit more of Spen just for the odd coffee now and then. Spen would come to Lealt to visit me, throughout which we would kiss as we both loved it but knew it wasn't good for 'us'. After many chances, Leo made himself understand and accept that I just wasn't ready for a serious relationship and we remained friends. When he came round every now and then to make sure I was OK and to catch up and I made him proper dinners, like Lasagne, which I enjoyed doing for him, I used to say I'd already eaten. He did comment and ask me if everything was OK and if I had any issues around food because he said he said I was "shrinking" and would hate for anything to happen to me, but I laughed it off, thanked him for voicing his concerns and assured him that I really was fine thank you, and, so anyway...

14iv-Spen's Return and Confrontation ~ A & E ~ Fresh New Start:

Confronting Spen.

I confronted Spen about what had happened in the tent that night in Scotland and he said he was so sorry and that it should never have happened and that he feels so terribly awful for it. I opened up to him a bit more about my eating, as he saw it when I went round to his as from him I made no effort to hide it or my behaviours for that matter. When we used to meet after work in Farringdon I would go to the gym and pace the streets and then meet him only to be faced with having to go to the Chinese to pick something up for dinner. I really tried but remember being so indecisive and unsure of the menu and about what I could consider having that Spen would become angry and frustrated with me for being so uncertain and dithering around for so long. On occasions he had tried to ask me what I thought had started off my problems around food and I never could answer him as the question I found uncomfortable and I didn't want to think about it or indeed acknowledge that my behaviours were at all wrong, after all I would always retort "it's just my choice! It's just how I am".

I had gone to the gym round the corner from his house while he finished work one day at the beginning of the year and we had something to eat afterwards. I had half a slice of dry brown bread and a bit of chicken and salad and a tangerine, of which I only sucked out the juice. He commented on his shock at how little I ate – I hadn't really realised to be honest, but it did make me think, but then it was infinitely easier just to forget and to continue listening to myself, as I could be trusted and only I really knew best, for me. I know what I need, I know what I deserve, I know what I can have, I know best...

My life was now, gym, work, meet new people, gym, work. I would have my set routines to complete at the gym and it had to be done properly. I would also attend Yoga classes in between my two work outs and by the end of my sessions I would feel better. I found a couple of groups that met up in London: one was mixed and one was girls only and I tried them both out. My gym was also females only, which I found more comfortable in getting on with my own thing, plus when I first joined I thought I would make friends in the area but once there, I had zero interest in pursuing this and kept myself strictly to myself, even getting upset and annoyed if someone was rude enough to disturb my routine, thus make me lose timings etc. etc. etc.

In September 2006, I went on a work course with my friend and colleague, Rav, to Liverpool. During this course I dreaded the meals we would be having together but I enjoyed getting to know him better and also I enjoyed doing the course immensely. In fact, we ended up staying an extra day into the weekend as we wanted to prolong our trip and our experience together away from home. Ravi looked after me well.

A & E.
By October 2006 I was working over fourteen hours a day trying to prove myself to my new team and managers. I usually worked through the day with no breaks and was attending a Management course I'd enrolled myself upon in Lealt in the evenings. I was also participating in a wind band rehearsal once a week and was dedicated to teaching private music lessons in the evenings. I was also heavily relying on my ever increasing trips to the nearest gym and had started to attend netball training after work, in the hope of meeting new people in London. My eating habits were ever changing and becoming stricter and stricter. As if I didn't have enough men in my life (I had been meeting up with Ravi in secret at the house he had bought and was decorating with intentions to rent out to a family and after one forceful experience followed by another freezing episode, tears and running away, I never returned). I was also arranging to meet new random men off internet dating sites. I began having serious problems both with my stomach and with my throat. Spen had come to spend the weekend in Lealt with

me and was staying the night and I was in serious, serious pain in my stomach. I had tried everything to make myself settle and after hours of restlessness, I could stand it no longer. I was crying in agony, sweating in worry and in the end as the very last resort, Spen believed how ill I was feeling and we drove to A & E, me scrunched up and crying in pain at the steering wheel, at 3 o'clock in the morning.

The doctor asked if I had been diagnosed with Anorexia and I had said no and shrugged it off as not right and I must hide it...but part of me wished someone would diagnose at least something! Please help me! Please! He gave me some tablets for IBS and I remember thinking that I need something to take the pain away right now. As soon as I left his room, I was in the toilet letting out my pain and it was the most relief ever. I had a lot of similar stomach problems in the next few months and my periods had well and truly stopped by this time too. But at least I had my trusty tablets that really seemed to do the trick after a while of being scrunched up in severe pain usually during the nights.

Fresh, New Start.

I was house hunting for somewhere to live in Stalbany, which was a nice area to live and as I was commuting into London for my secondment every day, it made sense to move closer. Plus, I was being confused in the relationship that was forming between me and my friend and colleague, Ravi, whom I had grown extremely close to right from that day he had walked into my office and sat at the desk next to me. We had shared more and more of our time together at work since then, particularly on all our courses at the beginning of our secondments. I was confused with religion: Christianity or Islam? Muslims can hide their bodies and this aspect appealed to me greatly, but in both religions sex in a marriage has to be acknowledged and adhered to by the woman at all times. Muhammad even raped a girl aged nine, I had been told by Leo. Ravi asked me to marry him and I couldn't bring this up, but it was constantly on my mind and I desperately wanted his view on it because I had only these one-sided bombardments coming constantly from Leo in addition to my own research that I tried to carry out mainly by searches on the internet. Ravi helped me a lot with finding my new place to live in London and I was able to confide a lot about my illness to him at that point and he really tried his best to help me, but it didn't work well enough. He was also my only friend that I let visit me on my second hospital admission.

If I was to remove myself away from this destructive environment I had found myself in, maybe I could break away and leave this life behind me; a new start. Maybe I could replace this fake smile with my old happy carefree smile? Please, try hard. It's My Fresh New Start.

On a three day work course trip to Birmingham that I undertook alone, on 7th December 2006 I remember walking around the food hall in the big department store in the shopping centre in the evening not knowing what on earth to get for my dinner. This is where I had ended up after walking around the city checking out the German Christmas Market and enjoying the atmosphere as I paced around at top speeds, never stopping. Missing a step would result in a little run having to be done in order to catch up with what I had lazily lost or been made to lose out on because other people were in my way. I remember taking in those smells of German beer that reminded me of Munich, of Pretzels, of sausages and onions and of sweet mulled wine, desperate to try some. But I wasn't allowed. I had to keep walking! Who did I think I was sauntering along and enjoying the smells! I spent a long time looking around the stalls and walking round the block, and again, and again, and again, before I bought a winter statue for my Mum as a Christmas present. It was then time for me to walk back and to find something to eat.

I found myself back in the town centre department store. Where do I start? What can I have? I was completely overwhelmed. I had a whole £20.00 allowance already paid for by my company, which contributed to my turmoil as I felt obliged to buy something simply because now I didn't even have the excuse of not wasting money on food for myself. This used to make me feel good and Angel was feeling infuriated at this extra barrier and was fiercely fighting to confuse me! I managed a healthy meal the first night of noodles and prawns that I saw being cooked right in front of my eyes, which made me feel a little safer although little did I realise how seriously I was taking this at the time. At the time, I didn't even recognise that I was having such trouble or thinking anything of it. I was just quietly and solitarily struggling, pacing up and down the food isles with my chaotic thoughts fighting and battling away for hours and hours and hours.

After having managed the Japanese meal, I then kept on eating, having felt greedy and wrong for even giving myself anything at all in the form of a meal. What on earth was I thinking of? I kind of felt obliged to have a meal as I had twenty pounds to spend from my firm and this was confusing enough in itself and I had called my Mum to help me decide on what to have for my dinner. I felt I should, somehow. In the end I spent it all on edible Christmas presents for my family so that the receipts would be accepted as food, but I had just taken it all home and distributed it amongst my family. After the meal however, usually a bit of sandwich or this rice or noodles, I would go back to my room and stuff my face in floods of distraught tears, having eaten the doughnut that I had bought to prove to work that I was eating, but I would spend all the rest of the evening '<u>S</u>', desperately wanting it all to be out of me, to feel clean and empty again. I hated the feeling of being full or of having eaten at all. I hated the guilt afterwards. I would hear these insane, sounds of constant, nasty, bullying screams in my head. Everything had to get out of me, I had to drink water, a certain amount, wait a certain number of seconds even jumping up and down or walking constantly in order to do everything I could to get it all out of me, every last bit. I hated myself for having ended up behaving like this – listening to the scream killed me and put me through torture...how could you eat in the first place you greedy loaf , now you *must* get it all out! You must...!

I would find myself collapsed on the bathroom floor, *ABSOLUTELY DRAINED*, my face *SOAKED FROM TEARS,* asking myself "How did you let this happen again? This is so bad for yourself!", but really I was more overcome by the immense feelings of *TOTAL NUMBNESS, MINDLESSNESS, CALM, EUPHORIA, A-B-S-O-L-U-T-E--R-E-L-E-A-S-E. . .* If I didn't fall to sleep on the bathroom floor, I would fall straight to sleep in bed, shattered, but with *NO THOUGHTS, NO WORRIES, JUST FREE AND CLEANSED. EXHAUSTED FROM THIS MENTAL STRESS RIGHT FROM TRYING SO HARD TO AVOID THIS BEHAVIOUR FROM HAPPENING, TO BEING OVERCOME BY THE EVIL DRIVE,*

THE PLANNING AND THE EXECUTION IN THE VIOLENT PHYSICAL EFFORT OF 'S'! The only thing I would be thinking would be the odd thought over how did this happen and making mental notes to myself that it must be the last time, yet at the same time making more important mental notes to MUST WITHOUT FAIL restrict, restrict, restrict all of the next day and never rest, must EXERCISE and walk everywhere. I am scared for tomorrow now... *please, please, please never, ever again. LET IT HAVE BEEN THE LAST TIME!*

If I wasn't starving away my badness, I was 'S' it away. If I wasn't 'S' my feelings away, I was exercising them away. If I wasn't exercising my emotions and thoughts away, I was starving them away...and so the cycle continued...

I remember arriving at the course the next day and I had made my lunch from the toast and jam I took away from breakfast, which I was going to try and have secretly on my own somewhere (just to stave off my stomach from rumbling throughout the rest of the course that afternoon), most probably I'd end up shoving it in my mouth really quickly while hiding away in the toilet and right before the afternoon session was about to begin for maximum last. But a lady asked me to go with her for lunch and I couldn't say no. She took me to a coffee shop and I took ages deciding what to have, never mind eating it. I couldn't believe I was going with her to a coffee shop to have lunch. I made a token effort but took my time eating it and was super chatty for me as it meant I could make it look as if I was not getting through it because I was talking. I remember her saying when we'd been there a while, "little and often, that's my motto". The next morning I remember walking into the course and there was a conversation going on about Anorexia, which abruptly came to an end when I entered the room.

This evil behaviour of mine continued however, even after I had prayed to God in desperation for Him to help and guide me to do right and to be strong and I promised Him that I would never do it again. I was confident that I had compromised such terrible enough consequences with Him that it would be absolutely sure to make me keep my promise and to stop. Firstly, because how awful would it be to lie to God? Secondly, I agreed with Him that if it happened again, he could take away all of my teeth, my greatest fear of loss, as punishment.

Back in London I would meet my work colleague and friend for a drink after work and would always dread her having invited others along in case I couldn't get out quick enough with an excuse of having to leave before food was brought up. When we'd had dinner, I'd rush home in desperation trying to be normal and deal with myself, but I was in such turmoil that I carried on eating when I'd get home and I would spend the whole night violently vomiting everything back up again, berating myself for my behaviour afterwards and dreading waking up 'hippo-ised' and too ugly and disgusting and fat to deserve even being in this world and on this planet the next morning and vowing if I wake up, that I *must* go swimming / gym / before work *and* after work and to plan my exercise and food and social life better in order to prevent this from happening ever, ever again. But it was never enough, it happened time and time again. It was impossible for me to stop. I would feel my puffy cheeks the next morning, my clothes would feel tighter and it would take me hours changing in the morning until I found something that looked just about OK to go out in. I would feel like I'd put ten pounds on overnight and I truly probably had.

After this behaviour, or if I'd missed a gym session or eaten too much or not restricted enough, I would feel absolutely anxious, totally conspicuous and large. I felt all attention was on me and that peoples thoughts about me being overweight or letting myself go or being an indulgent individual with no sense of control over my life, or not appearing perfect and sorted, which is what I wanted to convey, was being washed all over me everywhere I went. If I made it into the office that day, I hated walking down the room to get my printouts and would wait until the end of the day to do my printing, detesting myself for being so stupid and selfish to think that people would even notice you, but still being just too scared to do it. I still struggle with this problem even today.

When the letter inviting me to attend Jury Duty arrived on my doorstep one morning, I was so excited as I had always wanted the opportunity to sit on a real live Jury. I was chosen to sit on an interesting case and was needed every day. It was taking place in Lealt Town Centre and I would take my gym clothes with me for the morning and for the end of the day. At lunchtime I dreaded anyone asking me to join them and I would say that I'd probably go home, as I lived so close. But I would go to the canteen in the big department stores after I had worked out that I was unable to buy myself a sandwich from anywhere or even sit anywhere and order anything but a black coffee. I used to get out my poorly made tomato sandwich secretly while sipping my black coffee and look out of the window from my corner seat. I didn't have enough time to go home and return in time. One day I went to sit in my gym and watch television while I had a coffee, but this made me feel even more guilty just being there and not burning any calories – look at what everyone else is doing! Think of all the weight they are losing and you're lounging around watching television and eating food!

I returned to sitting in the department store canteen and on a couple of occasions I even cried over my black coffee and my squashed tomato sandwich. Why was I being so stupid? Why couldn't I just order a coffee with milk? Why was it I was only allowed to eat my homemade soggy sandwich? Why was I so stuck?

CHAPTER 15:

FRESH NEW STARTS

15i-Fresh New Start at the Girls' House:

Not So Easy.
I found a lovely homely place to live with a lady and four other girls and it was perfectly located very close to the town centre and also to the train station. I had my own tiny room but the house was cosy, warm and large and had everything there and the company of girls my own age. I thought this is just what I needed, but my eating habits were still awful and I was relying very heavily on my IBS tablets and peppermint tea to get me through both the days and the nights. Zach helped me move in there on Sunday 21st January 2007 and I took him out for dinner that night as a thank you to him. It was late, but we were also celebrating my new start. But I just couldn't hold it down... 'S'.

Mum came to see where I'd chosen to live on Sunday 28th January 2007 and we went to the local pub for lunch, which I had found extremely greasy and felt "very stuffed" afterwards and it obviously didn't help with my stomach problems at the time as I was ill in the toilet, the food having gone straight through me. When I got home I washed my hair and had a bath: 'S', so that the time I spent in the toilet wouldn't look suspicious to the other girls in the house if I came out with wet hair and made the room smell nice. The following day:

- **Monday 29th January 2007:**

Feel rough. Very. Was horrible to Ravi because he'd bought me a big orange juice and a chocolate bar. Worked with nice colleague. Netball! Was good. Met Spen on way home – Pub at Farringdon – had burger – horrible. Spen had my chips. Home. Bed.

I was still seeing Spen and I was still seeing Zach. I remember once inviting Zach to spend the day with me in Stalbany. It was my first Friday in the new house and as I had worked so hard during the week, I had already completed my designated hours and was entitled to a day off in lieu and this is how I spent it:

- ## Friday 2nd February 2007:

TOIL ☺. Gym at 9:30am. Zach came for 11:00am. Walked round Stalbany looking at restaurants, think he got a bit annoyed! Oh well. Home. Made sandwiches. Sleep. Went out to cinema but stopped off to have the sandwiches on the way. Sent a picture message of sister's husband's school to Kerry! Hemel Hempstead - saw film, very good. Back home.
Went out for meal at a Thai restaurant – Zach ate all the complimentary wholemeal prawn crackers so I couldn't have any – very annoyed – selfish. Parcels – very nice. Skewers of chicken satay. Zach had rice and chicken and cashews – didn't let me have much taste even though said we'd share – I had noodles with lemon chicken, which wasn't that nice. He finished it off though. He piled his plate high and scoffed, didn't speak to me throughout the meal unless I did, otherwise he just said "mmm delicious!" I didn't enjoy his company. Sorry. Even at the starters he didn't eat the carrot or cucumber. Really not sophisticated at all. Dirty clothes too. Rubbish. THEN...he had to go out for cash for the tip, leaving me in there! Went to rent a film on way home and stopped for lots of chocolate. Home – ate it – 'S' a lot. Went out for a cocktail, which I had to pay for, and his was more expensive, obviously! Back. Bed.

I used to ask Zach or Wil to take us out for a dessert if I needed to so I'd look normal to them, thus to my housemates, thus to my sister who phoned me thousands of times a day wanting to know my every move, thus to my Mum – but I kept going to the bathroom. On this occasion, Zach knew something was wrong and confronted me by knocking on the door and asking if I was OK and if I was doing something I shouldn't be doing, but I laughed and said I'm fine, telling him I had a stomach upset. He told me to make sure I tell him if I am hiding anything and need help but I had persuaded myself that he believed me and I kind of did have a stomach upset anyway, but not owing to reasons that I supposed one would presume. I felt drained and lonely. It carried on and the weekend routine became typical:

- ### Saturday 3rd February 2007:

Zach left at 10:30am because of the car parking situation. Shower, went to gym and had a really good workout. Washed hair in shower. Came back and dried it here. Good. Spen expected here at 4pm. Walked round shops then to train station to meet him. Walked to supermarket for fish ingredients, then to another supermarket and round the market for the vegetables. Home. Rest. Cooked ratatouille. Cinema in Hemel. 19:05 showing. Good. Spen has a very embarrassing laugh in the cinema – rude, arrogant, through nose and teeth, noisy, kind of hissing and horrid! Sorry, but it is very embarrassing.

Home. Cooked dinner. Went out for drinks. Home. Toast and chocolate: '<u>S</u>'a lot. Bed. Spen had switched off my electric blanket and was in my bed! I had a go at him and he got up and found the other duvet and slept on the floor for ages. I wasn't going to apologise! He did! My bed! Sleep. Used bathroom together in the morning like we used to!

- ### Sunday 4th February 2007:

Hello. Didn't make it to the gym today. Have a sore throat again. Got up 10 or 11ish. Shower. Breakfast with Spen: toast, jam, melon. Naps. Went out for a walk round the shops. Saw George my housemate in Wilkos. Bought two for one wash and go shampoo. Went to Pub for lunch where I went with Spen for the two for one offer: I had chilli con carne and rice and tortilla chips and orange juice and soda water. Tried to eat just what I could but it was all greasy and then I was stuffed and felt ill. Walked Spen to train station and on way back went to supermarket and bought red grapes (whole pack), chocolate bars (three double bars), got home, had bath: '<u>S</u>' everything.

Tidied room, internet etc. Toast and jam in the evening. Clara got back – nice chat – nice Sunday evening feel. Have my door slightly open now and radio on. Nice. Bed soon!

Netball tomorrow. Should I go to the gym in the morning?? Nah. Netball tomorrow. Tablet. Put ads on internet for clarinet teacher today. Ravi had been texting me all day – really annoying.

I stuck rigidly to my boiled noodles only dinners, with green vegetables and chilli sauce every night. Even when my sister came to visit, this is what I made us and she made it known to me that she had missed the meat. I used to have breakfast up in my room every morning, sneaking it up there as quickly as I could in my embarrassment at my dry bit of toast with a scraping of jam and my huge mug of tea. I planned when to come home after work so that I would have the kitchen to myself because I was embarrassed of preparing my meal in front of anyone and didn't like people watching me eat. I liked to take my time and preferred to be alone, just me and the television and / or magazine. If anyone was in the kitchen, I was anxious as I couldn't prepare my meal properly and it threw me totally off course having to eat my food in front of anyone as it felt so fake and uncomfortable and wrong, like I shouldn't be doing it and so I wouldn't.

On 15th February 2007, I embarked upon a short trip to Barcelona with my sister for the long weekend while her husband was away on a school trip. During our trip, I silently struggled with menus, always searching for the fish or vegetable option, hiding food and leaving food. One morning after our breakfast Kerry followed me into the toilet right after I'd been and I know she was looking for signs of me having 'S' but she didn't say anything and neither did I. I was just thankful that I hadn't done anything that time and therefore there was no sign of anything to give me away. I was grumpy around mealtimes and snack times and dreaded them coming yet at the same time I was thankful for having my sister there to rely on for structuring the day and making sure we had normal eating patterns. I didn't realise it or think anything of it at this time, only shame and trying to get my habits under control and stopped once and for all. To be honest, I always thought that she was doing it too, she just had to be, her secret and my stupidity. She was secretly laughing at me. Now I can see how my mind just twisted everything to suit *Angel*. Oh, my poor sister. I knew she knew I wasn't right and had problems but she would be sarcastic with it and it made me more defensive and stubborn and only increased my whole denial.

Returning to my routines and back to work for the first day was an absolute struggle after a whole long weekend of eating:

- **Monday 19th February 2007:**

Work. Not motivated at all. Had to get up at 7:30 this morning to move my car. Went to South Bank for breakfast from about 8:30am until 10am! Went to coffee shop and had coffee and fruit salad. Really wanted to try porridge, but I just couldn't. Too much noise in my head and stress arising. Looked in diary, read book, looked through Barcelona photos again. Went to work at 10am! Left at 4:30pm but it was wet and so no netball for me, plus stomach not right and throat feels wrong. Went to Farringdon – gym. Met Spen. Tired! Chinese takeaway. OK – rice, hot and spicy peppers, hot and sour soup. Bed.

- **Tuesday 20th February 2007:**

Work. Gym. Two boys in Super-Healthy Japanese fast-food chain knocked on the window and waved at me as I walked past – not sure, was it Ted and Rod from house-hunting? Funny!

- **Wednesday 21st February 2007:**

Work. Left at 3pm. Ravi followed me, grrr. He said I was "quiet and distant" all the way home. Really, really tired. Gym and washed hair. Met Danielle at 8pm and went to smart bar, really nice company actually. Left at 10:30pm. Home.

- ## Thursday 22nd February 2007:

Extremely tired so took TOIL.

10:15 – 11:30: Gym
11:30 – 12:30: Snack (nectarine and coffee)
13:30 – 13:30: Yoga at gym
13:45 – 15:00: Lunch and television programme
SLEEP – great ☺
18:00 – 19:45: Dinner (chicken soup, vegetables, spicy sauce)
19:45 – 21:45: Choir. Almost fainted.
22:00 – 23:00: Pub. Free glass of wine! Sat near conductor, who wants my number and email address for Orchestra ☺.
23:00: Left and went home. Bed.

My days had to be planned exactly and to the second, leaving no room for change or alteration. If I hadn't planned the whole day right down to the last second, or if something changed slightly, I was wrecked. The next day, I was offered the job that I had applied for at the end of last year and I was ecstatic yet apprehensive, for reasons explained below (Fresh New Start at The Boys' House). Towards the end of February, Zach was pestering me to go out with him again and wanted to get married but I didn't feel the same. The day after, on 25th February 2007, Leo had called and wanted to meet up and for me to edit something for him.

Having been eating the food with my family for so long and putting up a front of normality that was so far from the reality of my behaviours when I was alone, I managed to continue my unhealthy lifestyle. I met up with Wil again just before I moved into the boys' house and he was excellent at helping me to move in the way that he whole-heartedly applies himself to a task when assigned. Bless him. Unbeknown to him, I used him to help me to eat, in our trips to the Super-Healthy Japanese fast-food restaurant chain. I took everyone there. But my portions and choices got smaller and smaller until I was just ordering a side bowl of steamed rice and sharing the starter of edamame beans and putting on some soy sauce and then leaving most of it anyway and just drinking the free cleansing Japanese tea and tap water.

Angel Just-Rights

My life became a mixture of gym, early in the early mornings before work and after work and even after my netball sessions prior to meeting Spen. I joined the work netball team and attended strenuous training sessions after work in the cold where I felt my knees and hips hurt, I ran out of breath, I could hardly keep up and would go dizzy sometimes but I was determined to put myself through it and to not let it show and I would get freezing cold and would wear three pairs of tights under my trousers to keep warm and for extra support to prevent my knees from cracking and also it made sure absolutely nothing would wobble on my body but I enjoyed the feeling of having done exercise as a social and team event (which was also a reason for joining in that I could meet new people, or try to), but I was too intent on having to be the best.

I used regular amounts of coffee to keep me going at work and I learned how to re-direct the rumbling of my stomach to keep it quiet. I would eat my measly lunch on my own that stayed hidden in my bag by my desk, it went down to a fruit salad and then to going home by lunch time to have my cereal and watered-down red milk. I took jam sandwiches, which changed to tomato sandwiches to work in order to have at lunch time that I would eat at my desk in secret until one day I was disturbed by a colleague and felt so embarrassed. I then used to order a sandwich from the shop close to our office on my way to work and would unconsciously ask for less and less to be put on it each morning, always on brown bread and definitely no spread, to the extent that the nice lady commented on the state of my sandwich one morning and how it was "getting smaller and smaller each time", so I could never go back in there and I started taking a different route to work. Instead I would buy a fruit salad from the man on the stall at the end of my walk over Blackfriars Bridge every morning and have half of this for breakfast when I got to work with a strong coffee and the other half for lunch with a bit of powdered soup from a cup-a-soup to keep me warm. If I'd managed to induce laxative effect through having to run to the toilet throughout the morning and if I'd managed to have any fruit salad left by the time I was walking home, then I'd done particularly well that day and *Angel* delighted a lot. The day had gone well and I was in good spirits and more likely to spend time in the company of others, as a reward.

Sometimes Ravi, my close friend and colleague, would take me to the Italian for lunch across the road from work. But it was only on those occasions when I felt things were going OK and I knew that I could have a tuna salad, but there was always lots of tuna so I was a bit worried about that, but I'd only let myself go there if *Angel* felt I had been 'doing well' and deserved a tuna salad, plus I could always 'just walk a bit more' that evening or 'just do a bit more' at the gym that night or 'just have drinks' (i.e. pots of peppermint tea, fizzy diet drinks, water – anything to fill you up) for dinner that night until bedtime. In the end, I just used to leave the tuna that I thought was too much or just walk straight out and say I'd changed my mind if there was no tuna salad on the menu that day as there was nothing else that I could consider having – the concept scared me stiff. I would insist on going back to work via a walk through the park and by the river every time after having lunch at the Italian with Rav.

I used to buy special spelt bread from the bakery in Stalbany as an occasional treat at the weekends, very occasionally. But it had to last the whole week. I remember going with the intention of sitting in the gorgeous park a few times with my picnic and my reading book and enjoying the warmth of the sun on my skin. But I had to walk around the park for hours and up enough hills until I was dropping and had deserved to sit down, never mind eat. I would find a quiet spot where I could sit and allow myself to unwrap my lunch and open my book and switch off my phone and *enjoy* some time in the sun, look on at the families enjoying their games of Frisbee or playing with their dogs and sit quietly to take my time over eating my fruit salad and tomato sandwich. I even made this for myself and got it out with Wil, pretending it was mostly ham having bought a packet for him and just poking bits round the edges of my sandwich to make it look like I had a normal filling, but really I could even leave this bit because it was around the crust, so everyone stayed "happy".

Spen came to visit and I did the same with the meal I had with him, and with Wil. I used to feel safe going to the Super-Healthy Japanese fast-food restaurant chain though and let myself eat there in the evenings. I would invite all my friends to catch up and to go there, one by one. I wonder if they all knew it was the only place I would really go to eat. Not because I just enjoyed it in there, or liked the menu, or had vouchers, or wanted to use the offers, or because it was fresh, or because it was quick. I always spent ages looking over the menu just to make sure it hadn't changed at all and I was secretly, away from *Angel*, always trying to work up the courage to have something different, to try something new, but I would *always* stick to the same identical dish, because they never added anything healthier. Luckily they did two-for-one vouchers and Ravi even bought me vouchers to use there too as he just thought it was my favourite restaurant, which I suppose it was in a way; after all, it was the only place in which I would ever eat. I don't know if he suspected anything. I don't think he did. I still have the vouchers today, no doubt out-of-date and expired by now. I always chose the same safe dishes although desperate to be able to try something else yet never brave enough to do so but I was always keen to see what my companion's dish looked like (usually so much more exciting and appetising than my own dull choice) but I was always so glad that I had listened to my *Angel* and stuck to what I knew was OK, because I felt safe with it and could manage to appear at least to start it and talk to my dinner companion with a smile at the same time. I knew what and how this would be served to me and I knew I had done it before, so this put my mind a little at rest. Plus, it was always so huge that leaving most of it didn't seem too odd to anyone.

I joined dating websites and even went on dates with random men because I thought if I could deal with what I have dealt with then I can deal with anything. One man took me to a posh restaurant in London on Friday 30th March 2007 and I loved the atmosphere and enjoyed the night and the food was too well presented to eat almost and we saw Robbie Williams! But I managed to have this night out and to soak in a touch of the ideal world that I so wanted to be living in; not for me, but to make others proud. The next time we met, he drove me to a cheap American diner and ordered a big meal and he was insistent that we didn't share a pudding and that I should order a nice chocolate pudding for myself too. He ate a spoonful of his pudding, saying it was too rich and chocolaty for his liking and so I ate most of his too after polishing off my own in my anger and threw it all up afterwards in the restaurant toilet and the rest I spent trying to throw up in my room most of the night in my efforts to get it all out of me. Severe stomach pains would keep me up on all fours

215

for hours, sweating in the night and crying from the pain that I had inflicted upon myself through my disgusting behaviour, which had me now reaching out in desperation for my IBS tablets once again. After that, maybe he realised something wasn't quite right and thinking I was such a greedy pig with no manners, he never called me back. For me, having tasted what the nicer side of life could be like, it made me strive to damn well achieve this all the more.

Running the bath used to hide the noises, or so I hoped, at home in Granada too. I think my Mum knew something was wrong as she asked me to open the bathroom door one night at home, but I said I was already in the bath and was determined not to open the door. I did it in Stalbany too and in Lealt and subsequently in London. All my so-called 'fresh starts' were a waste of time. I was '<u>S</u>' into bottles in my room if I was scared I was taking too long in the bathroom and people were waiting to use it. I had hidden in my room stashes of things I would use under the bed in a suitcase. I used to buy things in the supermarket other than salad and fruit just so that my basket would look more normal and so I would put a chocolate bar in there or a packet of sandwiches or a cake, only I never ate it. I used to leave notes in the fridge to my housemates saying 'Please eat me' because I hated wasting food and I even thought of giving it to the homeless outside the supermarkets in London because I would never eat it and they would probably be so thankful for it, but I never did and felt terrible that I didn't have the courage to do this. I was afraid they wouldn't appreciate it and would prefer the money or that they might be offended by my offer of food. My behaviours were all absolutely overtaking me and draining me. I needed to CHANGE once and for all if I was ever going to be able to concentrate on getting that permanent promotion at work.

15ii-Fresh, New Start at The Boys' House:

Even Harder.
I moved into the boys' house down the road, as I was finding being in my current surroundings yet again too terrible and claustrophobic and I had to get away. This would be another new start; the final

chance. The place was located in between the train station and the city centre and so this was perfect for me. I had a large downstairs room so I would not disturb the household if I came in late and most importantly it meant that I had easy access to and from the kitchen. The lounge was in between the kitchen and my bedroom, which meant I would be forced into being normal in my behaviours around food. There was another bedroom next door to mine, which was at the front of the house, so this made me feel safe too. The house was big and comfortable and the boys were all laid back and cool.

But my eating and behaviours only got worse and worse. I stopped the gym and started staying in bed more. I changed my hours at work so I could be home by lunchtime to have my cereal with red milk and water with grapes. I stuck to the noodles meal only when the boys were in (probably twice in the whole time I was there) and I was staying in every now and then in my effort to look more normal and to socialise with my housemates, because they were all really nice people and I felt bad. But my stash was still there and the bath was getting blocked. I had, however, made friends with a group of really nice people whom I would meet up regularly with in Stalbany and I enjoyed their company a lot. I was still also going out most nights in London and drinking and meeting new people and coming home late only to get up for work early the next morning.

When I was offered the job in Kensington with a specialist team, I was ecstatic but terrified. I had gained experience in working with this kind of team on my secondment in Lealt and had really enjoyed and excelled in the work expected of me during my time immensely and thought I had definitely found my niche in this work. I was scared in having to go to a new office and face all the new difficulties in settling into a new routine, new people, new lifestyle, new colleagues and was particularly worried about the difficulties I would be facing in carrying out the shift work outside of the office due to my health and my disordered eating patterns. How could I participate fully in a job that required full awareness and attention to a situation and being expected to eat a three course meal in the process? How could I participate fully in a job that required full awareness and attention to a situation for long periods at a time and for long hours when I was prone to fainting? I was so disheartened as I knew Rebecca could be so good at this job and would enjoy it so much, but *Angel* was adamant that I couldn't, *no way...!*

On visiting the office where I would be working I was happy to see my desk all ready for me, and all the people were very friendly and I even took note of the noodle bar that was close to the office thinking if we go for lunch as a team, at least maybe I could cope with a noodle dish if I had to. To my surprise, I discovered that they were currently working closely with the Police on an operation whose details were to be brought to my attention by the nurses during my second and third hospital admissions. Although I had reservations and fears around putting myself in these situations deliberately through work, I desperately wanted to be involved with this project and felt it was my duty now to help others and I felt that I was meant to take this job and that I could really make a difference here. I wanted so much to accept this opportunity, but I turned the job down in preference to stay with that which I was currently with. That which I knew I was able to manage around my secret life of the disordered eating patterns I was following. Rebecca was still strong in her life ambitions, but all this change she couldn't cope with. *Angel* was winning; she was becoming stronger than ever.

Lucy and Sarah were two girls that I met at a London Girls get-together one evening and after this, they became my two best friends. I found meeting them easy after the initial introductions because these new friends knew nothing about me at all. We started our relationships with one thing in common: we were all at a similar stage in our lives with our own circumstances and reasons for having met at such an event. We were all going a bit crazy on the night life and drink and keeping ourselves busy 24 hours a day – for me, it was perfect avoidance, I suppose. We gradually got to know each other well and would look out for each other as proper friends would. It was easier at the beginning because I could be myself and not worry about not being liked or about saying the wrong thing because if this was to happen I could walk away from these people as easily as I had met them and just know not to be so thoughtless again.

I would go out in London every evening of the week if I could, and those where I was in Stalbany I would ask Wil to come to the Super-Healthy Japanese fast-food restaurant chain with me after I'd been to the gym, or to take me to the cinema to avoid eating altogether if I had already consumed 'too much' during the day. When I'd go out in London, I would spend the time getting ready and then make a piece of toast, by now it was always thin-sliced of only one brand *only* or nothing at all. I would eat it dry in the few minutes right at the last moment before I'd walk out the door, only I'd usually burn most of it and so it went in the bin scraped off and then I didn't like walking down the road with it to the train station anyway, as this is not how I'd been brought up, and so the rest ended up in the bin anyway. The whole motion was to make the boys think I just didn't have a spare minute's time to make a meal and they would be more inclined to believe that I was going out to meet my friends for food because when they weren't in, I didn't bother at all as I'd usually be running late for the train that I had to catch in order to meet my friends on time.

I did think one day that maybe the boys might have known something wasn't right with me. We were sitting in the lounge one evening watching a television program about the storyline of a girl with an eating disorder when one boy commented, "I knew a girl once who just ate fruit and her body turned against her. It was awful". They used to say to me "Are you going to give us the pleasure of your company this evening?" I really wanted to sit there with them and enjoy their company, but they all sat there with their meals watching television and I couldn't join in. I was scared they would notice and start commenting and asking questions. I didn't feel worthy of sitting with them and didn't expect I'd be welcome to because I was boring and never said or did the right thing or never said anything witty or intelligent. Better to hide. They even had an ongoing joke about my 'sleeps' that I regularly had in the afternoons and they joked about wondering if I really did have a job at all, owing to the hours that I worked and to those days that I could take off work as time off in lieu (which accumulated due to the extent of my travelling time) and for those days that I took as 'working from home' on my work laptop.

On my 'working from home days' I would work intensely hard all day. In the evenings I would spend out drinking and dancing with Sarah and Lucy and meeting new people and it was just waiting around for the train on the way back that I hated because it was cold and I would have to pace up and down the platform until the train arrived...*never sit down you lazy, undeserved being!* I loved spending time with my friends because we would always make each other laugh and were each, now I realise, going crazy at this time for our own personal reasons – we loved getting to know one-another, sharing stories, sharing ambitions and wishes, sharing drinks together, sharing laughs and sharing dares, dancing on the tables, speed dating, lock and key parties chatting up the boys – all just for fun and to build up our confidences with 'friends' who didn't know our histories and who didn't judge us and we began to form very strong friendships with one another.

We were each another person at night. Nobody knew the real person underneath that fun and flirty person letting their hair down with no cares or worries in the world. I think it made it easier for me to spend all my time on the trains – 20 minutes each way – because my travel was paid for by my work, as I was on secondment I had a season ticket, which meant I could use it as much as I wanted to and I felt obliged to make the most of it if the opportunity was there for me to take. When I'd arrive back home, I would make some cereal with my red milk and water or have some more grapes and a piping hot cup of tea and go straight to bed, only to start it all again the next day when I would get up to catch the 6:30am train to work.

One Friday, I had put in my contact lens incorrectly and it was bothering me all night. I had returned home at about 4am not daring to go to sleep and so I called my ever trusty friend, Wil. He offered to come round and to drive me straight to A & E as I had been advised by the NHS Direct Nurse over the telephone. Wil came straight away and drove me there, both smiling about the situation. They checked my eye and gave me an eye patch to wear and some ointment to apply. They also checked my blood sugar levels as I had fainted in the hospital and they gave me a cup of tea that they said must have sugar in it, even though I politely said I didn't want it thank you very much, but they handed it to me and said I wasn't leaving until I drank it. I went to sit in the waiting area back with Wil and gave it to him to drink. My friend, Wil, who would do anything for me and anything I asked of him and thankfully he didn't let me down today: he drank the tea quickly and gratefully with a cheeky grin on his face obviously being so happy to help me out and he seemed really pleased with himself that he had helped me out so much. Bless him. Mum came down the next day to help me with the ointment that I had been given and I was really grateful to see her. It was actually one time when I felt close to my Mum and I let her into my emotions and let her take care of me. This is what I had wanted for so long, but still I felt oddly overwhelmingly angry inside. My housemates were impressed with the eye patch; I wasn't! A few weeks later, I was out in London with Lucy crossing the road and a stray contact lens appeared in my hand when I rubbed my eye but I could still see perfectly! It must have been the contact lens that got lost behind my eye that night and only just come back round after its adventure inside of me! I felt cleansed and relieved to have an answer to this event and could put it behind me now.

I was fainting on my journeys back from London after work at 2pm and couldn't concentrate at work at all. I was getting it done and keeping up, but my friend / colleague kept telling me I was distant and kept asking "where do you go?" when we took our breaks in the old, now deserted, canteen downstairs, which could last almost all day at the worst of times and then I was delighted when I was put on backdated and continual temporary promotion and was getting a pay rise too due to the level of work I was taking on. Now I just needed to make this promotion permanent and I was there! Now I needed to be the best and to start putting together examples to use in my next Performance Appraisal.

Searching for any kind of training course away from London was a top priority of mine at work. I put myself on so many courses with work, mostly accompanied by my friend Ravi, but I dreaded the meals. I really tried, but after most of them towards the later courses especially, I 'S'. The worst course for my eating behaviours with Ravi was my final course on an evening in Birmingham (29th April 2007) where we ate at the Super-Healthy Japanese fast-food restaurant chain that I felt safe with. I was really struggling immensely at this stage and even rushed back to the hotel after our quick paced march around the town, to vigorously 'S' every last bit. I felt desperate but only now can I realise how pushed away and hurt Ravi must have felt.

We also managed to seek out cheap tickets to a musical while on one of our courses together and I remember being in such excruciating pain in the interval that I was rummaging desperately through my bag for my IBS tablets. These tablets had become my absolute saviour to instant relief. I thought to myself "look at what you've done to yourself, so desperately relying on your tablets like some kind of addict! You must stop all this!" But when I was relieved, I was so relieved. I would spend all night bent over on my bed on all fours on so many occasions trying to push the pain out and wishing for it all just to go away. I was constantly in tears with it, crouched over in pain, rocking and squeezing my stomach to try to make a difference when I was alone in the nights. Anything to make it go away! Please! I was in agony. I was exhausted. The nights were long and dark and lonely. But I had to keep a brave face, laugh it all off even, in the company of others. Smile.

I took another trip to Barcelona, this time with my friend Sarah. We became a little irritated on our last night because we just could not find those special restaurants by the sea that we had planned to eat at on our final evening. We had walked miles in search of these restaurants and we were tired and hungry! However, we ended up at a large, rather brash, tapas restaurant but with a wonderful view of the sea. I will never forget how delicious the swordfish dish tasted. We had a super time on holiday with lots of laughs and lots of fun. We could forget all our worries and it was especially nice being able to wear summer clothes and both return to the same hotel together at night, rather than making the long and dangerous journey home alone wrapped up in our coats, as was the case in cold, wet, lonely London.

By now, I think I had almost decided that marriage was just not for me and that if I can just have a relationship, on my terms and before it gets too serious, then this is what I will do. Because right now, this is all I can deal with.

CHAPTER 16:

AMIR

~

MILAN

~

FRANCE ~ EID ~ NEW YEARS' EVE

16i-Amir:

Meeting Amir – All Barriers Firmly Up.

On one of our nights out with Sarah and Lucy, we were in 'The Huge Hill', Brick Lane, about to leave for the night, when this guy started talking to me. He was interesting and nicely spoken and smartly dressed in a white shirt and black trousers and carried himself well and we chatted and got on brilliantly. He seemed sensible and I could see the qualities I look for in a guy: he appeared sure of himself and not pretentious at all. I explained to him that it was nice to meet him and that my friends and I were about to leave and go home. He said they were also leaving and that he had a taxi outside the bar waiting to take him and his friends to 'The Huge Hill' at Kings Cross and did we want to go there too? For me, that was a straight yes because this offer meant that I didn't have to find my own way back to Kings Cross in the cold, rain and dark on public transport when here was a nice, smart group of people, who had booked a taxi and were inviting us for a drink while I waited for my train, which the station, I knew, was right next door to 'The Huge Hill' at Kings Cross. Perfect.

Next thing I knew, I had persuaded my friends to comply with the plan and to stay out a little longer and so we were all being driven by these guys to Kings Cross. I could always rely on my persuasive skills to kick in when I needed them to; this was something I knew I had always been good at. I was only thinking, great they can stay with me until I go to get my train and I won't be standing on the platform all cold and alone for a whole hour and there was a group of us and a group of them and so the night all of a sudden had lengthened and had changed for the better. We did get there and we did go to that bar – Sarah continued her journey home, but Lucy stayed on with me and the group and we all chatted in comfort and warmth whilst waiting for my train. He was kind and seemed intelligent and we chatted a lot. He kissed me briefly at the train barrier as I left in a hurry, we swapped numbers and I made my way home.

He was a gentleman, strikingly good-looking, seemed clever, knowledgeable and proactive and appeared to be able to look after situations by applying the necessary levels of assertion. He reminded me of myself in a way, a few years ago when I still had my real confidence. He was definitely a business-type people person and knew exactly how to speak to different people in the best way. He was good at networking and connecting with people. We talked a lot on the phone every night and he asked me out to have dinner with him near his house at Canary Wharf. Nervously, but not wanting to appear abnormal, I agreed.

We saw a lot more of each other for drinks, coffee, dinner, spent time with friends etc. He was a footballer and a sports adviser and an ex-model and, to me, he didn't appear to eat much himself and so on our first outing at dinner, I thought he was perfect for me. He demonstrated healthy eating habits and so I was OK around him mostly. I wanted to appear as normal as possible. I didn't want him to know about any of my problems at all as I was still in denial of the behaviours and trying my best to make myself stop them and leave them in the past. I didn't understand them or acknowledge them. He used to say to his friends though "ah, she doesn't eat" I don't know where he got that from as I DID eat in front of him, but maybe even then it wasn't enough to appear normal; I don't know. I do know that I was excited to have finally met a guy who intrigued me once again, who I wanted to get to know and that this person even seemed to be similar to myself in a rather amazing way. We seemed to fit and to click and to have an understanding of each other that never extended to needing words for confirmation. I guess maybe we spoke a lot in actions and with this I – maybe him too – could feel secure.

16ii-Milan:

Short Break to Milan with My Lovely Stalbany Friends.
Very soon after I met Amir, I took a trip to Milan with two of my lovely Stalbany friends: Victor and Amy. We all stayed round at my house the night before. I so wanted to host an exciting and perfect proper pre-Milan evening at my house, and would have excitedly made it my business in the past, but *Angel* made them come round *after dinner*, making Rebecca feel like a terrible friend for not inviting and offering them dinner together as part of a fun pre-holiday get-together and bonding session at mine. I remember always having avoided travelling to Italy because of my intense fear of oily pastas and cheesy pizzas, even though I had always had a quietly hidden curiosity of wanting to experience the authentic Italian culture, which included experiencing authentically-cooked Italian pizza and their overall cuisine. My favourite meal used to be spaghetti bolognaise, but now I was particularly scared of this. It was definite no-no for me. Plus, as a child, I had said to myself that I would secretly 'save' going to Italy, now the more romantic parts of Italy, to visit with my soul mate…if I were ever to find him and was, in turn, able to make it work, that is.

In Italy, I remember my absolute dread at each meal coming. I dreaded not being able to read the menu, as Italian I knew none of and the menus were not in English. But each time I would pull out my phrasebook that I'd purchased in advance and my realms of internet printouts, including a range of holiday and basic living phrases and vocabulary with the largest section detailing those foods that I was desperate to avoid. Once, I even tried to ask the waiters to pick out the items on the menu with no cheese, but this request was met with a mixture of bewilderment and irritation and I learned that such things did not seem to exist in this country, thus confirming my fears. I felt so under the spot-light and I knew I was sounding like an extremely fussy eater because my friends knew I had no allergies or intolerances and so I was left always taking ages to order (nothing new) and felt so stupid and pathetic and slow and awkward. These traits I never wanted to possess in the company of my friends. I didn't want to turn into one of those fussy eaters in front of my friends, it wasn't that I *didn't like the taste of it*, I could eat anything really! It was something far more important and crucial than that, but only ever to me. *Angel made* me ask all these questions, she *made* me try to find the blandest item on the menu and she *made* me have to try my best to win because only then could life go on.

By the end of the trip I felt F A T, sick and absolutely disgusted with myself. I hated having my photograph taken but at the same time I enjoyed being with my friends a lot and felt we were all supporting each other totally on our trip, even at mealtimes although they didn't know it, and we had a super time being together and getting on really well. It was clear we were all thoughtful and considerate with each other and always looked out for and cared about each other's safety. I suppose, looking back now, it was this feeling of trust and safety and comfort that is the key to what really aided me with my eating and encouraged my more truthful smiles.

I got a little bit of period when I got home, which I was happy about underneath and it reminded me of what my health had become...*but more-over I felt like a failure and I felt stuffed.* Although this confused me, it scared me much more. I started exercising vigorously at the gym and fiercely 'S' again. I didn't know why I felt or acted in this dreadful way. I was overtaken by the wings of *Angel*, my shadow, as the mind of Micci declined.

16iii-Amir – Happy Ever After or Slippery Slope?

Daytrip to France with Amir.
Amir invited me on his work daytrip on the coach and ferry to France, which I graciously accepted. It was lovely. I love travelling

and especially on coach rides where you can cuddle up and sleep in each other's arms. We had a great time. We ate cock-au-vin, he chose it and I copied his choice, and we stopped later on for a coffee. He always tried so hard in encouraging me to have a milky coffee because he said "Go on, you'll like it", but I never did again after the first time, which was to keep him happy and to look normal. I loved falling asleep in his arms on that coach journey back. He was soft and warm and gentle and just gorgeous. I knew it was completely safe and so I *felt* safe and could totally relax and be blissfully happy for a couple of hours. *Wow.*

We spent a lot of time together after this outing and I would stay over at his friend's places in their spare rooms with him after our nights out, always keeping my clothes on I must add. We used to go to frequent a bar in Brick Lane where he knew everyone. It was really much more like gathering in a lounge at someone's home. It was just nice to be with him, rather than standing around for trains back to Stalbany at 2am alone and in the freezing cold. He joined me on the train numerous times to make sure I was OK, even though I made it clear that he would be coming back to London straight away. I was surprised at his desire to keep me safe and to look after me properly. He was fine about me not inviting him to my house he was very sweet in making sure I got home OK and this spoke volumes to me in that he had been brought up properly and that he was showing that he genuinely cared for my safety. Let's see if it would last.

On the odd occasion I would catch him watching me talking to his friends in the bar in Brick Lane with a smile on his face and he would quickly look away if I looked over to do the same to him. This made me feel special to him and I was happy because I felt the same way. I was still in disbelief that this person was choosing to spend time with *me* when he was clearly sought after by what seemed like every single female under the sun! Little things attracted me to him and it showed me he was brought up well and had gentlemanly values, which I find attractive and crucial qualities in a guy to base a relationship with and to hopefully spend my whole life with and make a family with.

We had spent our first evening in together sharing snacks, which I sadly just couldn't touch, and a couple of drinks in front of the television and he had shown me some of his most private hopes and dreams of past and present on his laptop. We were getting to know each other and I enjoyed and could relate to his ambitious side. That night we spent together, but he noticed my tears as I was saying no and I think it made him uncomfortable and he made a tiny effort to ask if I was OK but, as usual, I brushed it off as just being silly. I was shocked at my inability to control my emotions and felt stupid and weak! Still, he respected my signals and wishes but we didn't talk about anything. In myself, I was confused and upset and most of all annoyed at my uncontrollable silent tears and was thankful to just be content feeling him falling asleep in my arms.

Eid.
As our relationship progressed he appeared to be OK with taking things at my pace. I bought him a nice pen for Eid and we spent some time together having coffee in the lounge in Brick Lane and he took me to visit a charity to show me some of the work that he had done for them previously to help children in third world countries. Of course I expected nothing in return for Eid, as I did not celebrate this myself. He bought me something however and that night he made me unwrap the gift in front of him. It was a night dress. I thanked him and told him it was very nice, but I was feeling disappointed because it wasn't really my style and I knew that he was trying to tell me something and this scared me. I was now questioning his motives. Why did he have to put this upon me when it was all going so well?

Usually I would always sleep in my trousers and fully clothed. He told me to put it on and I said no, not tonight. I laughed a bit shyly. I didn't want to, no way, I knew his intentions. I knew men! He started to get irritated, saying "why, don't you like me?" And he started to get really angry and upset with me. I went into the bathroom to change into it but still I kept on my trousers and got into bed. It was a compromise. He was grumpy. I took off the trousers while I squirmed in awkwardness, he smiled gently and said "beautiful" and he kissed me. I certainly didn't feel beautiful. I felt awkward, fearful, bullied, anxious and fat. My thoughts were flying around in my head. His friend and his fiancé were sleeping in the room next door and I was next to the wall, so I knew I could bang on there or just scream out if I needed to, but in hindsight, how stupid and unrealistic was this thought? Would I ever have been able to do this, in reality? Of course not: You are strong and can say no! You must fight off anything that you don't want, on your own! Nobody is there to help you. I was not weak and failing! I was strong. I was me. I could deal with anything. He came and cuddled me from behind and started...

I always enjoyed kissing him, but I knew I didn't want anything else at all, definitely not yet, and maybe not ever with him. I told him where I was at, but he kept on in his persistent Scorpionistic attitude, which reminded me so much of Spen (also a Scorpio) at the time and I made myself a mental promise never, ever, to get involved with a Scorpio again. When he wanted something, he had to have it. I said no but he made out he was taking me as a tease. I was serious, I was totally fighting him then and I was crying. He was strong, *so* strong, and rough with sudden movements. I felt dirty all of a sudden and thought "how is this happening to me again?" No! I hated that I had put myself in this situation that was now totally out of my control. There was no way I could escape it. I *hated every second. Crying, tears streaming, stupid, dirty weak, idiot, idiot, IDIOT...!*

More silent tears back again; he was so cold afterwards and we didn't speak. We didn't discuss anything in the morning either. I got straight up and dressed and wanted to get out of there as quickly as possible. I just wanted to leave. How could he just ignore and not acknowledge that anything had happened, so easily? He showed *no* remorse. I walked away thinking "I am never coming back, ever. How could I have let that happen? Dirty, disgusting, slut of a person, you're nobody and don't deserve even to *live!*" I left the flat and immediately had to exercise, to push myself to the very extremities of my limits. I had no dignity left. I had to get home, wash myself out, prepare for a vigorous regime at the gym. Go, go, go go...no time to waste. Must text Sarah and Lucy...text anyone...need to go out...need to have alcohol...*need to forget!* Dance on those tables, flirt with those men and escape from being you. Be somebody else. Anything but this!

But 'this' carried on: the drinking; the staying at his friends' houses; the physical fight of me not wanting to, but him having to have it;

him getting angry and frustrated, and me crying; him ignoring, me self-deploring. How was it that he still wanted to see me when I was such a terrible girlfriend to him? I was so confused. He did try to ask me once, what was upsetting me, but I couldn't tell him, I didn't even really know myself. All I knew was that I liked spending time with him, a lot. I had found someone who was like me and I guess who was a lot like Spen. He was good-looking, well-spoken, clever and intelligent, confident, sparkly, everybody adored and loved him and all the girls were jealous because he had now openly chosen me. He referred to me as "my honey" all the time with a loving smile and a hug when girls still had the nerve to try and steal him away from me, but he knew how to play them and he – maybe playing me too, I never found out – would always make me feel safe that *I* was his chosen one, and I believed him. Every time I had a plan or I was determined that I wouldn't let him win in the physical sense, that I would do what *I* wanted to do and only what *I* wanted to do, *it never worked*. I betrayed myself and berated myself on my way home more and more each time. How has this happened again? And again? And again?

New Years' Eve.
OK my New Years' Resolution was to give up everything bad for me i.e. my '<u>S</u>' and being in a position where things could go wrong, no matter how I had planned to control a situation or put plans in place to avoid events happening that I didn't want to happen. This I was to put firmly in my past.

On New Years' Eve we met at Amir's friend's house to enjoy a home-cooked meal and good company before making our way out to our favourite bar in between watching the fireworks from Tower Bridge.

Firstly, Dear Reader, I couldn't believe it was a meal of *dumplings* in three different *SAUCES* and a nasty fattening pudding! It made me feel ill. Could this be any worse? Smile, be strong. Look, it is fine...everyone else is eating it too...it is fine, it is fine, it is normal...it is not wrong...but *is it OK...?* Afterwards, we went to our usual Brick Lane bar to celebrate and had a nice dance and a great time actually and then drove to Tower Bridge to look at the fireworks in the rain. It was nice as he showed and pointed out to me all the places that were dear to him and his family when he was growing up. By then, we had consumed a couple of drinks and returned to the bar, which felt like our own private party as the bar was small and comfortable yet situated in the buzz of Brick Lane and I felt safe around the people I had grown to know and be around. I was supposed to leave when I heard from Wil and to meet him at Kings Cross to get the train back to Stalbany, stay at my house and then drive home to Mums for her annual New Years' Day curry lunch. This plan ensured that I wouldn't be stuck overnight with Amir, instead I would be *safe* and happy and free from harm with the lovely Wil. But this didn't happen so smoothly because plans changed due to phone receptions at midnight being blocked and I was forced to get in the car and head back to Amir's friends flat. I was silent. I was frozen stiff for the whole journey. *Please NO! Not tonight! I will not, I cannot let it happen. Not tonight!*

I managed to get through to Wil by text, much to Amir's disgust and possible jealousy that he was texting me at this time of morning. Wil was going to stay in his office for a couple of hours, which was close to the train station we were supposed to have met at and I was to meet him there in the morning. Amir and I went through the whole fighting thing and he had his wicked way, again, through my fight and my tears and my fully dressed being. He was *so cold.* I had kept all my clothes on again, but still he had managed it. I wanted to leave then and there, but I stayed until early in the morning when I quietly let myself out of the flat.

I had nothing to say to him. I felt so dirty all over again, so alone; I couldn't believe what had happened. I hated myself for being in that situation, yet again. What a complete and absolute idiot I was. I wanted to die and didn't care what happened to me on my journey to Kings Cross. Weak and failing in life even when I had *planned* to *ensure* that my evening meant everything would be OK. An organised, planned, new-found control of my life to start off the year with – not quite! I must deserve this terrible punishment and torture that seemed to be ongoing for me whatever I did to try and live a safe, happy, normal, ambitious and fulfilled life. I was worthless and clearly my fate was not to have a place in this world where I achieve anything I strive for. I must have done something terribly wrong in my past or past life somewhere, to be dealt this deck of dastardly deserved cards that was so set in stone for me, no matter how hard I tried to achieve anything slightly opposite to that which I feared most. To me, this world was a terrible place and my position within it was of no worth what-so-ever, not to me nor anyone else. I was a total failure, a waste of space and never good enough or able to achieve even the simplest of things.

As I paced my way home with these intense feelings of hurt, disgust and severe loneliness inside, I felt a strange sense of realisation that at least now I knew that through my years suffering confusion and disturbance of intercepting thoughts and feelings of 'just not fitting' into this world, always being 'different', being 'wrong' and 'stupid', 'weak' and 'dirty', just 'not worthy' and 'destined to fail', and will 'always be a disappointment', 'never good enough', seem 'determined to upset all Beloveds' etc. etc. etc. I would no longer battle my tormenters and shove them out of my mind as ridiculous and untrue, as why should they be untrue? I accepted that actually, it *is* what I deserve, I *am* unworthy, look at what I have done...if it happened and happened and happened again and again and again, it was only because I had let it each time and I deserved it. I realised maybe I felt safer in rejection, pain and suffering, distress, worry, anguish, fear and cruelty and if I wasn't shown it, in desperate efforts to feel safe and secure in this world, I would be subconsciously seeking it out and afflicting it upon myself. I am strong, I can deal with anything, I may as well make some money from it and at least then I can buy nice things for my family and treat my family and make them proud of me in seeing that at least I have achieved promotion at work and able to spoil my loved ones by buying them nice things.

The bus on the way home came across a woman lying in the road. I had to get off in the middle of I don't even know where. I became increasingly unaware and didn't even care about anything that was going on in the world around me. I wasn't destined to live and be happy, but at least I could fulfil my role in keeping the peace, and in keeping others content. Do the right things; say the right things; be there to help those who needed it, and smile.

I made it to Kings Cross and met Wil, who was so kind-natured that he didn't even show his annoyance at my behaviour, bless him. I didn't deserve his kindness, but I needed it. We made it home in time for the family New Years' Day Curry...'<u>S</u>'... Moreover, I was worried about being pregnant, although I also knew that this was highly unlikely. If I was, I would have kept it because I still really felt something for him and believed we could have had something together. But also I wanted to make him realise his irresponsible actions had consequences to ruin his life too.

CHAPTER 17:

HELP ~ VALENCIA ~ HELP

17i-Stalbany Help:

After some time and back in Stalbany, I sought help at my local doctors surgery because my eating was causing me so much pain, confusion and problems in all aspects of my life and I knew that I couldn't hold down a relationship as what I thought had been dealt with clearly had not and I just wanted to get it out of my system and get on with my life. I was shaking in the waiting room while trying to work out what to say. Should I stay? Should I go? I seemed to have been there for hours but they had fitted me in at the last minute, so I couldn't walk away and I wasn't going to. I had written 'disordered eating' down on a piece of paper in case I couldn't get out my words and I didn't want to leave having just avoided bringing up what I had made such an effort to bring out today. I was determined to get some help in how to continue on with my life – marriage and relationships really scared me and I knew I had real problems in this area and wanted someone to tell me how to get over it and have a happy and healthy relationship with a man. That is all I wanted.

I did manage it. I absolutely cried my eyes out uncontrollably and felt so silly and surprised that my saying this had made me so upset. As I was in the process of looking for somewhere to live in London with the aim to be in walking distance of work and so that I could lose myself in the big city, which would help me carry on being at work (and also so I could carry on with my nights out), he advised me to register with a doctor in London and he said he would forward a letter to my new surgery so that I don't have to go through explaining anything all over again.

17ii-Short Break to Valencia with Amir and Friends:

Amir was going away to Valencia with his friend and his friend's fiancé, who was Spanish and I got on really well with her as she was quirky and flirty and I could see the relationship she had with her fiancé was equal and loving both ways. I was deciding if I should go or not as my sister was expecting her baby in February and I didn't want to be out of the country at that time. This is what I told Amir and that is what I told my family and myself at first too. I knew the baby wasn't likely to arrive during this time really though. I so wanted to go away with them, it was only for a few days and I absolutely loved travelling and I knew he would take care of me. Part of me thought I hardly know the guy really, but I felt like I did and I felt safe with him in this world, I don't know why, because I felt we knew we were both alike. Except my worry were the nights. I talked it through with my best friend Sarah, who had inklings that I wasn't at all happy with all that side of things with him. She came up with a plan that couldn't go wrong – to tell him I was on my period – and if I stuck to my story then everything would be OK and we would all have a fantastic time! I decided to go and we were both really pleased and excited.

We did have fun, but my plan didn't stick. He was too pushy and I was too feeble and weak. I tried to tell him that I couldn't etc. but I couldn't even get the words out that I needed to for my plan to work and instead my default was to communicate in riddles and body language. I was so annoyed with myself. So that was that, subject to days of this and with no excuse. I cried afterwards every time and hid in the bathroom, washing my face and running the tap in order to hide my tear-stained face. I knew he knew, but it was completely my problem. I went round Spain feeling dirtier and dirtier, filthier and filthier each day, feebler and weaker, and I hardly spoke a word to people, even those I was on holiday with because I just felt awful and undeserved. Keep up the fake smile. You let it happen so suffer in silence, you tramp! Look at you! You deserve nothing. Do the others know? Of course they do, it's all a joke to them all! You're the joke. I was desperate for someone to be on MY side and to pull me away from this, to help me out here. I was looking at strangers in the street, desperate for someone to just know and to take me to safety and to protect me from any more harm. I just couldn't speak out, how was this happening to me? How weak am I? Where was the voice of Rebecca?

17iii-Move to London – Prague – and Help:

London.

I moved to London. Ravi helped me move, he helped me find the place too, which was hard work. I was still working so hard to gain my permanent promotion and wanted to show my family that I was doing exceptionally well and so I was signed up as an escort, which meant more money, more hours distracted socially and being paid for it, meeting other people and building up my confidence, it was London and I was not going to be recognised by anyone I knew, I could be someone else completely – I thought I could deal with this as I just needed to put on my fake face and keep safe i.e. Accompany people to shows etc. although to dinners would be difficult (but I could specify this) and be pleasant and get paid huge amounts of money for doing it and I tried to persuade myself that it is really confidence-building therefore it is a good thing for me to do. They used company taxis to pick you up safely and you remained in complete control of identification, telephone numbers, hours worked etc. and so I felt it was well-contained and that I would be able to put on my work game face but also work on my social skills. But I was even too scared and weak to go ahead with this plan. I felt pathetic and timid. I had let my family and friends down so much. Back to the original plan – I just *had* to get that promotion!

I still saw Amir. But I gave up completely in staying over at his friends' houses with him. It was easier now that I was living so centrally and it meant that I could always make my way home to my own flat, alone. Once inside my locked-up flat, I could be myself and I felt safe in these confines, but I was depressed and hated my life. I told Ravi of my struggle with eating and he tried his best to help. He took me out and to the cinema, to musicals, to anywhere I wanted to go and he treated me so well. I trusted his brain and his mind, but I didn't trust his intentions. His intentions I disliked. He started to ask me why I blocked him out, why I didn't speak to him, why I go distant, why does my hand not feel safe in his? Why can I not hold his gaze? I was longing just to tell him, it feels trapped and unsafe and out of my control, I didn't want to feel anything I wanted to run and detach but that was just me. That was just how I was and was something that I, and only I, had to work out and to deal with, to accept or to work on and not to expect others to hear about it at all...and so I never spoke out, as who wants to hear that rubbish? You're strong, you're all-together, you're sorted, you're not struggling really, think of all the people who are so much worse off than you, you selfish idiot, how dare you! So selfish, get on with life! Smile.

Ravi asked me to marry him again. He bought me very expensive jewellery and looked after me at work. He said I was made from his ribs and that I was his eyes and that we were meant to be together. There always was something there, I admit that I personally felt it the very day that we met in the office, with no mistake. But it stopped at a deep friendship for me because how could I ever consider 'being' with him, a devout Muslim? He even wore a beard, which suits him, but I found it uncomfortable and disturbing, and a hat. We were from different worlds; I told him this, yet he gave me all the promises he thought I still wanted to hear.

I remember going out for dinner after seeing a show once, he was not taking no for an answer, his offer of dinner taking me by surprise. I ordered a salad. I couldn't help myself. I ordered it without chicken and without dressing, but with an additional side salad for us to share (I felt bad for suggesting another dish, even though it was just salad and it was to share). I felt so embarrassed when a large bowl just of lettuce and croutons arrived! I don't think Rav noticed until I immediately put some of the side salad of tomatoes, cucumber and carrots onto my plate in an effort to make it look a bit better. He was great and just continued to smile and tell jokes, which distracted me and made me feel better. I left the croutons.

At the end of April 2009, Amir and I spent our best ever evening together, from my point of view anyway. He had invited me to a launch party with his friends, except this time a few of his female friends would be going too, a couple of whom I already knew.

Usually it was just me and his mates and only rarely their girlfriends, but tonight it was a group of males and females. Amir picked me up in his friend's car. He commented on how nice I looked and stated that he loved my dress and he said all the right things to me and ensured I was safe and in good company throughout the evening. I spent most of the night dancing with the girls, but checking he was OK too. He was so lovely towards me that evening and we all had a genuinely good night. I felt happy and like I was finally fitting in and being accepted for once in my life. I felt like I was amongst friends, finally. He was playing football early the next morning and so wasn't staying over at mine that night. We cuddled and kissed in the car on the short journey back to my flat and he made sure I was back inside safely. I felt happy and content and clean and orderly and had no worries going through my head, for once!

I felt happy and proud that this person to whom I held such high regard, was still choosing to acknowledge ME, over every single one of those beautiful, young and intelligent females that forever flock to and surround his charismatic and charming being all day and all night long, as "My Honey". This is a concept that I had struggled with from the very day that Amir had approached me and my feelings of insecurity and disbelief in his continued efforts at pursuing me and attending to me and showing his care for ME, grew evermore confusing as time went by, which I was able to speak about and analyse over and over with my best friend Sarah. I was growing closer and closer to Amir emotionally, but never yet letting down my guard, ever. Still sensible. Nothing's secure; nothing's safe. Beware.

During a night out with Sarah, I spoke to Amir on the phone as he wanted to join up as we were all out and about, which was fine by each of us. We were in Kensington, which was a part of London that we were not yet familiar with and we had a bad time trying to get back to the centre of London. We even ended up in the back of a group of lads' car on a dual-carriageway until I suddenly became scared and demanded they please take us back. I was back on the phone trying to explain to Amir our where-abouts, but I was getting confused with Kensington and Kensington High Street, being unfamiliar with the area and so he spoke to Sarah, who has never seen eye-to-eye with Amir and it is in her nature to always speak her absolute mind to anyone, anytime. She has no qualms in using her natural assertiveness and this I was happy to learn from her, little by little each day.

But tonight, Amir was becoming stressed as I informed him that Sarah would be coming home with me tonight because we were getting tired and it was getting late and I couldn't let my friend make her way to North London all alone. He still wanted to come round and I said I would try and sort something out. I explained the situation to Sarah and she became upset too. I said that she could sleep on the spare bed in the lounge next to my room. She would be comfortable there. Problem solved, or so I thought.

As soon as we got in, Sarah climbed straight into my bed...Amir turned up and saw her pretending to be fast asleep...he was livid and stormed out. He's never been like that before, but I totally understood. To be honest, I was livid at my "friend" Sarah too and yet, I was too feeble to make any assertive stance further than purely pathetic. Amir had left, it was our first falling out, Sarah was in my bed pretending to have passed out. I had messed everything up once again. I felt tiny, unworthy of having a life to live in this world, an utterly terrible girlfriend and friend; I should just be left alone with nothing there to destroy.

The next day, Amir was very angry towards me and said I had spoken to him like I was someone else that night and that I didn't treat him like a boyfriend. I was confused as I had tried my best and I could have sorted something out. I was so angry with my friend though and I still feel she had aided the split between Amir and I. Maybe that is what she wanted because she herself was single and I had found someone I felt special with and was spending my time with him more and more, though never at her expense. I wrote in my diary in those weeks while I was locked away from the rest of the world in hospital, that in reality maybe Amir (having also been drinking that night) didn't realise who he was speaking to on the phone and maybe, just maybe, he thought my friend Sarah – who is always very direct and to-the-point, of rudeness sometimes, especially to people whom she does not get-along with, I suppose and also with the consumption of alcohol too – was me! I felt terrible for thinking these thoughts about my best friend and put my head down, hoping I would feel differently in the morning. I never voiced my real feelings to Sarah because our friendship was too precious to me to potentially throw away.

So the morning after, I was distraught and felt hopeless, useless and like a terrible person. I wanted to make it all right again and tried to be really nice to Sarah. In my stomach and my heart, I was aching for Amir to think better of me: I respected him so much and didn't want him being disappointed in me and thinking terrible thoughts about me as a person. About my lack of abilities I could deal with him knowing these weaknesses as I believed them myself and would be the first to admit my lack of knowledge or ability, but about my pride, my integrity and my general manners and respectability as a person, I could not contemplate him being left with this view of me. Whatever I was, I continued to hold my morals and attitudes towards others, whoever they maybe, my priority.

Prague.
I went on holiday for a long weekend with Sarah. We had a good time, but the weather spoilt it a little as it was cold, especially after the weather we experienced on our wonderful first holiday to Barcelona, which was lovely and hot. I had opened up more to her in a coffee shop one afternoon when we were sheltering from the wind and I told her about some of my disordered eating behaviours. She was great. She listened carefully and gave me sound advice and I felt she was so supportive of me; I couldn't have asked for a better friend and I knew I could trust her as my confidante. I told her I had been to my doctors and he was going to refer me to a therapist and she was happy that I had sought help by myself and told me I had done the right thing.

On our penultimate evening, we returned to a club that was most renowned in Prague. It was big and the music was good and it wasn't too far from our hotel either. At the end of the night however, as there were so many stairs in the club and we had spent a lot of time walking up and down these all evening, we were sitting by the sides of the dance floor with sore feet and I was contentedly refusing to get up and dance any more. I was tired, but happy. We were having a good chat together and making the most of our holiday to build on our friendship. I never felt judged by this new friend and she never got angry. We were very similar to each other in that we were both easy going and wanted to enjoy life, but we had our ambitions and morals too. A lot of men approached us and asked us to dance at this point and I was able to say no to everyone because I was so tired and it was early hours of the morning and we were ready to go home for the night. Also, I didn't want to cause a fight! But because of this, there was a fight that broke out over me. I felt awful as the group of guys was thrown out of the club, which made us have to stay in there for a little longer, just to make sure they'd all disappeared completely.

On our final night, we returned to our favourite restaurant for dinner and back to our favourite bars as we had planned a quiet night of winding down our holiday and spending the last of the change we had left and just relaxed in laughter. However, we met a familiar guy sporting his black eye from the night before. He was with a large group of guys around the same age as us, and he approached me. I spent the evening getting to know him only to discover that he was a musician in the Royal Marines, who went to school with Spen (I questioned him in such a way that I wouldn't give anything away about him and that confirmed to me that he genuinely did know Spen). He was telling me how Spen used to bully him on the school bus.

My friend was chatting all evening to another group of guys from Ireland that we had made friends with previously and both groups seemed to look after us really well, always ensuring the two of us were safe between ourselves too. It was this night where we had our best time and ended up very irresponsibly sleeping in through our alarm clock, rushing to the airport and just missing our plane home! Very, very, very poor behaviour and I take full responsibility for not setting my alarm before falling asleep. Whoops. I am so sorry for putting you through the stress and the rush at the airport that morning Sarah, please forgive me because I think that I didn't manage to even set the alarm and it wasn't that it just simply didn't go off. Now I admit this and I am so sorry!

After we had sorted ourselves out for the night, I think we were both quietly pleased in a weird way because we saw the sun that day, we had lovely chats, we relaxed and found a really comfortable hotel closer to the town centre with a lovely shower. We also saw my Marines friend from the night before during the day and he came right over to our bench to say hi and we walked around Prague together, both in search of an internet cafe 1) for him and 2) so Sarah could send an email to her workplace letting them know she would be back in the office a day late! We kept bumping into our new acquaintances throughout the day and also that evening, which we all found hilariously funny.

On our return to England I restricted severely for days, unable to go to work out of desperation after my indulgent holiday. It started by being unable to consume the sandwich we'd bought to share on the plane journey home. Owing to the fact that I couldn't pick one out for myself, my friend said that I had to share hers then, now that she knew about my struggles. Once on the plane, I pretended to eat my half, but made such a mess and left it. I just couldn't. It *had* to stop! I had struggled silently in many ways on holiday, but Sarah was so understanding, plus she is a very light eater too, which made eating slowly and leaving food half way through a whole lot easier for me because when she stopped, I stopped and I was so grateful because if I ate slowly, then nothing looked odd. Some nights we had the BBQ in the street while watching the football in the square. This was easy as the sausage could be squashed in the napkin it was served in and went in the bin with the ketchup anyway. I know Sarah wouldn't really have said anything to me anyway because she didn't get angry and I was my own person; we respected each other and it was a big sausage anyway. After my dinner of a half-eaten ketchup sodden bun, I just wanted the alcohol: spirit and mixers and the odd glass of wine if I needed it to feel better, a good old flirt with a nice gentleman and an evening filled with dancing.

I couldn't face Amir. I couldn't even face work – I'd get ready in the morning, berating myself all the way for getting the bus and for being so lazy for not walking and then I would have to stay on the bus until it stopped at Hampstead Heath, where I knew I could go on walking for hours, up and down hills. Otherwise I would plan, plan, plan to go straight to the gyms and swimming pools; I'd count in my head always to distract my thoughts and then I'd plan the rest of the day, the evening, and the week.

If I had to stay indoors through being far too fat and large and selfish and undeserved to taking up any room at all in the outside world, sometimes I would be all ready to walk out of the door to work and yet I just couldn't face being in the world and I would have to call in to let them know I was working from home or taking time off in lieu of the hours I had already worked. I felt far too disgusting to be seen in public and was just too scared to be in a public space such as at work or at the supermarket, instead I would rearrange all my furniture in my bedroom, I would search the internet for the lowest calorie brands of whatever I could eat and figure out where I could buy it; I just couldn't see how I could ever live a normal life? No matter how hard I tried, it never worked. What was I to do? Who could I tell? I needed help.

Help.

I started seeing Pam, a therapist at a London Hospital, but I couldn't get my words out. I just wanted someone to know everything and to tell me how to have a normal relationship and to help me with being able to be normal in my future so I could get married and have children if I chose to. This wasn't how my life was supposed to be turning out. Someone just tell me it is possible.

When I was with Leo and getting to know Ravi, I was unsure of the religion I wanted to follow and was finding that I was basing it totally on the rules of marriage. When I was going out in Stalbany, I had decided that I didn't ever want to get married and be belittled and feeling like this for life ever after, until death do us part; no way, I just couldn't cope with it and I didn't have to if I wasn't in a serious relationship or married. When I met Amir, it all changed and I was thinking that maybe, just maybe, I could give it one last chance. But now I knew I had no hope of a happy life, be it married or not! I was finding this world unbearable to be a part of and didn't see my point in life. I was giving up and wanted it all to end. Mum, I am so sorry, I know how much you wish to see me married and leave my family home and I wanted this too, but just cannot see it happening. Instead, I see a life of distraction and death that is so much closer to me now.

My friends and I were still going out at night and they were totally understanding of my desire to avoid the certain places we would be more likely to bump into Amir. We did walk right past each other in the street once when I was with my friends and also my school friend Suki, whom had come to stay with me for the weekend and I was showing her round my favourite places in London. I had walked straight past him, as I tend to keep my head lowered when walking around, although I am always aware of people around me but he had grasped hold of my hand as we walked past and stopped me to talk. He looked tanned as he had also been away on holiday the same week I had been to Prague. I still loved him, but we never TALKED. He was pleased to meet Suki and he was most polite in offering to show her around London properly, as it was home to him; this City is where he grew up. I know he was thinking about bringing business to his friend's restaurant too, as by now I knew how his mind worked especially where business and networking, opportunity and prospects were concerned.

Our lack of communication and strained relationship was entirely my fault and for this I could blame only myself: I would always try to be brave-faced and act all not-bothered and as usual, this is how I acted right now. All smiles, but really I just wanted to talk to him and for him to tell me how he felt. To tell me that it wasn't all a game to him and that I did actually mean something to him. I just wanted to hold his hand tightly, to kiss it, to hug him and to never let go. This is how I continually felt around him and I thought he could pick this vibe up from me, mind-read I suppose, but why would he? When I was always so standoffish with him and so superbly brilliant at being quiet and game-faced and as if I didn't have a care in the world for him? Why should he show any real love towards me either?

When we had said goodbye and walked on around the corner, I couldn't hold in my silent tears any longer and my friends noticed. They were so brilliant and said he wasn't right for me anyway as he seemed arrogant. Typical me choosing this type! What was I thinking? Suki, I am sorry for dragging you to the "exciting new contemporary curry restaurant" near my house – because it offered a low fat diet curry with brown rice that *I* could have; I am sorry for dragging you to Camden Market – so *I* could get away with having the chicken noodle soup that we could eat in the street and that made *me* feel safe; I am sorry for dragging you to the busy, crowded and noisy Super-Healthy fast-food Japanese restaurant chain – that *I* felt comfortable with...and to Little Brother, who visited me also the weekend after and with whom I did exactly the same. I am so sorry.

I met two other guys in whom I saw potential for a long-lasting relationship, while out in London with Sarah and Lucy and I decided they were worth seeing again. One was a lovely, gentle, clever, down-to-earth chap from Australia and I had met up with him and his friends a lot, with Sarah, and even stayed at his place a few times. He lived in a lovely large house and watching films in his lounge was really comfortable and nice. He was kind and gentle and we actually hardly even kissed when I stayed over – he just held me all night, me in my jeans, and we talked. The other guy was from South Africa, unconnected totally to the above. He was also very gentlemanly and would make sure my friend and I were constantly happy and would arrange for us to enter nice places free of charge and would ensure we always had a glass of whatever we chose to drink, just to feel looked after was wonderful. He was also as gentle as a butterfly, yet full of personality and charm. I felt safe with him too and although he subtly tried his hardest to push things with me on a couple of occasions, I could tell he totally respected all my signals and signs, no matter how very, very slight, and he also respected anything I managed to say. Both parties started to ask me out for dinner and there were only so many excuses I could give until it became apparent that I had met these people at the wrong time in my life, which was finally pointed out to me calmly by nice guy number one. I HAD to sort out my life!

The last time I remember visiting my Mum at home for the weekend was on the Saturday night where the ritual in our house was to have a take-away and watch television. I dreaded it all, but had to keep my ill feelings to myself. I was watching an A & E program with Mum and was feeling really unwell to the point that I was so scared I was on the verge of having to ask her to drive me to A & E as I had been advised by the hospital in London. At the time I felt unable to breath and I texted my friend Ravi to tell him. I couldn't tell my Mum. How was I supposed to mention it all now? The whole story! My therapist had told me to get myself to A & E if I felt unwell, but it would be such a shock to my poor Mum, to hear her daughter just come out with – "Mum, I'm not feeling well, can you drive me to casualty please? I need to go right now." I think now, I must have been feeling scared and panicky too, being alone with my thoughts and feelings and this probably didn't help. I couldn't go home again because I needed to know the hospital was there if I needed it. I didn't want to involve my poor Mum, she'd be distraught and I could work this out for myself. I'm strong. Carry on. There's nothing wrong with you! Get on with your life, stop being so selfish! Keep them all happy. Smile.

Before my nephew's Christening I tried to go shopping for a dress and it was so stressful. I couldn't think, I felt tired and faint and worried about not being able to get home without fainting, I couldn't decide which clothes looked right or even what looked half OK as nothing did and nothing fitted. I had taken bits of fruit and crackers in my bag all wrapped up to take in the changing rooms if, and *only if,* I needed it in an emergency – *No, just a bit longer, you are still standing are you not? Well then! You are strong! Look at you! You don't need it, throw it in the bin!* – I hated myself so much. How was I going to face everyone at the Christening? I hadn't been home for a long time or seen the family for a while either. I ended up buying two possible dresses, to which when I finally returned home, I made a couple of alterations to each of them. I was stressed out completely but couldn't rest.

In the end I decided to wear one of my summer dresses that I had worn once before for my friend's wedding and again at another friend's birthday party who was from Eton at his home and so I thought it looked OK. I put a cardigan over it, but it should have been a big jacket. I thought Mum would be pleased with it as it was summery and below the knee and not 'cheap-looking', or so I thought...

The next day I woke up feeling fat and sick at the thought of being in this public situation and wanted it all to be over already. As soon as I came downstairs having changed into my chosen dress at my sister's house before the Christening, I straight away received my first comment from my sister's mother-in-law, "oh, what is this tiny frame all about?" I pretended to laugh and shrug it off and quickly escaped into the conservatory and then back upstairs. Then from my Mum, "are you trying to be the thinnest? You look terrible. Are you anorexic? Are you? I'm taking you to the doctor". She had threatened this numerous times in the past, I think in an effort to just try and make me eat more and look after myself. Next was my brother when we were sitting down at the buffet, "finish it then Micci, go on", "you need to put some weight on Mic!" I made up some excuse and didn't bother.

I had made a token effort to look normal, what else did they all want? Comments followed from our babysitters / cleaner / gardeners / window cleaners / maid and butlers / my Auntie, etc. I was glad to get back to my flat. I avoided going home to Mum after that as I was so afraid of what I would have to face at mealtimes and I couldn't do my exercises and stick to my routines – I couldn't hide anything anymore as I was so terrified and rigid and losing all hope. I wanted to sort myself out without worrying her and without my secret eating rituals and routines coming out! I was embarrassed and ashamed, what would they all think?! I was scared of being 'found out' and didn't want anybody's attention...Only today I realise that I was doing exactly the opposite, unbeknown to myself at the time: I was desperately hurting and crying out for help and attention. I couldn't speak it and so I was compelled to show it in my actions and in my body frame and all subconsciously. My family still think it's about vanity, superficial and all about looks and hence this is reflected in their continued annoyance having interpreted the tiny frame and aggressive behaviour as defiance and selfishness and always asking "why are you doing this to yourself" and "It's the worst thing you could have done to the family, it's killing everyone" and "if your sister loses her baby, it's all your fault". But I was not Micci anymore. I was lost to *Angel*. Rebecca had no choice in the matter.

My Mum was to pay me an impromptu visit and I just knew that she knew something was now seriously wrong and that this could be hidden no more. My actions were now speaking my torture for me and this was to be just the beginning of my journey through hell...

I hadn't had a proper period for years and underneath everything all I wanted was to be happy again. I just wanted to be normal and to actually have a future. It used to scare me that I didn't get a period but now I felt safer that I hadn't had it and the scary side became just a murmur every-so-often that was easier to just block out, ignore and not to listen to that anymore, as everything else had taken over and become so much more essential and necessary and important to me. *Rebecca* didn't matter anymore. She wasn't supposed to have a life or to live out her dreams. This was purely fantastical! Now I possessed an inability to experience any kind of joy in life.

I had vanished to Angel Galore.

BOOK 2:

WHO AM I?

CHAPTER 18:-

...DIARY ENTRY TAKEN FROM TWO DAYS PRIOR TO

HOSPITAL ADMISSION 1...

- **Wednesday 13 August 2008:**

Woke up at 11am. Mum calling, whoops. Phoned her back saying I'm working from home today. She said she's feeling OK and will come and visit this afternoon / evening. OK. Text Ravi straight away. Got up. Big breakfast: grapes, melons, some crumpet, tea, dried apricots, strawberries. Quick; need to think. I cannot have a meal tonight! Must tell Mum truth – so I can go home at weekends etc! Good chance. Don't delay it. Spoke to Ravi. Called Mum back. OK, today's the day. Washed hair, cleaned room, got bus to Kings Cross. Had some more dried apricots by the way – scared. Met Mum 14:30pm. Oyster top-up. Bus-ticket. Home. Rained! Watched favourite daily chefs programme [as usual, I would come home from work to watch this and enjoyed it; it made my not eating easier and it made me feel safe]. Cup of tea / coffee. Deciding on evening meal or afternoon tea and train times / plan...Very thin, are you anorexic? Laughed loads, sorry Mum. Oh I had some crumpet and grapes while making the tea and while Mum was in the toilet, by the way. She asked how long no period. Over 2 years. Why not tell me? Can't believe it's happened to you...you had everything...why...what have you eaten? Come home. Mum was fainting, lay down, glass of water. Post came! Hid letter; opened it in the toilet. Appointment 3:00pm tomorrow. Coming with me! I cried a lot. Mum was fantastic.

5:30pm went tube to canary wharf shopping. Bought cardigan. Felt ill on tube. Tea / coffee at coffee shop. Had fruit salad and some salad / vegetables. Nice choice. Home. Get ready. Kings Cross. Met Sid. Drove to Angel, Covent Gardenish. Talked about today. Nice advice. Cranberry and soda x 2. Sid opened car door for me; he is an absolute perfect gentleman. Nice drive home right to my door. Actually enjoyed our kiss goodnight!

11:45pm got home. Ate two beans and sugar snaps from left over lunch – thanks Mum – plus couple of grapes, milk and hot water. Replied to couple of texts from Ravi and went on website. Sent Lucy a flower and Little Brother's wife. Can hear men's voices downstairs, bit annoying. I'm empty, might have to eat something. Drank some cold milk and water left over from when I got in.
Headaches. Anyway…my thought was: did Amir realise in his drunken state that that night he was speaking to Sarah and not me on the phone mainly!? I love you Mum. Hoping I am OK to go home at weekends. Finally.

3:30am: Cannot breathe. Not slept yet. Switched on Olympics swimming – butterfly. Ready to stay up until 6:30am rather than eat...

4:30am: Still battling over whether to eat something. I want to go to sleep…but I also want to wake up…thin...

5:00am: Still up. Just heard Big Ben really clearly!

CHAPTER 19:

HOSPITAL ADMISSIONS ONE, TWO,

AND TWO POINT FIVE

19i-Hospital Admission One - Informal:

"But it's just me, Micci...I don't DO this! I can't!"
My Mum and I were left waiting for two hours owing to "staff shortage because an incident has occurred in the dining room", we were told. Mum was in tears. She kept saying, "I wish your Dad was here". I was trying my hardest not to pace the corridor, unable to sit still next to my dear Mum, instead all-the-while determined to at least stand and never – *don't you dare!* – consume even a single green grape or a crumb of cracker that I had taken to carrying everywhere with me in my bag, just in case, including here. The nurses arrived, introducing themselves and then lead me through the locked doors away from my Mum and into the clinic room to see the doctor in order to start the admission process with an interview and examination.

I remember now collapsing and Carole, the Charge Nurse, announcing "I'll bring some milk". She turned to me and asked "how do you like it?" In my confusion and state of disarray by this time, I answered "I don't really drink milk..." and upon reading her face in reaction to this "...skimmed, with mostly water" followed by a shy "please". I remember her response well, because I was left trying to work out exactly what she had meant by this statement: "we work against the anorexia on this ward" and on her return, she stated "it's semi-skimmed. We don't lie to the patients here. You don't have to use the straw; I just thought it might help". When the nurses searched my bag before my Mum left, they took away my grapes and my bits of broken up cracker wrapped in cling film! I immediately sensed fear inside of me and pleaded with the nurse that he let me keep it *"please, just in case, I'll keep it in my room! I won't tell anyone"*. I was shocked at my own words. I felt embarrassed. More-over, I felt terrified.

Mum said to me "just show them all how it's done and be a friend to everybody, you haven't really got a problem, you just need a bit of help to start eating again, that's all". I believed her as I thought like this too and so I took the advice of my Mum 100% on board, although my reactions to what I was expected to do, i.e. eat all this food, no choice about it, were more shocking to me than I could ever have imagined.

The inpatients had no choice about eating what was placed in front of them six times a day; we were all being made to do it. I was more confused than ever and didn't understand why they were all making me eat all this food that seemed to be the same as all the others who needed it so badly, unlike myself, and why did I struggle to eat it anyway? Why was I suddenly being swamped with these overwhelming emotions that I could not control?! I felt stupid. I found I only would have a voice and a high level of assertiveness bordering on aggressiveness when in the dining room and when I was being pushed and pushed and pushed into territory that gave me such intense fear. I was being asked or made to do things that I just could not do because it was far too scary and it wasn't what I did! I was forced to voice my concerns because it seemed I had no choice in eating this food, to my horrified discovery when the staff barricaded the doors to the dining room shut, standing in front of them, not allowing a single person to move a muscle until all patients had finished their complete meal put in front of them. If a patient went over the 45 minute time limit at a mealtime, then a high calorie energy drink was slammed down in front of them – in addition to their meal – and every patient was kept in the dining room until that one patient had completed their requirements in full, after explaining to the whole group of sixteen other patients of course, loud and clearly upon the staff's demand, the reasons as to why everybody was having to remain under this prolonged torture in the dining room for so much longer rather than being able to rest in the lounges all because *you* haven't eaten what you have been expected to. I just found again and again that I couldn't possibly! It wasn't right, it wasn't allowed, and it wasn't me. *I* couldn't do all this! Inpatient units are incredibly competitive places and I soon became the most hated patient on the ward, or so it felt.

I was able to note down my torments in my trusted diary, on my first full day in hospital, Saturday 16th August 2008, as follows:

"6am got up – exercised. Weighed. Plan was to not eat the bread and butter. Sat there from 8am until 10:30am. Cried and cried. Peer pressure. Ate the fruit. Not yogurt. Now cream, energy drinks, sugar, bean bags, aprons, moved tables, noisy etc. Had to eat it! Or they force-feed cream and thick meal replacement drinks. Lunch – fish and cheese sauce, swede, apricots and custard, coffee as lax. One hour rest. Couldn't '<u>S</u>' or have drink after that.

It's 14:45. Milk at 3pm. Then 20 minutes rest. Might sneak a coffee in and hope for runny pooh. Not sure what getting tonight. This *is* awful. Can't '<u>S</u>' after the hour! Dreading bread and butter tomorrow. I don't know what to do. Might have a bath later to exercise in peace!

18:00 – Macaroni *cheese*! Nurse took it away with lump of cheese hidden under the knife! Yogurt. Coffee. '<u>S</u>' yogurt a tiny bit. Text Rav back. About to start exercise. 21:00 for an hour. Macaroni cheese! I'm full of milk, cheese, butter. Dreading bread and butter tomorrow at breakfast. Can't wait to have some proper exercise! Feel bad because haven't spoken to Mum – she thinks it's easy "for me". I'm surprised at how hard it's been."

...And the next day...

"Nurse gave me loads of his time today speaking about my world and real world. Good chat."

...Almost two weeks later...

Dietician's Note – 27/08/2008:
Rebecca is finding it very difficult to eat, and has had meal replacement drinks on some occasions. She finds it almost

impossible to articulate the feelings she is finding so difficult, or even to tell whether they are physical or psychological.

Nurses Notes – 24/09/2008:
Rebecca really struggled with snacks today. Today it was Bounty Bar and Angel has not given herself permission to eat chocolate for a long time. She was given support and it took her one and a half hours to eat it. Praise was given even if it took her a long time.

I remember that chocolate bar nightmare. I had gotten myself through it by chopping it into tiny pieces with a knife and fork, separating the chocolate from the coconut and eating tiny bits at a time, first coconut, then chocolate, hating myself more and more. I couldn't believe I had done it. It didn't feel good; I had failed severely and cannot begin to write down the racing thoughts that were speeding through my mind. I was angry with that nurse who had sat there with me for making me do this! But she was one of the loveliest, most kind and caring nurses on that ward – she was my primary nurse.

But this *'me'* was allowed – or forced / encouraged – to come out from hiding in the safe confines and surroundings of hospital for the first time ever. I spoke little but enough for me about this, to other patients and felt such immense relief in that some of my thoughts, feelings, anxieties and fears were actually shared by others and I was no longer alone with my struggles and no longer alone with my own thoughts that I feared to be so abnormal! But I didn't give them chance to understand all of me and I couldn't expect anyone to as I didn't understand myself and I gave little of myself away as my mask was still firmly in place. I was confused, but at least I was no longer totally alone anymore, although I, as the majority of all other patients on that ward, may have appeared two-faced or scheming, but underneath *Angel's* shadows, Micci was still there.

But the support of the other patients who also had similar thoughts and struggles didn't help the depth of my struggles subside. Why was I the only one who was unable to control her feelings and actions? I felt stupid and laughed at. I felt they all thought I was an odd-ball and a fraud and why on earth is SHE here? Why on earth hasn't she just gone home yet?! I felt the patients and staff alike were laughing at me and wondering why on earth I hadn't discharged myself when I could have done as we could give the bed to a soul in desperate need of it like everyone else in here instead of me, but my Mum said I had to stay and I felt like I would fail everybody if I didn't and so I did complete the whole three months treatment, for her and for myself in order not to fail but it was absolute hell and I vowed never to return there, ever again. I understand that saying 'never say never' now, because I really did mean it when I said I'd never return to this ward ever, ever again, but...

After meals was the worst. I felt just terrible, so dirty. I felt humiliated and such a failure for having let them make me eat it and therefore be allowed to win and to laugh at me in my loss of control and I wanted to die in a deep black hole rather than continue living. Why did I cry uncontrollably and why did all these emotions come out in floods of such immense tears? Why were these images haunting me? Go away, don't think about it, don't let it hurt you anymore, be strong, you're still alive, you have everything in your life, get out of here, go back to it all, go back to being *you* and what *you* know is best for you! *You don't need this! Be strong and leave, right now, GO ON..!*

Psychological Therapist's Notes – 25/09/2008:

We spoke about a mini formulation of Rebecca's decline into anorexia:
Rebecca described always having been a perfectionist and always having been very driven and goal oriented at work. She then experienced two romantic relationships ending and the death of her father (whom she was close to) and over focused on her drive at work to reach the 'top' at the expense of her health. Around this time she started attending the gym more and restricting more and was then admitted to hospital. It is unclear whether there are more events that Angel holds back in discussing. She hints at this and then

257

moves off topic. She has beliefs about not showing emotions in front of others and 'just getting on with it' when she is struggling.

She is aware that I am on leave for two weeks and that she will be meeting with trainee clinical psychologist.

This psychology session was the best I had been involved with to date, but it made me angry and frustrated in that here was someone I felt comfortable with and she was leaving me to go off on leave for two weeks, plus subsequent to which she would be commencing her maternity leave and so I wouldn't see her again most probably. I couldn't deal with the rest of the treatment program. I exercised 24 hours a day: in between snacks and meals, in the mornings, after dinner, all evening, at night, throughout the night on the hour every hour. My alarms were all set in case I fell asleep and then it was disaster. When I was put on hourly observation checks where my door had to remain open, I would use the sound of the connecting door to listen out for staff and also the reflections in the picture frames that hung on the walls outside of my room to check that no-one was watching me. When my door was documented to be locked at all times, I would use the lounges and the corridors, wherever possible, as long as I wasn't being watched, I continued with my exercise.

I had my routines: I used to have a morning run in my room for an hour before breakfast every day, at nights I would run in my room and then go into the toilets and do laps in there with a mixture of wall presses in between and then it was back to running in my room. I timed everything down to the second and always a bit more, or a few more, just to make sure or just to make up for the lazy feeble repetitions that had been counted when they shouldn't have been counted, or it wouldn't work. I needed a change of scenery from my tiny room because my sight would go weird and wobbly and shudder and I would get annoyed with the same songs going round and round on the radio and then it happened by the time I'd finished my routine each time in the toilets too and so I would go back into my tiny room and start all over again. Sometimes I would be so thirsty and hot and sweaty and so desperate to get rid of those extra calories that I would drink the tap water to help wash them nicely away. I knew exactly how long my exercises took and how long I had to do each for and how it fitted into each hour; walk, run, jump, reps to the minute, timed to the second, exercises that I just made up completely, but I could feel my muscles working, so it was toning something and so it was worth it.

Mum, I am sorry: I would ask you to bring me more shampoo bottles just so I would have two of the same weights as equal weights to use on my arms while I paced in my room and would not have time to phone my family and would get angry if I had spent too much time on the phone to them instead of using the precious time exercising rigorously. Kerry, I am sorry for never answering your calls. But we never TALKED either. I would also pretend to read the huge dictionary in the lounges during rest periods while lying on my back with my arms up. By the end of the hour rest, my arms would be killing but I had won over a little control and it felt more OK that I had then suffered for that meal I had just eaten, a bit more – just the slightest thing made a huge difference to how I would cope in the next few hours / minutes / seconds of each day in that environment.

Then the night checks would be coming and so I would be sure to jump into bed when I heard the door opening on the dot, every hour. I would hold my breath so that I wouldn't be caught panting. On the hour I would either pretend to be writing in my diary or sleeping or just standing at my desk, sitting on the floor, unable to sleep and clenching my mobile phone or reading some material or writing in my diary.

I couldn't sleep. I couldn't rest. Not after eating all this food. My brain was on overdrive and I had far too much energy that I had to get rid of somehow and I didn't want to think about anything. I wanted to feel exhausted and empty and numb and counting my repetitions distracted my brain as it was able to concentrate on something repetitive, timings, always busy, always moving, get it all done, plus a bit more just to make sure...

Selection of Hospital Notes:

...Right ankle has intense swelling...She needs to see the ward doctors for an examination...Rebecca was observed limping and dragging her right leg...Superficial abrasion noticed on her

259

hand...Rebecca has been observed by staff to be walking with a limp...Right ankle swollen, left ankle worsening...Possibility Angel has been exercising during rest period. When inquired by staff, Angel specifically denies it. Staff continues to have similar concerns regarding possibility of Rebecca having sustained right ankle injury...Recently staff has also noticed some abrasions on her arm. When specifically asked about it apparently Angel reported to staff that she slipped in the bathroom. Details unclear...She was seen by a member of staff exercising in her bedroom doing press-ups...Observed Angel exercising in the adolescents area...Angel was seen by a member of staff exercising in the quiet lounge this evening...Angel was active at start of shift, observed in corridor...Continues to do regular exercise on the ward...Angel has been caught exercising in her room and has been told she might have to have meal replacement drinks in additions to her meals if it happens again...Angel was seen by staff exercising this morning in her room and when she was asked the reason of her action she said she was anxious about breakfast...Pass was cancelled for two days as Angel was observed to be over-exercising...Her door has remained open to monitor her (over-exercising in bedroom)...Night staff reported that Angel has not been sleeping at night and has been engaging in over-exercising...Reports have been made that some staff have witnessed her to be running around the hospital grounds during passes...

I couldn't concentrate on reading a book or on the television as my mind just wandered and I would have no idea what I had read or what I was staring at on the television even. It was the same every day, over and over again. If I missed something or something went wrong or I had been disturbed, I had to get rid of something, hide something and not eat it at all, work extra hard on reps and running and pacing. I just had to. I continued to the point where my knees would feel like giving way they would feel so weak and even one of the nurses used to say "you can't walk straight" and "we need to sort your wonky knees out" and my feet would be so painful I could hardly walk properly down the corridors or in a straight line and it was really had to work at hiding any struggle in walking as it was so painful and weak, but the fear that I would be put on supervision or that I would be given extra meal drinks or that my life in there would be made any more unbearable than it already was, terrified me.

Nurses Notes – 18/09/2008:

Rebecca struggled with afternoon snacks, and was tearful. I met with Rebecca for 1:1 session. She expressed feeling angry that the anorexia had changed her personality from being pleasant to becoming stubborn. Said that she now realises how much the anorexia had affected her social life and other activities. Angel informed me that she does not exercise in her bedroom, later I was informed by a member of staff that Angel was in her bedroom over-exercising. Remained settled for the remainder of shift.

I hated how I'd become so secretive and deceitful. The scales every morning was a lot to deal with and it scared me stiff. That figure at 6am every morning, would rule the rest of my day: good if the figure had decreased and very bad if the figure increased. If it stayed the same I had to work extra hard to ensure that the next day it went down. I remember on my last day, when I was about to be discharged the nurse came into my room in front of my Mum and said there was no weight recorded for me that morning and that they quickly just needed to weigh me before the consultant could agree the discharge! I was immediately reluctant and said I can tell them what it was and rummaged through my diary, desperate to find it in writing for them. I'd written it down myself. I was refusing by prolonging tactics, as much as I could, because I had been falsifying my weight by drinking water each morning, every day for the last month. It had made me ill doing this every morning and every time I had to come back to the ward on the train. It had all taken *a lot* of time calculating and planning. I felt awful and deceitful, but I *had to do it in order to ensure I was discharged from this place.* I had no option but to follow the nurse and right at the last moment, there was a knock at the door to say that the charts had been found – such a narrow escape for me, I just wanted to leave right then and there, quick, get me out now! After I had left, the belief dawned upon me that this was done on purpose in order to gage my reaction, but to let me go and maybe just expect to see me back further down the line. There was nothing else they could do for me. They had saved my life by feeding me up, but they knew I would be back as my issues would come back to haunt me. They had seen it all too often. When I left, one nurse casually stated: "see you in three months' time". Not me. No way.

Mum was amazing throughout my stay, but at the time I kept thinking "why is she making sure I stay here when I could be back at work? I'm OK now. I'm fine! I'm eating again! All this food and that's what they all wanted!" I thought I could always trust my Mum to help me and to sort things out for me, but not in there. I remember the charge nurse coming to get me from my room when Mum had come to visit me and he said I needed to go back to the dining room to have my (high energy meal replacement) drinks because I had not finished my pudding earlier. I was pleading with Mum to stop him taking me because *I didn't need all that food.* I was crying and begging but he calmly took hold of my hand and forced me back down to the dining room telling me that because my heart was so weak he didn't wish to force me any longer and could I please walk properly. Once again, I was there for hours through my defiance and sheer tears of confusion where the dictates of *Angel* were winning all over. But I knew the consequences if I didn't eat or drink.

Afterwards I would be furious and angry and depressed and would be made to sit down and have rest period – I would always choose the quietest corner to be alone with my thoughts and tears. I just wanted to be removed from this world. Furthermore, after this torturous episode, I could trust nobody. Not even my Mum because how could she let them take me away and agree with them and even say to me "It's only a drink Rebecca, just go and drink it and then come back!" How could she say that?! My mum didn't understand!

When I was later allowed out on my 'passes', I would race right into the woods that I'd sought out close to the hospital and would do laps upon laps upon laps while trying to get rid of anything that was still left inside of me at the same time right until my time had run out and I had to return to the ward. What a life I had managed to get myself into! I wanted to go home badly and had no desire to put on any more weight at all. I admit I did feel better within myself and my personality came back a little, which I loved, but I hated the way I looked and just felt unbearably fat and stuffed full to the brim and I hated this. I felt like I couldn't eat for the rest of my life I was so full. I was scared about getting back my period and that was a major reason behind all my excessive activity levels and not eating so many potatoes and the continuance of my 'S'.

Especially one time in the dining room when I was refusing to eat my dinner, all I could think was 'you're all stuffed up, no way can you eat this plate of food with stuffy potatoes – you'll get your period back for sure!' I remember Carole sitting with me, the other 17 patients staring at me, shouting at me, accusing me of being selfish, giving me hugs and support – but after it all – *I* would be the one left alone, crying uncontrollably in a pile in the corner behind the sofa, wrapped up and hidden, desolate and shamed, away from the world in a blanket, sobbing out my heart in fear and dread and listening and believing my screams... 'How could you! Now there's no rest for you...! They got what they wanted...how could you?! ' and so on and so on... No! I didn't want to feel stuffed. I didn't want these emotions. I wanted to feel numb and there was no way I was risking getting through all those stuffy potatoes, *I* couldn't, because I wasn't good enough at my illness like all the others were. They could do anything and eat anything and smile to everyone, but I couldn't. You shouldn't even be here! They're all laughing at you, confused why you have the nerve and the dismal face to even sit at this table and eat the same food as the other patients here. You should be staff helping them! What are you doing here! I did try to tell my primary nurse that 'I don't want my period back, I'm scared', but her response was just that they are normal and that every healthy woman has to have them. That was it, so I kept my thoughts to myself, silly girl.

When I left hospital, I went straight back to my life with only fifty minutes a week to attend my outpatient appointment for "support" (as they all called it and this term I never understood). Whilst going straight back to the big wide world to live and work, I was faced with all the stresses and worries of life returning to me and I immediately defaulted or "relapsed" using the only coping mechanism I knew – return to the security of *Angel Just-Rights*. Smile and avoid. The following diary entry is taken from the day after I left hospital, Friday 14th November 2008:

"Stayed in all day. In bed. Television, internet. Got up 11am when Mum called. Skimmed milk and water – hot. Strawberries, slices of apple, coffee. Bed. 15:00 – same, plus cereal. 16:00 – fruit and apple slices, tea. 22:30 – cereal. Bit of bagel as well and prunes (about six today). Zero activity though. Fat. Dunno what I'm gonna tell Pam - THE TRUTH. Struggling. Truth! Long day catching up on sleep. Depressed. Zero exercise. Tomorrow must do weight, Hoover and tidy room."

...And the next day...

"Amy text wanting to meet for lunch. Too scared and depressed and fat. Told her I was going to see Kerry. Jay rang. Missed it. She wanted to meet up at the shops. Feel awful. Mum rang at 12:45 – getting breakfast – Mum wants me to go home. I can't face eating and would have to there. Little Brother rang – spoke to him. Had cereal and milk and water, three prunes, about six strawberries and a bit of bagel and tea. Feel guilty. Will wash hair after Hoovering etc. in order to burn. Need to go shopping for an apple. Run out of chewing gum. This is no life. I'm depressed. Need to tone arms and body again. NO EX. Amir text loads. Clapham with Sarah and Lucy."

I hadn't dealt with anything at all in hospital and just wanted to lose a little bit of weight, to be happier, to be *just me* again, but it kept going and going down and down. I walked everywhere even though my bone density scan had now told me that I had Osteopenia and in parts of my body my bones were now just point one away from Osteoporosis but still, I missed work instead to walk anywhere and everywhere and to go running at the gyms; always a bit more than the day before. I couldn't eat a thing without it coming straight back up again, even a slice of melon in the end. The more I counted calories, the more I became afraid and the more I became exhausted. I would spend ages in the supermarkets. Once I broke down in the supermarket, abandoned my basket and ran out crying.

Whatever it came to, it had to be less. It was always too much. I was terrified and just wanted to be normal and I didn't know what to do. I remember not getting my way after making a point of being assertive in my Performance Development Appraisal at work and I was so upset that I packed up my things and left work, crying all the way home via the shops and I knew what was coming and didn't want anybody to stop me. I felt alone and shut myself away stuffing my face... I knew it was coming and I gave in to it but it was my only way of coping. I couldn't deal with life anymore. I was worth nothing. Failed again. I realised I was totally out of control, I never wanted to do this ever, ever again. After S every last bit, I was exhausted, my heart beat irregularly and my eyes were throbbing.

I turned to severe anorexia. I was still striving for perfection and still believing I could reach it, with the only friend I wasn't afraid of: *Angel*. But as part of my therapy work, I was told to write a letter to myself in the way of thinking about where I want to be in three years' time. This I found to be extremely difficult, although I managed the task, which was written a month previous to what was to be my second inpatient hospital admission (Appendix A: Letter to Rebecca).

Still, at this point in my life, I just knew I couldn't eat, nothing would make me eat. Even feeling so ill, fainting in my flat on numerous occasions, banging my head on the corner of my chest of drawers, having panic attacks and being taken off to hospital after lying on the floor of my flat having collapsed unconscious for which must have been a significant period of time, being taken in ambulance to A & E all scared stiff and alone, yet I still couldn't eat and most definitely outwardly refused to be admitted to any kind of A & E ever again for fear of being put on a drip as I was threatened with one time – this was my absolute worst nightmare I would never allow.

I wanted to punish myself. I had to. Maybe I partly was trying to avoid the stress and maybe I feared the growing responsibilities I was facing at work and was avoiding these, no matter how much I enjoyed my job and the people I worked with, I was hurting and in confusion and my self-esteem and confidence had completely plummeted. I had to feel in control and the only way I knew how, was to withdraw within, running to *Angel* and clinging to those empty promises and lies that I'd prioritise over everything that really mattered in life. Losing weight was now my achievement. It was a guarantee that I wouldn't 'get fat' if I did what I believed I should do.

Angel Just-Rights

My life became tinier and tinier but bigger and bigger in compulsion and chaos. I soon ended up back in the place I said I would never return, not me, never: inpatient hospital care.

I could not believe that this had become my life.

19ii-Hospital Admission Two - Informal:

"It's all TOO MUCH! ...Why is it so hard for me to just comply?
What is this great fear?!"
When I arrived at the private hospital late at night with my poor
Dear Mum right there by my side, I collapsed on the bed straight
away. I was glad of the level of help I was given in here although I
hated being restricted to having to be wheeled down to the dining
room in front of everyone in a wheelchair when I could still walk! It
was slow and gradual and I could deal with this rate of increase in
taking food. I managed to give myself another week of losing
weight while I was here because I had stretched the truth a little in
my first interview and told them I had been eating less than I had. I
felt terrible for doing this, but I was scared stiff that I would be put
straight onto a full diet that I wouldn't be able to cope with and so
they put me on a restricted diet beginning in quarter portions and
with this I felt relief.

I still exercised in the bathroom, but not so much. Only stretches
and star jumps as it was forbidden to exercise in the bedrooms and I
could not risk being sent away to that other hospital like last time.
My room was comfortable (I even had my own television and my
own heater) and my quarter portions remained a relief. I was always
grateful for my smallest portion and dreaded it being increased as no
way could I ever eat that which the others were expected to. I wasn't
even made to drink the high calorie substitute drink I found out
when I refused it after struggling to complete a meal once.

This is where I faced my fear of spread though. I managed it in
quarter portion once, which was more than I had ever done
throughout my first hospital experience in London, where I was
allowed peanut butter instead of butter or margarine on everything,
even with the omelette meal, ploughman's meal, cheese and biscuits
etc. So I was pleased at my progress with this. I still had a lot to
overcome, but for me this was a big step that I was proud of and
from this I felt a sense of achievement.

My funding ran out and I was unable to stay in this hospital, where I
was losing weight anyway and the plan was to transfer me to the
first hospital. Although I was adamant not to be transferred here and

267

I found my meals here increasingly difficult to complete on hearing of this terrible news, there was no choice in the matter now for having lost even more weight even while in hospital. I was told that not only was I in the critical stages of Anorexia, I was also deteriorating and was on the verge of a cardiac arrest due to heart arrhythmia and was warned that I would be put immediately under section and taken against my wishes into treatment, should I disagree to the transfer.

I was transferred by ambulance, with my Mum at my side. Upon arrival, I informed them that I wanted to get better and I meant it. It was easier at the start as the new soft diet enabled me to choose things I felt just about OK with and I had watery frozen omelettes every night for two weeks, which meant I began to feel OK with eating this meal. I struggled immensely with the dreaded thick and creamy Greek yogurt at breakfast times and refused to come down to the dining room one morning to face it until all the patients were made to leave their own breakfasts and to come up to my room to help me decide to come and have breakfast with them. Their peer pressure made me agree to at least come to the dining room and sit there, so their cereals wouldn't be going anymore soggy than they already were, thanks to my selfishness.

I spent hours in that dining room. Thankfully they compromised with me and allowed me to change this to the thin and watery soya yogurts, which I accepted as long as it was raspberry (which had least calories, was purple and was full of fibre rather than fat like in the Greek yogurt) but I kept my reasoning to myself. The fact it was also thinner and runnier in consistency than the Greek yogurt that would coat my throat meant I didn't have to sneak in the water from my hot drink in order to make it more edible. The texture was more just like a drink and it didn't taste of much either and so there was no risk of getting caught 'watering it down' and therefore having this soya alternative replaced with another bowlful to get through. Obviously I didn't speak any of the above reasons aloud to the nurses as they would be considered "anorexic" reasons to 'avoid' certain food types, and thus unacceptable to be changed, ever.

Dietician's Notes – 18/03/2009:

Angel Just-Rights

Angel particularly dislikes foods with a thick fluid texture such as Greek yogurt and custard. I have agreed that she can replace the drink of choice at breakfast with 200 ml semi-skimmed milk, and omit Greek yogurt, until she is having the full breakfast, when she can choose an alternative.

I began to open up a little about my past and about my struggles with eating and about my present struggles with eating, now that I wasn't constantly terrified with all I'd be faced with in the dining room and not being able to manage even touching it with the spoon. I dreaded my sessions with my therapist, but she was the best I could have asked for and I began to feel comfortable with her and we worked together well, I felt. I tried to talk as much as I could, but I got stuck. I wasn't allowed to say anything. It's a secret, it can never be told, and it can never come out, buried forever. Forgotten forever. I stopped talking and instead tried to talk about how my week had been and how I can help myself when I'm off the ward, which was helpful to me too, in the short term. But I knew that I needed help in moving forward with my life as I knew I still could not do it on my own; I know that whatever I do, whatever plan I put in place, always a disaster. I need help therefore I need to really open up and talk in order for someone to be able to even know where to begin in helping me.

But I can never talk.

My voice had been lost again. I was stuck. I remember writing notes just saying 'Thank you' or 'Sorry' and passing it to members of nursing staff. I would walk away slowly, acknowledging that I appreciated their help, support and understanding, even if at the time it had seemed so unfair or completely wrong and I had shouted and screamed at the staff in my distress, but on reflection I could see the logical reasoning of it and was so, so, so, so grateful and thankful to the staff for acting upon helping ME and putting their foot down and I wanted them to know that Rebecca could see their reasoning and appreciated their help so much. Yet I could never say so or admit it with my own voice. It was only when I really tried on my passes that I realised and had to accept that my expectations of actually doing it if I really had to were totally unreal. My belief that I could stop my behaviours, at any point, was totally untrue and false. I had been kidding myself all along. Were they all right after all?

But when it all got too much, I would simply run away.

Nurses Notes – 08/06/2009:
Telephone call made to Rebecca's mobile, no answer and message left. She returned the call moments later, she reported that she was at her flat and had been trying to return to the ward all day but was finding it difficult. She stated that when on the ward she is faced with all her problems and experiences flashbacks, which she cannot cope with. We talked about how she was coping at home, Rebecca said that she still needs help and wants to carry on the work she has been doing as she feels this is the only way she will be able to get on with her life. She agreed to come back to the ward tonight, she estimated it would take two hours so should be on the ward by 11pm.

Psychological Therapist's Notes – 09/06/2009:
We explored what had led to Angel going AWOL (Absent With Out Leave) and the difficulties associated with permitting herself to return to the ward. She feels overwhelmed with flashbacks and memories and this plus working towards improved nutritional health was becoming unbearable and she felt that she needed a break from this process. We considered the pros and cons of this approach, as well as how difficult she finds it to ask for/accept help and support, but how important this is for her.

We continued with exploration of her past experiences. Rebecca finds it very difficult to hold responsibility where it belongs, leading to her being self-persecutory and full of self-blame. However, through exploration we could identify that she feels anger towards her parents for not recognising what was happening to her, as she was unable to communicate her distress openly.

Psychological Therapist's Notes – 16/06/2009:
It seemed important for Rebecca to be able to explore the reasons why she is finding it so difficult to return to the ward after periods of leave, leading to a situation in which she loses weight which in turn prevents her from being able to access practical aspects of the programme that would be particularly beneficial for her (such as canteen group, cooking group, shopping).

Rebecca found it extremely difficult to initiate discussion around what happened at the weekend because of feelings on 'shame' surrounding her behaviours. Initially she was extremely reticent to speak about this but, with encouragement, she was able to explain that she had binged and vomited on her first night at home. This used to be a regular occurrence and she was trapped in the starvation/binge cycle, which she had been able to manage to date on the ward.

Thus, due to the fact that she had binged and purged, she believed that she must have put on a substantial amount of weight, and therefore could not return to the ward and associated treatment programme until she had lost this weight. We discussed this cycle in more depth and thought through some strategies that she has attempted to utilise in the past to manage this, as well as means by which she could potentially begin to work on this cycle now.

Rebecca does find it exceptionally difficult to talk about herself and symptoms, and to ask for support. She believes that she should be able to manage independently of others, but is beginning to recognise that this is possibly not the most helpful or appropriate strategy for her.

Occupational Therapist's Notes:
Cooking Group – When shopping, Rebecca did appear anxious about the portion size of the prawns and needed reassurance. When selecting her vegetables Rebecca again struggled with recognising a suitable quantity but responded well to guidance. When cooking, Angel tried to negotiate on the weights and appeared to be quite anxious at times. She cooked her meal independently but again needed to be reminded about quantities and then required reassurance...Rebecca still appears to be struggling with portion sizes and tends to try to quietly push boundaries....OT observed that Rebecca appeared to be role modelling to fellow patient who was obviously struggling. Although Rebecca appeared anxious at times she coped well and was given positive feedback.

Psychological Therapist's Notes – 21/07/2009:

...It seemed important to appreciate that the healthy part of herself had been able to return to the ward and that she remained motivated to work towards recovery. However, we also worked towards thinking through means by which she may be able to approach staff to talk through her anxieties and fears rather than holding them inside and leaving the ward, as she would do usually. It seems, at a more general level, that Angel struggles with any form of confrontation which means that she is left feeling misunderstood, unheard or ignored which is hard to tolerate, and we were able to draw links between this incident and her not being heard throughout her childhood when she was in a highly traumatised state. Through this, it does seem that Rebecca is prepared to work towards approaching others and working through difficulties instead of internalising problems.

Rebecca continues to experience flashbacks leading to her feeling frightened and/or terrified. We considered means by which she could approach these memories in a slightly different way, not berating herself for her weakness or thinking through how she could have done things differently; rather treating herself with compassion and kindness for surviving these experiences in the best way she could at the time and turning her anger and frustration towards those who placed her in these frightening positions. Rebecca is going to attempt to work towards this during the week.

Psychological Therapist's Notes – 02/09/2009:
Rebecca engaged well in discussion regarding her brother's wedding, which was difficult for her to manage. She has a tendency to focus on others experiences rather than her own, but was able to relate how uncomfortable she felt in this environment, both because of others comments towards her and the sense of loss of the years between her sister's and brother's weddings. She seems to be left feeling unheard and misunderstood. Through exploration of her experience at this event, we could identify the feelings of irritation and anger towards others and Rebecca could recognise for the first time her own anger towards those who have 'hurt' her for leaving her with feelings of loathing and disgust. We were also able to explore anorexia in relation to these 'hurters' and how reflective the illness is of the external 'hurt' she has suffered.

Through this exploration Rebecca did seem more motivated and determined to begin fighting back against the anorexia and we were able to consider what would happen if she did not start to battle against it. She is going to draw up a list of challenges to anorexia in terms of what she is 'forced' and 'coerced' to do by the illness and what, in comparison she wants and needs for herself. Through this it will hopefully be possible to start to develop small goals and essentially 'harness' her negative feelings into positive action against the illness.

19iii-Hospital Admission Two Point Five – Formal Under Section:

"Nobody can help me because I can't let them and I can't help myself".

After the room search revealed the weights that I had hidden in the lining of my bedroom curtains and also the weights that I had sewn into my shorts that I wore to be weighed in the mornings, in addition to my bottles of water, my stash of chewing gum and coffee wrapped in tissues, sachets of vinegar, my hoard of anti-depressant tablets that I had taken to hiding amongst a box of teabags in my wardrobe, and my pedometer, I tried to carry on with the treatment, but stripped of all my "safe" and "anorexic" coping alliances, immediately I was finding "it's all too much!" I was experiencing those spontaneous eruptions of overwhelming stress, panic and fear and I asked to leave by discharging myself that day. My holding section was, that afternoon as I recall, altered to a section fixed to last a whole six months. Suddenly and drastically, now my weight was 5kg lighter (which was lighter than they had apparently calculated) my life changed:

I, *Angel*, was terrified at what they would do to me and make me look like and I immediately rejected everything and star-jumped and exercised continuously in my room in the dark with my curtains closed and my lights off and towels stuffed under the door to stop any shadows escaping, constantly and without ever stopping, every single second of every single day and every single night when I wasn't in that horrific dining room. When my feet and knees, brain, eyes, teeth, hands, shoulders, back, hips could take it no longer, I introduced other exercises that I could do in between the running and the jumping. Always be active; weight must not move up, even by point 1. This was serious. I was absolutely petrified. Everything had to be frozen. No change what-so-ever. I was put on anti-psychotic drugs prescribed to me without my consent, I refused to take this medication and would be warned each time by the lovely night-staff that "if you refuse to take it, we will call the emergency team and ensure administration another way". I hated that this Olanzapine made me so lethargic and drowsy and I was petrified of the size affect: weight gain.

At the same time however I, Rebecca, had felt the hugest "weight" being lifted from my shoulders as I was no longer choosing to do this for myself. But I still couldn't actively help myself in any way or indeed let them help me either, because I was so petrified and so my life became a living hell.

Nurses Notes – 07/10/2009:

...Angel remains detained under Sec 3 MHA 83...She has not been eating for the past two days...Rebecca has remained upset and will need support to start re-feeding.

Psychological Therapist's Notes – 08/10/2009:

...Rebecca explained that it is impossible for her to manage her emotions in any way and the only means of doing so is through symptoms and distraction, which she has been currently utilising to date. The main emotions she struggles with are fear, terror, anxiety, and anger and she feels that these will become overwhelming, unbearable and impossible to tolerate so she has no option but to utilise the strategies she has developed in order to prevent them from escalating. In addition to concealing weights (as were found in a recent room search), she also utilises purging and exercise as means of preventing memories and associated emotions from being experienced.

With regard to engagement in the treatment programme, Angel explained that she feels this to be utterly impossible as the emotions are too unbearable for her when she attempts to eat. We considered 'can't' in relation to previous work, rather challenges to be worked on and overcome. With this in mind, she has agreed to start attempting to engage with treatment and we talked openly and honestly about the alternatives if she continues to refuse.

Nurses Notes – 09/10/2009:

Following a further day whereby Angel has found it far too difficult to feed herself and concerns that she was restricting fluids, discussion with her Consultant and senior nursing team including her primary nurse, Angel was assist fed as a life saving measure. She had her afternoon snack with a lot of staff support. However she refused to have her dinner, staff tried to encourage and support her through her meal but this was to no avail.

Psychological Therapist's Notes – 13/10/2009:

...Angel was initially reticent to attend her therapy session...She is desperate to feel 'numb' emotionally and to feel an internal sense of cleanliness and symptoms of anorexia provide this for her; she is thus highly reluctant to work through the process of permitting herself to eat anything. She was able to recognise that she is feeling extremely angry and outraged regarding the assisted feeding, particularly as she feels she was doing her best to engage in eating over the weekend.

Through exploration of her recent experiences, we could identify how entangled her 'hurt' history is with her eating disorder, which makes working on one aspect alone very difficult for her to contemplate. She feels exhausted and hopeless that things may be different so has essentially given up trying. It seemed important to confront and challenge this position with regard to the ultimate outcome of her continuing to starve her body. She could take this on board and, by the end of the session, did seem willing to make an attempt towards feeding herself.

Angel has found it especially hard that staff and patients have been 'nice' to her as this is unbearable for her to experience. Rather, the experience of assisted feeding is more akin to what she expects and we could explore how her history is in some respects being replayed on the ward – we are the 'hurters' and that feels essentially safer because it is known. She did remain engaged throughout the session and is willing to continue this process when we meet again.

Nurses Notes – 14/10/2009:

Angel struggled this morning because she slept in and was therefore unable to do her exercise routine she usually does before being weighed and before breakfast. Angel needed support to get weighed as per her plan. Angel then went to the dining room and completed her plan, however she did try and negotiate less. Angel approached me for a one to one to try and reduce the meal plan steps that we agreed yesterday...

During my time out, when I was put on my own special compromised meal plan in conjunction with the work I was doing in therapy, I had the 'head space' to think about my life, my behaviour, my past, my future; everything. This is when my 'flashes of clarity' were shown to me and I was determined to write this down while I was in the moment (Appendix B: Hospital Headspace: Rebecca's Clarity Flowchart) and was able to take this along to my therapy session.

Psychological Therapist's Notes – 15/10/2009:

Rebecca engaged very well in our session today and it was possible to openly and honestly explore a range of difficulties that she is currently struggling with. Rebecca had completed a flow chart which outlined how trapped she becomes in various situations and, through consideration of a very simple example, we could see how trapped she becomes in life generally and within anorexia in particular.

We could identify that particular difficulties are concerned with remaining in connection with those who could potentially support her. Her expectation of others is that they will treat her poorly, being judgemental and critical at best and 'hurtful' at worst. In a way this is easier to accept as this is what she expects and fits in with her belief system that she does not deserve thoughtfulness and care and that others are dangerous. In this respect she is more readily able to push people away and remain essentially safe in isolation. It is more difficult to manage when she experiences positivity and care from others as this means that the other essentially 'gets into' her which feels uncomfortable and intolerable as this does not fit with her beliefs. However, the result is that, equally she has to push the care away and again remains in isolation.

When isolated and alone and not in relationship with others, the anorexia becomes more dominant and powerful and the only 'way of being'. However, through exploration, she could identify for herself that aligning herself with the anorexia was akin to aligning herself with another 'hurter', which is not something she wants for herself. Additionally, through attempting to turn things around on her own, she is also increasingly coming to recognise that anorexia does not provide her with the sense of 'control' she is seeking, because she cannot choose to 'act' against it.

Through this exploration, we thought together about means of beginning the process of managing the anorexia and associated eating, through working towards separating herself sufficiently from the anorexia to be able to be open to the support from others that she knows she needs. In the immediate term, we considered that she will 'freeze' when it is put in front of her and panic as a result. To assist her in starting the process, the member of staff placing it in front of her needs to say quietly and calmly 'it's alright, it's right'. She will then offer herself further reassurance through a cue card. I will meet with her briefly tomorrow to review the effectiveness of this approach.

Psychological Therapist's Notes – 16/10/2009:

...I shared my concerns with Angel regarding assisted feeding, in that it in some respects replays 'hurts' in relationships as she stated that, through this method, 'the staff are doing what they need to do' (something that she has stated in relation to the 'hurt' she has suffered). By physically giving herself the food, the only change for her would be to therefore physically do something different to prevent herself psychologically feeling as though she was essentially succumbing to further 'hurt'. This did make sense to Rebecca but I am unsure whether there was sufficient time for us to work through this concept fully enough to make a difference for her at this time.

Psychological Therapist's Notes – 21/10/2009:

...We continued to explore more fully the flow diagram Rebecca had presented a week earlier. It seems apparent that Rebecca struggles significantly with extremely black and white thinking, leading to a position in which she is either a failure / useless / pathetic / weak / helpless or strong / achieving / successful. Through this understanding we were more fully able to explore the positions she finds herself in situations more generally and on the ward specifically.

Through consideration of schema mode work, we were able to begin the process of labelling and naming her experiences and could see how she flips from one mode to another. On the ward she becomes the 'detached protector' (cutting off and distancing herself from others through various means) or the 'punitive parent' (self-berating and punishing herself for any supposed wrong doing) as a means of protecting her 'vulnerable child' (that vulnerable part of herself that is anxious, terrified, and fearful of harm). Through this exploration there was very little by way of the 'healthy adult', which could offer her reason, compassion and thoughtfulness.

As a result of this, Rebecca does feel it may be possible to explore again her experiences of 'hurts', i.e. accessing that vulnerable part of herself within the therapy, essentially working towards processing the experiences of the vulnerable child whilst building towards becoming a healthy adult.

Rebecca does find it useful to write things down to bring to sessions and I have encouraged this, although not expecting or structuring this (to prevent myself as perceived as the punitive parent).

Nurses Notes – 26/10/2009:

...The emergency team were called and Angel was assisted with feed. She was very resistive...Staff stayed with Angel until she had her shower. Angel was in the lounge with staff. Angel was engaging with staff and peers and she was saying she finds it very difficult to cope with dinner. She informed staff that she may take Promethazine pm prior to her meals.

Ward Round Notes – 27/10/2009:

...Psychologically she is generally making way. She appears to be a passive recipient of re-feeding and this is how she appears. She appears to be very emotionally cut off and has detached herself from the re-feeding process. She feels hopeless at the moment and struggles to have goals to work toward...

Psychological Therapist's Notes – 27/10/2009:

...Through exploration it was apparent that Angel utilised the strategy of 'justification' for managing the majority of her meals and snacks during the day, appreciating the fact that staff had made certain compromises regarding her menu plan and not wanting to 'lose' this. Through this process of recognition she is able to justify for herself managing breakfast, lunch and snacks and, seemingly because she has made an active decision to eat at these times, she does not feel out of control and overwhelmed by emotions.

However, she cannot find for herself justification for managing the evening meal and fear and panic regarding the possibility of overwhelming and unbearable emotions means that she cannot contemplate this meal. We explored her fears regarding emotions and it seems that she fears the 'humiliation' and 'shame' of showing her degree of distress to others. Developmentally, it seems that negative emotions particularly were not permitted expression and had to be concealed in order to maintain calm and equilibrium in the family home.

Thus, it does not seem that Rebecca has experienced scaffolding or containment for these emotions previously, and the uncertainty of what may happen in relation to emotional expression prevents a risk of doing things differently.

This did make sense to Angel and she could identify for herself that 'hurts' and 'punishment' (as she understands herself to be in the position of in relation to assisted feeds) is essentially more tolerable because it is known. In order to do something differently means managing the unknown which feels quite unbearable. We thus worked very hard to reframe her thought processes and, by the end of the session, Rebecca shifted perspective slightly, moving from a position of 'I can't' in relation to the evening meal to a position of 'I don't think I can' (which does leave the possibility for change open to her). We finally appreciated that it is exceptionally hard for Rebecca to trust others and to be supported by staff, as this is unfamiliar to her, but it does seem imperative that she can experience the containment that she can receive when experiencing distress, thereby enabling emotional expression and processing.

Primary Nurse's Notes – 28/10/2009:

...Mrs. Parker reported that there has been little contact with Angel as she does not appear to be picking up her mother's calls. Mrs. Parker reported that in her last conversation with Rebecca last night, Rebecca had reported that on waking every morning, she wishes she could have died in her sleep...Angel has not reported any self-harming or any suicidal thoughts.

Psychological Therapist's Notes – 28/10/2009:

...Angel was quite withdrawn and 'cut off' during the session, showing how she is managing her distress through 'numbing' herself to what is going on for her. We attempted to think through strategies she had utilised to be able to manage her evening meal yesterday, but she was not able to verbalise means she had used other than attempting to cut herself off psychologically from what she was doing.

It still seems that emotional expression in the presence of another is extremely difficult for Angel to contemplate but I did put forward to her the idea that, by remaining cut off from other sources of information/resources, the only relationship open to her was one of the anorexia. At present she is struggling to think further than managing each day and there was the sense that anorexia is the solution rather than the problem to be thought through, thus we named the ways anorexia has impacted severely and negatively on her life, that we had outlined together in previous sessions.

At present, it is apparent that Angel is struggling with ambivalence with regard to contemplation of change, and any thought of change is overwhelming as it feels insurmountable.

Dietician's Notes – 28/10/2009:

Angel is needing frequent assistance with eating. She is now talking about what she finds most difficult about eating, and we have agreed a meal plan which allows her to avoid the most difficult foods, and keeps the total volume manageable for her.

Angel Just-Rights

Occupational Therapist's Notes – 02/11/2009:

Art and Craft Group (on ward) – Angel attended the group and spent some time initially looking through the materials. She needed several reminders re rest period boundaries before she sat to start making cards. She was able to sit for approx. 4-5 minutes before she needed to get up and search for more materials, after choosing not to allow me to pass these to her. At 11:00am, after rest period, she chose to stand up for the last 30 minutes.

Angel initially was quiet in the session and spoke very softly. She did not join in with all of the conversations, but did grow more sociable after 11:00am. She started a shape making workbook and took the materials away with her to continue on the project in her own time.

Psychological Therapist's Notes – 10/11/2009:

...It does seem that Rebecca is developing a greater insight and awareness into the problems associated with the illness, rather than the illness as perceived as a solution to problems and, as a result, at present it does seem that she is motivated and willing to continue to work towards gradual and incremental change.

Finally, we were able to return to consideration of the 'huts' and the impact this has on her life generally and in relation to her anorexia. Rebecca agreed that, however frightening for her, it is going to be an important part of the process to 'name' her 'hurters' so that she does not continue to be controlled by their 'secrets'...

Dietician's Notes – 18/11//2009:

Angel has not been able to use the meal plan we agreed, and had lost weight. We have agreed a plan which is not likely to achieve weight gain, but should prevent further weight loss. It will need to be increased to achieve weight gain.

Psychological Therapist's Notes – 19/11/2009:

...Rebecca does seem very depressed at present and feels a sense of hopeless and helplessness regarding her current situation and the

future. She lacks motivation to engage in any activities and her day is spent in a negative ruminative cycle that impacts on her.

We considered the meaning of depression and means by which it is possible to begin to work towards change. Angel is very isolated at present and does not participate in ward activities. She remains much of the day in her room and only tends to socialise/spend time in the company of others in the evening. Thus, her day is spent ruminating on her current circumstances and thinking about fears regarding the next meal, which she could recognise is not helpful for her.

Psychological Therapist's Notes – 24/11/2009:

Exercise Group – Rebecca attended today's session. We spent the first part reflecting on the previous session and why this group was so difficult to stay in. Rebecca shared that it had felt very overwhelming to face up to her exercise problem but that she would like to try and tackle it for when she is discharged. Today's session focused on the CBT maintenance model of exercise and a scenario that illustrated it. Rebecca felt it was very relevant to her and became tearful at times but was able to reflect how much it reminded her of her problem.

The group was positive as members felt some relief at being able to understand their problem better and to realise they are not alone. Rebecca managed to stay until the end of the session this week.

I remember another event that had significance to me and to me only. On the anniversary of my Father's death, I was still in hospital and not allowed home. One of the nurses came into the lounge where I was lying on the settee and he said "Come, I got a job for you Parker". He wanted me to count all these bags of coins he'd collected from a charity event and wanted it all sorting out so it could be taken to the bank. I was glad of a job to get stuck into in all honesty, a job to do well, no matter how small, and to take my mind off everything, plus I was so bored and wanted to do something helpful. I thought how significant this was as I was asked to do this on this particular day and related it back to how my Dad used to call me 'Miser Micci'.

Maybe it was the best thing for me to have stayed in the hospital for that day and maybe I was in the right place for everyone after all the complications and misunderstandings and rising emotions that went with it all at this time (I was granted leave, then wasn't, then was, then wasn't and there were issues over the reasons for it being taken away around my Mum not being happy with it etc). I guess this helped me see from Mum's point of view too and to think of HER MORE and to even think that my Dad was looking down on me and was there for me in spirit too.

However, I began to lose hope of ever getting better in hospital, my hope was dwindling and I was giving up: A half-life was no life, and the life I wanted and thought I had, was impossible to get back now it was just too hard, I had tried and had nothing left to fight for Rebecca, that soul lost inside this wasted body, anymore. I had lost all hope and all my strength and could see no way out. What was the point? I'd done such terrible things to myself that I couldn't stop my unhealthy behaviours if I ate and if I didn't eat I still didn't get peace in my head. All I got, whatever I did, was incessant screaming from this horrendous bully and guilt and fear. I was not capable of leading a normal life, I was bound to get ill again or to remain ill, and that was no life at all – simply existing in a no-life as a slave to this soul-destroying eating disorder – for me to continue slowly killing my whole family more and more each day. I wanted to die and be left in peace from it *all*. At least then I'd be with my Dad; my Mum even said to me, "What you're doing is even worse than when your Dad died. At least there was an end to it all" and she was right.

Psychological Therapist's Notes – 01/12/2009:

Rebecca continues to feel trapped, despondent and despairing. She currently feels unmotivated and, through exploration, this seems related to the fact that she does not experience a sense of progress/moving forward. However, through reflection, she was also able to see that this lack of progress was also internal, that she was unable to prove to herself that she could continue progressing forward with regard to challenging her eating disorder...

...We continued to think together about disclosure of 'hurts' and how and in what context this may be able to happen for Rebecca. We thought about this in relation to anger between her and her mother, and how the 'secrets' of her past were preventing them from being able to enjoy a fuller and more open relationship. Rebecca became very tearful at this point and stated that she would like to be able to open up to her mother and be supported by her. We thought through means by which this could be supported by the ward in family sessions, but Angel feels that she would like to be able to achieve this in her own time and when on leave. However, she may be willing to think through how she may broach this subject in our session together.

Psychological Therapist's Notes – 04/12/2009:

Angel was feeling very distressed and tearful regarding changes to the seating arrangements in the dining room and the majority of the session was focused on what was causing her anxiety and considering this further in relation to her 'hurts' history, and means by which she manages her fears of harm in the present. Angel finds it incredibly anxiety provoking to be in a position in which she cannot be fully aware of what is happening. She is hyper-vigilant to any danger and, by placing herself in 'safe' positions, she manages her anxiety more effectively. By being placed with her back to the room with staff and patients walking behind her, she feels extremely unsafe and on edge. She was feeling motivated and determined to be able to manage her lunch, especially given the change to her care plan and not wanting to lose any passes she is being given, but was fearful that she would not be able to manage given the situation.

It seemed important to respond proactively to Angel's exploration of her fears, as she does find it so difficult to be able to disclose when she is finding something difficult to manage. As such, it does seem that she requires positive reinforcement for her efforts in this area. Thus, Nurse and I discussed the seating arrangements in relation to her past experiences and agreed that it would be beneficial to respond to this distress and alter the seating to accommodate Angel.

Psychological Therapist's Notes – 08/12/2009:

Exercise Group – Rebecca attended today's session. We began by summarising the Maintenance of Excessive Exercise Model which was introduced last week. Rebecca shared that from reflecting further on this model she was beginning to realise how her exercise was not helping her and was only making her thoughts and feelings worse in the long run. This led on to today's discussion about the thoughts and feelings associated with exercise.

Rebecca engaged well in the session and shared some of the positive and negative feelings associated with her excessive exercise. As a group we looked at new ways of feeling these positive feelings and new ways to neutralise negative ones.

For homework Rebecca said she will do craft/knitting to feel good and will talk to someone when she feels an urge to exercise.

Psychological Therapist's Notes – 10/12/2009:

Rebecca described feeling more engaged in the treatment programme and supported by the team, particularly now that she is feeling a sense of progression both on and off the ward...

...As a result of feeling more supported and engaged with the programme, Rebecca was able to think in the therapy session further about disclosure of her traumatic experiences...

...In relation to this, and thinking about her life more generally, Rebecca does recognise that she needs to disclose the 'hurts' to her family, her mother in particular. More recently she feels she and her mother are developing a closer relationship, more reminiscent of the relationship they had when she was a child. We explored this at some depth, in relation to the barrier that her eating disorder has created. Rebecca now recognises that, to enable this process, she does need to be able to talk to her mother about the 'hurts'. We discussed various options in relation to this and Rebecca is very protective of her mother and concerned about the impact of the

disclosure on her, but was able to take on board that the team are available to be able to support her mother through this process. I have discussed this with ... and we will arrange a time for this meeting.

Psychological Therapist's Notes – 11/12/2009:

The session was concerned with considering further the possibility of disclosure to Rebecca's mother during the planned family session next Tuesday. We explored Angel's fears in relation to disclosure and the potential impact this may have on her mother. Angel thought her mother would blame her for her traumatic experience but, through exploration, could recognise that this was probably a projection on her part, as she still holds the belief that she is somehow to blame for the 'hurts' occurring and being ongoing. Rebecca would like a closer and more open relationship with her mother and realises that the 'secrets' she holds about contributing and maintaining factors associated with her eating disorder prevent this from being able to happen.

Through this process, we attempted to continue the process of disclosure within the therapeutic relationship. We explored her earlier experiences within the home environment, but Angel was unable to disclose who the perpetrator was; she still feels that she has to protect him and thus by answering any of my questions she would 'accidentally let slip' who it was.

As a result of the work during the session, Rebecca feels that it may be possible to disclose the 'hurts' that has occurred in her adult life but believes that information regarding childhood 'hurts' would be too difficult for her and her mother to bear.

Psychological Therapist's Notes – 15/12/2009:

Family Session - ...Social Worker, myself and Angel met for a few minutes prior to Mrs. Parker joining us as Angel had decided that it would be inappropriate to do disclosure work during the session. She felt that it would be too overwhelming for her mother to hear about the issues that have contributed to the onset and maintenance of her eating disorder at this time, firstly because she would be left with the information and the two of them would not have an opportunity to talk further after the session and, secondly, because Angel does not feel she has spent sufficient time with her mother recently to be able to talk to her about the 'hurts'.

Thus, the session was predominantly concerned with the theme of communication, as well as means of managing over the period of Christmas leave.

Mrs. Parker was able to describe the distress she experiences in relation to Rebecca's illness. She feels desperate and somewhat helpless and hopeless to be able to be of help to Rebecca, which is expressed through anxiety and frustration. She described remaining in a state of 'shock' in relation to the illness, as Angel had concealed the extent of her eating disorder from the family until she was admitted to hospital a year ago; she described herself and the family remaining in a state of shock that they had not been able to move forward from. Additionally, Mrs. Parker struggles because she does not know what she can now do to assist Rebecca. She cannot understand the illness and feels confused and bewildered as she does not know where it stems from. It is as if 'the illness has come out of nowhere'. She feels desperately saddened regarding the impact that anorexia is having on Rebecca's life, particularly as she feels that, prior to the onset of the illness, Rebecca was doing exceptionally well in life.

It seemed quite clear during these interactions that Mrs. Parker was asking for answers with regard to underlying issues but Angel was not able to disclose during the session.

Both Rebecca and Mrs. Parker could recognise that the illness does impact on the closeness of their relationship. Communication is predominantly based around anxiety, tension and frustration regarding eating and leads to lack of mis-understanding on both sides.

What had been helpful in relation to this with regard to recent home leave was that there was a specific plan in place concerning menu planning, which both of them could work on together. This did enable them to enjoy some of the overnight leave, talking about life outside of the eating disorder. They both agreed it would be beneficial to have a similar plan for over the Christmas period, so that they both are working within the same framework.

During the session Rebecca did struggle to find her voice but was able to say what was helpful and unhelpful in relation to communication styles. Finally, we discussed discharge and the potential benefits of the day care programme. Both Rebecca and Mrs. Parker were able to vocalise their fears regarding discharge and what may happen in the future.

Psychological Therapist's Notes – 16/12/2009:

The first half of the session was concerned with reflecting on the family meeting that we had yesterday. Rebecca feels somewhat frustrated and irritated with herself that she was not able to disclose the 'hurts' during the meeting, particularly as she experienced her mother as being open to this and actively asking for explanations regarding the onset and maintenance of Rebecca's eating disorder. Through reflection, Rebecca does feel herself to be in a stronger position to be able to talk about it outside of a structured environment but to be supported by staff through this process. She is going to consider this further but also recognises that she will still be somewhat frustrated as her mother will not know the full extent of the 'hurts' (she is currently not ready to talk about what happened during her childhood).

We continued with our exploration of the 'hurts' and the impact of it on Angel's current life. Angel struggles significantly with flashback, particularly at this time of year, as the most current 'hurts' was worst during November to February. Angel finds it very hard to move out of the cycles of the flashbacks when it is occurring and it is as though she feels she has to 'play the video' all the way through. We discussed grounding techniques and means by which she can be more in charge of the process. For herself, she is going to attempt grounding through focussing on an object in the room she is in. However, she has also accepted that she may need some help from staff to ground her at this stage.

Psychological Therapist's Notes – 06/01/2010:

Angel Just-Rights

...Rebecca has found therapeutic intervention beneficial, particularly with regarding to considering her cognitive processes and challenging unhelpful thinking styles. Angel has also found it beneficial to begin the process of disclosure but is finding this work much harder to tolerate. She still holds a strong belief that she should be able to forget about the past and move on with her future and is continually frustrated when this is not possible for her. Additionally, she is a very private and independent person and it seems that needing to work through her traumatic past is a sign of weakness for her. We have been able to challenge these perspectives to a certain degree and, in this respect, she is more open to the possibility of working through her 'hurts' experiences. However, she does continually oscillate between positions and work needs to take this on board.

CHAPTER 20:

HELL OR HELP?

20i-Angel Parker's Hospital Hell:

Unhealthy Behaviours I ABSOLUTELY *HAD TO DO*, that I WISH and HOPE NEVER to go through, EVER again.

•   Shouting, screaming and swearing at my Mum down the phone over my own frustrations and fears making it always about the food when really it never was. Unforgivable.

•   Over–Exercising: Pacing and running everywhere; completing exact numbers of sets, repetitions, routines I had to get through in between dining room sessions and all afternoon from 4pm until 6pm where I could catch up and do 'always just a little bit more, just to be safe or just to make sure', until my head ached constantly from the sheer tension, my teeth grew loose through the strain, I developed hard bits of skin and abrasions on my hands through resistance on the hard floors and walls from repetitions, I couldn't walk on any part of my foot or at any angle on my feet without severe pain and they were swollen (which I could blame on oedema to keep the nurses off my back), my knees would feel like they would give way and snap at any moment and my back and body ached in the mornings, yet I kept going with it all, always plus more. I would Hoover my room three times a day and make my bed and walk the corridors and the only time I could sit down was when I was in the dining room or in rest periods and even then I had to get up more than any of the other patients in the room and I sloped off unnoticed many a time to the adolescents corridor to go running during the hour of 'rest period' slyly around the corner or even in my room, which sometimes was missed being locked as it was down that forgotten end of the ward. As soon as I got up after rest I wasn't allowed to sit down again until the next dreaded dining room experience.

- Absolutely being in pain through over-exercise in knees, ankles, feet, also in arms, back, brain, teeth – everywhere – but having to keep doing it, never, *ever* stop and if caught, at least jingle a foot or a toe or stretch something as much as possible. *Never* sit down! *Never* relax!

- Resorting to cutting myself in the showers to let out some pain. Something I never wanted to do but I had to find an escape for these overwhelming feelings that I was getting swamped with from eating all this food and feeling so full. Luckily, this never really worked for me as it just dripped away far too slowly under the water and it didn't hurt enough. I was never brave enough to cut myself properly for fear of it not being able to stop and then I'd have all my razors taken away from me, which would be another nightmare to deal with somehow. Only in the days afterwards did it hurt when it would rub against my clothing for weeks and I became scared of changing in front of my Mum when she had so thoughtfully bought me a new item of clothing to wear, always hoping I was the next size up and never was. I needed *more pain, more punishment* (assisted feed after assisted feed in later admission, as much as I absolutely and completely just dreaded hearing the rustle of plastic aprons walking down the corridors, getting louder and louder, signalling to me that they were coming for *me* and then hearing that knock at my door as they came to get me and force me down the corridor to be shoved on the beanbags and gagged with five syringes at a time congealing, suffocating and choking me literally with thick, globby high calorie milkshakes, replacement meals, liquefied mars bars, double cream etc. etc. etc.). One of the nurses noticed an abrasion on my arm the very first time I cut myself and was angry with me, saying "you've got a lot of work to do" before walking off. I dismissed it, but now I know he was so right. I used my upper legs for cutting after that and only dreaded being weighed in the morning in my pants and bra, but I got through this by managing to be weighed in shorts and a vest top that I would pull over the marks on my legs, and so I was allowed to keep the razors, thank goodness.

• Using laxatives to induce diarrhoea so I'd at least 'feel' empty. I had never turned to using laxatives until I was in hospital for the first time. I tried to use mints, coffee, prunes, or anything with a bit of fibre in but it was never enough to work through the amount of food I was consuming every day: 3,000 calories to put a disgusting figure on it, if not more. I bought a few different types of laxatives when on leave once and I remember wondering how much to take and when the best time was to take it because I didn't want to be absolutely running to the toilet desperate, only to find them locked for an hour or engaged. When I'd taken them, one of the patients asked me straight out after dinner that night, as she could apparently see I was in severe pain in the dining room and after the evening meal that night. All I'd managed to achieve was a severe stomach ache and wind. Great, I'd even failed at this. I didn't try it again. It hadn't worked and I was aware of the dangers and the lack of effects it had on actual weight loss anyway, so I left it alone as something I really didn't want to get into at all, feeling stupid for even thinking it would be a means to a 'quick relief'. I was just desperate to have everything out of me, the emotions of fullness and flashbacks, to feel *empty, uncontaminated, cleansed, drained of impurities, light and free and happy and back in control.*

• Chewing gum to the point where I'd have terrible stomach ache.

• Preoccupation with researching items from the menu on the internet so that I knew exactly what it was, how it was cooked, what it would look like, so I could choose the option that I could persuade myself must have the least calories, definitely the least fat, would be easiest to eat, then I'd have to work out how to eat it because I couldn't see myself getting through it at all, even picking up my fork and starting it for that matter, otherwise etc. I had to spend time planning the best way just to get through the meal in order to be able to even begin to feel (*hardly*) bearable with myself afterwards too.

• Wearing my pedometer and calculating exactly the very least I *must* do each day, plus a little bit more, because I can.

293

- Trying my absolute best to appear shorter in height than I actually am, in order for my BMI targets (body mass index) and thus weight targets to be lowered. That way I could reach the 'unsupervised table' quicker, where there were less beady eyes constantly upon you and a lot more opportunities to have more personal choices at snack times and puddings and the dietician was more likely to listen to you like a human being and participation in groups such as 'canteen group' and 'cooking group' was allowed etc.

- '<u>S</u>' after meals in my socks or in the cover of a cushion whilst hiding in the telephone booth after meals and waiting there for an hour until someone unlocked my door so I could slip into my room and quickly change my clothes then put my things in the wash straight away. Hide the guilty face; smile in the corridors; everything is fine.

- '<u>S</u>' my yogurt pudding and apple in the sink IN THE DINING ROOM KITCHEN while the dining room was still full of staff and patients when I was pretending to wash my hands in desperation to get this out of me. This vomiting reaction was natural now, especially after consuming things like chocolate and yogurt.

- '<u>S</u>' after meals in an unlocked bathroom, but failing that, into tissues and then into the bin and covering it over with tissues. If there were no tissues it would come out by the fire exit door in the adolescents area, which was farthest from anywhere and it lead outside; hopefully it would trickle out of sight, anything, as long as it was no longer inside of ME.

- On occasions where there were no unlocked bathrooms, no tissues with which I could hide my mess in the bin, too much to fit in the fire exit gap to trickle outside and out of site, when I had been stopped for leaving piles of tissues in random places all over the hospital, even stuffed into my clothing and down my pants, when there was no other way out and I was desperate, it started coming out in the corner behind the adolescents' plastic settee because I couldn't keep anything inside of me for that hour that the toilets remained locked. I had to get it all out of me and straight away. It was a reflux action that I just could not stop. I felt dirty and disgusting, full of 'seepings' from the poison I'd just taken in and full of overwhelming emotions that made me feel like I wanted to die right then and there and that was the most important thing in the world that I had to do as, in addition to these unbearable feelings of disgust, the screams of *Angel* were shrill and never shirking – my shadow did not leave my side particularly at these times! I didn't know what on earth to do with myself. I actually wanted to die.

I longed to join the others in the lounge area at 'reflection group', which started after evening meal, but as the staff were in there too, I was safe in that no-one would question my whereabouts at this time and *Angel* had worked out that if I positioned myself near the room of the group at the very beginning of the group in making people think I was in the group and vice versa, I could disappear without a soul knowing! I hated myself and my sneakiness, but if I could get away with it *I just had to.* The only other option was to try to tell someone, or to not eat, which would cause the other 17 poor patients to be kept in the dining room, hating me and shouting at each other until I explained myself to the other fifteen patients as to why I was not eating, like everyone else.

- Hiding food (in my pockets, down my socks, up my sleeves, even down my pants or left in my mouth as I left the dining room) and smearing food (between clothing under my sleeves, in my hair, under the tables, never into my skin for fear that the fat would penetrate into me unless it was my fingers, which I could wipe and wash) i.e. biscuits, thick pastry on the quiche, blocks of cheese, whole margarine sachets, nuts from the sponge puddings, egg yolks, sandwiches and the fillings, toast, pitta bread, burgers, buns. Also being falsely accused of hiding food, being marched out of the dining room and strip searched by nurses in the toilets.

- Hiding myself like a child in my room, under tables or behind the sofas or round the corners just wanting to be away from everybody, refusing to go down to the dining room and being forced by the nurses into the dining room and to my seat and having them blocking the doorway, the nurses taking my hands away and trying to force food into my mouth.

• Buying bottles of vinegar while out on my passes and stealing sachets to hoard in my room and downing three quarters of a bottle or numerous sachets before a particularly difficult meal in order so that I could even begin to even touch it with my fork, never mind get it down my neck and then keep it inside of me. I used it initially to help me get me through the meal. Just so I could feel safer in that my stomach had been lined, which prevented 'seepings' of horribleness into my body and thus stopping the contamination getting in, usually from the cheesy and greasy, oily meals mainly. It made it that bit easier to 'sit with' in the rest period, although it also made it so much easier to '<u>S</u>' afterwards too while absolutely burning my throat at the same time.

• Downing bottles of vodka and wine. In desperate efforts to make myself relax and just be able to eat the dinner without thinking about it for goodness sake. But this made things a thousand times worse and ended in even more struggles, embarrassment, more floods of tears, and more untouched meals.

• Drinking bottles and bottles of disgusting toilet water in the mornings that I filled up my empty shampoo bottles with before I was weighed. I couldn't show myself an exact and true weight on the scales – no, that was far too scary. It had not to have ever been real, instead it had always to be a bit more, just so I knew I was in control and I was convinced that every single other patient on the ward was falsifying their weight a lot more than I was for goodness sake! In addition, I feared that they would up the diet or put me on toilet supervision or take my passes away or do something awful if the weight wasn't going up. I was violently '<u>S</u>' in towels in my room or back in the toilets after having drunk so much water on a few occasions before breakfast. Sometimes it was just water, which was OK and I felt better after this. But other times it would be all this awful globular green stuff and water before breakfast that I was violently retching up. On a couple of occasions I felt very dizzy, I had blurred visions and felt extremely tired at the breakfast table in the mornings if I hadn't '<u>S</u>' the water out of my system before breakfast and I was still full to the brim with water, and then plus my three course breakfast and two drinks!

• Drinking shots of raw coffee granules mixed with cold water from my toiletry bottles before meals.

• Holding my breath to stop my heart from beating during the assisted feeds because when it got unbearable and *Angel* took over my acceptance of punishment and inability to even think about being alive tomorrow after all this cream etc., I just wanted to die. But I didn't want to make myself fat, if it was going to happen I wasn't going to take the blame for the state I would be left in. It wouldn't be my fault. I wasn't eating!

• '<u>S</u>' all my yogurts and assisted feeds into the plant pots / behind the sofas / into tissues that went into the bin, into the towels that I was made to sit in after the feed for an hour while on one-to-one supervision and I would lather up so much soap in the shower afterwards while washing my hair that I could manage to get rid of the rest of it, if not all of the remains, without the nurse's beady eyes noticing. I had to be extremely careful or I'd be going through it all over again. It went anywhere, as long as it wasn't left inside me. It had to get out of my body. Out of site out of mind.

• '<u>S</u>' everything else that was inside me into spare bottles, making sure everything came up after the rest periods was horrible and could go on for hours. Routinely I would wash them out ready and waiting for my desperate behaviours should they happen the next day. I had separate bottles for drinking water and for '<u>S</u>'.

• '<u>S</u>' while walking down the road after completing my whole lunch and my cheese and biscuits at dessert so that I could leave straight away to see my friends in London – anything to get away for an afternoon and to not do a rest period. I hated myself for this too and was crying out for someone to keep me in there please, at least until after rest – in which case I wouldn't have completed my lunch or have been able to go into London – and I found this prison-existence extremely unbearable, so this option they gave me was the only other option, they knew and I knew.

• Pulling out my hair where each hair had to be 'just perfectly right', indescribable are the specific regulations it had to pass before it could be pulled, but when each was found, there was a certain sense of dull excitement and relief followed by a feeling of pitiful gratification. I can liken it now to when I used to pull out my eyebrows (Book 1: Secrets Out, Part 2, Chapter 4). I still carry on with this when I'm alone – sometimes for long periods of time, knowing full-well that it is wrong and always underlying the feeling that I am destroying myself and must force yourself to stop it – but it doesn't help. I now have to wear my hair in a different style to hide the fact that it has all been pulled out in specific places. I hate myself for it, but still I will do it again.

• Counting calories, restricting, and worse of all the compulsions of food behaviours in the dining room that reached a terrible stage. I couldn't stand it, I just wanted PEACE from it all – I would think about it from the moment I woke up, calculating, calculating, calculating what the smallest amount I could get away with giving myself was. I made it up to a number of calories that I would maintain my low weight at so as not to induce any further attention on me by way of the dreaded assisted feeding. I know the dietician had calculated my maintenance diet plan to include a level of exercise, which I hadn't asked her to, and this annoyed me because I wasn't even exercising I don't think, and so I had to adjust this a little more. I was always compelled to overestimate the calories in my calculations in order to 'make sure': a nurse asked me "are you limiting yourself to 300 calories per meal?" I laughed at how he'd got it so wrong. I was aiming for more. I would spend all day calculating and calculating writing down and scribbling away in my room how I was to do it each mealtime. Each day. I was in hell. I wanted HELP; I just *couldn't let anyone help me.* I saw no way out

– no hope of peace with a normal life – I had given up. I wanted rather to be dead than to continue living through the sheer hell of this life. Just do the bare minimum to keep them at a safe distance from wanting to push me, give me any attention, put up the threat of more assisted feeds, the torture for which I didn't now crave – so long as the food and the feelings were kept at bay, I needed no other punishment.

• Spending my entire passes pacing and running up and down a shaded bit of the park area or even sloping off to the nearest gym for a work-out when I was desperate and lying about where I had been. Mum, that time you spotted me on the station platform, yes, I had been to the gym. I am sorry!

• Absconding from the ward when on passes / leave / being let out to attend Day Care and being hunted down by the Police and driven back to the Hospital in the back of their van in the early hours of the morning like a dangerous and convicted criminal.

20ii-Rebecca's Clarity; Parker's Harsh Reality:

I completed a time-line of my life (which I am yet to be brave enough to take to and to work through in sessions) when I was in hospital and on the period of time out to find my head space, I had moments of clarity (Appendix B: Hospital Headspace: Rebecca's Clarity Flowchart), only in-so-far that I shouldn't be expecting to be able to manage when I am out on my own, because I always thought that I 'could always just do it' if I needed to, but actually the reality of it is that I simply couldn't and needed to be able to admit and accept this sad fact in order to even have a hope of managing some kind of normality or reasonable meal plan and routine to ensure I can pursue a half decent quality of life, ever, ever again.

CHAPTER 211:

DAY CARE

AND THE MOTIVATION TO MOVE ON

YET STILL NO STRENGTH TO DO SO

My discharge from inpatient hospital treatment came on 11th January 2010. Prior to this I had been, sporadically, attending Day Care and returning to the hospital for the evenings. I was, at this point in November 2009, once again secretly falsifying my weight and clearly demonstrating an inability to take myself to attend the Day Care service and to carry out what was being expected of me and then to return to the hospital for the evening too. Consequently, I was put on supervision so that it was impossible for me to run away or escape en route, both ways. Upon discharge from the inpatient unit I found full-time Day Care a huge struggle at first, but at least I could please my anorexia by having my own time in the evenings and in going home at weekends rather than being imprisoned in that hospital 24 hours a day.

I was however, continually questioning myself, 'how do I move past this?' I would ask. I tried eating everything expected of me at Day Care and Rebecca began to feel better for it. This nutrition was helping me and keeping me alive. I would get terribly panicky in the evenings though, as if that plane was about to crash and there was absolutely nothing I could do. I felt like I'd done something terribly wrong if I ate and stuck to my meal plan at all after being in Day Care where I'd receive all this care and attention and such listening ears, the help and support, only to then go home and do it all again; but all alone! That was just craziness! I just stopped completely and made myself go out and see my friends in order to not be alone in the flat with my thoughts blasting around my head. I tried both to eat and to socialise a little, and it worked at first but I would get tired and freeze in the cold on the way home! Then I just saw my friends without eating and they were really good about not revisiting old haunts because I didn't want any reminders or to even start bumping into anybody that I didn't wish to.

One night in the past, I was with my friend Sarah and realised that she had chosen a seat in a bar right opposite none other than Spen! Obviously this had happened without her realising it as she had never met him before. I couldn't believe it. I discreetly informed her and we moved away. Luckily he was with a girl and I made a point of not looking over. We finished our drinks in hiding behind a pillar before leaving. I received a text from him saying "Hi to you too ;) x".

When I was meeting up with my friends in the evening however, I could do what was on my meal plan no longer. In this way, I didn't suffer the battles all evening in my head and had not this severe guilt extending to urges to commit suicide to contend with afterwards while on my own. I just had the guilt of not doing what I am told I should be doing and therefore apparently "not helping myself" to get better, but this guilt is just more like a bad feeling that is easy to just brush aside and to worry about another day. In other words, the easy way out, short-term, I suppose. Anyway, at least I was coping with Day Care, which was a step in the right direction. Maybe the rest will come slowly in baby steps, right?

I started to have dreams and couldn't sleep at night. I have always had trouble remembering my dreams, and then I stopped dreaming at all. But recently I have been having really vivid dreams that wake me up with a start and they're not nice. In the past, particularly in the Stalbany days, I had learned the only way of staying safe was in the company of my friends: dancing in their company and staying in crowded places for as long as possible only to return home in the early hours of the morning when it would be getting light very soon, and therefore safe enough to at least rest my head for an hour and wake up during the daylight, should I experience a horrible dream in which case I could get up and go out or distract myself counting at the gym...

Mum, remember that time at home, when I selfishly woke you in the middle of the night feeling all shaky and faint? (Saturday 10th

February 2010). I am so sorry I couldn't talk to you and explain exactly what had happened. I am so sorry and I cannot thank you enough for looking after me and for not being angry at me. I felt awful, as I know you were so tired and I disturbed your sleep and even dragged you downstairs. Now, if you wish, you can read about what was really going on for me at this time (as follows at Interlude: II B1)...

...Interlude II...

INTERLUDE II

DREAMS

A:-

Week beginning Monday 15ᵗʰ February 2010:

1.   *I was sitting in a coffee shop with Kerry and Little Brother. I had chosen a ham sandwich with lettuce in it. I tore half of it in half again and opened it to make sure that it looked OK. Then I started to eat it slowly and subconsciously. There was a lady sitting at a table on her own, close to the door of the shop. She wore black hair and big lipstick. She was looking over at me and she said "are you sure you deserve to be eating that bacon sandwich?" Quietly and nervously with my head hung in shame, after pausing, I replied with "it's ham actually, and who are you?" She spoke smugly down to me, smirking: "I work behind the desk at the dentist, what on earth has happened to you? I know all about you, I've read your notes" I grabbed the beans that had appeared in front of me as I stood up throwing back my chair – the beans were from the five bean salad I used to feel safe with at the hospital, which, towards the middle of my admission two, became a meal I could only allow myself half of as I was convinced that the heap of beans just grew and grew and grew, bigger and bigger and bigger each time I was served this meal until, even this simple salad meal became a threat for me to ingest – I threw the beans straight at her in a rage. She stood up and shouted something, then shook off her black wig and walked out of the shop.*

2.   *I was at home in Grenada on my own and opened the sliding doors into the Old Lounge Wing. I saw a huge fluffy white cat sitting on the chair and thought, OK I'll leave it there, I'm not going anywhere near it! So I closed the doors and left. I went to lose myself in playing the piano and was enjoying myself immensely.*

Then I went to look again in the lounge and my two year old nephew came running up to me at the doors. I was shocked.

My poor, neglected nephew looked tired and flushed in the face, like he'd just woken up. Was I supposed to have been looking after him? I had no idea that he was even here in this house! Anything could have happened to him upstairs - the cat was there, there were stairs there, there was the fireplace, oh my word I felt terrible, I picked him up immediately and asked him if he was OK. I felt irresponsible and how could I not have realised and how could I have just left him like that, to instead enjoy myself getting lost in my music and taking pleasure from my musical talents within myself?! How selfish! Kerry was back in the kitchen and I took him through to her.

B:-

Saturday 20th February 2010:

1.   *I kept waking up with a start and a beating heart. I was hot, tossing and turning, my head aching, heart racing, finding it hard to breath.*

Turn over! Bury your head in those covers..! Must seek sleep: the only possible reprieve wherefrom Angel you may just concede to peace...just a seconds leave...

Dropped off. Woke up, suddenly, panic and fear, sweats and tears; I wake with a start and a fast beating heart.

Really have the feeling that someone is in here with me. Someone is behind me. I listen intently, am I dreaming this or imagining this? No, this is real. I can definitely hear breathing, definitely. OK, do not move, and pretend to be asleep and keep still. Is it Mum breathing? No, it is too close behind me. Is it male or female? Please be female. Not sure. Please be female; please be Mum, sister, friend. But no...

I hear a noise now and notice shaking. It is male and there; preparation... I feel immense fear. It is definitely male! Feel alarm, threat, terrific panic and fear.

Listen. Listen carefully and keep calm, do not move, stay still. Remove. This isn't happening, stop breathing, close your eyes, freeze, worry stiff, waiting, notice head aching, ignore.

Breathing less - wake up to a heart beating, it's pounding fast and hard, open eyes, think - have I just woken up from a dream? Listen carefully, can I still hear anything? Only my heartbeat. Is it real or just a dream?

I'm scared. Wait, don't move. Smell; try to feel a presence, sense anyone? Deep breath. Turn around. Alone. It was a dream. A nightmare. Switch on the light I cannot go straight back to sleep now I feel unwell.

Heart beating, can't breathe. Thinking how on earth can I do this? I gave myself a hot meal with Mum's support tonight and it was a middle-safe meal that I had managed. I need to eat and I did, but I fear the evenings in London alone and dealing with this panic and immense feeling of losing control, like that crashing plane so high above the land, the feeling of having done the absolute wrong thing and how could I have done this? Intensely high anxiety levels and panic after eating – cannot sleep if I do – dizzy, nightmares and worry. Cannot sleep if I don't – can't breathe, dizzy and worry and panic that I'm not doing enough to help myself to "get better". And this is just around a life filled with medium-safe only foods! I can't live like this. I can't live! I can't help myself! Nobody can help me! I'm unable to let anybody help me! I have ruined my life and I can't get better! I'm scared!

Get up to put on big light and feel so sick, sweating, shaking, cannot breathe.

Try to make my way to the toilet but feel very faint, divert into Mum's room. Hot, shaky, feel sick, sweating. I just want to be better, RIGHT NOW. What have I done to myself? I HATE myself. I HATE what I have BECOME. Look at me!

Mum made me lie down on the bed and very slowly I began to feel a bit better. She suggested that I stay in her bed. I needed a drink, a cup of tea, or probably milk, but I couldn't say it for ages. I wanted her to go back to sleep and to not be disturbed by me anymore, but I reported what I needed and poor Mum came downstairs with me. I had some milky tea. She put a plain biscuit by me and told me I need to eat it.

I actually managed the milky tea and the biscuit within 45 minutes. We went back upstairs. I slept with my light on, hating myself.

Failure. Disaster. Guilt.

CHAPTER 21II:

DAY CARE AND THE MOTIVATION TO MOVE ON

YET STILL NO STRENGTH TO DO SO CONTINUED

I stayed at home for an extra couple of days before I felt safe enough to go back to London and be on my own. I can admit now that I was really missing the service of Day Care and I didn't want to not be there, for once, because I was feeling ill again and lacking in energy to do anything or to even think for myself clearly, but I was too frightened to travel on the train and be all alone. My thoughts alone would kill me.

When I arrived back at Day Care, I had written down the real reason that had kept me off and managed to tell the Dietician, just because she was the first person I had a one-to-one with and also because I trusted her. I merely informed her that I had experienced a dream and that this was the reason I hadn't been well enough to return earlier. I didn't give or show her the piece of paper that I had described the dream on as it felt silly and I didn't want to sit there while she read it and I didn't know where to go from there and she was the dietician and this meeting was to speak to me about other issues i.e. my food and my meal plan. At least I had been honest with the staff so they knew the real reason, which I sensed they had already worked out for themselves as it was evident in her response to my honesty, which made me feel better for having shared this with somebody. I was pleased that I had been able to move away from keeping all my troubles to myself anymore. A baby step, I know. I was realising that the staff had already clearly accepted that I am the one who must learn to find and use my voice WHEN I FEEL OK TO. Rebecca, it is not their responsibility to push you to speak, you have to take the responsibility.

Since being open and honest with the Dietician at Day Care and since getting my new meal plan prior to my week's reflection, I feel I have been managing my meal plan better at home with Mum at the weekends. I am especially happy that I can push myself to do the hot evening meal with Mum's support, but since I came back to London I continue to struggle with making anything else for myself other than a slice of bread, lettuce and beetroot and half a carton of cottage cheese or a slice of packet meat (bought by Mum and brought back to London with me, as is the bread) followed by half a yogurt and fruit. On the last day of my week out, I did stretch to buying the 'be good to yourself' mini pots of humus that come in pots of three. I thought as I had bought it once before, it was something I could do again and I needed to help myself somehow, so I made this a change for me. I think I was worried that I would go back to having cereal for dinner to make a change from the cottage cheese and that would have been a big step in the wrong direction. I just know I can deal with what I was giving myself and it eased the battles in my head and the anxieties and panics. I just wanted to keep myself well, so that I could live and stave off fainting attacks and concentrate on my week out properly. I still have the humus in my fridge two weeks later...because *Angel* tells me it is only protein that I need to help me, *never stuffy carbohydrates.*

Anything I do on my own without support, I cannot deal with. I get panicky, I can't breathe, and I think I have done something terribly wrong. I don't want to start dreaming again, but I don't want to not be able to sleep through feeling so light-headed and unable to breathe and panicky that I worry about silently slipping away and about my overall health and long-term health implications worsening.

I want to be able to eat anything without feeling insecure or disgusting and dirty and out of control, fat and full of emotion, overwhelming images and thoughts and memories flooding my mind so intensely that I wish no longer to be alive. I just want a break from it all and for it all to stop. Please! But I want to be able to eat and be healthy and gain back my strength, have my period and build up my brain, my muscles and to not get tired so quickly and often and to be comfortable with all of this. I want to be able to visit my friends and family and stay out with my colleagues without making sudden excuses and constantly planning, being scared of anything that may involve food or a sudden change in plan and feeling like I have to run and act on these impulses or feel unsafe and overcome by the plane crashing analogy, just because I have eaten a piece of cake, a larger jacket potato or an extra 0.2 mls of milk than the next person in the queue.

I want to take the support of others and to always believe that they are helping me, that they are right and to not have to believe my own extreme doubts and fears in believing everyone is really laughing at you and thinking you're a fraud and should just get on with your life and stop messing around, you're fine. Instead, I want to be able to feel confident and have the faith to listen to them and to take their support and BELIEVE their advice over my own negative thinking. I cannot persuade myself that I am not being laughed at secretly, that there is a secret that everyone is not telling me; a conspiracy. I am still half sure that I was never sectioned in the first place and that it was all a way to try and get me to do things. But then I think why would they bother to lie to *me*? Unless my Mum had asked them to, in order to make it sound more serious than it actually was. But again, why bother? These are professionals doing their job! Then when I didn't get my letter to say my Section had ended, and I remember others getting this straight away (or so I persuaded myself to believe so adamantly), it made it even easier to accept it as having been untrue all along. It sounds terrible but I really do half believe it still even now as I write (written prior to reading my hospital nurses notes, which was my main reason for requesting these – to read the written facts so that I would believe it actually did happen).

The only thing that persuades me, to a miniscule extent, is the fact that I don't have my period and that my bones ache and this makes me scared of long-term health issues and I realise I am already almost 30 years old and my life is disappearing right in front of my eyes, yet I cannot see it. This existence is always more important, safer and I am in control and think I can live like this perfectly well, thank you for your concern but look I am really fine; except I am obviously in reality so far from 'fine' and 'in control' of anything: I continue day after day with this horrible, lonely, fake existence, this unhappy, intolerable prison of inflexibility, rules and restrictions. Before I know it (and probably only if I am "lucky") another twenty years will have passed and I'll be living exactly the same isolated life as today; the same day over and over and over again and again, and again, and again except maybe in a wheelchair and with zero support and all through my own doing...

I hate people hugging me or touching me lovingly or in a caring way because I feel I don't deserve their love and they should be mean to me because that is what I can deal with and I feel wrong, weak and a joke if I am not the person to initiate the contact, when I feel comfortable to, yet I am *never allowed* to take this step, as much as I want to speak out, help people, explain myself, give my Mum a hug or comfort a fellow patient, I know not how, I am afraid and scared and no good at it anyway, and fear fierce rejection after saying or doing the wrong thing, which is bound to happen from me and spoil everything BECAUSE I DON'T HAVE THAT SECRET UNDERSTANDING and I just can't, and am not meant, able or allowed to do it, therefore I can't. I have little confidence and low-self-esteem, I suppose. I don't know how to deal with being told nice things and I find it extremely uncomfortable. I don't want to have to have those barriers constantly up to hide behind, I don't want to be distant from others to make me keep feeling safe and just to live by my shadow, I don't want to put up this false front anymore - I am tired and want to be ME - I don't want to turn to using alcohol and going out or visiting the gyms excessively simply as a means to distract myself. I just want to be Rebecca again! I just want to be content with no burdens to carry around weighing down my shoulders 24 hours a day. No more secrets, no more fear, no more uncertainties; where's my cure?

With men I just freeze and think they're having a go at me or being derogatory or suggestive and I get defensive and begin to hate them exceedingly for this and be wary of them on the inside, but be smiling on the outside. I need to keep my dignity, but I feel I have none left and never will regain any. I tell myself I am strong, but really I am weak, dirty, feeble and degraded. I just want to be able to get on with life, but this is what I have tried so hard to do. Last time (Book 1: Secrets Out, Part 5, Chapter 17) I learned it is just written to end always going wrong for me and that I am weak and incapable. I scare myself having accepted that I thought it would be easier than it has been to even start to get better even when I have decided to just go for it, it never happens, I always get terrified, and I always stop and it has made me realise that what I thought I had

310

control over, it has a complete evil control over me and over the direction my life has and is taking and that I cannot push this away no matter how hard I try. Thinking that it might actually be impossible for me to get better from this, it scares me rigid and I lose the hope in living each next second.

Day Care: please help me to get my life back, help me recapture a real me, whoever that may now be. Please.

CHAPTER 22:

RETURNING TO DAY CARE WITH

POSITIVE QUOTES AND AFFIRMATIONS

- It's not about the food.
- Don't start getting better tomorrow, start here, now, today, as tomorrow never comes.
- The food won't kill you, your illness will.
- "I am always doing that which I cannot do, in order I may learn how to do it" (Picasso).
- Don't be afraid of life, it is worth living, live this day as it will never come again.
- Today, I can do the extra mile.
- Thoughts provoke action; think healthier thoughts to provoke healthier actions.
- Negative thoughts will never help; they will always hurt me.
- Allow help, support, and normality as a reprieve from self-destruction.
- Everybody is in charge of the direction of their own boat; every second you live is your life, your future.
- The fear is worse than the action.
- Do what you need to do and not what you don't.
- Listen to those you trust and believe they are trying to help you.
- Only YOU are with you 24 hours a day.

CHAPTER 231:-

...DIARY ENTRIES TAKEN FROM THE FIRST WEEK

BACK AT DAY CARE AND

THE WEEKEND OF MOTHERING SUNDAY...

-Curry Day
-Shift: Security, Happiness, Hope
-Back to the Bad Days

- ### Thursday 11th March 2010:

Dreaded going to Day Care but thankful that I was at least going to have a meal and some nutrition and some support. My weigh-in this morning told me I had lost a little weight, but I still felt absolutely F A T and nervous and anxious on my bus journey there. I had got up early to wash my hair and shower and I had eaten my breakfast as normal, well maybe a slightly bit less here and there quickly. I know, "I'm only fooling myself" but I let myself off today, as I was facing a whole day of eating to get through, so I let myself off with it and didn't berate myself too much for doing this either.

I was thinking I would walk, at least part of the way, but no, actually why should I?! I would get the bus as I had learned to and I would enjoy it. So I did, but it didn't help my guilt when I would see other people taking as much time to cover the same distance as me, on foot, and I felt even guiltier for sitting on the bus when I could be being active. People must be thinking "why on earth is she not walking!"

Go away.

It was curry day and I had told myself, OK just go for the Dahl curry, rice and vegetables because a) I had done a Dahl curry before, b) There was so much less compulsion to separate and have the constant worry and battle against this all the way through the meal, and c) It eased the worry of not knowing what kind of sauce the chicken would turn up in all morning. So that was that, I had thought it through and decided that was what I was going to do.

I chose it. But then I was worried that it might have been the lentil one that came up and I had no idea what this one was like, but then, surely this would be better than the other option still? I changed my mind at the last moment as I saw on the list that it was chicken Buna, which said to me, probably quite dry with not much sauce and quite different from the Korma or the dreaded Masala, my greatest fear, and I had done this Buna once before, when everybody else was having it, which they were also doing today. It still made it hard, but at least we would all be doing the same thing together; we were all in the same boat. And why the hell SHOULDN'T I? Well, as I knew what I was expecting, that was that; hard but hopefully manageable.

It came up as the dreaded Masala! I couldn't do it. How could I put this inside me and sit with it? Today! Talk about in at the deep end. I tried to wait until the end of the queue until everyone else had served themselves. I managed to serve up the green beans and the rice, but I couldn't do the chicken. It wasn't what was supposed to have come up. It wasn't what I had ordered. I couldn't take it, I wanted to go home.

Chloe (staff) did it for me. It seemed like loads of chicken and a horrible amount of sauce! Through my tears I asked her if I could please go home now and come back tomorrow. She tried to remind me that it is either this or the other thing i.e. inpatient hospital admission and she asked me if I could remember the quotes that I had put on my reflection form after my week out. I tried to remember, but I couldn't think of these right now. But hearing her rational voice and advice helped me to remember what I was doing here. I immediately thought of what I would HAVE to eat at that hospital and of my positive quotes and was determined that I had to stay out of hospital.

Chloe also told me that my Consultant had come back into the office that day especially to ask about my quote from Auntie Ann by Picasso as he wanted to take it on to his new job. This actually spurred me on too. I don't know why. Now thinking back, maybe it gave me a hint of self-worth and usefulness, I do not know.

There I stood sobbing my heart out in the kitchen, holding this huge plate of food that I had to eat. Chloe helped me leave the kitchen, but I stopped outside the dining room. I was flooded with tears, it kept coming back, my fears, and I felt so ashamed of myself when the others were silently doing what they were here to do and eating their meals. Even if it was all a front – why couldn't I be that strong! Weak and failing...Chloe asked the other patients to help me and I heard them all saying nice things to me from inside the dining room. Chloe took my plate in for me – I couldn't walk in there with this plate of food that I was expected to eat – she laid it at my space at the table, there it all was, waiting for me to devour. A nice creamy curry for you Micci, there you go – enjoy, you greedy bitch... You can already feel it seeping Rebecca... Chloe had really helped me so much and I was so grateful to her. I tried to compose myself before I walked in; having those few seconds away from that plate, really helped refresh my perspective.

I sat down and tried to keep myself composed, concentrating on the others' conversations. They were obviously struggling silently and they were really helping, in that we had the same thing to deal with on our plates, even though we all had very different struggles, we could relate to a struggle when we saw one. I kept as strong as I could. Thinking, 'start to get better today, NOW! Not tomorrow, as tomorrow never comes'...and I've realised the connection that makes this so true – that tomorrow never did come for my Dad and that is what upset me so much at the New Year Party [Book 1: Secrets Out, Part 3, Chapter 9] when I heard this playing. My saying. My personal motivator. Determination set in. 'The fear is worse than the action...The fear is worse than the action...the fear...'

315

I was the first to step forward to serve myself with the dreaded jam roly poly and custard pudding and I felt good that I had completed the whole meal. For once, I had carried out what was expected of me, just like the others! I even ate my dinner that was on my meal plan that evening and I also managed to give myself my meal-planned night snack and I was really, really happy.

Today I had defeated one of my greatest fears. Thank you Chloe, so very much.

- **Friday 12ᵗʰ March 2010:**

The world had not ended. I found getting up a bit difficult and was dreading weigh-in. Only put on 0.1, which was not expected at all. I thought it would be sky high after yesterday and had been dreading it, hence the reluctance to open my eyes and find out, and so the morning was a good one. The day before I had taken a huge leap of faith and had faced and overcome something major to me. Small, baby steps were being made in the right direction and I was happy. Maybe it would all show up the next morning, but I couldn't think like that and was able to let this go, not completely, the thought was always niggling, but I tried my best to ignore it and not to let it disturb me too much because anyway, I wouldn't know for sure as I would be waking up at home back in Granada, far away from my scales (I had started leaving my scales in London at the weekends now) and so I would not know what my weight was anyway. I think, subconsciously, this made it easier to ignore and to get on with the day at Day Care with all my might. Anxieties showed through, but I successfully completed the day. Another fantastic feeling.

When I was waiting for the bus that morning, I experienced a glimmer of that actual feeling of SECURITY and HAPPINESS! It was a strange feeling. Warm and nostalgic but not horribly weird; it was just nice and I tried to hold onto it. I was feeling HOPE and that there actually is life worth FIGHTING for and to be excited about. It made me realise just how bad things had been for such an extended length of time, in terms of my mood. I had received a text from Spen the day before, which I think, now, may have helped towards re-igniting that feeling, which is probably a bad thing, but at least I know I CAN at least feel good again. I can feel glimmers of hope.

At Day Care we were going to the canteen today, so there was always the choice of a safe jacket potato and tuna or beans, or the possibility of stretching to a whole sandwich with the support of the others, or even daring to go for one of the actual menu options.

But apart from this, FOR THE FIRST TIME EVER at Day Care, I had been distracted from my thoughts of lunch for the duration of the whole morning group, from just after 11am until about 11:45am! We were doing an art class that required total attention and I didn't even realise that I hadn't been disturbed by thoughts about lunch until I glanced at the clock and realised the class would be finishing soon and I went to the toilet and then it hit me.

Oh my word, what am I going to have from the canteen?! It's lunchtime right now! Argh. I tried to quickly run through my options, realise what I am feeling is a safe option for me today that I could cope with, trying not to spend too long in the toilet on my own being undisturbed with my thoughts and worries. I was still a bit confused and anxious when I was going downstairs...

In the canteen, the other patients were all having sandwiches. I tried choosing one, but all I got stuck on was a) finding one with JUST under or JUST enough calories that would be acceptable under the rules, b) making sure this was OK and manageable for me to eat, in saturated fat levels, c) making sure that the filling was not encased in mayonnaise or a horrible dressing that I would be compelled to smear all over my plate as much as I possibly could, d) making sure that the filling didn't look like simply too much to be able to finish both halves of and e) making sure my choice was brown bread. HELP. I wanted to try and choose a sandwich as everyone else was doing this today and so I thought I would seize this opportunity to face my fear and this restriction that meant I can never have a whole sandwich. So I asked Lilly to help me choose one but I couldn't do it. I couldn't voice my overwhelming, silly, concerns and worries and fears. I told her I would have a potato, but even that was scary as I was put off by the sheer size of them today! Lilly calmly looked over and actually agreed with me, calmly telling me not to worry

317

because we can 'do surgery' on them when we get upstairs and serve.

OK, so I think potato it was. I hoped the others didn't think I was greedy for choosing a hot lunch for myself. At least Lilly was having a hot lunch too, so it made me feel a bit better about my choice. But for me, I would have felt even greedier sitting there having a whole sandwich for myself with a huge creamy filling, which I didn't feel able to do, personally. I wanted to do it, particularly as the support of the others was there today too, but I guess I could surely do that another day. Baby steps.

I felt stupid for taking so long. As if that wasn't enough, I was then jittering around the fridge bit. I took the melon pot and decided it was far too big and that I would have an apple or pear or something from upstairs instead, so I then put it back. Lilly came over and reminded me about the cheese pot I needed. I felt awful, I had completely forgotten about the cheese, even though I knew I had to have it and was prepared to. I hoped that she didn't think I had just tried to conveniently "forget" it on purpose, because I really hadn't!

I felt so pathetic for my idiotic dithering around over something so simple and felt hugely thankful towards Lilly. I felt idiotic and pathetic for making such a fuss and being so indecisive and stupid. Lilly cut an edge off the potato upstairs and then the size of it was bearable. I had raspberry yogurt and an apple for pudding. I really wanted to try the blueberry one and hesitated in the fridge for a few seconds, but I stuck to the raspberry as a) I knew it was highest in fibre, b) I had done it before and felt safest with it, c) I knew I struggled with yogurt anyway and didn't want to make things even more difficult for myself as that one was higher in calories too! No, not today. Stick to justification in fibre contents. Decision made.

Lunch over. I went for the walk in our break again, which was nice. Why shouldn't I have some fresh air and be sociable and talk to other people, hey?!

Weekend planning group that afternoon: All I intended to say was that I was going home for Mother's Day, no real plans. I felt so much better when Lilly prompted and gave me the opportunity to talk through as much or little as I liked of the events of my week out. I did feel better. She said I was eloquent and logical. I felt so much better afterwards. OK, I felt a little guilty for taking up so much time in the group, but I don't usually, and it all just came spilling out and they were really helpful and actually I don't think I did take up that much time. I was really hot and sweating when I was speaking but was so desperate to get it all out.

Snack usual, the apple and cereal bar. In the summing up at the end of the day, everyone was positive and felt they were making steps and being supportive to everyone else. Felt nice and maybe there is some hope. I just hope I can keep it up and make it work out.

Left the Day Centre and walked a bit with patient x. Went in to book her hair appointment with her. Felt good doing this as I know she likes to be with someone. Walked to supermarket and bought Mum's flowers and cupcakes that I had seen yesterday and I hoped I could join her in having, after much deliberation I did decide to buy them, thinking I could decide if I wanted to bring them out or not on the day. Went to buy some cottage cheese for dinner but they didn't have any...no big problem. Bought a flump and had this instead. Well, it's Friday. I felt a bit freer and lighter already.

Wrapped up presents at home and spoke to Little Brother on phone. Checked email etc. Left for train. Just managed 7:30pm. Had my meal-planned dinner and then tea and toast with Mum! Well, half, but good as thick sliced so double really! Felt OK about it ☺ bed.

- ### Saturday 13th March 2010:

Got up desperate for loo as usual, dressed and came downstairs. Mum came down a bit later and I had already prepared my fruit and yogurt and milk and put it back in the fridge so I didn't have to annoy Mum doing it all in front of her. Mum had a go at me telling me I was sneaky being on my laptop and scolded me saying make sure I don't send off for any funny things on the internet. Spent all morning on laptop trying to get letter to Mum sorted but it kept going and going and going and now I have missed the post anyway and I might just turn it all into a book for whoever the hell wants to read it.

Angel Just-Rights

Had half a toast with Mum and some apple and coffee at snack time.

Made scrambled egg (2 egg whites only) half a toast, tomato, tomato ketchup, lettuce and brown sauce and beetroot while Mum ate her poached eggs on toast with her back to me preparing my food. Poked the egg yolks down the sink behind Mum's back and added some ketchup and tomatoes to the mixture to make it look a bit yellowy. Did it in a dry pan and added a spoon of cottage cheese to the salad on the plate. I didn't really need this cottage cheese today and I guess it is just habit and something I feel safe with. I suppose I also needed to feel completely satisfied in that I wouldn't have to 'pick' later or afterwards. That way, having a taste would settle my buds and it wouldn't be constantly on my mind calling me to the fridge all afternoon until tomorrow lunchtime when I'd be allowed some, possibly.

Some apple and two teaspoons of raspberry fat free yogurt for pudding. I am getting worried because we are obviously not going to town today and there is ¾ of an apple left in the fridge and no more tangerines or fruit of any kind. Anyway, Mum tried to make a bit of conversation but I know she still hates me. She said she is going to tidy up in the greenhouse. I told her not to and that Little Brother can help us with it when he comes tomorrow. She is absolutely knackered. I am not watching and helping her wear herself to the ground, I can't. Plus, how dare she say in one breath I don't want you helping in the garden, look at the state of you, and then tell me she's going outside, hinting she wants me to help her wear herself out. If Mum wants me to help or to do something, she has to say yes when I ask, not get angry and say horrible things to me. It makes me angry and yes, maybe there is a hint of defiance even, if I really analyse every single tiny minute emotion.

Mum was in the garden most of the afternoon from 3 – 5pm. I went to bed because I couldn't watch her wear herself out and I knew she'd give me all the little jobs that didn't matter, so there would be no point in me going up the garden to help her anyway. I wanted to go back to London and go to the gym for some real exercise. Either that or just go to sleep, blocking out the world.

Went downstairs to find my snack at about 5pm and my rice cakes had been thrown out. What should I have? I am saving the apple for pudding and / or for tomorrow morning. No other fruit. Plain biscuit? No milk (only the green top).

Had apple and yogurt in the end. Mum told me to have a milky drink, I said there's no milk and she stomped off to town, not letting me stop her. I stayed in the house and immersed myself in watching my favourite food television program where people go to a dinner party five nights in a row and cook for one-another, really loudly, with my bit of apple and yogurt and my super huge mug of piping hot tea.

Mum back. She had bought two apples, a fruit salad and some milk. No tangerines. Oh well.

Dinner was haddock, wedges, fruit and yogurt.

Snack of cereal sprinkle, milk and water.

Did jigsaw all evening and then got laptop out in the lounge while Mum was watching television all evening. Mum was horrible to me, looking at me disgustedly and accusingly, saying, "What are you doing?!"

A pretty horrid day. I don't know if Mum hasn't spoken to me all day because she is still angry at me or because she isn't feeling well, or if she has something on her mind. Night.

- ### Sunday 14th March 2010 (Mothering Sunday):

Got up when I heard Mum get up and go downstairs. Decided to go for the cakes to make her happy and so I took them downstairs along with my card.

Gave the card to Mum and she said she didn't want all this – meaning the words I had written inside the card and the wrapped up present – but then she opened the present and I explained how I thought we could all have a cup-cake together for pudding or at snack time that afternoon. This made her really smile. I was glad I had done it and not bought something that was expensive for the sake of it as I knew Mum wouldn't have thanked me for doing this for her when there are other things that would make her happier.

Little Brother arrived and we drove in his car to town to pick up some things from the DIY shop. We arrived back home to the curry lunch. I really tried. OK, I had to make my lettuce and tomato too, but I did try the curry, a little. AND I felt more able to do the chicken as I had got over my ultimate fear on Thursday, although it wasn't that kind of sauce.

We did some gardening and helped with some things that needed doing around the house and then soon enough it was snack time. I was hoping that Mum had forgotten, but she got the cakes out. We all had one with our cup of tea. I left the icing on top, but ate most of the rest of it, with some mango from the fruit salad (as I needed some fibre to push it through) Mum had bought me the day before. She wasn't particularly happy that I sat there eating it and said afterwards that it doesn't count because I have left most of it – meaning the icing that was on the top! I suppose I had left some. To be honest it made it even worse that I really didn't enjoy the taste of eating it as it was vanilla-flavoured sponge and tasted a bit weird, in addition to everything else.

So I was left feeling like I wished I hadn't even bothered and felt ill and lonely and was left totally on my own to deal with my bully intruding on my thoughts and my feelings berating me fiercely that I had done so wrong for having just eaten it. Fat, greedy thing...you're definitely not having anything else today...you certainly can't have dinner now...half milk and half water for you at snack time...just so you don't stop breathing in your sleep. SHUT UP AND LEAVE ME ALONE; I WANT TO DIE AND HAVE PEACE FROM ALL THIS! Little Brother gave me a lift to the station in his car on the way home, bless him.

- ### Monday 15th March 2010:

Day Care - Didn't get weighed today at Day Care as there was a lot of people and there was no time – flexible.

Angel Just-Rights

Bean and Tuna Burrito, quite nice actually but such a lot of tuna and horrible goats cheese on top, but I always try and have first pick at serving when it is already portioned so that I can choose the smallest and the one with the least cheese, so the cheese I dealt with as others were having more than I was. Eves Pudding was quite heavy and pretty huge too.

My key worker told me I wouldn't be allowed to change therapists and this angered me at first, but I really tried to listen to the reasons she was giving me and to take on board the advice that the team had spoken of. I agreed to try again, taking their advice. But I still felt angry and that I didn't think it would work. I found my snack especially hard to do after this. I really was struggling to start those oatcakes, but I did. And I was proud that I didn't let *Angel* beat me. I knew I was making progress after this.

...Interlude III...

INTERLUDE III

DREAMS

A:-

Monday 15th March 2010:

1.   *I dreamt that I was sleeping in my Mum and Dad's bed with 'him'! I was wearing my pyjamas. This was another recurring dream of years ago. I did used to go into my parents' bedroom on some mornings when I was little at the weekend and I suppose their bed was safe and comforting. In the dream 'he' was a lot younger somehow and I kept getting up and was carrying him in my arms like a baby. In the dream I was back in the bed, asleep and when I woke up, I looked down and was naked and realised that he was doing horrible things to me, hiding under the duvet. What on earth was going on?! I awoke. Disturbed.*

CHAPTER 2311:-

...DIARY ENTRIES TAKEN FROM THE FIRST WEEK

BACK AT DAY CARE CONTINUED...

- **Tuesday 16th March 2010:**

Lunch was Malaysian Salmon and jacket potato (nice salmon but big and a little sweet and the potato was hard) and syrup sponge with custard (very big and very plastic in consistency, but at least not much syrup at all).

- **Wednesday 17th March 2010:**

Had meeting with therapist. Waste of time as just did family tree yet again and she had forgotten everything I had told her in the weeks / years previously. We did canteen today and I had a jacket potato with a tomato, mushroom and onion sauce thing! Was nice. Fruit and yogurt.

...Interlude IV...

INTERLUDE IV

DREAMS

A:-

Wednesday 17ᵗʰ March 2010:

1. *I heard footsteps in the lounge area outside my door and thought it must be my flat mate going to bed. I saw myself waking up from my sleep and seeing the door handle of my room being opened slowly. I was scared, thinking 'why was someone coming into my room and who was it? Is it opening? Is it?' I was trying my best to look and to really see, but it was blurred to my vision rather like when you try so hard to keep your eyes open when you are so tired, but nothing works. Here, I was awake and yet my body wasn't working. I was hearing the footsteps, seeing my door handle moving and then I saw my housemate coming into my room! I was terrified. Was he really there? No he wouldn't...he can't be...but he is! ...Isn't he?*

I couldn't wake up properly, I was paralysed. I couldn't move or see. (Sleep Paralysis; Book 1: Secrets Out, Part 4, Chapter 14].

2. *I dreamt that my housemate was moving out and she said she was cooking a meal for everyone. I said how nice that would be. Then I changed my mind and said actually I'm not a meat-eater. It was curry.*

3. *I dreamt that I was in a room with a few people who were my friends and I was lying and relaxing on the floor with them and the television was on. People were watching a film I think. I was next to this man emanating Leo* [Book 1: Secrets Out, Part 4, Chapter 14] *whose aura shone safety, trust, security and comfort to*

me. We were obviously 'getting together' and people were noticing us moving closer and closer together on the floor, slowly.

We ended up cuddling innocently in each other's arms, he was warm, shielding and gentle and I could sense he cared and would never hurt me and I felt the same for him. I enjoyed feeling so safe in that room amongst other people that I could clearly feel comfortable being around and in being close to him at the same time; this was nice and I wasn't scared, because other people were close-by and visibly aware of what was occurring, and they were keeping an eye on the situation in a normal interested and playful manner. They were there with me and supporting me. It seemed they were approving and thinking it was 'right' and 'good' and sweet and I suppose I was reassured by this rather than feeling alone, confused and afraid. It felt normal and nice and safe because I knew Leo too.

CHAPTER 23III:-

...DIARY ENTRIES TAKEN FROM THE FIRST FULL

WEEK BACK AT DAY CARE COMPLETED...

- ### Thursday 18ᵗʰ March 2010:

Curry day. Another patient went for the Dahl curry, so I did too. I didn't feel brave enough to do a chicken curry again this week. It came up as the lentil curry. It was very similar to the can of lentil that I had opened a few days before in my flat when I had run out of lettuce and was feeling brave as it had been in my cupboard for ages! I was relieved it was green and didn't look that nice, but it tasted exactly like those lentils in the tin that I had given myself at home, plus I think I was lucky to get a measly portion today, so I felt OK at eating my lunch today. I can't even remember what the pudding was now!

At least I know I can deal with either of the Dahl choices now and I can just do the chicken if I feel brave (probably never will ever again!) so at least I don't have to dread curry day so much every week now. Phew.

- ### Friday 19ᵗʰ March 2010:

Just three patients and one member of staff present today. I managed to wangle another canteen day☺. Tiniest jacket potato, tuna pot and smidge of salad cream added when we got upstairs, which I smudged around the plate anyway, so... I wanted to do it with cheese like I usually do, but she said it had to be mayonnaise or salad cream and although I tried to negotiate with her, I was secretly pleased that she had said this and not given in to me because a) it is more normal and b) I LIKE the taste of salad cream. AND...I was kind of forced to try the blackcurrant yogurt today, with melon, as there was no raspberry left! Great lunch actually and I engaged in conversation too! Hard as always, but manageable and I had been flexible, with the salad cream thing, and we had nice conversation today too, just the four of us.

Left Day Care with another patient and I walked all the way home for once. I decided to stay in London, where I could make progress with my writing. Felt bad for not going home and as the night went on I really wished that I had decided to go home to spend the weekend with Mum...

CHAPTER 24:-

...DIARY ENTRIES TAKEN FROM MY FIRST

WEEKEND SPENT ALONE IN LONDON...

- **Saturday 20th March 2010 and Sunday 21st March 2010:**

Really, really disappointed how much I am still struggling on my own, nutritionally.

I met Sarah for cinema, but it was expensive and there were no two seats together so we decided to go for a drink instead. We went to a bar we knew in Leicester Square and I slipped right down the wet wooden stairs and was shocked. Had a diet coke and we had a good chat. In the next bar I ordered another diet coke but I didn't touch it after tasting a sip and thinking it wasn't diet. Sarah noticed, she was really good, and commented that I hadn't touched it and that I had better not be thinking of calories, which I was getting petrified about, yes. I admitted it and she said, "don't do it to yourself!" She was right, but I still COULD NOT touch it.

I can see the life I want to live and can only imagine that I will be battling off the other that never gives in forever. I will never be completely free. I don't think I will ever be in peace unless I am dead, and even then I cannot imagine being free from the noise completely.

But as long as I have HOPE, I have a chance. Do not give in. Never give in, because if you give in – as I did in hospital admission two point five – the pain and the distress of living every second of every day in this life still lingers on and on and on until not being in this world appears all the more enticing: to be finally released, set free, both for my family and from myself. Let me go...!

So accept that it will win sometimes and accept that only 'baby steps' will help, but never give in to the fight against it: FIGHT FOR YOU. Learn to separate disgust from fear and face and accept reality. Live, do not hide your face or shut tight your lips from speaking or bite out your anger on anything and everything that isn't edible i.e. pen tops or the duvet cover or your fingers and your thumbs, be open and seek back your confidence, be eloquent, be involved. Do not hide your face from help.

...Interlude V...

INTERLUDE V

DREAMS

And so it continues…

A:-

Saturday 20ᵗʰ March 2010:

1.   *Rather similar to the recurring teeth and cigarette paper dreams from childhood, only this time I was naked on the toilet at home in Granada and all this rice kept spilling out of my mouth like I was being sick, except I wasn't; it just kept producing the same things and spilling out and I couldn't stop it and the toilet door was open and people could see, but no-one was taking any notice or helping. I was in tears that it was happening to me and that I couldn't make a door appear or stay closed and I was trying my best to cover it all up as much as possible but it wasn't working and it wasn't stopping. I was so embarrassed. I was ashamed. I was humiliated.*

The toilet theme has been another recurring dream ever since childhood and can take many different variations with me, but it will always involve me searching for a toilet constantly in public and continuously, desperately searching for somewhere that is private or that actually has a door because there is never a door or a curtain and I am always naked. I am always striving. I am always humiliated.

CHAPTER 25:-

...NEW HONEST-TO-SELF DIARY ENTRIES ~

BACK AT DAY CARE...

And so it continues, with honesty...

- **Monday 22nd March 2010:**

Woke up, immediately realised today is the beginning of another struggle. Got up around the same time as usual at about 7.30 - 8am and started my routine. Toilet and wash and dress, in bra and knickers and two hair bands and my watch ONLY, ready for weight. Get out my diary and pen to check yesterday's weight and ready to write it down today. Don't trust the scales so I do it again. Still don't trust the scales so pick up my laptop and step on the scales holding it. Scares me to realise that the hospital want me to be carrying this weight of my laptop around with me 24 hours a day! Why me?! Then step on them again, just me, and it gives me a different result! Step on holding my bag, then again, just me. A real weight, I hope, write it down and put it away making a mental note that these scales just cannot be trusted. Great, another set in the bin. Tell self: I really shouldn't buy any more. Thinking I should walk there today.

Been thinking you should miss breakfast altogether today. Been thinking you should have gone to the gym this morning, you lazy thing. Been thinking you should at least really be doing exercises in the morning again and why the hell aren't you?! Go on, you clearly need to! Do it now! Every second! Look at yourself! Feel it! NO,

Angel Just-Rights

GO AWAY! Stop bullying me every morning when I am brushing my teeth and looking in the mirror! I know I need to, but leave me alone! Checked arms; checked legs; checked body.

Got dressed and drew curtains, opened window and drew back bed covers. Breakfast as usual these days. Tea, a tangerine (plus maybe quickly and sneakily put half an apple on my plate too if my greed takes over) and a couple of teaspoons of yogurt. I stopped doing the sprinkle of cereal with 150 ml milk and 150 ml water at the weekend, even though I want to and know I CAN do this if I was to really force myself to, but I don't. Put the jug in the cupboard so it is out of sight and then it isn't there to tempt you, you greedy pig! Go back into bedroom and put breakfast on the table. Don't forget to get the tablets out and to shut the window and to make the bed.
Have breakfast watching television and reading / writing the plan for the day. Make sure you start at the latest by 8:45am as you need to be ready to leave by 9:30am after washing up and you cannot rush and gulp it all down you greedy thing. Leave flat by 9:30am to get bus; it's too late to walk there now, think of how lazily you've already started the day!

SHUT UP! Breakfast is usually the only meal I take my time over and can 'enjoy' and my bus journey to Day Care is the only nice time I allow myself to not be busy and allocate my thinking / worry time to, so LEAVE. ME. ALONE!

Look, she's making the same distance on foot as you are larding away on this bus, see, you can feel it already getting worse and look what you're about to go and do all day! Get off the bus now and walk quickly so you catch up! Quick, go now, now, now...!

In community group today one the patients had talked about how she was taking her son swimming at the weekend, but on the bus he was screaming in pain from a tummy ache and she was ignoring him and he ended up walking down the street with faeces falling down his trousers. It made me think, I know it is hard to tell whether kids are telling the truth or not of course but, was there an element of her illness urging her on to go swimming for herself? In this case, I truly believe there was not, because everybody is different and struggles with different issues. But it really scared me that I would be affected by my illness one day to the extent that I would put myself first and ignore the needs of my nephew or my niece or anyone that I care about. Because, to an extent I already have! But doing this to a vulnerable child scares me and doesn't give me hope for my abilities in the future as I know how strong this compulsion and desire can get to the point where nothing else matters in the world unless you get that exercise done right then and there.

Vegetable burrito with carrots and fruits of the forest crumble with custard. Everyone else nabbed the cereal bars at 3pm snack today, so I had to have the rough cakes that turn my teeth fury.

And so it continues…

- **Tuesday 23rd March 2010:**

We decorated the Day Care room with the new furniture today. Felt tired with my cold. Taking pain killers.

Fish cakes with leeks and apple strudel with custard. Had a fruit bar thing today at 3pm as the others chose this too and I didn't want those filling rough cakes because you have to have three and they make my teeth go fury. There were no cereal bars that I usually have, so I guess this 'change' was good for me.
Text Ravi to say I couldn't meet him. I couldn't be bothered and felt a bit ill. Plus, nothing was going to get in my way of watching the first episode of the new series of my favourite television programme about people, food and lifestyle. I made my dinner in time for it, I ignored poor Little Brother's calls to watch it, I ignored Kerry's calls to watch it. There was a section of the programme following "anorexics" and it shocked me because the state of them looked awful...but my height is more than theirs and my weight is less! I just think they must all be a bunch of liars about their weights. I used to think the same about the patients in hospital, and at Day Care too for that matter, because no way can those weights be true as they would all be put in hospital like they threaten me with.

NO WAY. I came to the conclusion that it was an untold secret I was never to know or be let in on, similar I guess, to the untold secret in Chapter 5 etc. and the untold secret that I was never really sectioned. They're just playing mind games with me to make me fat. Why me? Logic tells me otherwise, but I continue to believe the screams as they're louder and harsher and always there with me. To me, they are real, true and safe. This is what I MUST follow.

There was an announcement at the end of the program informing viewers that one of the girls featured had died a week after filming.

Lies or no lies – if I continue only to turn things around and manage to CHANGE only when absolutely forced to, and little by little at that, it will almost certainly, and one day sooner, end up being JUST TOO LATE for me too, like my Mum always says to me that "you leave everything to the last minute and one of these days it will be too late". I must ignore my screams and follow those who know best who are in the majority here!

This shock made me question my extreme lifestyle – is it that this possibility of surviving each day so close to death was something that comforted me and kept me feeling safe because it provided me with a way out? An escape? Because everything is far too scary in the real world...desperate to feel safe...and if I was to succeed in anorexia, I would lose my life to it ultimately and then I'd be free...but that would never happen to me because people are making a fuss over my weight even now and for what reason? I could never be thin enough. I would just die or remain alive, but be left with ailments because I can't even do anorexia properly unless I lose more weight...!

- **Wednesday 24th March 2010:**

Day care closed, due to future planning review.

Today I went to Oxford Street and upgraded my phone. This afternoon I actually bought a prawn mayonnaise sandwich from supermarket and ate some of it with some fruit for my afternoon snack! Then for my dinner, I had some more as my chopped up open sandwich with added cottage cheese for my protein booster as stated on my meal plan. And then I spoke to Mum on the phone and she was brilliant as usual, giving me just enough support etc. and I was left feeling strong and ready to jolly well fight for myself, and while I was preparing my night snack with the hot chocolate orange that I really enjoy before bed, I helped myself to a good part of the rest of that delicious sandwich, AND IT FELT DAMN WELL GOOD!

Brief Evaluation of Diary Entries:

Finally I was listening to the real world that was good for ME and not to the evil voice I thought was *'just me!'* Can you understand how difficult this is to live with, day in, day out, and to have to trust and to keep reminding yourself of the simplest of things? To keep telling yourself 'ACCEPT what those you trust are saying; ALLOW them in and speak yourself out; REMEMBER who you used to be and discover who you are; REVEAL. COMMUNICATE. **LIVE.**

•   **Thursday 25th March 2010:**

Curry day, but it was OK. I chose the samba lentil safe choice today and it was like the bright yellow one that Mum used to make. Lilly let me replace the end bit on my Bakewell tart with a softer middle piece, thank Goodness for that.

Exercise group – Well I've done it before on the ward and at that time it reduced me to tears to see exactly what I had been doing and feeling for so long without even realising it was being detrimental to my health, written down and finally explained. It wasn't just me! This time round, I tried not to think about it all as I have already worked through this in my head and I don't feel the need to go there again (maybe because my diet is so limited at the moment in reality and urges to get to that gym really scare me that I will end up in my bad habits at the gym again).

Although it rubbed in my thoughts that I go through every morning now-a-days, around not exercising in the mornings, guilt at being on the bus, not catching the bus a stop later or getting off the bus a stop earlier and feeling embarrassed that people on the bus must be thinking why on earth didn't she get off and walk sooner?! Why on earth is she even on this bus in the first place?! There could have been more room for that woman with her poor baby and push chair, selfish girl! But it made me realise that I am fighting for MYSELF every time I don't give in to it and this makes me feel differently.

- **Friday 26th March 2010:**

It's just me, patient x, and patient y at Day Care today, with three staff. News that made me think today was about a patient who had left the Day Care centre yesterday and twisted her ankle before she had even got out of the gates. She had called the Day Care staff to let them know, as she couldn't walk and didn't know what else to do on her own. She didn't return home that night until 9:45pm. This scares me and shocks me to realise how you can see somebody one day and the next it can ALL be changed with a bit of news, and all so suddenly.

Chicken casserole, which again I thought was pork, but maybe it is the way it is cooked. I think it must be fried first or charcoaled, I don't know, and I don't wish to know, which makes the pieces a bit burned...or I wonder, maybe it's grilled...?

Spent all of 'rest period' staring out of the window trying to decide which train to catch home...6:30pm? But then I would walk into a kitchen at home in Grenada with the table set and a meal cooked, ready and waiting for me to sit down and eat with Mum when I got in. 7:30pm? To arrive just before 9:00pm, probably the safe bet as I could leave before dinner and arrive home too late for dinner. 8.30pm? I could have dinner at my house and arrive at home for snack, but it is a bit late for Mum and selfish of me, as it would almost be time for bed by the time we got back.

Patient x and Patient y asked me what was on my mind and I was open about my ruminations and they both really helped me.

Conclusion was simple: go home, have dinner around 7:00pm as usual, treat it like a normal day, catch train home at 7.30pm, which is a compromise. Thank you girls. I should have voiced my battles rather than wasting that whole hour and being no further towards making a decision.

Weekend planning group was REALLY good thanks to Jill (staff) and patient x. Jill made me realise that I need to let Mum in slowly, but thinks that I haven't started to because I am scared I won't be able to stop, just like my Auntie Ann letter to Mum – completely right, and I had not seen this staring me in the face! They suggested containing it somehow, i.e. talking for 15 minutes outside on a park bench and when we leave the park bench, the conversation is left there, not to be brought up again, forgotten for the rest of the day, until we next both agree to open up that box again on the park bench, or coffee shop or wherever we choose as the place for it to be allowed up for discussion. Excellent idea. Thanks! But how bad have things got for me to be having to do this?!

We had snack downstairs in the canteen. I had to have one of those cake things at 164 calories compared to the 120 calories of the usual cereal bars but there were none left today and I didn't feel right thinking of myself sitting downstairs and scoffing my way through three dry oatcakes, and a piece of cut up fruit and no-one else was doing this either. That's not really normal is it? But patient x was doing this cake thing too, with a pear, and the saturated fat was only 0.6, so I thought OK I could do this today and I did. Granted, yes, I walked quicker on my way home and I didn't manage my dinner at my house in London, but I was flexible enough to do this snack and I did have a light dinner when I arrived home at Mum's too. So it wasn't a complete disaster. *Angel* was assuring me that patient x had planned to do that cake bar, probably for a week, and was able to deal with it in her own way somehow, but you? You were greedy and will be enormous for that tomorrow... Poor patient y from the inpatient unit was texting me telling me she was back almost at admission weight, poor thing. I could cry for her.

INTERLUDE VI

DREAMS

A:-

Friday 26ᵗʰ March 2010:

1.   Absolutely horrific dream. Cannot even remember it properly, only trying to escape and climb over this wall but not making it and being raped and raped and raped, trying to escape; raped. Still in my dream, I turn up for Day Care the next day unable to speak and trying to hide everything inside with fake smiles on the outside. I try to carry on as normal in getting up, calling Mum, then I am on the bus, walking into the hospital, but it was all different surroundings, different places I didn't recognise and it was A&E, not my usual ward.

A patient from Day Care was there, patient x, and she knew something was wrong but I couldn't speak, just tried to cover up my emotions and tears and overwhelming fears, shock, repetition in my mind over and over again of the fresh experience that I couldn't get away from, yet had an inability to speak about this thing that I had been through and that I couldn't stop relaying in my mind or even tell anyone about, through shame. I was simmering up and bubbling away inside, more and more and I kept having these outbursts where my tears would fall right out in floods, uncontrollable, and I would be in a very public place and overwhelmed by this wave of emotion, yet nobody was helping – they noticed, but ignored, not knowing what to do or how to approach me. I was desperate to say something, but knew not what or how?

Angel Just-Rights

How could this have happened to me? Again and again and again? How? How? How?

I woke up, disturbed, firmly gritted teeth and frowning intensely, actually crying silently yet with no tears. I put on my electric blanket and got up and out of bed, it was 6.30am. I went downstairs to the toilet and then came back upstairs.

*I had been thinking that maybe I should let my Mum take us to see Kerry and the children today as I **really** was feeling that I needed my family around me. I wanted to feel loved unconditionally and accepted and safe, I needed kindness and around children this is usually the case and I love my nephew and niece. I didn't want to carry on living otherwise, being in this world was unbearable and I wanted to go to sleep and never wake up; hiding myself away in the dark, deep under the bed clothes, covering my face with my arm, biting my bed covers and turning my face away from reality. Old habits really do make me feel safe, hidden and distant from this harsh, unsafe place.*

Trapped; completely trapped and hurting inside. In pain and utter torture, never relenting and isolated with this, alone and with no choice. I wanted to let Mum in on what was going on for me, but how was I to bring it all out now?! Just like that? Where would I start and how could I?!

I opened my curtains to let in some daylight and got into bed, comforted by the feeling of warmth from the heat of my electric blanket. I turned it down and lay there looking out of the window, eyes transfixed on nothing, just vacant and staring wide open not daring to shut. I was trying to remember the dream more specifically, but I couldn't. Why now? How? Leave me alone!

I was craving reassurance and rigidity and needed to feel safe. I was dreading my breakfast. How was I going to even pretend to make my cereal when I had been skipping it all week and now all I wanted to do was to waste away and die off quietly and alone? Let me be free from this world, release me from torment and neglect and fear. Why haunt me with such vivid dreams that seem so real all over again, and again and again!

Angel Just-Rights

Mum seemed a bit happier last night and more receptive towards me and it felt nice. I really hope she was today too. Please Mum, be on my side, I still feel like I might break down in floods of uncontrollable tears right now, from the feelings I have left lingering over from that horrific nightmare just now.

CHAPTER 26:-

...NEW HONEST-TO-SELF DIARY ENTRIES ~

WEEKEND AT HOME...

- ### Saturday 27ᵗʰ March 2010:

After that nightmare I was worried about how I was going to do breakfast as I hadn't been having cereal at all for the last week, or was it two weeks? But I went back to sleep with the curtains open and before I knew it Mum came in at about 8:45am ready to start her cup of tea and the day ahead. All I wanted to do was to stay in bed, I can't get through today.

Downstairs, I joined Mum and made my tea and sat with her.

Kerry phoned and was trying to encourage us to make up our minds about if we were going to visit her today or not. I was put out because yesterday Mum had said that Kerry had asked if I wanted to go and visit tomorrow and I got angry saying she hadn't asked ME. I needed to calm down and see it rationally. But I was annoyed because when Kerry is alone through her husband going to football or parents evening for example, she expects us to feel for her and to come running. HELLO?! Alone constantly here! Mum and I! Plus, I had come home to spend the weekend with Mum, not to share Mum, and it was another stress I suppose that I hadn't planned for and was annoyed that I hadn't got a present for the children and thought I could have been looking for one during the week, lost out on a chance to walk more and spend more time out of the house wandering around on my feet instead of sitting loafing at home, as that would have been a purpose for a specific purpose. And so I was annoyed that the whole event hadn't been planned out and organised properly. I felt LAZY and that I could have achieved something else during the week, if only I had known.

Mum had her cereal and then set the table for me. She said she had read the meal plan and weighed out how much cereal I was supposed to be having – 30g – and it was two handfuls and this is what she did, plus a bit extra! Great! Even worse than I thought! I went back over to stand by the radiator to calm down. I find heat and warmth a comfort to my *Angel*. I sat down at the table with my fruit and couldn't even look at any cereal.

How could I explain that I was dreading even the sprinkle of cereal with skimmed milk and water today, never mind a big, huge bowl of cereal that was just a random amount shoved in the bowl and that actually Mum, I hadn't done this since being in hospital when I was forced to and even then I was suspicious of the amount I was given, not to mention my extreme fear and shame experienced those times I had been served the end of the packet crumbs, which meant I had twice as much as I should and twice as much as everyone else was having! Mum stormed out in tears after calling me deceitful and nasty, awkward, killing the family and just plain defiant. I got on with my breakfast feeling terrible. I put on Saturday morning cooks television very loudly to block it all out. I felt safe with this program as I knew its presenters, I knew its structure, I knew its layout and I knew it would keep my attention. I felt selfish and nasty underneath everything, but I had to have my rigidity this morning and nothing was going to stop me.

I poured the random cereal back into the box and left those in the bowl that had stuck to it, adding some milk and mostly water and shoved it in the microwave. Lord only knows what on earth I thought I was doing. I burned my tongue on the liquid trying to get it down quickly as it did look like dish water and I then threw most of it down the sink.

There. At least it looked as if I had continued to sit in the kitchen with my fruit and at least tried to have some cereal. I am so sorry Mum. I washed the bowl up and left it on the side to drain instead of putting it away, just maybe it would make Mum happier to see it when she came down, even with a little bit of remnant flake sticking there for added effect. I hated myself but tried to block it all out. Later, before snack, for which Mum had her toast and I had my coffee made with water, I poured some of the milk out of the container to make it more believable... What WAS I doing?!

During coffee, I was standing at the kitchen table writing this entry and Mum asked "Why don't you ever sit down?!" She called me "the most ignorant person". She hates me and can't stand the sight of me, and I understand why! I can't come home next weekend, and it's Easter – Thursday right through until Monday! Help!

Going to Kerry's now. Dreading it all but at least I can play with the children after the long boring lazy car journey, God I feel bad already. Can I go?

- ### Sunday 28th March 2010:

Bad day at home with poor Mum. She drove me to the train station and said she doesn't feel like going anywhere when she sees other girls my age with families because it makes her think even more about what I have ended up with i.e. nothing and that I am heading towards a life on the streets. I realised, or hoped, that Mum isn't angry at me, REBECCA, THE LOVING DAUGHTER, she is angry at me, ANOREXIA, THE EVIL ILLNESS, for what it has done and continues to do to this precious life and soul that she had brought into the world, full of love and looked after so well, gave everything to and gave up everything for and this is how she is repaid.

And that is exactly what I am angry at too. How me, with the illness no longer hidden from family and close friends but now very much out in the open for all to see, is keeping up the fight to hide Rebecca, the daughter, friend, colleague, auntie, sister, and, more importantly, the extent at which it is destroying my family and their lives in themselves it seems.

No, it is time to accept that I have been in denial and that I AM ANOREXIA! That there is no way out, only to search my whole being for that voice of Rebecca, who has been silently lost – completely mute and vacant from soul – for over twenty years having been slowly and painfully overtaken and over-ridden by the most evil voice of Anorexia.

I know exactly what my 'baby steps' now have to be and I know exactly what I have to do in order to use IT, MY VOICE, as the KEY to unleashing my final chance to freedom and happiness. It will be hard, feel outright impossible, but I HAVE to have this faith and keep it and ensure that the candle goes on burning, as only then will the lights keep lighting the path and the wind keep blowing me on, pushing and encouraging me down the right and only route: My only chance to be free from this grip of devilish existence!

I WANT TO BE, JUST REBECCA, AGAIN. I WANT TO BE JUST ME! I WANT the senses that glimmer of happiness had made me feel for those few seconds, back again and I want it 24 hours a day! I want to be happy. I want to be free. I know I have "a lot of work to do" (Book 2: Who Am I, Part 1, Chapter 20) in order to get past this and am ready to re-live my past in order to live any future I still hope to have left open for me.

CHAPTER 27:

A POEM ABOUT ME
A Poem about Me: Micci

Yes that's me.

Look and you'll see.

My hair is tied up away from

My eyes that seek out the good and detect all the lies.

My arms, they reach out to help those who are near.

My hands produce music, 's reduced some to a tear.

My heart is so warm, silently simmering inside.

I'm learning to 'live', to take life in my stride.

I never give in until I succeed.

My friends know I'm quiet, but let *me* take the lead.

I live to run risks, to laugh and enjoy!

I hope to create lives and not to destroy.

I dreamt that I *will* be headmistress, you'll see.

Now all I dream of is to be free.

It's all clear as can be.

That's positively

absolutely

me.

BOOK 3:

THE BIGGER PICTURE

Angel Just-Rights

CHAPTER 28:-

...WEEK OF DIARY ENTRIES ~

BEFORE, DURING, AND AFTER EASTER...

28i-...Diary Entries taken from Easter Week at Day Care...

-Try To Enjoy

-Day Care Review

-Meeting With Manager

- **Monday 29th March 2010:**

BBQ chicken filling with jacket potato and green beans followed by lemon and poppy seed sponge with custard. It was separate, separate, separate and then the pudding was actually nice tasting, but far too big and got stodgy. But still I did it.

- **Tuesday 30th March 2010:**

Everything was telling me not to go into Day Care today, go to the gym instead. Called Mum about six different times throughout the morning, was late for Pam and she was really angry and annoyed with me, only had half an hour with her today and she said could I go and make my snack with cold milk but I said no. Lou (staff) came in and made me fill my cup up a bit more. Whoops.

In my session we spoke about how to approach telling Mum more and being more open. Decided to take a few points from Auntie Ann email and have a conversation about it. Got a lot of thinking and planning to do now. Milk nearly made me cry as had to start and finish it quickly when I'd finished my session with Pam.

Had an off-the-cuff 'feelings group', a general check-in as they hadn't planned anything for us to do this morning. I was honest and told them how I was feeling sick that morning, because I think, of the review and Mum coming and also because of the email from my manager who wanted to meet for coffee. I remembered, with reminders from what patient x contributed to the group, about the reading I was doing last night and how happy I was with my personality, how comfortable I felt in being myself around my friends and without even realising it, just taking it for granted. Listening to patient y's contribution also made me think that there are choices in life, not just what we feel we have to do to tick the boxes, but to do it for ourselves. Patient z was talking about realising that she has to let people know how she is feeling, maybe by letter and Lilly straight away came up with writing it and then editing it.

Called my manager and arranged to meet Thursday at 5:00pm.

Dreading it.

Five bean goulash with rice and cauliflower followed by coconut rice pudding. Main was OK, just tomato with a few beans but the pudding was pretty horrible as it was far too sweet for me.

Again, no group had been planned for the afternoon, but we did finish the group on a positive note. Lou made us all spend two minutes writing some words about one other person in the room. I wrote about my key-worker Lou herself, finding it hard at first as there were so many words I could have put down, but I contained it using each letter of her name. It was particularly nice to do this because this morning she had announced to us all that she would be leaving in four weeks, to start a new job closer to her home and I hadn't congratulated or said anything to her, so now at least she knows that I respect her and have treasured a lot of her support and guidance, and tried to at least listen to her advice because I trust her and know she makes sense. Patient x wrote about me and she wrote 'thoughtful, determined – willing to keep fighting, intelligent, hopeful, under estimated'.

- **Wednesday 31st March 2010:**

Felt ABSOLUTELY FAT AND HUGE TODAY on the bus. Terrible. Shouldn't be in the world and certainly shouldn't be taking myself off to a day of scoffing food down at Day Care! But when I was sitting on the bus, I knew I had LOST weight and tried to think what was making me "feel fat", despite this.

Well, I was absolutely dreading my review and Mum coming later and her staying for dinner. This logically thought out, I still couldn't trust my scales had told me the right weight and I went on feeling "just terribly fat…"

Tuna and bean burrito with beans and carrots and bread and butter pudding with custard! Burrito usually is stuffed with tuna, but I got first pick so took the smallest and today it was cheddar cheese on top rather than that goat's cheese like last time at least, but mine had loads underneath! Managed to get rid of a bit on the table and threw some on the floor too. Well.

Met Mum and went for coffee in the nice cafe. Poor Mum was freezing. Review, lost weight rather than maintained and this was the deal. Another review next week or hospital. Great. Mum upset. Oxford Street. Got home to landlady who checked room and wanted me to sign a contract.

- **Thursday 1ˢᵗ April 2010 (April Fools' Day):**

Got up late again today because went to bed so late and couldn't sleep because of hunger and also dread about seeing manager today and getting through Day Care.

Got changed a hundred times in casual / work / smart outfits and in the end I wore black trousers, which now fit as opposed to fall down (size 6) and my new long black shirt thing and the long wool grey cardigan that Kerry had given to me in hospital to keep me warm, my low heeled black shoes and my long black coat, put on my necklace and my perfume for added effect. This is how my manager would remember me, not as the pathetic thing in ripped jeans and trainers, sporting a vacant look on her face. I don't know which is the 'real me' anymore!

Had a big spoonful of coffee in my cup this morning I couldn't help it. Called Mum about fifty times before going into Day Care this morning and tried to ask her what the curry was that was written on the menu. When I got in I had trouble choosing my menu option and then Lou came in and reminded me straight away that we were supposed to have a meeting at 10:00am and I had assured her that I would make an effort and be here on time but I had honestly completely forgotten about the meeting this morning! Felt awful about it, especially after having given her my word. She told me I had to take more responsibility and had to at least hold my weight and be truthful about how I'd done this week.

Chose Dahl curry and chocolate sponge with custard today, after much, much deliberation, but it was the right choice in the end; definitely safest as the chocolate pudding was just plain sponge.

Exercise group was OK, really seeing it from a different perspective to last time, which was my first time round. Don't want to be reminded even more of the exercise I'm not doing anymore though, as if it's not hard enough having it in my head from morning until night every minute of every second of every day as it is. But I guess it just makes me stronger, and I mean in reality and truthfully and in a healthy way, stronger.

Weekend planning group was good as Jill understands, and I quote her own words, *"Angel* of old, ha-ha". I love Jill, she's just great.

Had a new blueberry cereal bar today rather than the current one. It was less calories, but not as nice although I told everyone I prefer it to the raisin one just so I could choose it without people really knowing why. Oh dear. Haven't reached my goal of even doing a different biscuit in the morning snack even once this week – been a tough one.

Met manager – He apologised for not keeping in contact with me over the last year and said he needs to slap his wrists for that! Good chat over coffee and I feel better about going back to work now and even looking forward to it a bit. He said himself that it is 'baby steps' this time and I admitted to not getting caught up in the fight for my band 7 again.

Just have to worry about getting through the dreaded Easter weekend now.

28ii-...Diary Entries taken from Easter Long Weekend Away from Day Care...

-To Join In Celebrations With The Family, Or To Abscond?

-Realisations

- **Friday 2nd April – Monday 5th April 2010 (Easter Long Weekend):**

Couldn't get up for ages as deciding what to do and when to go home this weekend and how is it all going to work out? Plus I had more cottage cheese last night and finished the pot of yogurt in my efforts after speaking with Lou and so now I feel even more anxious about being weighed this morning. But it was OK.

355

I ate the wrap that Mum helped me to buy on Wednesday for lunch! With extra cottage cheese because I only planned to eat half of it! Felt good, but guilty that I had been so greedy and so I didn't have any yogurt, just a tangerine for pudding. But I did have the whole wrap and on my own! OK it was at 3pm, but I did it! Decided to go home as it was the best thing for me and the family. Got things ready in a rush while I had decided and before I changed my mind, dreading it underneath though, all the while.

Home and Mum in a better mood it seems. Mum asked me if I'd had dinner and I was honest. She said she'd made a beef dinner in the slow cooker to have with potatoes. Told Mum I don't eat beef or cheese when I'd said no thank you to the beef and her suggestion of jacket potato, cheese and beans! I said to her that she didn't have a clue and she said "no I don't unless you TELL ME." I said, but you just tell me I'm certainly mental and need serious treatment and storm out in a rage. I was standing by the fridge for ages trying to decide what to have and how to make something up that would be right and manageable, and politely asked Mum to leave me alone to do it and repeated myself, calmly, until she did leave and I could continue trying to think and then I went to sit in the lounge with her to eat it.

The rest of the evening Mum and I spent in separate rooms: Mum in tears, which made me feel even more ill with myself. She was blaming herself for not spotting my problems earlier and said she was too caught up in looking after Dad, but this so is not true Mum. Mum didn't even say goodnight to me and I felt so sad.

- **Saturday 3rd April 2010:**

Still in bed. Poor Mum yesterday. Thinking about breakfast: hope Mum goes out of room so I can prepare it normally, but no. Do it properly? How can I? I'd have to go for a long run afterwards and I don't want to start that again. Plus, I might have those reactions again and start 'S' and I couldn't handle that and it would be back to square one again – Fake...

...Being Fake: OK it will make Mum happy to see me eat, but the unhealthy behaviours I use to cope will return and I have been working so hard to ignore these impulses. I'm scared to start eating normally.

Should I compromise? Have what you can manage and slowly increase intake. Do it FOR ME. Then we can go to Lilton or anywhere we choose. Tell Mum what you HAVE been doing; tell Mum what you THINK you can manage; tell Mum you are trying your damned hardest!

Getting up now. It's a really nice day and I could REALLY GO FOR A RUN or maybe just a walk in the village, but I WON'T do either. Mum thinks it is awful that I don't even visit the Churchyard anymore, but I am scared to even do this because I know I will be overtaken by *Angel* and have to power-walk all the way up the next lane too...

Got up. Checked face, arms, and legs. Try to tell self that when I am making more progress then I can tone up more when I am reaching a healthier place and I will have more energy to do so...

•   **Sunday 4th April 2010 (Easter Sunday):**

The rest of the weekend went OK as Little Brother and his wife and their dog came to visit. As did Kerry and her family and so it was a busy house on Sunday and I got through the meals and snacks alright in my own token effort but was pleased I joined in with everything and even managed a small chocolate 'nest' at afternoon snack time, which everybody had. Mum was less so pleased and told me "You've had nothing. Get a sandwich or something for yourself now" right after the three-course meal! Not helpful.

•   **Monday 5th April 2010 (Easter Monday):**

On the way to the train station, Mum had commented on just how surprised she's been at Kerry's ability to take to motherhood so well, as she always thought it would be me, Rebecca, that would be the one to get married and have children first, be the family person, and not Kerry. I was in agreement with this comment, although I knew it was for no other reason except that Kerry was the clever one who was supposed to have the high-flying career (which, incidentally, she has achieved along with her perfect family) and Micci was good at other things like childcare and everything else, but oh Mum how I wanted to cry out to you that yes, I agree totally with what I had dreamed and expected of myself to be completely in opposition to this shell of shame and disappointment that I am now left with facing every single day!

A large part of me now regrets only one thing: that I was so unbelievably innocent, naïve and trusting enough to believe that Spen had actually CARED about ME. Never did I think twice when he walked me into all those chemists, drove me to all those doctors surgeries in the middle of the night, accompanied me to all the walk-in-centres, to Boots etc. etc. etc. when clearly he didn't care in the slightest, only for his own selfish ends.

Only now have I realised that maybe I had actually been given a gift of having his baby on so many occasions! Yet through what I thought was love, had become 'the norm', was an evil aftermath of betrayal and torture for ME because now I realise that I may be facing a life with no family and no children of my own, and all because of my own silent self and my inability to think or to speak as my double life of confusion slowly impaled.

- **Tuesday 6th April 2010:**

Today, on return from Day Care I was told that a new housemate would be moving in next week. This confirmed to me another factor telling me it was time to entrust in experimenting in small changes. After all, this was about to be forced upon me now, and wasn't that how I worked best?

CHAPTER 29:

CONFUSION TO CONCLUSION?

Real control handed back to Me – Bright Monday:

From the very start of the Easter Bank Holiday weekend – hearing my manager project that all can be well with my job and my feeling inspired to return to work being supported by my team through those 'baby steps', returning home to my Mum actually verbally requesting from me "You Have To Tell Me!" right through to the end of the weekend and the discussion between my Mum and I in the car about hopes, dreams and expectations verses reality – had confirmed to me that something had been my guide and was, once again, there by my side.

I believe that throughout the last four weeks (Friday 5th March 2010 – The Day of The Auntie Ann Event and the week of my Time Out on Reflection, through to Friday 2nd April 2010 Good Friday – The Day I was taken home to Mum and the week that celebrates the resurrection of Christ and the day I finished the writing of the contents of this Memoir, being specifically on that Easter Monday or Bright Monday or Renewal Monday) a guardian angel, here God, has been explaining to me and enlightening me, using only ways that I would be sure to understand, be safe and feel comfortable with, thus able to accept, this dreadful journey he has taken me on.

This Easter Monday 5th April 2010 He was telling me that those I love and who love me are ready to hear my cry and that this book has been my preparation, having achieved it with Him guiding me every step of the way. I am now in real control of my future and I have to continue to communicate in the way that I have been shown. I have to take responsibility. I have to make the changes.

Easter Monday and the conversation with my Dear, Dear Mum: He has handed me the final sign of permission to grasp THAT KEY firmly in my hands and to turn it in the lock. He has told me that NOW is the right time to reveal my true self from that fake reality I have kept secret from everyone in the world, in particular from those whom I so cherish, for the whole of my life that I can remember. It is time for me to be the real Rebecca, as Kerry and Little Brother came to life, so now should she.

To reveal the torments I thought had Been and Gone...Happened in the Past...Dealt with...Dead and Buried...but which had really been left there to Rot...Silently Festering Away...The Steaming Stench growing ever denser by the day...Revelling and basking in its sly parasitic way...Clinching itself firmly...Snug and Profane...Assured and Secured in the new home it adeptly chose to ride...Retrained and made Wane by its poisonous cloud...Quick to discern any faint remnant cry by the thundering storms...Silencing tears through its making of rain...Detecting desperate times with an ambushing eye...Driving all the more to determine no room for the sun or the moon or a hint of blue sky...To Shine a light in its dwindling, dying providers eye...but then in one gust, so strong and so bright in this wind shines sun's rays, which recovers the sight in this power that blows away dust, to reveal a path free to take where you finally have YOUR SAY.

Him who has placed the key back into MY POWER, where it belongs: The only soul, who can find the REAL STRENGTH enough to throw it out there, naked for all to see, to burn in hell and never to rise again, **IS ME.**

CHAPTER 30:

DEAR FAMILY:

THE NEXT STEP IN CHANGE, BUT HOW?

Do You Agree By Not Turning This Key;

No Future Can Be For The Tell-Tale Like Me?

My Fate Lies In Death! It's Just Me And My Stench;

Together With Pest I Will Rest (Tick!) Conquest.

No Need To Despise As Uncertainty Dies;

Along With Hushed Secrets And Lies That Chastise.

In Battling On I'm Prolonging The Con;

For All This Is Selfish And Woefully Wrong!

As Eyes Fear Revival, 'Til Lids Finally Sleep;

My Battles Incessantly, Gruellingly Steep.

Mind Racing! Heart Thumping! Adrenaline Troubling!

Sweating Disgrace From Dire Screams In My Dreams!

Angel Just-Rights

All I Am Asking Is A Moment In Peace;

The Noise, Rage, Fear And The Fight Just To Cease.

Show Me The Lock That My Keys May Release!

Then Maybe They'll Trust Me Godmothering Dear Niece?

Promise One Thing To Me, Each One Of You:

Never Solitarily Stew!

Don't Keep All Inside! Don't Think 'Must Abide!'

Really Listen And Take Care Of YOU.

You May Trust In The Bible, Believe And Have Faith;

As, With Him, You'll Eternally Be Safe, As It States:

"...There Is Nothing Concealed That Will Not Be Revealed;

Or Hidden, That Will Not Be Known"

"Therefore Do Not Fear Them" As, In Fight Or In Flight;

"All Secrets, Will Come To Light" (Matthew 10:26)

Accept They're Your Truths, Bravely Leave More Than Clues;

For All Worries Can Be Worked Through (So I'm told)

(Epilogue: Thanks and Pledge).

Angel Just-Rights

Confront All You Feel And Respect That It's Real;

In Time You Will Heal And Begin To Reveal;

That Spirit Inside, Waiting Patient Their Cue;

Is The Wonderful, Real-life, True Renewed You.

NOW IS MY TIME TO CHANGE.

NOW IS MY TURN.

...Interlude VII...

INTERLUDE VII

DREAMS

A:-

Friday 9th April 2010:

1.   Mum and I were in a department store shopping together and we were looking at the nightwear. I saw some nice black and white pyjamas, which turned into a night dress that was also black and white and was reminiscent of the one Amir had bought for me that night [Book 1: Secrets Out, Part 5, Chapter 16], but then it turned into a burgundy colour (my favourite colour) and finally into burgundy bridesmaids dresses (as at my sister's wedding), which I commented on being a nice colour. Mum said "No, you have to think about the colour suiting your bridesmaids, I don't like these".

Mum was taking it seriously, as if I was shopping for the perfect dresses themselves, for the bridesmaids at my own wedding. But I was thinking "What if I don't want to get married?" but Mum was saying I must.

2.   I was in the cinema with Kerry and Little Brother and we went to sit with 'him'. The younger Wil, whom I had never known but had seen photos of, was sitting with his friend Karl and some other friends a couple of rows further back. They were whispering and pointing at me and my family circle and I was feeling awkward.

'He' was in tears and had absolute fear in his eyes and I could see Wil's friends pushing Wil to say what they had obviously talked about and decided must be said here; now; today. The seats were

getting closer and closer until there we were, all sitting there in the Old Lounge Wing at home in Granada: Kerry sprawled across the settee all relaxed, Little Brother on the other chair, Wil still agitated and whispering amongst his friends, 'him' on his own, also younger, and Mum sitting in her green chair by the fire. The television was on and Mum seemed to be oblivious to the increasing whispering and agitation going on. I was silently willing that everything would just calm down and be peaceful.

I could see the sheer fear in 'his' eyes, but he was being brave. I kept telling him "No, don't!" and opened up my arms for him to come and sit next to me, but he wouldn't.

I heard Wil then suddenly say "If 'he' won't speak, I will". 'He' whispered, "But it's...!" I said "Don't!" Mum was trying to look like she'd not noticed the whispering and that something was wrong.

'He' moved to sit on the low stool in between Mum and the television. I said "Don't!" 'He' was now crouched on the floor in front of Mum's feet and said "...We weren't just..." and the rest faded away.

Mum said she couldn't believe she was hearing it, what must the neighbours think? Can they hear? She was in tears, frantically looking at the walls as if they had ears or holes and all the neighbours were standing there listening in, shocked and disgusted.

I motioned to 'him' to come and sit with me and he did, he was just like a small child that fit tightly protected in my arms, but I could still tell it was 'him'.

Kerry started to speak and I said I didn't say anything because I was worried about Mum not being well and this all being too much for her. I asked Kerry how she knew and she said she had sent a text to Wil from my phone pretending to be me and Wil had told her that he knew something wasn't right from our relationship we had together.

CHAPTER 31:-

...DIARY ENTRIES ~ CHANGES...

31i-A Weekend of Small yet Significant Changes, FOR ME.

-Experiment: Record Thoughts, Feelings and Actions; Before, During, After.

- **Saturday 10th April 2010:**

Breakfast – Thoughts / Feelings Before:
Decided to have 150 ml semi-skimmed milk and one block of cereal for breakfast now rather than 150 ml skimmed milk and a sprinkle of porridge / cereal flakes as the oats come up to the top if put it in the microwave and the bowl appears to be full even though there is just watery milk underneath. Will have tea and an apple in replacement of the juice that I am supposed to have. They allow this in hospital so I know it is OK. Actually no, I will have the 100 ml of fruit juice as my plan states, rather than the fresh fruit that I usually have, because I would probably get away with having just one tiny tangerine and that is just cheating myself, right?

Nervous about going to do it NORMALLY and won't distract myself by reading the paper, but I will make an effort to talk nicely to Mum instead. Mum really made efforts to speak to me last night and after my dream too, I need to start today. Going now. Not even getting changed first as I usually would.

Feel happy but very unsafe, but Mum is here and I can come and occupy myself with getting ready for the day when I finish and write down my thoughts etc. Wish me luck. Bye for now. Oh, I'm feeling

I can't do my yogurt today after getting so upset over it yesterday at lunchtime so I am leaving that out completely. Feel OK as changing the rest of my breakfast and doing this bit completely properly.

Breakfast – Notes:
Went downstairs. Poured semi-skimmed milk. Got out block of cereal and put it straight into the bowl. Put 150 ml water in with the milk, as I usually do with the skimmed every day. Mum said "Why are you putting water in with it? It's like you're not having it. Right, you haven't had it. It doesn't count. It's no good Rebecca". I retorted with "It's still going in! I'm still having it!" and I stormed back upstairs immediately, saying "I'm not having anything then, I don't know why I try".

Was going to get ready for the day and carry on with my routines, as I usually would have, as I was still very angry. There was now no way I could go back downstairs and do it now. I started to write things down and felt my heart beating hard out of anger and frustration that I was so determined to do this change in having a normal breakfast before it all started to go so wrong. Started panicking and thinking "Should I? Shouldn't I?" FOR ME?

I decided that I will still have it with the water, as I had already measured it all out in the jug and I actually couldn't do it otherwise at all – it will just taste like cream and stick to my tongue and I couldn't then sit in the car simply idle for the following two hours while on the journey to Kerry's house – and I AM still having it, and it DOES still count. Maybe tomorrow or next week I can try without the water but today, I am going to beat my anorexia and do what I said I would do and I will stick to what I was prepared and ready to go downstairs and do, previous to getting angry. Without water is just too unmanageable today. It's either with water or NOTHING.

Going back down to do it now, feel awful, shamed and humiliated but holding onto fact that I am doing right, for me and so ignore the horrible feelings and ignore Mum telling you it doesn't count, because it does...

Breakfast – Thoughts/Feelings After:
Did it. Feel bit rubbish but Mum was good as she was talkative and at least I can get on with life until snack time. Leaving for Kerry's at 10:30am – 1 hour.

Mid-Morning Snack – Thoughts / Feeling Before:
Plan to have coffee and plain biscuit for snack. Can't do 200 ml of semi-skimmed milk again no way, because will be just sitting in the car straight away for 2 hours and then going straight into lunch, which I couldn't do. This is what I can manage.

Deciding on the biscuit – I don't know if I'll be able to do it when it comes to it. Thinking cup of skimmed milk? Don't know…good calcium but bad being skimmed. No. Coffee and biscuit. MUST DO THIS WHEN IT COMES TO 10:30AM OK?! Have the semi-skimmed milk tonight for supper. SORTED.

Mid-Morning Snack – Notes:
OK. Mum was having toast as usual and this confused me and I tried it too: I put it in the toaster and sat down with it on my plate with my coffee. It looked huge and dry and I thought well I have to have even more bread at lunchtime today, so I changed it for a biscuit. Feel bad but ate it all!

Mid-Morning Snack – Thoughts / Feelings After:
Let's get going now. Dreading lunch but will have to do it.

Lunch – Thoughts / Feelings Before:
Going to have a sandwich from supermarket or from coffee shop like last couple of times. Taking an apple with me for pudding. We'll have a hot drink from coffee shop when we're there. Might see what Mum is choosing for pudding or maybe Kerry might get cake out when we arrive, I don't know! No way can I do yogurt still.

Lunch – Notes:
Wrap from supermarket – went back to car and had it all, except the dry end bits. Apple for pudding. Mum didn't have a pudding at all! I left half of it for later because I was obviously taking ages and Mum wanted to go back into the coffee shop for a hot drink before the sun went in.

Lunch – Thoughts / Feelings After:
Feel full. Had to rush it a bit. Had nice sit in the sun with Mum outside at coffee shop though. Looked for cereal bar in service station while Mum bought some flowers for Kerry in another shop, but feel too stuffed to even think about it. Just want to not be in the car sitting down!

Tea – Thoughts / Feelings Before:
Knew we were going to end up being out of the house for it. We were at a Garden Centre sitting outside in the sun. Very nervous about what was going to be on the menu...

Tea – Notes:
Chose toasted teacake. Mum and Kerry had the same. Dreading it coming with butter smothered all over it, but it came separately to my relief! Thank you! Only managed half of it because it was twice the size of the hot cross buns we had a choice of at Day Care and I thought this was OK. Also, Nephew was enjoying his ice-cream and was still hungry for teacake and jam and so I gave him some. Well I am his Godmother!

Tea – Thoughts / Feelings After:
Felt OK as had been actively playing with Nephew a lot today.

Dinner – Thoughts / Feelings Before:
Nervous of potatoes and salmon. At lease the potato is portioned and I can try to compare everything size-wise to Day Care routines and rules rather than my own skewed thinking.

Dinner – Notes:
Salmon, jacket potato, salad AND vegetables (mange tout and baby corn), fruit for pudding as still can't face yogurt. Had dinner quite late by the time we got back and got it ready, although preparation didn't take long and I was pleased at this; thank you Mum.

Dinner – Thoughts / Feelings After:
Stuffed but OK I suppose, as Mum is here. Feels like I really pushed the boundaries as I had ALL THE POTATO. Really happy I managed it though and quite sure that my meal was enough, I think. Really need to get some more alternatives to yogurt. I have

portioned ice creams, but couldn't do that tonight as well as everything else and it is later than usual too.

Supper – Thought / Feeling Before:
Couldn't face doing another semi-skimmed milk as still full and usually go straight to bed / sleep after snack as so tired and couldn't imagine being able to do this at all, I would feel panicky and unsafe, insecure and I hate that feeling especially in the dark silence of the night.
Glad Mum is here, but ultimately I would be on my own with it all...

Supper – Notes:
Tea with milk and half a rice cake.

Supper – Thoughts / Feelings After:
OK but annoyed because I had to pull out all the tiny chocolate bits, which I have never had to do before, maybe just the odd one, but I couldn't allow myself to eat even one chocolate bit tonight and it annoyed me even more because the chocolate bits are SO miniscule! Usually I can eat the whole half rice cake (equivalent of a biscuit in calories) but I was feeling on-the-edge and scared I think, about having done the bigger dinner and tea and lunch and snack and breakfast and everything else more properly today. Plus, the chocolate rice cake was initially bought to help me introduce myself slowly back into eating chocolate without 'S' even just the phlegm or danger of starting a binge / vomit cycle.

So pleased that my eating was a lot more normal today. Felt so much safer and less head stress that I knew exactly what I was going to have and was taking responsibility for doing it properly myself. A relief in a way. But I couldn't have done this without Mum being there by my side, even though any arguments may have arisen; I knew that if I got distressed of course she would be there for me.

Drinks – Thoughts / Feelings Before:
Uneasy at having more milk in tea and coffee but tried to ignore this. Didn't feel safe having it, but I did have it and am glad I did (worried now though, but hey...).

Drinks - Notes:

Tea and coffees, juice at breakfast time, one bottle of water, water in the milk and juice too.

Drinks – Thoughts / Feelings After:
Even more milk.

So nice to drink a bottle of water rather than bottles of fizzy diet drinks to fill me up! Pleases my Mum and pleases myself too!

31ii-First Full Week Back at Day Care and String of Confirmation Signs that my Guidance Is Ever Present.

-Changes, Changes, Changes Everywhere.

- **Monday 12th April 2010:**

Maintained my weight exactly, thanks Lou!

- **Tuesday 13th April 2010:**

Our group at Day Care this morning was on 'Change!'

I really enjoyed being silly in this group and realised that I don't actually need to know exactly what I have planned for the day as I would be more inclined to worry about it, spend time thinking of ways to avoid it and not be able to apply myself in the present and engage with others at that time. I felt a glimmer of what I, 'Well Rebecca' used to be like, laughing and joking with friends with no worries – as opposed to being constantly fake – and enjoying the moment and I want this feeling back!

We were also given a worksheet that split up each area of life, with a column to complete, entitled 'How will things be in my life this time next year, if a) I don't make changes and b) I do make changes.' I completed this quickly and it confirmed that which I already knew: that I would have to face the very things that I fear most in this world, which means changing today, in order to make my life bigger, free my soul and be able to enjoy living in the moment, where I belong, after all why shouldn't I?

This evening my new housemate moved in! She seems lovely, a bit younger and excitable and asks a lot of questions, but I also finished another part of the Memoir tonight, which I also find significant...

...This week, everything is screaming out at me "time to change!" but how do I do this?

I need help, I need inspiration; I need to feel safe!

•   **Wednesday 14th April 2010:**

Today I was told how to take the next 'baby step' to change!

In the meeting with my community local health team, my Doctor had returned (the last time I saw him was right before my second emergency hospital admission).

We had a long meeting and at first I was irritated by his continued questions that seemed to be too similar and never-ending but it took me a while to realise that maybe I had all my priorities wrong and was trying to force myself into doing something that I thought was the next step, but clearly was not.

I had discussed the fact that I felt I was not making any further progress in my therapy sessions with Pam and was almost blaming this on the relationship I had with her, my therapist who I'd been seeing for over two years and I was frustrated at having to still carry out the same exercises with her each week, yet two years on! I could be right in some points as I feel frustrated when leaving the sessions because I haven't gained anything or learnt anything new or spoken about anything I need to.

But my doctor made me realise that maybe, although I had addressed my secret demonic past (in the outburst of this Memoir writing) that I was not in a strong enough position to DEAL with it yet and I think he is totally right in this! I need to re-prioritise my recovery and now that I have my truth written down, I can finish the paper version completely and THEN concentrate on my nutrition and social and work lives and only then, when I am stronger in myself, can I choose whether to, how to, to whom, deal with or finally bring out my other life – once it is forgotten forever – please!

This evening our new arrival at the house, called a house meeting, which is something that we never had in the past in this house share. I was scared and worried that they'd bring things up that I had done to upset them or annoy them, but this was far from the case.

I realised that it had been only me that had isolated myself from them, everyone, in the last few years particularly as they responded to all my inputs and involved me in decisions etc. When they were swapping phone numbers, I didn't ask anyone for their number, feeling like why would they want my number? Then my phone rang and it was them calling me and I suddenly felt nice, included, and happy.

I made an effort to try and laugh and joke with them even though I wasn't feeling it inside at all, but it made me realise just how awfully unsociable I had become and I hated this, it made me angry and loathe what I had done to myself and of what I had not made of my life!

I did want to stay and talk to them, but I was freezing cold and so retired into my room after the meeting to get warm by my heater! I was feeling scared that it would become a real sociable house and I would have to leave myself out and look weird and even though I so didn't want that to happen, look what I had just done! Plus, I didn't have my dinner that night because I was so scared to go and spend time in the kitchen as I was thinking they would think I was greedy, they would be annoyed I was spending a lot of time in there, preparing my food and what on earth was I doing for so long, greedy girl! I was then scared that they would see me taking all this food into my room, shutting the door and thinking of me indulging in my salad and apple. It was easier not to, and to make a bigger snack before bed and so that is what I did.

- ### Thursday 15th April 2010:

Curry day at Day Care again...will probably have the Dahl option and vegetables today and then the pudding.

This morning I had a long key-working session with Lou. It began at 10:20am and was supposed to last 10 minutes as we have snack at 10:30am every morning.

But it lasted until 10:55am. When we walked back into the room with everyone sitting at the table with their empty mugs, I thought maybe they won't notice that I had missed it, but they did. I made my snack with Lou in the kitchen and was made to take it into the group room and have it in there!

The room is tiny and there were a lot of us in there today. I asked Lou if I could have it quickly in the other room but she said "What have we just been talking about?" and I replied "Yes I know, sitting in the lounge with my housemates is a small step to change" and I knew it would be good to practice this in this small room with all my peers: they would know how I was feeling, they had eaten their snacks and knew I had to have mine and so I went inside and sat down.

I felt so subconscious, I always do in there anyway but here I was the only one with a mug of milk on my lap and a biscuit to get through, with everyone in there watching me! I know they had all had theirs, but this was different. I froze with it on my knee and my thoughts were racing...

"Fat, ugly imbecile, look at you greedy thing and look at everyone else. Go on then, they're all waiting to see you take your first greedy sip of that thick, creamy milk..."

I couldn't do it, my thoughts were absolutely terrible, so strong and my tears were welling. I was stuck. There was nowhere to go to escape. I imagined seeing myself still sitting here with it on my lap, or discarded on the floor at the end of the group at 12:00, lunch time. It was just getting worse. My tears welled up and I turned to

Jill and asked if I could just go out for a minute and she came to sit with me in the dining room, bless her.

I felt awful for taking her out of the group and for not being able to have the snack in there, but knew I could do it quicker and in a bigger space, away from prying eyes and thoughts. I couldn't have expected anyone to encourage me to 'have it' in the group room either, as it wasn't fair on them and it was group time, not snack time.

I was so thankful to Jill for sitting with me, I did only take a short time; I just wanted it done and I knew I had to, and was feeling really bad for being in this situation and just wanted to make it better.

I told Jill that I had changed my priorities after the meeting yesterday firstly with the doctor and secondly with my housemates and I was realising just how much this existence IS NOT ME: REBECCA that my family used to know that my friends used to know that EVEN I used to know and it made me angry! I jolly well was going to get better!

At the end of my key-working session I had also felt (at least) that I had spent the hour with Lou very well indeed and had asked her if she would mind writing a summary of our session, as I was bound to forget everything as soon as I left the room, which was usual for me now no matter how hard I tried to make my brain work: a section of the summary is as follows:

-New housemate – good for Rebecca, bad for Anorexia.

-Current low weight – may lead to inpatient admission ("Your immediate response was 'I have to do this, I know, but I don't know how to'; suggesting you are currently stuck") if this is not turned around by me outside Day Care.

-Addressed past – but not strong enough to deal with it and have re-prioritised health and nutrition and life skills as top-of-the-list with adopting positive coping mechanisms to deal with after thoughts and behaviours subsequent to food intake including re-building my life healthily and Day Care to help with this.

-Patterns and logic – really help me putting things into practice (Lilly rightly suggested I look at things in patterns) and how the main challenge is managing the negative thoughts that intervene at every positive attempt.

-Experiment – This weekend my 'experiment' is to not tell myself "I have to do this", but "I will try this" or "I want to do this" and keeping the bigger picture in mind.

-Key Point – Be aware of the voice that is negative and take responsibility for your actions; do the opposite!

- **Friday 16th April 2010:**

Did canteen today and I chose to have the chocolate chip sponge and custard for pudding rather than anything else! Plus everybody followed! And it was nice.

- **Saturday 17th April 2010:**

Awful thoughts starting from the moment I open my eyes. Breakfast, the day etc.

Had my block of cereal! Left by 9:30am. Got bus and called Little Brother, Kerry and Mum. Paced from last bus stop – Tottenham Court Road to Marble Arch end of Oxford Street to shop I was aiming for. Bought two pairs of trainers in sale, was looking for Lou's leaving present and card and found three options I can go back to, all from the same shop: Pretty notebook and pencil, necklace, flamingo key ring; all around same value.
Whilst looking, I bought a little necklace that is a gold chain with a silver butterfly and a black clock face at 12:55. I bought it as it is significant to me in that I can constantly be reminded that precious time is ticking away and every second counts now...

...Interlude VIII...

INTERLUDE VIII

DREAMS

A:-

Saturday 17ᵗʰ April 2010:

I was arriving at my Town Music Festival in time for my Piano Class, in which I was playing one of my exam pieces that I actually did play in the festival in real life once, and to which I had momentarily forgotten my chords (also, unfortunately, in real life!)

I walked through the Church where it was being held and everybody was getting ready. I was wearing my glasses and in real life I had never dared to do this (feeling inadequate and humiliated and angry that my eyes didn't work) until I went to university and started to wear contact lenses.

Anyway, I went into the practice room / hall in order to put my bags down and to have a practice before my competition class started, only my glasses had disappeared and were nowhere to be seen and I had no contact lenses with me! I walked over to the piano to see if I could play without 'seeing' and I couldn't!

I had to withdraw my entry from the competition. I felt sad and isolated due to my own careless doings. I was sitting in the room thinking about this, while the class took place, when a man enters from my previous music schooling / some guy from the television – I can't put my finger on the face. He 'comes onto me' and I manage to control the situation so we are kissing and cuddling and it is nice and feels safe as there are people also close-by.

377

Angel Just-Rights

When it was time to leave, my Mum appeared (she'd been watching the class) and we left together. We were in my secondary school car park and exited from the Old Hall part of the school. We started walking towards our car when we heard an old woman's voice shouting.

The old woman was being told to get out of the school, near the Old Hall Exit that we'd just come out of ourselves and she was wearing a pure white gown and had long white hair. People in the car park were beginning to watch. She walked past my Mum and I turned when my Mum said accusingly and so the old lady could hear her distaste at her behaviour "Who's that?!" The old lady started to shout at us and become even more furious. My Mum was really tall in my dream, but I was on guard of her and trying to step in to resolve the lady shouting and my Mum looked scared on her face and had tears in her eyes.

The woman turned into a man in a suit, but he was still big and I became confused but carried on defending my Mum and trying to defuse the situation as best I could. I was standing up to it in between her and the man to protect my Dear Mum who was very tall in my dream, yet tearful. I managed to diffuse the situation, the man left out of the gate and we got into the car.

CHAPTER 31III:-

...DIARY ENTRIES ~ CHANGES CONTINUED...

31iii-First Full Week Back at Day Care and String of Confirmation Signs that My Guidance Is Ever Present, Continued.

-All Lights Are On; You Have To Take Responsibility
-Final Desperate Chance To Change!

- **Sunday 18ᵗʰ April 2010:**

Today I went to meet Sarah. The sun was shining and I couldn't say no because I was the one who had asked her in the first place, plus I wanted to go really.

I called her when I got there at 13:30 and she said she was grabbing a burger on the way and so I told her I would be in the supermarket close-by.

I looked at the sandwiches and fruit and drinks. I was disgraced at what I bought for myself after much stress, which reminded me of the reasons I stopped putting myself into these situations in the first place because of the stress it caused me: a diet coke and a mini packet of apple slices. We went to sit in the courtyard in the sun and I drank my diet coke while she enjoyed her delicious-looking burger and orange juice. If only I could do that! I felt fat walking around as it was, even without having had my breakfast and now my lunch. I couldn't even get my pathetic apple slices out. How can I ever get better from this? Just want to go home and die to be honest.

Sarah asked me, "Do you ever want children?" I said "Well I'm not sure". But then when I – Rebecca – had chance to think, I said "Well in an ideal world I would have children tomorrow, with my gorgeous loving husband and live at my nice house with my nice new growing family" and it made me happy thinking of the life I dreamt as pure fantasy, once a far-away possibility but still a possibility in becoming real, but not now.

Sarah was telling me not to "put off" looking or making "it" happen any longer because it will get harder and harder, more impossible, more impossible and she is right. She is seven years my senior, came out of a twelve year relationship when we met and has now met a guy that she is deciding whether to have children with or not, before it is realistically too late for her.

I know my dreams of the life that I want are still there from childhood; those are my real dreams, certainly not this existence! Where has this gotten me except from friendless, lonely, almost jobless, having lost all my skills, hope, motivation and my ability to live? Why shouldn't I actually chase my dreams? I can still do it and have it all, right? Only I can actually make my dreams come true: Family; holiday; job; actual friends; being present to and for my existing family. How nice would this be?!

Sarah was telling me of the "just nice", contented and happy feelings that she'd felt while simply sitting in the sun with a glass of wine and some olives, but with the new love of her life, on the holiday they'd returned from that week. To feel love and to have someone who loves you and to love back can be the most amazing thing and those feelings I want to experience again, it just seems impossible for me to ever reach that place, no matter how hard I try now. Even my relationship with Spen had ended because of *Angel*. I want to grasp my LIFE QUALITY RIGHT BACK more than anything, but I get so scared and terrified and petrified and I give in to *Angel* every time and this angers me!

I told Sarah about this memoir and she made me realise that actually, when the time is right, I don't have to show it to all my family. Maybe just inform my Mum that I have written something and then to give her the choice of reading it or not, and only my

Mum. I need my life, I need my health and actually, 'Secrets Out' may not have the horrific consequences I foresee.

I just fear that if death doesn't take hold before my secret life is out, it may ensue after all is revealed, which would be so much worse for everybody. So then, is it better to keep my whole story a secret until I die, in which case I may as well give in to *Angel* right now and die as soon as possible for the sake of everyone?

CHAPTER 32:-

...DIARY ENTRIES ~ HONESTY...

32-Be Honest With Yourself First!

-Admit Denial!
-Final Straw

- **Monday 19th April 2010:**

Lost a lot of weight. Worried they are going to recommend the ward. Need to look for my passport or get my memoir printed and do my suicide note. Sorry. I need help; I don't need to be turned into a zombie and be spoken to like an imbecile. No way. Not again. Thanks, but no way. And if they recommend the ward then they can put everyone else attending the out-patients service in there before me! Must show them my choices are getting better at Day Care so at least they can see I am really trying and coping – I can just start walking there too – no! Well I have Wednesday off, so I suppose that is OK. I hate this.

Today in 'Goal Setting Group', Lilly made me see that my inability to spend time in the kitchen at my flat this weekend, and in the evenings because my housemates are around, is the anorexia! I had not been aware of this before but I guess it is true. Everyone else in the group could see it except for myself. Great.

The thing that stops me is the voice. Severe guilt, greedy, paranoia of how they'll be thinking I am spending ages in the kitchen, in there yet again, how long do I spend in there greedy thing! And then hearing my plates and the kettle and the microwave and taking it into my room to indulge in. It's better not to. You don't need to, you're strong.

Lilly pointed out that I'd had it for so many years that I wouldn't see it and that it is hard to be aware of it. I realised that in all the house shares this was definitely a trend with me and even in my halls at university and at other peoples' houses I visited, as in Scotland at Spen's sister's house.

I remember in The Boys' House, I cooked a three course meal for Wil, just to say thank you for helping me to move. I enjoyed doing it all but something stuck in my mind that day...

...The boys were interested in what I was cooking and I had no problem what-so-ever in sharing with them at all, in fact I wasn't shy and I was making jokes and laughing and enjoying myself. I did feel a little guilty about taking over the kitchen, although I was neat and didn't really take it over at all. Plus, it was a very big kitchen with ample room for us all to be cooking at once, if that happened to be the case. But, I said to them, "don't worry, I won't be doing this every night!" and they replied "Oh, why not? It's good" It stuck in my mind because I would never prepare a meal for myself, never mind spending time on a lavish three course meal all for myself. But at the time I didn't say anything and just laughed it off, but it did stick in my mind as feeling strange, on my part, yet I couldn't put my finger on it until now.

I had made a starter of mushroom and goats cheese bruschetta (which Wil could enjoy while I prepared the main dish) followed by fish stew and rice (which I ate a little of with him too and there was some left for my housemates also) and then I treated Wil to his favourite pudding (which he polished off whilst he watched television and spoke to my housemates and I could clear away in the kitchen).

...Thanks for pointing this out to me Lilly.

- ## Tuesday 20th April 2010:

Filled half of my mug of milk up with water from the tap AT DAY CARE (!) this morning ☹!

Printed an outline of the Memoir out for Pam today. She started our session by informing me that she'd had to put my name down on the ward waiting list and had applied for funding. My heart sank.

Awful day at Day Care today for pretty much everyone. I think they were all getting at ME when they were all talking about being honest. Only at the end of the day when I was asked to stay and have a chat with Pam and Jill, did it confirm it to me when they told me that the ward have a bed free and want me to go there straight away. I straight away said "I'm not going!"

Jill explained very simply to me that they really fought my corner to negotiate my staying in the Day Care program so long as I comply with the putting on of 0.5 kilos a week until I get up to what I weighed on coming out of hospital and I agreed.

They both were open with me about falsifying my weight in the past and asked why I hadn't done the same this time and I said because I didn't want to be dishonest and I really do want help getting my health back and my life back in all honesty and not in lies. I had seen others manage to and I wanted to too.

I could see that they were concerned about me as they said "can you see where you're at right now?" I know it's slipping, maybe too much, but I kept saying I AM making changes, not huge ones and not constantly, but I am trying! And I don't believe I have gone down that route and given in again, and I know they don't believe me, but to me I haven't, not until I give in to walking AND THE GYM, WHICH I HAVE NOT DONE!

I think maybe I need to realise for myself which chapter in the poem that we were given in our group on 'Change' today, it is exactly where I am fitting right now.

Angel Just-Rights

Training day for Day Care staff, so all patients had a day off.

Went to Leicester Square Trocadero to pick up Lou's present.

Caught bus to Waterloo and then got off and walked just because I thought it would be quicker and it was a nice day. Met Ravi at 4pm at Leicester Square. Went for a coffee at coffee shop.

He annoyed me a bit because he was obviously trying his best to get a seat in a really quiet, deserted part of the coffee shop or downstairs and I wanted to sit in the window to look out in the sun! I was assertive and it felt good to state my need and keep to it! We had a nice chat and then after an hour, I had finished my coffee and was feeling rather tired and again, I was impressed with myself for being able to communicate the truth to him and it felt good. No Secrets. Nothing Fake.

I felt irritated for a second time because he was obviously trying his absolute best to stay longer in any way that he possibly could, even though he was supposed to be going back to work and I kept repeating that I was tired and needed to get home, but still he didn't budge until I had really pressed on the fact that I wanted to leave and this made me feel good too that I had been able to do this and that it had worked.

I think he wanted to bring up more subjects, but I was making a quick exit. I really was tired and feeling a bit ill and needed to get myself home for dinner. I couldn't deal with anything else right now and I had said before I'd met him that it would only be for an hour.
Didn't have dinner until 9pm tonight. Felt so ill. I prepared it in desperation and in front of housemate again as she came to do her washing up. I had tried to go into the lounge to speak to them before I went into the kitchen so that they would leave me alone, but no. I saw her looking sneakily at what I was doing and I felt awful and nearly walked out until she'd finished, but remembered Day Care and persisted on with my preparation, for me.

I made my cut up lettuce, cut up beetroot, half a carton of cottage cheese (as housemate was watching me do it!) two wrap things left over from yesterday (10kcals each) and tea and then quickly took it back to my room.

Had snack at 10:30pm: Apple, milk with a sprinkle of hot chocolate AND ONE SLICE OF TOAST WITH MARMITE AND THE LAST TWO MINI WRAPS (10KCALS EACH)! I had been feeling so absolutely faint and ill, I had to. I hadn't had anything during the day hardly, and it is only the bread that I should have had at dinner time, lunch time and breakfast time is what I told myself for justification and the trying to making it OK and not feel overwhelmingly wrong...all the while trying to tell myself it is not going to do anything, it is OK, tomorrow is more likely to come if you DO have something to eat and the only way to do it is to change your ways...right now.

Still felt so ill and was scared to go to sleep. Felt very, very, very, very unsafe indeed and as if I would have a panic attack at any time. Couldn't breathe. Felt FAT. Great all this is starting again...

Thinking about having a block of cereal or biscuit, even a chocolate! Mum says to keep up your blood sugar levels, but I just couldn't persuade myself to and the fear of starting an awful binge and vomit behaviour cycle all over again was not worth trying chocolate over. Chocolate would be the easiest to get down, but also dangerously the easiest to get up again too, which was the horrid natural reaction I tended to suffer with eating any kind of chocolate, amongst a range of other things too.

HOW AM I IN THIS PLACE ALL OVER AGAIN? I'M ANGRY. Wish it was time to get up and to go to Day Care. I am so tired but scared to fall asleep in case I don't wake up again – but for me Rebecca, a part of the real me it would at least set free...

...NO MORE TURMOIL. No more worry, efforts, no more FIGHT AND BATTLES in my head. No more feeling ill or downright selfishly sorry for myself! I have EVERYTHING to live for! I am so lucky, I have everything! Life is fading away.

Angel Just-Rights

STOP.

I am STUCK.

I am TERRIFIED.

I want it all to END.

I feel maybe I am heading towards Chapter III of the Poem? Or maybe I can still head for chapter IV; yes, please!

I just had a dream, which is why I wrote this diary entry right now; it's my final straw...

...Interlude IX...

INTERLUDE IX

DREAMS

A:-

Wednesday 21ˢᵗ April 2010:

1.   *I returned to Karl's house (The colleague / friend that I worked with in Lealt and through whom I met Wil) after a night out and he was preparing an oven meal: Ratatouille Lasagne and asked me if this was OK. I was confused as Ratatouille I could handle, whereas Lasagne scared the hell out of me! But I said yes, to be polite and because he was preparing his dinner too and I could deal with it later...*

2.   *I was now in a completely different room and was sitting at a long wooden table. Miss Muller (whom I had met during my inpatient admissions and who incidentally, hated my personal Angel Just-Rights) was sitting right down the other end of the table but I could both hear and see her making a fuss over her prawn and noodles soup dish!*

I see her picking up a king prawn, mumbling on about it being "huge! Look at it! You expect me to eat that? Am I an imbecile?!" etc. etc. etc. In her usual ironically comical way – with a touch of the real Miss Muller's personality, I suppose. She gets up to walk out and I take a deep breath and follow her, something I would never have dared to do on the ward, but this time I just cannot believe my eyes and my ears because compared to the terrible things that we had both been made to eat on that ward, particularly as I know she likes seafood and finds it more manageable above anything else (except her beloved fruit), this dish was as safe as it could ever have been, for her. I was thinking that this had gone far enough! She was looking even worse than I had ever seen her too, poor soul!

I try desperately to MAKE HER LISTEN TO ME, for once! Trying to tell her "It's a prawn! One Solitary Prawn! Think of what we have faced (meaning the food) in the past hospital and thank your lucky stars that you are here having prawns and dry noodles with a bowl of pure hot water!"

Do You See...?

~

Honestly?

~

How Bad Can Things Get?!
It's A Never-Ending Set:
Always To Beat;
Always To Win;
Must Feel Strength;
Keep On Top Of That Power!
Must Keep Control;
Only Way To Remain Safe;
Trust no-one, Not Yourself, Not Her And Certainly Not Him...

~

But Until When?!
The Definitive, Ultimate, Final Last Hour?
Until Sudden Death?

~

Do You See?

~

...IT CAN NEVER...
...EVER, EVER...
...BE ENOUGH...!

CHAPTER 32I:-

...DIARY ENTRIES ~ HONESTY CONTINUED....

32i-Be Honest With Yourself First!

-Angel Parker!
-**Very Brief Dream**
-**Responsibility**

- **Wednesday 21ˢᵗ April 2010 Cont.:**

3am: Look at you! Look at yourself! How can you be so weak to have these headaches, creaking bones, collapsing knees, hurting hips, shortness of breath, aching brain, weakening joints, fat arms, fat legs, fat face, fat fingers, fat bum, fat tummy, fat chin, fat cheeks, fat being – undeserved. Tired and scared, seeking solace in sound: television, radio, stillness of the outside world and the rising sun, the singing birds, that stillness. The Millennium Wheel coloured in its changing lights standing tall over my city that I have used only to hide and to try so hard to achieve: job, career, perfect husband, family – none ticked – just left bear with terror and exposed...

FAT. UNDESERVED. UNABLE. ALONE. ALLOWING NO HELP! TOO WEAK TO END IT ALL. EVEN TO FREE YOUR FAMILY! MAKES NO SENSE: Aim to protect, but actually gradually, slowly, torturously, cause and prolong THEM SUCH PAIN, POOR FAMILY.

I cuddle myself. DESPERATE. Curled up in bed in a ball. Nowhere to go. Which way? I still want my life, but it's FAR TOO HARD to face and even to try and say...

391

Please make me better! Understand how hard. Understand ME.
I AM SORRY! I AM TOO WEAK TO EVEN DIE!

FATTER CHEEKS – BUT NO – I KNOW THESE ARE supposed
to be the real lies – BUT AREN'T! Where's the secret I'm missing
– how can *I* be THIN? It's impossible for ME...for me; I'll just be
taken away – as I'm too weak to end this torture myself any other
way. I am sorry!

●   **Thursday 22nd April 2010:**

Curry day again.

*...This morning, in the little sleep that I caught, I briefly dreamt that
I accompanied Kerry to an antenatal class but when we arrive, it is
a class full of "recovered" anorexics who all have a bump and we
are all tested by having to eat this cake!*

●   **Friday 23rd April 2010:**

Today I felt pretty ill. Doing canteen day today. Really can't face
yogurt still so I will have to have the hot pudding. Spent all of
relaxation thinking about what on earth to have...main meal is easy
as I can have a jacket potato or a wrap and even a sandwich again if
the others were doing this too.

But pudding?! OK yogurt and fruit – can't face this still no way.
Fruits of the forest crumble my worst nightmare for fear, but I know
I would enjoy it too probably but only if the crumble isn't too thick,
that is. Yuck. Or there is the cheese and biscuits option. I want to
show them that I am trying and I am very worried about weigh-in on
Monday, thus the awful hot pudding would really have to be
'choice' number one.

As soon as I decided this, I wrote on a bit of paper straight after
relaxation: "Please can you help me to choose the hot pudding
today? Thank you!"

...and put it in my pocket in case I needed it downstairs in the canteen.

When we got downstairs, I looked at the crumble and it looked OK. I was in the queue for the salad and gave the note to Lou and we discussed it properly and she was there for me 100 per cent. Done. No backing out now. Actually eating it was pretty horrible as it was a lot of crumble, but I did it all and I hoped Lou and the others were pleased that I had taken responsibility for my own actions and had stood myself in good stead for the weekend. A step away from that inpatient threat!

In goal-setting group this afternoon, Lilly was pushing me to be honest with the group, and I was. I felt terrible for it, as I had to admit I was clearly struggling, but they were all supportive.

I really listened to Lilly because I know she is extremely good at picking things up about individuals and working with this. She smacked the nail on the head when she mentioned two words:

Deserve.

Trust.

I MUST be honest with myself. I HAD TO change my thinking, if not my perception.

I power-walked to King's Cross to catch the train home that evening. I couldn't help it after the extent at what I'd done. It wouldn't do anything to my weight; it would just make me feel better.

- **Saturday 24th April 2010:**

Today Mum and I went to Norin and had a lovely time together ☺. I felt ill for most of the day, but didn't tell poor Mum.

393

Jacket potato (all!) and haddock for dinner like I had done last week when I had maintained the weight. OK.

CHAPTER 33:-

...FINAL DIARY ENTRY ~ TWO FINAL POINTS...

BELIEVE in Yourself, before you can TRUST in Others:

-Bath-Time!
-Mum and Kerry

*   **Sunday 25th April 2010:**

Had a bath and washed my hair while Mum was watching the London Marathon on television.

I was about to look at my toes, when something in my head said:

"No, don't! You don't deserve to wear sandals and have nice toes and legs! Get on with the dip and get out! HURRY UP, COME ON!" I hid my body back under the water, closed my eyes and put my face under too, as usual; out of sight, out of mind.

But then, I thought: "Actually, no! WHY shouldn't I? WHY shouldn't I make myself look nice, feel nice, be nice, be pleasant, make myself comfortable, pamper myself even, just deserve! Because I do deserve...don't I?" I began to pick up the soap and really wash myself properly and have a 'Mindful' bath as much as I could. I can't say I enjoyed it much particularly but it was a freedom that I hadn't allowed myself for so long.

Now, I was thinking differently: "ACTUALLY, NO...

-I DO DESERVE to wear sandals, like everybody else! (No, you don't rah rah rah rah rah!)

-I DO DESERVE to wash in soap properly! (No...!)

-I DO DESERVE to take the time to look after myself! (No...!)

-I DO DESERVE to feel comfortable, calm, contented and nice (No...!)

-I DO DESERVE to EAT (No...!)

-I DO DESERVE to be in nice clothes...

-I DO DESERVE to have nice hair, nice arms, nice legs, a nice body...

-I DO DESERVE to be the nice person I once was and can be...

-I DO DESERVE my personality back...

-I WONT HIDE ANY LONGER!

-I DO DESERVE to be happy! LEAVE ME ALONE!

-I WILL LOOK AFTER MYSELF AND LIVE MY DREAMS!

-I DESERVE A JOB!

-I DESERVE FRIENDS!

-I DESERVE A FAMILY!

-I DESERVE MY OWN CHILDREN!

-I DESERVE TO BE HAPPY!

-I CAN AND I WILL.

-LEAVE ME ALONE, I HATE YOU!

-I CANNOT BATTLE YOU CONSTANTLY BUT I WILL RELINQUISH *YOU!*

-THANKS, BUT NO THANK YOU! NOT ANY MORE! NO LONGER WILL *little you* **OVERWHELM AND DECEIVE ME WITH YOUR LIES AND FRIGHTEN ME WITH SELF-DEFEATING THOUGHTS AND BULLY ME INTO UNHEALTHY ACTIONS LEADING ME TO DEATH!**

-REBECCA WINS!"

I had egg on toast for lunch. I haven't had an egg for longer than I can remember (without slyly discarding the yolk!) OK, I didn't have spread, but I had two boiled eggs and the runny yolk of one! And I felt better for it too! Two fingers to my old friend, now fiend, I don't need or want you in any part of my life.

After lunch, Mum told me that Kerry had invited us both to stay overnight at her house with her next weekend as her husband is away on a school trip and she needs some help. I mentioned to Mum that I felt uncomfortable being at my sister's because she doesn't understand my situation, even now at almost three years after my first hospital admission, I don't feel she has any patience with me what-so-ever. Mum said it was 'you, and the way you take things because you're ill'. Mum said she wouldn't go to Kerry's if I wasn't going to come home that weekend and then I felt selfish and horrible but realised Mum was putting me and my health first, bless her so much, I didn't deserve her.

On the journey to the train station, my Mum and I were diverted due to the St. Paul's Parade in town and through this, I saw an old lady walking across the road who was extremely hunch-backed and I thought to myself, please don't let it be too late for me, please!

This weekend I had been more open and honest with Mum about my fears and my continued struggles, for example when I carried out the poached egg on toast at lunchtime, because I had been open with Mum in order to try to get her to understand that having an egg was, although extremely sad, but still, a big deal to me; Mum was amazing in her support then. In the car, she told me that she wasn't angry with "me now" but with "me all those years ago" for not telling her, and she said she was mostly angry with herself, for not intercepting and stopping it all earlier.

I told Mum that I, as the illness, did everything possible in order to hide its existence and that is what I had done in order to continue the secret. Mum beats herself up about not noticing and confronting it earlier, but I know how well I hid everything until I was absolutely desperately giving up in exhaustion and when I finally recognised I was totally out of control and in need of help and support to continue living in this world. When I realised for myself that I could not do this on my own and needed help other than from myself and my best friend Ravi, this was when Mum came down to London to learn just how severe my struggles had become and also shockingly to her, of my impending emergency hospital admission that was to become real, just two days later.

Angel Just-Rights

I am sorry Mum! And thank you. Mum, I don't know how I would have told you otherwise as I was not coming home to see you at all by then.

On the train back to London today, I called Kerry and she asked me if I wanted to stay at her house next weekend along with Mum. I said thank you and I'll think about it. I even voiced my worries to her about that biscuit incident on my Nephew's birthday...

...It was snack time in the afternoon and I thought we would all be faced with a piece of birthday cake (simply put together by my sister as sponge and I knew I did sponge as pudding every day at Day Care and so I was planning to try to have this today, if the situation arose), but this didn't happen. Knowing that I had to have something, I asked my sister if I could have one of the chocolate fingers and she said of course, help yourself...

...When we were having tea and a biscuit a little later, Mum asked if I would have a chocolate finger with my tea and I replied "no thank you, I had one earlier" and immediately I heard my sister sarcastically, and with a bullying tone and look on her face, say under her breath, "Well have another one then!" spoken in a very quick and quiet harsh tone. I asked her what she just said and she made something up about her hair and I didn't say another thing at the time, but I'm actually not that stupid you know Kerry...

...So today when I brought up this example of my worry, Kerry didn't admit to it at all, but she did say that she promises that she won't be thinking of saying anything and wishes to have me there for the weekend.

Oh OK Kerry, it is very kind but I still feel she is a lot of 'just all talk' and IS thinking horrible thoughts in her mind, I know she is thinking along the lines of: "just say the right thing no matter what you're really thinking...she's your sister...otherwise she won't come and that means Mum might not come either".

I don't know what I'll do yet. I just want to be normal. I wish I was less paranoid, less self-doubting. I want to be able to have even a little trust (rather than baulking from all humanity, being in my eyes all encased in malevolence at first sight and in every comment and every sly smile, I must be missing something. How can people laugh and be happy anymore? How was I satisfied with life and able to carry on? How did I ever cope? How did I ever trust:

...With my colleagues...

...With my housemates...

...With my friends...

...With my family...

...With myself

...Within this world!

Where is me? I want her back!

CHAPTER 34:

THOUGHTS FOR LIFE – MUMMY AND DADDY

~

CONCLUSION

Thoughts for Life – Mummy and Daddy:

My First Memory with Dad.

Whenever I am at the seaside, seeing the very final shallowest part of a wave on the sand reminds me of my Dear Father. It is a memory that I treasure and will never see in the same light, ever again, no matter how much I look for it because when you are little, everything seems so different, uncomplicated and enticing and you think you will never grow up and lose this innocence. I sometimes think that if I returned to Scarborough beach, which is the location that I gather the memory to have originated from, maybe I could recapture this nostalgic scene perfectly? Yet part of me, although a little unsure of returning to the scene for fear of recounting nothing in my feelings but a solemn regret and longing for the past happy memory to return, I wonder if staying away and accepting this memory as something special that can never be lost or spoiled is far more special to me than attempting to recapture something so special? Obviously, I would not wish to spoil this memory or to replace it. What if I am disappointed with my return trip and it touches me with nothing at all? For a life without Anorexia means I MUST MAKE LIFE-SAVING, SEVERE CHANGES INVOLVING MANY, MANY TERRIFYING UNCERTAINTIES, OR I WILL DIE.

I LOVED MY DAD. IN HIM I COULD TRUST. HE WAS JUST AMAZING.

My First Memory with Mum.

Mum used to leave me at primary school in the classroom in the mornings. I would see my Mum's blue Volvo car parked outside the school. She would get into the car and drive off without me, having dropped me off in the morning, just leaving me stuck here with the teacher with the red lipstick on her tooth.

I used to cry and cry and cry, as my Mum had left me all alone for another day and I wanted her to be with me and always be by my side. When Mum heard about my distress on seeing her drive off every morning, the teacher tried distracting me with books and Mum even later bought my sister and I teddy bears for "not crying for a week at school". But it wasn't until my Mum TALKED to me and said:

"If you miss me, just laugh and say oh, Pot!"

I remember this only too well and must have looked back at her totally bemused as I asked her how or what it meant. My Mum just repeated it with a bright face and a happy chuckle, which I can still remember perfectly to this day.

So the next time I saw my Mum waving to me as she was driving off and away from my classroom and back home without me, leaving me all alone with the teacher with the red lipstick on her tooth, I remembered the conversation we had together and I said to myself:

"Oh, Pot!"

Immediately, I chuckled out loud and, smiling, skipped over to pick out a good book with the other children. For a moment, I was being just like everyone else and I remember really feeling warm inside, all thanks to my Dear Mum who solved something so simply and all it had taken was COMMUNICATION AS THE KEY; other's will take care of me.

I LOVE MY MUM. IN HER I CAN TRUST. SHE IS JUST AMAZING.

Conclusion:

I Am Ready To Speak And Reveal...

...To Mum, Who Is Ready To Listen And Learn.

~

Kerry Has Promised To Be Patient And Understanding...

...Towards Her Sister, Whom She Says She Is There To Support.

~

Little Brother Is About To Start His Own Family...

...Little Brother, I Am Eternally Here For You.

POSTSCRIPT: A NOTE TO MY DEAR FAMILY:

LIVING IN REALITY...AND THE FUTURE:

So Now, May You See, This Intricate Me;

Bit By Bit, My Whole Life's Been Revealed.

The Happy, Kind, Carefree, Loving Rebecca;

Whose Secret Side's No Longer Sealed.

Creative, Considerate, Cheeky And Fun;

Friend, Sister, Niece, Daughter, Aunt, Colleague, Estranged Hun.

Slowly And Certainly Swept Underside;

By This Wickedly Crafty, Long-Cherished Cruel Chide.

She Wanted For Nothing, Was Playful, Fulfilled;

Yet Her Brutal Bold Bully Bred Brightly Strong-Willed!

Disguised In Fake Highs, Charming Mirage Did Mask;

The Secreted Sad, Laden Mind In Life Task.

With Fiend In Distractions, Behaviours, And Actions;

All Silent Hurt Rests Undisturbed.

Only Voices Are Heard, But To Her They Assure;

Instant Relief: An Addictive Results-Proven Cure.

Angel Just-Rights

Blinding Flashes Of Strain, Sourced By Such Repressed Pain;

Gush Out! Explode! Uncontrolled!

Fear Terrifically Reared! Panic! Chaos! Denial!

Floods Of Tears Drown All Harshness Untold.

As Uncertainty Reigns, Default Overwhelms;

Fight Or Flight? No, I Pathetically Freeze. Stagnant.

Nothing's Safe In This World! I've Indefinitely Tried;

Many Times Ne'er To Hurl Myself Unto This Tide.

Hence, No Future Can Be! For Just Micci, As Me;

Unless Those Whom I Love Can Be Willing To See.

How Once Beautiful Flow'r, Became Plagued By This Pow'r;

And Lost All Of Her Strength Through Her Infinite Wrench To Fight For Her Right To

Be Free.

Deal With The Moods, Bravely Confront All Foods!

Disperse Of The Fears And Unleash Sultry Sneers.

Begin To Heal Faster, Away From Disaster;

Secured, Reassured And Encouraged By My Family.

Angel Just-Rights

With Your Help And Support I So Want To And Will;

Endeavour To Set Us All Free.

In Expulsion Of Hurt, I Aim Ne'er To Revert;

Rather Discover, Who Is This 'Rebecca'?

The Real Life, True, Present 'Me'

CONCLUSION:

OPEN HEARTS AND OPEN MINDS

MY APOLOGY EMAIL TO AUNTIE ANN

Dear Auntie Ann

Thank you for your letter, I wasn't sure after last week if I'd hear from you again.

I am so sorry for the way that my behaviour made you feel and to cause so much upset for yourself and for Mum. Everything that you put in your letter shows such understanding.

I had tried to get the timetable from my Mum numerous times the day before you arrived. Mum knows I need to plan everything and that I need to know exactly what is going to be the plan. She knows I plan things to the minute. We even have a group at Day Care where we discuss our plans and worries for the weekend, so that they can help us with ways to deal with our anxieties. Mum gave me the impression that you were popping in for coffee and to pick up the jigsaw and that you knew about my hair appointment at 12. I tried to ask Mum if she wanted to take me down to town earlier so that she didn't have to interrupt or cut short your visit through having to take me down to town in the car, but she said no. I felt bad and selfish that you were coming to have coffee and that I had an appointment at a really bad time and couldn't take myself to town and was dragging your chats with Mum away.

I then saw the lunch out in preparation and immediately thought that Mum had planned for us all to have lunch together and she hadn't told me! First I was angry and shocked because Mum is aware from the day before, how much I was struggling to have what she wanted me to have at lunchtime. But for me, actually sticking to my new meal plan yesterday lunchtime was an accomplishment, but it isn't enough for Mum. I felt alone in that how could Mum think I could do this? Did Mum think I could just do it if you were there too? Scenarios were going through my head. I tried to calm down and think about it rationally, but I couldn't see myself doing it, it terrified me. I just wasn't ready, especially with no warning, and I wasn't going to put myself or people that I care about in a situation.

I know Mum was just doing what she thought was best, out of desperation and I feel for her, the last thing I want to do is to hurt and keep hurting her. I didn't act like I did to hurt Mum and especially not to be rude to you and make you feel unwelcome at all! Please forgive me. I was petrified and had to escape. If I had stayed, then it would have been a disaster and Mum would have ended up in tears and hurting probably much more, at the extent my behaviour may well have reached.

I am so sorry for acting the way I did. I don't want you to think I went out of my way to hurt you, I wasn't cunning, I didn't want to run away but I had to. I was nervous about seeing you anyway, as the day before we had met my old primary school headmistress in town and Mum had turned round to me and said something like, "God knows what she thought seeing you looking like a walking skeleton". I still have yet to contact any of my old friends, and still avoid seeing my friends except for my three very best friends only in addition to the patients and nurses at the hospital because I am ashamed and embarrassed and I want to see them when I am well and ready.

You are right when you say in your letter that I need to say how I am feeling and I have spent all week writing everything down: 10 chapters entitled 'No More Secrets'. And thank you for your invitation for coffee and / or lunch. Like I say, if I know exactly what I am expected to do, I can deal with it and take the support I am so lucky to have. I just need time to plan and build myself up to accepting that I am going to do it and that it is the right thing to do. I need to feel in control – it is all about the control with me, certainly not the looks.

I hope this makes sense. I haven't really spoken to Mum much, but I hope you don't blame her for anything, or me. I certainly don't feel blame or anger and all I can do is to apologise, try and make you understand how desperate and terrified I felt and say thank you for always being there and trying to help me, you always manage to cheer me up and I so look forward to hearing from you and talking to you and hearing your funny stories. I always have.

I am just going to send this now as if I read it through then I will probably re-write everything and just send a pathetic 'sorry'. I hope I haven't written too much and please ignore any spelling mistakes.

I hope to see you soon and make up for my behaviour somehow.

Take care,

Love Rebecca

Xxx

A2:

AUNTIE ANN'S EMAIL REPLY TO ME

My dear Rebecca (or should I call you Micci?)

I am going to comment on just a few points from your email as anything else can be covered in my next letter. I am so glad that you sent the email as it has made things a lot clearer to me.

First of all I need to let you know that now you've explained how you feel and why you acted as you did I do understand. I'm not going to blame anyone for what happened because you and your mum are experiencing such desperation that I can only try my best to put myself in yours or your mum's shoes and it's a very difficult thing to do. I wonder if all that happened on Friday was for a reason. I'm a big believer in fate and as I've told you in my letters, I'm also a big believer in writing things down. It's a way of getting things straight in your mind. Very often after something emotional or important has happened to me I write it all down whilst it's still fresh which means I can then read it back later. It's amazing how quickly you forget minor details. I am so glad that you have written 'No More Secrets' as I think a great outpouring such as this could help you release some of the feelings and tension which have been building up. I do hope so as this could be a real step forward towards your recovery. The only reason I didn't bring back the jigsaw was the fact that when your mum and I read the instructions for using the glue we realised that the yellow edging pieces which you'd left in the box were meant to be a gilded frame so that you could hang it straight on the wall without it having a frame made for it. It would be difficult to have it framed professionally as it doesn't have a straight edge and it probably wouldn't look as good so we

410

decided to wait until you had fitted the pieces to it. Don't worry about me blaming anyone because I don't. I don't know how I would act if I was your mum and I don't know how I would cope with the problems you have. I will always be here for you.

Lots of Love, Auntie Ann Xxxx

B1:

HEAR AND ACT

i: Making Progress.

12/05/10

ANOTHER SHOCK OF facts hailed down onto us today during the Dietetics group at Day Care, which was on teeth. This was a subject I needed to be spoken at me, but that I absolutely dreaded. Feeling certain throughout the session that my Mum had clearly been on the phone to the staff at the hospital and informed them of my unhealthy behaviours she was witnessing at home at the weekends in that I seem intent on continuing from one weekend to the next weekend at home with my Mum snacking on "bits of fruit". It scared me sufficiently enough for my night snack that evening, I felt able to enjoy a whole slice of toast with marmite, in addition to my mug of milk with some hot chocolate.

ii: Silent Signs Still Securing Support.

13/05/10

THIS MORNING I awoke early and decided to get up straight away. I ate an apple, as I had been put off oranges and if I wanted to get better then this is what I had to do, no matter how uncomfortable things felt, I had to keep reminding myself that I want and deserve to be well, if not for myself, but to ease the pain on my family at least. I had been writing my acknowledgement page to Auntie Ann, just coming to terms with the ambiguities found between the everlasting shadows of *Angel* and my real-life guardian, Auntie Ann, who was there for me all along when I realised I was now running a little late and so I made my way to the bus stop, as usual.

Angel Just-Rights

Upon arriving at my bus stop, I was approached by a man in a suit who said to me "May I please give you this just to read?" and I replied directly and with confidence "Yes, of course. Thank you" and he handed me a small leaflet and then went to sit back down to continue with waiting for his bus. I looked briefly at the leaflet and then put it in my pocket, thinking to read it properly while on the bus journey. I noted it was entitled '*Enjoy Family Life. Can families really be happy? How is it possible?*' and after realising that it was a religious leaflet, checked to see if the man in the suit was wearing a dog collar and he wasn't.

I was amazed and dumbfounded: I had just left my flat with the specific aim of returning home today having thought up and decided on a title for my Memoir and here I was standing at the same bus stop that I stood at every morning waiting for my bus, having just been handed a leaflet on happy families which, on closer inspection, included a selection of quotes to the exact effect of the one simple question that had plagued my mind for the last ten years of my life's increasing struggle.

As soon as I caught my bus, I was wishing that I had spoken to the man, just to say thank you and I pulled out the leaflet from my pocket and searched for a contact detail and it was then that I discovered that it was something I had never even contemplated that may turn out to be my calling – in reaction to the beliefs and attitudes of those I grew up close to – if you remember, I was troubled by curiosity and confusion in one area of my life particularly and had expert examples and sources for information (through Leo and Rav) and thus from both sides of the coin, thus implementing a time of intense juxtapositions and curiosity and confusion in my life: Christianity or Islam? And then I was shown Catholicism in the Bright Monday Events, yet I felt entirely comfortable with none of these. Now, Jehovah's Witnesses had come to me, which I open-mindedly decided not simply to wave away but will aim to and try to explore *for me* in my first 'baby step' in reforming *Rebecca's* values and beliefs and thus living my life as is as far and as fully as can be.

iii: Learning To Live.

14/05/10

TODAY, IN THE Day Care group entitled 'Dealing with Anxiety' I was taught the label attached to the behaviour that I had demonstrated at 'The Auntie Ann Event' that day. It is referred to as 'The Controlling Mode' and when utilised to the extreme in order to keep one's life small and risk-free, can spread devastating effects through the sufferer's quality of life and their well-being.

Action point: I MUST MOVE ON!

iv: Outpatient Therapy Session.

17/05/10

TO WHICH FOR the first time ever was I able to begin sitting down to, with my milky coffee and biscuit, exactly five minutes early rather than late!

During the session today, I realised I had learned some most important messages...

MOST IMPORTANT MESSAGES

i. For Mum.

MY DEAR MUM and I possess extremely similar personality traits, in contrast to my sister, which, I now believe, is a reason attributing to the fact that Kerry and Mum have always managed to communicate in a much closer manner between one another than myself and my Dear Mum have ever been able to muster. We are too alike.

In the last few weeks, I have been actively working on opening up the channels of communication between myself and my Mum. I would like to share with you one recent and brief yet meaningful, slightly reflective moment relevant at this stage.

This weekend gone, I did not touch a single orange and even cut down my apple and overall fruit intake too, which I was proud of and my Mum also had, to her absolute credit, taken note of my change. Thank you, Dear Mum.

Yet, your comment "are you not even eating fruit now?", having noticed my baby step challenge that I had set myself 'knowing' in a mind-reading-kind-of way that the Dietetics Group on Wednesday had been tweaked, if not tailored, for my specific purposes (or so I was selfishly convinced) and yet changing my constant snacking on fruit for that such as a normal curry and cake meal, was somehow still not enough! This, I felt, echoed her thinking that:

"If only you would eat the food, you would be able to do everything!"

Dear Mum, yes, if only! Did this happen in hospital when I was seen "happily" eating away at every last crumb on that full diet

415

menu I was forced to consume? Day in, day out I downed horrific three-course breakfasts, thick laden lunches and dinners, excessively huge chunks of cake, crumble, pies complete with cream or custard, doughnuts and chocolate three times a day, not to mention the snacks, all the milk and the biscuits and the thick yogurts from early morning until late at night…? No. My weight stayed constant when I complied to the full diet menu, I wore myself out, my mood deteriorated behind closed doors, my health, both long-term and short-term became stressed and strained and every part of my soul and my being was silently crying out in pain, both in mind and in body, SILENTLY ONCE AGAIN, BEHIND SUCH FALSE SMILES; my life was switched back to double entendre: smile to the real world, everything's great, everything's going just fine, see, I'm eating the food, I'm enjoying the food, everything and more that you're asking me to! Yet behind this façade, the mental torment in my troubled mind, my actions from morning until night I had no choice over, simply desperately fearful and overwhelmed, all alone, by 'feelings' I'd be overcome by safe faithful friend in my only soul mate who could take away this angst and give me relief: My *Dear Angel Just-Rights*. Rebecca's entire life was resolved again to pure isolative torture, absolute relentless sheer hell. However, to all in the outside world who welcomed or chose or desired ignorance, then they could simply reason:

"It's Micci! She's eating! She's Back! She's Well!"

I have trusted and listened to the thoughts that I have for so long that I cannot help but trust in them when I need to be looked after, no matter how ill, unhappy and alone they have made me. But I have tried so hard, my family and staff, to be truly strong and to eat, to not behave negatively and to live as I used to, but it is IMPOSSIBLE not to revert back to my safe coping behaviours that I use TO SURVIVE. Mum, show me a healthy way of coping, of dealing with my absolute fears, wishes to give in and commit suicide when I am forced not to use my behaviours; please find me a way! Please find my path to life again! Please understand and make it possible!

Dear Mum,

Before Pride, Comes A Fall.

Angel Just-Rights

I Have Learned Slowly The Only Possible Way For Me To Recover;

Is Through Minute Baby Steps!

Back to my Most Important Message: At the very end of this weekend as we arrived at the train station and were sitting in the car, my Mum had chosen to offer a fact to me regarding a family member's action that was carried out recently. This fact was spoken and was then followed swiftly by an abrupt:

"…And that's all I need to say."

…except for the decisive hand movement, arms folded, knowing look, quivering lips, shaking voice, anxious, hurt, upset eyes…

Dear Mum! Initially this angered and frustrated me in-so-far as here you were actually telling me, actually instructing me almost, to be a miracle mind-reader (Book 1: Secrets Out, Part 1, Chapter 2). I was expected to know what you were thinking and how you were feeling and to sit with this, as you had unfairly been doing to yourself and I could see the effect this was having on you. It made my heart ache.

I realised that my poor Mum was left holding onto the feelings being experienced, with no outlet to talk about them and this upset me immensely. Knowing full-well that this does not work, I saw it as my duty to try to urge you, Dearest Mum, to explain your logic, explore your emotions, unleash your true feelings unto your daughter, unto me, just me, I was here hurting with you, for you, willing you to open up to me so that I could offer you understanding, comfort and care, for you Dear Mum, as you wish happiness and freedom for me.

No more conveyance in anger, rather search deeper for answers. I wanted us to be able to talk rather than staying stuck in being so keen and intent to remain in what we know and feel safe with and trust. We are each being stubborn in our growing lone struggles, by quashing and accepting all horrific emotions and brushing all feeling aside, no matter how desperate and angry or upset we may be. It is natural to feel and we cannot squash these or hide these

417

inside our heads and our hearts. They will always come out in the end and I remind you:

Bible: Matthew 10:26

"…There Is Nothing Concealed That Will Not Be Revealed;

Or Hidden, That Will Not Be Known".

"Therefore Do Not Fear Them" [As, In Fight Or In Flight];

"All Secrets, Will Come To Light"

(Book 3: The Bigger Picture, Part 1, Chapter 30)

Thus you stating:

"…And That's all I need to say. I'm not saying anymore"

…I found less than appropriate. At the time I was pushing Mum simply for the reason explained above in that I wanted her to know and feel that she was not and did not have to be or deserve to feel so alone and isolated with her thoughts and feelings. Day Care has taught me that it IS OK to share. I wanted to relieve her of this, she must talk; I am here. I am listening. I am hearing.

In hindsight, I was selfishly in desperate and childish need, from you as my Mum, to role model to me. In order for me to be given that permission, to feel and accept that impending care and understanding, to know that reassurance from my Dear Mother IS there, to validate to me, that simply speaking out aloud IS OK to do! Rather than being left or silently expected to be clever and intelligent enough to be able to decipher the silence, the puzzle, to mind-read and thus to ultimately just guess the endless uncertain possibilities, one of which must be right? Or am I missing something simple? I am not clever, like Kerry. I am not a mind-reader either. Why am I not able to work it out? Why is it being kept secret? Why don't I just know? Is it wrong to talk..? It reminds me of my struggles with Maths. Even when I was given extra lessons to help me grasp the subject, I just couldn't. I wasn't destined to understand. I wasn't supposed to understand. Things were not supposed to be talked about. If it needed explaining, you were a dead loss. I was a dead loss. I was never expected to pass my eleven plus. I cried out of happiness when I did. I enjoyed and excelled at German and was ecstatic with my A star grade at GCSE because this was better than Kerry managed! When I was taking my driving test, I didn't try with my heart and soul to pass, until the fourth time lucky, because Kerry passed on her fourth test and so it was OK to fail until then. When the fourth test came, I was a state, owing to the pressure I was feeling to make sure I passed, without fail! Must prove myself! Must, must, MUST! I loved being better at Kerry when it mattered, but it always felt wrong (like the netball Book 1: Secrets Out, Part 1, Chapter 1), rather than an achievement. Because unless it was Kerry, anything Rebecca did was not as good or didn't matter so much, or was not considered as important. She was Kerry's underachieving shadow.

Dear Reader, you too will now be aware that my Mother and I possess tendencies to communicate in actions and body language, myself rarely in words but in riddles, especially when it matters the most. It is just the way in which my personality and our brains are put together. By now, you will know that both my Mum and I are also sensitive individuals, maybe just more prone to certain thinking styles, maybe more likely to push them to the extreme, to the negative or the positive.

On one hand, for me, I know it is OK to talk because this was confirmed to me by my friend come confidante, Sarah (Introduction:

No More Secrets, A1). Plus, now I see that this is how my sister lives. Kerry 'is who she is' and lives by trusting in her own confidences and abilities in what she 'knows' to be right. I have seen (and am sure she is aware of herself) that although this acknowledgement of this great 'pink elephant' standing in the room has the potential to upset people on occasions, at least it is being heard. So commonly it is the 'simply unspoken', while clearly and certainly 'there', that is quickly and neatly swept away and left; out of sight, for the mites to bite away at, bit by bit.

Not anymore. Mum, I have learned (although my *beliefs* remain too stubborn to change) that talking is not wrong. It is healthy and strong and not weak nor complaining and does not mean one is stupid or simple nor naïve nor wrong. Please, I can see in you what I hear in me and I want you to be open and express yourself too in so that you too can feel and be free. Please do not hold anger nor upset inside any longer. As I have been shown, now I urge you to speak and set to one side, lay resting your pride. Relax and heed from all those who **love you so very much and want to care for you, your voice and your worries, your emotions and feelings, not simply your anger, Dear Mum. I LOVE YOU SO VERY, VERY MUCH.**

ii. For Auntie Ann.

THIS COMING WEEKEND I will be attending the Christening Ceremony of my niece. It is two years since the Christening of my nephew, which was a prominent point in my life for both my family and I (Book 2: Who Am I? Part 1, Chapter 18).

Now having found myself in this tiny life of such severe strict rituals and routines right from the hour I wake until the time my head may touch the pillow, I realise that I have fully disengaged from everything in life other than literally Day Care (originally agreed so as to escape hospital and persevered though threats of re-admission and sections) and spending the weekends at home usually in Granada and only in the confines of the family home, never venturing out (occasionally I would have to visit my sister and her children, which is now always planned and forewarned to myself and always contained within the safe confines and surroundings that is along with my Dear supportive, helpful yet worried, thus angry, dutifully devoted, caring, loving Mother); I had in the past couple of days particularly been experiencing these familiar thoughts and screams all in insistent crescendo, of:

"...*SIMPLY MUST STAY IN LONDON AND 'PREPARE' FOR THIS*

STUPENDOUS SOCIAL OCCASION AS BEST AS POSSIBLE...!"

...as was fully my intention: *I had to go to the gym, I had to be toned, I had to starve myself, I had to be thin, I had to wear the best clothes, I had to have my hair perfect, I had to show everybody I am coping and have it all worked out, I have the perfect life, I have the perfect job, I have the perfect future in line, I have everything together*... No matter how much I tried to tell myself "No, this is wrong! Day Care would remind you that this voice is your Anorexia. It wants you to isolate, it wants you to work, it wants you to starve, it wants you to punish. Tell it to go away. Fight its voice. But *I* know I don't have voices, *it's just me!* But look where "just me" has gotten you! (Book 2: Who Am I? Part 1, Chapter 20) Listen to those you've learned to trust in Day Care. Now you have to try. Turn it around. Do something very different. Experiment..."

I fight constantly to dispel it all from my mind. "So-called logic" was inevitably being over-shadowed by that which I have always known and trusted in best, that safest and only way in which *I knew,* or thought I knew, to cope: I was successfully being drawn into running right back towards that sheltered safe wing of my stealthy long-standing trusty guardian – *Angel Just-Rights* – whom would absolutely delight in putting on the strain, once again, and rejoicing in having reignited that flame to ensure the harrowing demise of Micci...but now, of also HER FAMILY...! No.

And so I was brave and voiced my worries to those I now trusted and from this, I was able to see that for those whom I would usually aim and in my efforts to *'just must!'* show and impress on so highly to ensure they all only see that I have achieved and truly succeeded and acquired the perfect life, are the very ones for whom I would push myself to those very wretched limits far up and away in the sky and out of the reach of anyone, including myself, in the real world here and now. I have been weak and destined to live as such a failure, maybe through pride with distraction or maybe even with both just in fraction but always, *just* too far away and *just* out of my grasp, which is just as far as far as can be in those greedy eyes of *Angel Just-Rights*. Until death is reached will she never be happy. Not anymore. I give one final try; for my Dear Family and for I.

In fact, I was able to see that in my Auntie's consistent supportive writing of her letters, the surprise visit to the hospital, bringing me the jigsaw and helping me to start it while opening up our relationship through efforts at calm conversation, trying desperately to help in any way possible and, without fail, each and every week over the last few years had I received a letter from the Wentworth family – all this time my Auntie chose to dedicate not to my brother and not to my sister, but to me – she has been there throughout, never judging, but offering comfort and understanding to me, not supporting *Angel* or illness nor shadow nor failure, but caring completely and purely unconditionally, softly urging along that lost voice of Rebecca to begin to speak and return. Forever, Dear Auntie, you have been there only for Rebecca. You saw and cared only for the niece who was hidden, terrified; unwell. The girl whom you knew and respected as: 'Rebecca: Always Just Right As Just Her'.

iii. For All.

THIS IS WHERE I am at: I tell myself it is all feelings and thoughts that can be spoken through and not body fat growing out of control, but facing my emotions and being truly strong in encouraging my life to get bigger, separating right from wrong.

I need to take small steps (for Rebecca) or I know it is only two outcomes that are destined to occur and that both will end my life in sin:

Angel Just-Rights

1.   I will try too hard and to achieve too quickly (Micci Parker) only to once again fight against all the help offered along the way (*Angel Parker*), or

2.   I will simply exhaust, lose all hope and give up properly this time and do right for myself and moreover for my family (*Angel Just-Rights*). Either way, *Angel* will delight yet again. But she will win either way to extinguish Rebecca this time fully away.

Therefore I have to, and as of today I now do, accept that my past life of fake success has now ended. I ultimately disastrously failed myself and all others who know me and having completely derailed, I now admit and accept that I absolutely, to *Angel*, **have lost everything, plus every tiny sap of my pride and will not grip onto anything of my past life any longer.**

This is what I want! I now have understanding into my personal illnesses and can accept help, support, comfort and care. I am starting now to build up a trust in others and to gain back into my life those subtle quiet risks and dares that may begin to stretch me once again and hopefully allow some 'real life' back in. I can finally open my eyes to the colours and wonders that do exist in the world.

I am sorry to all of my "friends" from whom I have run terrified and abandoned so selfishly. I am sorry to all of my family from the bottom of my seemingly stone cold heart.

All those above, I also thank for not giving up on me. Mum, in all your devoted journeys to that hospital, only to be greeted and thanked by drowning in all those horrid outbursts, tears, words and screams that came from my sordid lips, of blame, of anger, of frustration through fear and desperation that I so severely inflicted upon my poor, poor, poor, poor undeserved family. I can never, ever make up for this. Never, ever, ever.

Believe it or not, I, Rebecca, always absolutely looked forward to seeing you every single time and I wished I could have seen you every day, except *Angel* was so angry with me, and this I selfishly took out entirely on you. I have been evil to you, Mum and I cannot say a sorry in this world that would mean enough, EVER. Nor can I ensure that you understand it wasn't me Micci who was angry – she was so desperate to see you, to accept your love, care, comforting arms around her, to allow those hugs that you offered, to laugh and joke with you, to enjoy the time we had together, desperate to be happy and to relax. Micci was always still there underneath.

But Angel was angry, she was livid at me: "Tell your Mum not to visit...What? Your Mum is HERE? HOW DARE SHE?! Why didn't you tell her not to come and make entirely sure that she didn't?! Anything to get out of exercise! You MUST exercise alone in your room after that sick dairy lunch! You must! And again before snack! Don't let your routines slip remember those scales that will surge right up in the morning! Tell her to go back home! Quick! Go! NOW...! Cannot lose a second! No! DON'T YOU DARE sit down! At least make your bed, go on, walk to the laundry room, stretch to that top shelf only! Step up onto that stool, look it's there for YOU because YOU need it so much! It was put there especially and only specifically for you. And again, and again, and again...go on! That one wasn't a proper one that one cannot count, must do ten more for letting that slip! Did you feel the strain?! No? I say, get back on it again, again! Get more towels than you need! You need to exercise those arms! Another one! Change the bed! Hoover the room! Quick it's been 10 minutes – go to the toilet's NOW and do your routine – QUICK! Hurry, it's nearly dinner time now and you have to fit in two more – Mum must go! Hug? No time. You haven't even deserved that breakfast you had this morning how DARE you – get back to it....NOW...!

My shadow is with me 24 hours a day. Those I have gained a trust in clearly can never be with me eternally, unlike my shadow. It's easier to follow the voice because I know it numbs my feelings and keeps me safe; yet also I am told it is wrong.

To life I give one more chance. If through / after this should come no hope / it just be too hard, too exhausting to cope, then will I with no further choice in the matter give up, give in and wilt foolishly away in sin.

I thank the amazing staff and patients at the Day Care program for their absolute consistent care, comfort, efforts, support, non-judgments, honesty, confidential and professional attitudes demonstrated and upheld every single day that I have been attending the program in the last six months since leaving the hospital ward after my long-extended admission. You have all helped me to see there is good that exists in this world, there is care and there is comfort and there is safety in life and I admire the understanding and insight and help, the natural empathy that shines out in each and every one of you that is more than anyone could imagine may exist among four small walls. Jill, Lilly, Chloe, Lou, Carole: I thank you all, for doing so much more than your job asks of you and for your striving efforts into making me smile every day. I thank you for slowly opening up my heart and my mind once again. I thank you for helping me learn. I thank you for helping me trust again in those within the unit and also slowly within the big wide world. I thank you for making my soul and my being bigger and better. I thank you for always being there for me no matter how angry, aggressive or scornful I may have been. I thank you for not giving up on me. I thank you for saving my life.

Today, 18th May 2010 I felt "normal" as I ran easily and without effort for my bus from which, I walked home with a spring in my step and noticed that I even managed, for the first time *ever*, to reach the top of the stairs to my flat without having to almost stop. My wish is to grab all those traits and gifts that I have been lucky enough to still have sight of and I know and hope are still there waiting for me to firmly re-grasp those skills and more, that were given to Me, Rebecca Parker and that I selfishly over the years, shunned and destroyed. Baby steps and understanding I will aim to cling onto.

Whoever I now may be, I wish to reclaim back enough respect and be content with leading a good life on this earth. I accept that being perfect in every aspect of life and striving to reach such unrealistic goals and achieving expectations far from reach in order to have the life that others judge me on gaining, just far too high, is not real life and is not possible and is just too far away, especially for me now, to ever reach. I still have restrictions in my life and without these I could not go on living, but I am challenging them every single minute of every single day. As with the voice who tells me I am so far from perfect or even from just being OK, even if I still believe in it, I have learned to challenge and level with it to some extent at least.

Angel Just-Rights

I have suddenly been hit by all events, thoughts, feelings and realisations that have happened over the last twenty years of my life that I feel I am waking up to and am reliving so much that I have missed out on experiencing and sharing those times with others who *were* present, at the right time. I was always fully aware that:

"Things never hit me until a couple of weeks/months subsequent to the event"

…yet only now can I understand why.

Every single thing that had happened and every feeling that I had pushed away rather than allowing myself to stay in that moment with, be mindful of the present and experience, enjoy, laugh, cry with others, I have missed these stolen years to a solitary and cold existence with *Angel*. Now I wish to miss no more of this life that I have been blessed with by my Dear Mum and Dad.

Rather aim to be content, live step-by-step in the present, laugh and cry through my journey of recovery, remember logic, as spoken so clearly and simply by trusted Day Care staff when fear and dread overpower my soul and drown me in torments leading me back into my own small, crazy world…

…My Final Two Most Important Messages that I have learned for myself and hope that if any part of my story may touch and help at least one other person, this part just may…

B3:

FOR MY READER:

i. MESSAGE ONE! IT'S NEVER ABOUT THE FOOD!

- **Thursday 20th May 2010.**

Today was the day that a member of the group was to bring in a **Birthday Cake.**

Specification, to pass as **"Birthday Cake":**

1.   Must have cream.
2.   Must have jam.
3.   Must have icing.

Rules regarding the **Birthday Cake** occasion:

A.   Everybody must have a piece at 3pm snack.

This I was dreading and didn't think – no, I knew – I would not be able to do this. I was angry that this had been imposed onto us with no choice in the matter and personally, I was being flooded and plagued by memories of my dreaded ward experiences. I admit this may have been heightened by the recent addition to the Day Care staff of a particular member of staff who was the charge nurse carrying out decisions around my assisted feeds on the ward. Having said that, I did have one of the best relationships with this nurse during both of my admissions because she knew and could speak to my anorexia very well, especially during those feeds ("well, done Rebecca, that's super, fantastic" when I'd spit it all out in every direction possible) most of which she would have led. But also, she could speak to and somehow I felt she knew Micci well too and, incidentally, it was through the work I was doing with this nurse, that I created my timeline of events that really helped highlight my negative behavioural patterns.

An emergency meeting was called right at the beginning of the **birthday cake** day and I will never forget the moment of clarity that I experienced as it flashed right across my eyes and right through my mind. I have replayed this round and around in my mind in desperate efforts never to forget the meaning that I saw in this and the poignancy that it gave to me right at that time.

Carole, you called the meeting to talk about the piece of **birthday cake** that was filling the Day Care room with hushed dread. A dread that nobody dared talk about or bring up, instead it stood as the 'great pink elephant' in the middle room with us all, never to be acknowledged or approached or spoken about. This impending expectation – to eat a piece of **birthday cake** – was creating tensions and anxieties and fears so intense that it could be felt bubbling up already at 9 o'clock in the morning and the staff wanted to create a space where we could talk about this atmosphere. It was approached by the staff with puzzled faces, together with the words, as follows:

"There seems to be some tensions created around this birthday cake today...? We don't see where the confusion or upset lies...? Because it's a normal social thing to do, amongst friends and colleagues...? It's a piece of cake [puzzled looks] What can happen?" (Three shrugs and three confused faces later...)

I suddenly and so automatically released a quick chuckle in response to Carole's comment and the three nurses' similar body languages being clearly conveyed, all sitting there in a row, like an army of bewildered soldiers. Yes, it is a piece of cake, that's all! Simply a piece of cake to be enjoyed in a social setting amongst friends, used to celebrate a birthday – no fears attached, no dread, no worry no concern, no questions absolutely necessary to be asked, no anxieties arising, no impeding on the day, on thoughts or actions and behaviours and decisions made throughout the week, no feelings of uncertainty, nothing unsafe in this, no 'I cant's; not alloweds; nevers', just a relaxed of course I can...and for a split second, I too, saw it just as a piece of birthday cake, for the first time in almost thirty years!

I can still remember this moment as clear as crystal: the comment and the shrug and facial expressions of Carole and Lilly and the other member of staff who were sitting there in a row with puzzled looks firmly streamed across their faces and maybe this was their tactic against the illness prevailing so strongly in this room, but it worked for me and I try now to hold onto this flash of normal and realistic thinking and feeling around food with all of my newly-found might.

Thus, we went on to explore:

"So, what is this really about? Because It's been brought to the staff's attentions that there is intense anxiety between the group and we're worried that this has the potential to blow up in many explosive ways throughout the day, if we do not address and acknowledge that this is going on before we start the day. What is really going on to make you all so distressed over doing what is simply just a normal activity as enjoying within a social occasion **A. Piece. Of. Birthday. Cake?**"

Because it is NOT about the cake, or the steak, or the Brussels sprout or even the portion size, the consistency, the colour, texture or amount. It is about the feelings and emotions that I (and maybe my peers) so solidly "always must just" default and enfold within. Yes, we all had our worries around this cake and they were all different and personal to each one of us, yet we were all using food to show, to enact, our real distresses!

Angel Just-Rights

"Keep quiet, you'll deal with it of course you will! Remember you're Strong. Smile."

Upon searching my soul, I realised that my own intense fear in this case was that I felt I had *No Control!* No choice or decision was my own and for this, I felt *Imposed Upon! Punished! Humiliated* for having to go ahead and do it, no questions asked, no help for me. I felt *Angry!* I *Despised Those Imposers Of This Threat!* I felt *Shamed! Belittled By Those Onlookers!* Those onlookers, whom I absolutely believed, were secretly sneering and smiling inside of themselves at having won. They were imposing this big fattening piece of cake upon me – something I detested and hated and didn't want, but I had no voice to speak my worries, instead I stuffed the feelings that came along with it all – immense S*hame! Inflicted Degradation! Helpless disgrace!* While I was being made to consume this wicked, vile cake, they would be sitting there all smiles, enjoying taking pleasure from my pain and thinking why on earth is *she* accepting the eating of this? What a joke! She doesn't need to eat this cake! Look at her, how funny. We win. That was easy. They would be fully aware of my pain and distress, yet *calmly acting oblivious, paying no heed or attention to the distress, simply disregarding* totally ME.

"See? Accept this is your fate. You don't need to speak! You're not worthy, you do not matter! But with me, you are strong, remember? We can deal with anything! This is nothing! You are different. Keep others happy. Smile and you'll see. YOU CAN'T. YOU have to be PERFECT. Stick with me and you'll always be safe..."

But in this instance, the rules had actually been rethought and the staff had apparently previously decided that actually we WOULD have a choice, as this is what Day Care is all about – it is not hospital inpatient care. Day Care is there to encourage patients to learn to take responsibility for themselves, which is far from the strict rules enforced on the inpatient ward. Immediately then, I could contemplate even just thinking about TRYING the cake, rather than feeling this immediate absolute fear and dread where I freeze right then and there on the spot on that sofa, desperate to run yet just so impossible to move a muscle! *"You must fight!"* Allowing my

430

default reaction to keep me safe and to overrule, defy, block it away as simply and purely, *"I can't! Not me! I'm different! I need to work and I need punishment! I don't! I can't! No way!"*

At Least Now, I Understood That It Is Not About The Food.

It Is Simply A. Piece. Of. Birthday. Cake.

I Can Do It And I Want To And I Will!

In honesty, I didn't choose to eat the cake for the 3pm snack that day, but I learned far more about my illness from that day than I woke up in the morning thinking I would.

I Am: Anorexia.

I Am: Angel Just-Rights.

No. Not Anymore Thank You!

I Will Now Be ALLOWED To Speak, Disclose, Thus Explore, And Understand,

And To Break Free Of This "*Safe*" Tiny Existence In My Routines And Rules

Self-Imposed Day-By-Day And Gradually More And More Over The Last Almost

Thirty Years.

I Take RESPONSIBILITY For Having Created My Own Harsh Reality

In A World Believed Guaranteed As Doomed For Myself

And That My Purpose And Pleasure Comes Solely From Ensuring And

Maintaining Brighter Futures For All Others Whom I Care.

This Is "Just Me": This Is My Duty. This Is My Destiny. I am Just Different.

This Is My "Just Desserts".

I Will Now Not Simply Hold Secrets And Thoughts Anymore

Enfolded Inside Of Me As The One And Only Who Can Ever Know The Truth.

This Is *Not* "Just Me": This Is *Not* My Duty. This Is *Not* My Destiny.

I Am Human Too.

This Is *Not* My Worth. This is *Not* All I Deserve.

I Am: Rebecca.

I Am: Micci.

I Have To Believe:

I Am Just Alright As Just Me

ii. MESSAGE TWO! YOU WILL ALWAYS BE MORE SPECIAL AS JUST YOU!

- Friday 20th May 2010.

Since Uncle bought me the jigsaw carry case two weeks ago I had not contacted him or my Auntie until today because I had been unable to call her and thank her for it, which would have been the most appropriate form of thanks and yet my delaying and avoiding of this for two whole weeks, told me that I was just not ready to set myself up for a private conversation with her; not quite yet. To my frustration but acceptance, I was still functioning in baby steps.

However, I am aware that in two days' time I will be seeing my Auntie and Uncle at my Niece's Christening and so deciding how to thank her before this event comes around on Sunday 23rd May 2010, I put as priority in my thinking. This morning, I wrote a draft email to Auntie Ann (Epilogue: Immeasurable Thanks and Pledge), after which I left my flat and just knew that today was going to be the day that would "open my eyes", and it was…

Lunch decisions were very difficult today. It was a hard menu, consisting of the following:

1) Battered fish and chips
2) Vegetable pie
3) Paella
4) Jacket potato with chicken, sausage and bacon filling
5) Peas or mushy peas
6) Apple Crumble or Cheese and Biscuits

My thought patterns unfolded, as follows:

1) No way!
2) Not had this before. Didn't want to have 'pie' i.e. pastry.
3) I had this a couple of weeks ago as it was supposed to be a fish Paella but it came up as mixed meat – I identified salmon, chicken, other kinds of meat, chorizo – and I struggled with the chorizo so I knew I could not do this. I asked Lilly if I could leave the chorizo again (no-one noticed I left it all last time!) and she said no. This option was out.
4) Sausage! Bacon! Well I could do this at a big push…I had seen it before and it looked like tinned tomatoes, which

433

would be OK as I could just try and serve myself the chicken and not the sausage or bacon when it came to it.

So I chose number 4) Jacket potato with chicken, sausage and bacon filling.

Our first group of the day was the final part of 'Anxiety Management'. We talked about control and boundaries and I **was able to voice clearly for the first time ever** how I felt over the **birthday cake** event and how my having to do something makes me feel fearful if a choice is taken away from me. I felt it was the first time I had ever spoken out, having only just realised how 'things' actually made me feel rather than just reacting and communicating negatively as if my life depended upon it, through food. However, when lunch then came up, it looked completely different to how I had expected and imagined in my head. I could not believe my eyes and my tears were welling.

It was a very thick, creamy pinkie-white sauce with the blocks of meat coated and covered over completely. It was worse than the "dreaded chicken masala!" (Book 2: Who am I? Part 2, Chapter 23i). I was distressing away quietly inside – frozen to the ground in that kitchen, tears brimming, thoughts whirling, voices screaming, arms itching, hair pulling, body rocking... "Could I even go near this?" I made myself last to serve and tried to change my mind to the Paella, which looked OK and I could have served myself carefully enough to leave out the small circles of chorizo I now realised and was kicking myself hard, even though I full-well knew the answer was "No" to changing my choice at the last minute (a rule of Day Care), but the Paella really did look OK and just so nice and bearable and "dry!" that I was longing for it at this moment when looking at the meal I was expected to consume. I felt dirty and humiliated for making such a wrong decision, but still Lilly didn't let me change my meal.

At the table, another girl struggled to begin her meal "because of the taste and it will literally make me sick afterwards". I tried my hardest to encourage her stay as I knew it was because of the sauce and nothing else, underneath it all. I knew this for a fact, because we had a conversation just between ourselves the week before, when I had done exactly what she had done today i.e. stepped forward to serve first, knowing full-well that it was impossible to do, but at least it is trying, and then running away. But I failed to make her see sense today, and she left. To this day, she insists it was "just the taste" that had put her off (honesty really does have to begin with yourself and I find it amazing that I see these things so clearly in other people, but I can see myself in that situation months ago and it confuses me completely to think how my struggle must have looked so superficial / defiant / mentally blocked)...but still...

Could I do this? I had been trying not to think about how I would feel afterwards when it was all lying there inside of me *seeping away*...and this upset me a lot, but I managed to speak out my worries to the group and to Lilly at the table when I was asked, which upset me even more(!), but I held onto the fact that I did not want this to impede on the rest of my life, like it had already taken away so many seconds, hours, days, weeks, years of living my 'life' already, having replaced each second of these years with solitary self-infliction to torture, pain and isolation!

I was now feeling *anger*, not with those who were actually sitting there *supporting* me, for once, or even with myself for having to do this, but mostly with those who had given these feelings and beliefs to me in the first place and the impact that this had taken on my life and my family, especially in the last few years. I was also angry at myself for having let this happen without knowing! I understood the meaning, finally, of the famously well-used word "support", although still confused and hating it right now at this moment!

Taking five minutes in the quiet room, I tried to talk myself round: I didn't want this to rule me for the rest of my life, why should I let it?! I am angry that my life has taken this route for so long and will not take this anymore. I am trusting in others – that is being strong, not weak and cowering away... But then, *if I wait long enough the decision will have been made for me as they will all have completed their meals and I will have to go home then anyway...phew...*Look! There you go again – Avoidance! No more Rebecca, no more!

No! Stupid! What are you thinking! Don't let them trick and laugh at you! RUN!

Why me. Why Should I? Another patient is in there doing it, how can I let her down and how *weak am I really being?* This isn't being strong. I have to get back in there and at least try. For me, Rebecca. Others believe in you. You trust all others in that room don't you? Well, they are not laughing at you! *Yes they certainly are, you silly, silly, gullible girl!* You chose the food. It is not poison and it is not punishment! It is Lunch. A social activity. YOU chose it. Remember, it is just a piece of birthday cake. If you don't face it now, you never ever will.

Remember all you have realised this week Rebecca, you cannot give in now. Plus, today is the day that will "open your eyes"…keep it going…for you, Micci, for once – FOR YOU.

I was determined to try to SEPARATE THE FEELINGS FROM THE FOOD and to remember Carole saying simply "It's A. Piece. Of. Birthday. Cake." And how I saw that flash of immense clarity in this, which had even made me impulsively chuckle! Come on! Even if you don't see this now, Rebecca, do it for you, Micci, you know it makes sense really. You know you can...

…And so I decidedly left the quiet room and on my way back into joining the others, I got as far as the door handle and walked straight back up towards the quiet room. *What on Earth am I thinking?! I can't do this! Go home! NOW! THIS IS YOUR DECISION? WHAT ON EARTH ARE YOU THINKING?! YOU CAN'T! YOU WILL PAY FOR THIS AFTERWARDS! LATER! TONIGHT! TOMORROW! RUN! RIGHT NOW WHILE YOU CAN! GO GO GO!*

My hand was on the door handle to the dining room and I was on my way to pick up my bag and leave, when I walked straight into the path of a nurse who had come to look for me in the quiet room and she handed me a tiny rock from one of the groups that I had missed when I was at home in Grenada, ill, after that horrendous nightmare episode (Book 2: Who Am I? Part 2, Chapter 21i, Interlude II B1).

The stone was small and grey and on it was drawn a fine tiny purple butterfly. I was in no state to see the significance of this symbol at the time and am grateful to the nurse for explaining its meaning to me right then and there: Freedom to fly away, and drawn in my favourite colour purple.

How could I walk away now? It was wrong. Micci needed to be truly strong in herself, to regain her life, to release those severe evil "butterflies" that were impaling her stomach and she needed to face her ultimate metaphoric fears that she found so intensely in food. Only then can she start to think of flying away from her cold secret destructive world – *running away* from the world that will give back and allow her access to all her favourite things is no longer a choice and definitely not an answer! Thus, I re-joined the others at the table. The staff could do no more for me. I had to do it for myself. The patients and staff in the room could not have been more supportive in any way what-so-ever. I had covered my food in pepper but I ate the peas and I ate the potato and I even managed to really engage in conversation in order to simply try to be normal and calm, because that was real life and that is what I wanted!

OK, I did have to separate the meat from the sauce and fiddled around with the ketchup. Everyone had finished their meals and were talking nicely and pleasantly, really making efforts to take away focus from that which we were all finding so hard to do that day: To eat. But I was struggling when it came to the last and worst part of the meal, over-taken and over-shadowed by *Angel* once again.

I took a deep breath and asked that if they wanted to leave me to carry on alone while they continued into the kitchen to get their puddings, then it was OK with me. I felt awful that I was still sitting there with what I perceived as the most disgusting meal in front of me, growing and growing in size and repulsiveness and I felt dirty for having to sit there and eat it. I just felt so humiliated, but Lilly and the other patients wanted to stay at the table to 'support' me. I just wanted to be left alone so I could run quietly away; I was ready to leave.

So now in this predicament, I started to break down. Terrific waves of fear all over again. But I was determined to do this and I started to eat the meat (my portion was mostly sausage rather than chicken, just to make it even worse!). I didn't taste a thing of the whole meal. At one point the sheer fact that I was sitting there eating this vile seepage would have made me refuse straight out. But after the conversation around trust, control, boundaries and rules in relation to anxiety and behaviour, and also because another patient had finished the same meal, and apparently "enjoyed it", I could tell myself that it was OK to do, that this was *only Angel's perception / belief, only her problem* and although it almost choked me through my distress and tears, I finished the sauce by covering it in the jacket potato skin to hide it and to feel a miniscule little bit better that I was eating it in conjunction with the fibre of the potato skin and hopefully that this might just push it through and out of my system that bit quicker, and I also ate it with tomato ketchup and ended up washing it down with water. This is when I had my real breakdown when most people had left the room for pudding, but thanks to another patient, I accepted her comfort and warmth and care and went on to complete the cheese and biscuits pudding too.

Although, at the moment, I may still have to:-

- Separate and organise every component of the meal perfectly and literally.
- Cut up the components of the meal literally.
- Rationalise textures and consistencies. Avoid tasting, avoid chewing, avoid looking at the meal literally.

But now I will try to remember, always strive to rather:-

- Separate the food from the emotions.
- Break down things in life into simple baby steps.
- Recognise that you are not being outspokenly punished or humiliated or laughed at or controlled by others without a choice – these are only your perceptions and these are only your thoughts – ignore *Angel* as she will only lie to you and cause you hurt and pain.

Rather trust in these people: the staff, the patients, even in your family and maybe one day you will find trust in your friends and be able to eat with others. They are not punishing you, they are not humiliating you nor are they consistently there to silently laugh at you or to harm you.

Let them help you. Let them in. You CAN talk. You CAN win. It IS OK, it IS alright; the strength and determination is there and always must come from within.

B4:

EMAIL UPDATE TO AUNTIE ANN:

Dear Auntie Ann & Uncle,

Thank you for your last letter, dated 14th May 2010.

I must really apologise for having been so quiet over the last couple of weeks. I've been doing a lot of work and the hospital are hopeful that I will be able to return to work, gradually, starting from next month. At the same time, they have extended my treatment for another three months, which is a plan that I am actually wonderfully pleased about and for once, I am in agreement with this as being the best thing for me.

Baby Steps Work Best.

Now: THANK YOU SO MUCH for the jigsaw carrier that Uncle and yourself have bought for me! I was stunned when Mum directed me to it at home and couldn't believe my eyes.

Although reluctant at first, I have actually been using it every weekend and allowing myself slowly to enjoy that bit of comfort that it brings to my life and I feel more and more able to sit with this and thankfully accept your lovely gift.

It is so more perfect than you can ever know and in so many ways; it is so thoughtful and extremely kind of you both and means so much to me.

THANK YOU BOTH!

Angel Just-Rights

Having said this, you REALLY SHOULD NOT HAVE done this for me in the first instance! Because my knowing that your support, understanding, only wanting the best for me, really means everything to me. I have realised a lot of things only in the past couple of weeks, and with the help of the amazing staff at Day Care, I have been able to recognise just how much your absolute support has been aiding my recovery in so many subtle yet significant ways and without myself even having known it at the time and really, right up until this week.

As always, it is lovely to hear your news and I look forward to the next instalments of 'A week in the life of the Wentworth family'! But please never feel like you cannot ease or end your letter-writing to me as I recognise how devoted you've been with your time and effort over me in the last few years and I cannot and will not ever 'assume' that your support is unending in any way should you choose to stop writing.

Do you have special plans for your birthday next week?

Well, it looks like the weather is set to be beautiful over the weekend and I look forward to seeing you and catching up at my Niece's Christening on Sunday.

Best wishes and thank you many, many times over again!

Lots of Love,

From Rebecca x x x

B5:

SUMMING UP AND THANKS

i. Summing Up Of The Week

DURING THE 'SUMMING UP' of the week session this Friday afternoon, I could acknowledge that it had been a positive day for me today, even after all my distress. I had done it. I had stayed to face my fears. And I know what it had meant, for me. This week, I had learned a lot.

Carole and Lilly both said to me nodding "it's the voice that has been found" to which I would agree and for this I thank: Trust. Experiments. Acceptance. And "a lot of work!" (Book 2: Who Am I? Part 1, Chapter 20).

OK, I am not going to go home and cook this meal (probably will never, ever eat it again in all honesty) but it was a baby step in fighting back for an improved quality of life. The meaning behind having achieved this under my own decision, with correct help and support, means I actually have something to fight back with now and this is what gave me so much more real strength.

My distress never seems to get any better, yet, but now I know I can do it with fight and for me, and I understand my underlying difficulties and have been able to voice these concerns more than before. I feel more confident to believe in the staff that tell me "believe me, it does get easier". I know some days will be better or easier, harder or more difficult than others, but I now amazingly actually possess the voice to fight back – here is the real strength – I WILL LIVE MY LIFE.

GOODBYE *ANGEL JUST-RIGHTS*, where all feelings and emotions are forever banned. Here I fight and prevail as Rebecca who WANTS TO AND CAN surmount endless unrequited trails of fake power, shameful indignities and metaphoric fears. I WILL be set free from every lone and extreme incessantly harassing

442

impulsive action and thought that forever plagues my being and overwhelms my soul with worries, great intense fears and terrifying dread, manifesting in uncertainty seemingly unbearably imminent, decidedly absolute torture and harm proving always to somehow secure its efforts unto the seeking out (usually, until now, finding and overriding, manipulating and controlling) once naïve, unsuspecting, indecisive and silent, silly, stupid, dim-witted, coy unsuspecting little me.

ii. Message of Thanks.

THANK YOU TO all those who have remained by my side in support of Rebecca instead of for *Angel* as although I did not at all see this at the time, you have been there for me consistently offering your unconditional comfort, safety, love and encouragement in your understanding towards what you all will have known as my – also your – very difficult, seemingly futile, long and slow journey of acceptance to finally embark on recovery. You have never lost sight of Micci through the spiteful over-casting shadow of *Angel Just-Rights*.

I have learned so much. Most importantly I have learned to recognise that when all is lost, give up fighting *against*, but remain true in belief and in trust so to NEVER GIVE IN. Instead, begin to re-learn through experimenting, testing, evaluating and of course accepting. As I have now learned that COMMUNICATION IS OK. In fact it is very necessary, it is crucial, it is special. Communication is not stupid, nor weak nor feeble. Communication is how we interact. Communication is KEY.

Thank you, all of those who have remained patient in your support, always listening, always helping, never scorning, never judging. It is from you whom I have derived clear trust and support and feel able to continue using this care and comfort in helping me to build upon the foundations we have made, to continue my growing responsible and utilising this new strength in order to regain the ability necessary to bravely face, to manage, and to treasure, the most important times in life: The here and now.

Never Give In!

My Eyes, My Heart, My Mind Are Open.

For, Although My Shadow Will Eternally Follow

In Each Step Taken By My Soul,

I Know That This Journey: It Is OK, It Is Right

Sit Through It, It Will Pass And I Will See:

My World Is **NOT** *About To Come To That Crashing, Tragic End Way Out Of My Control!*

"IT'S. JUST. A. PIECE. OF. CAKE."

It's Never About The Food!

Instead, Listen And Think Logically By Entrusting In The Trusted And Above All:

Find That Courage Within To Recover Your Voice And Be Brave And Therefore Begin

TO COMMUNICATE. TO SPEAK. TO WIN.

Nephew's Christening, May 2008

Mum Angrily Asks Me:

"You look anorexic! Are you?! You're the thinnest here! Are you trying to be the thinnest? Look around you! You look awful! I'm taking you to the doctor!"

To Which I Laugh And I Shrug It All Off...Keep Quiet...Smile.

(Book 1: Secrets Out, Part 5, Chapter 17; Book 2: Who Am I? Part 1, Chapter 18)

Niece's Christening, This Sunday 23ʳᵈ May 2010

Same Time, Same Church, Same Reception, Same People

I Now See Reality In My Eyes, Heart, Mind, My Destiny, Because I Am Different:

"I can never be perfect enough, just perfect or just right and be safe always.

Therefore, I can never be thin enough, happy, satisfied or content enough; not me."

Unless, As The Most Perfect Anorexic Whom Of Course Lies Cold, Alone, In Death.

So Maybe I *Couldn't* Attend The Reception After The Service,

Which I Openly Spoke About With Kerry And With Mum Before The Day:

Carefully I explained that this was not primarily about avoiding food,

I was now pleased to have and to take the support of my family.

But moreover, I was not yet ready to embrace the social event of the whole day.

The Baby Step That I Did Complete, Free From Tears And Intense Fears In That

One Hour Church Service Was Made Possible By You, Dear Mum:

Having you by my side throughout, I fought the brimming tears and the irrational

fears right through. YOU helped me more than you can ever know that day and

here-forward. Thank You, Dear Kerry, Dear Nephew, Dear Mum, Dear Auntie

For Now I Have Spoken, Your Patience, Your Respect, Your Comfort, Your

Understanding Has Come.

iii. I Ask...

WILL I EVER find comfort, safety, happiness, security, trust, even just a touch of solace in this world? Perhaps through friends, or even in a relationship? Personally, I still doubt I can ever have or deserve this anymore. I feel such a thing is so wrong for me to seek and so far out from my reach; rather punish, because I can deal with that which I know best.

But I am re-learning in those baby steps to re-gain the simplest trust in others, to re-open myself, to retain my self-worth and to live my life for me, as well as for those whom I care and who do care for me.

May I aim to take every day with commitment, strength and flair.

iv. I'll Remember...

THOSE WHO HELD out their hand, even to that distant remnant cry of ever-fading Rebecca. Those who offered their constant, unwavering, unconditional love and support

To the Micci they once knew. Those who never judged nor accused, never condemned nor reproached. Those who never stole bold, sarcastic looks with intent to hurt her soul. Those who helped ease her guilt and negativity. And those who never left her sinking in her shame and filth and to bear all her selfish struggling only furthermore alone...yes! I felt the shame and the disgust! Yes! I heard the accusing cries of defiance, of awkwardness, of blame and of mistrust! Please understand I, Micci, am sorry.

I'll remember those who continued to cherish the fragile soul of Rebecca who ended so weak and frail. I'll remember those who always believed in me and who never forgot me. I'll remember those who never once aborted their guidance and attentions from Micci, a child so desperate for support and comfort and love; the child afraid to speak. I'll remember those who remembered Rebecca purely for who she is: for Micci, of course just alright enough, always, as just you.

FINAL RIDDLE:

HERE BEGINS MY REAL RECOVERY

To Endowed Furtive Phantom, Today I Pronounce:
[While Sinister Shadows Lay Siege To My Soul!
Piercing Shriek! Frantic Flounce! Ensues Firm Tragic Goal!]
"Goodbye And Goodnight, *Innate Angel Just-Rights."*

Now Micci 'Just Must', Reach Out, Speak, Entrust;
In Humans T'help Fade *Angel Parker* Away.
[Exclude Angel Parker!? The Mind Will Construe:
Sheer, Eventual Disaster!] Help, What **Can** I Do?!

Utter Frenzied True Panic! Dread, Distress Fright, Fear!
Angel's Swift Wings; Strong, In Haste, Reappear.
So Lowly And Loyally Down They Do Swoop;
Vanish All Logic! To Safety I'm Scooped! (Excessive Exercise Coping Model)

These Wings, Though Enticing, I've Learned How They Dupe;
The Sensitive, 'Easily Led', Fragile Group.
Help Micci Maintain In Herself No Disdain;
Rather **Talk** Through Her Rage, Remain Present. Engaged.

(HERE BEGINS MY REAL RECOVERY CONT.)

Calmly Hear And Accept, A Secret's Been Kept.
Baby Steps Fall On Queue, Soul To Trust And Renew.
As Rebecca Restores, So Micci Matures;
Re-learning T'Involve, Being Present; T'Heal, Solve.

Micci, Seek Mirth, Please Dear Spec On This Earth;
The Help – Trust It's Right As You **Can** And You Jolly Well **Will**
Conquer This Blight!
Trust, Reassurance, Support Near Or Far;
'Though Struggles Stay Constant, You're Driving Your Car.

Laugh! Dine! It's OK, Your Brakes: They Are Fine;
Believe In Rebecca And Keep Her On Par;
(See, You Can. You're OK. You Are Still Alive)
You're Micci; You're You: Just Alright As You Are.

'Micci Just Alright'

For No Angel, Nor Shadow, I'll Give Up This Fight;

My Aim's To Live Freely, With Choice Day And Night.

When All's Blurred And Uncertain, Frighteningly Bleak;

Solace, Comfort, Trust, Safety, In Loved Ones I'll Seek.

~

And Try To Remember I AM Human, Because;

Purely, Perfectly Unconditionally I Am Loved.

So I CAN Live My Dreams And I CAN Flutter Free;

As Micci:

"I AM Just Alright As Just Me!"

New Reality:

"I Am Always Doing That Which I Cannot Do,
In Order I May Learn How To Do It"

Picasso

EPILOGUE:

THANKS and PLEDGE

EPILOGUE:

IMMEASURABLE THANKS AND PLEDGE

I. TO MY MOST MIRACULOUS MUM

Tuesday 25th May 2010 – Today I was spot-weighed and after every excuse under the sun and a lot of unnecessary wasted time on *Angel's* part, this clearly resulted in a very real weight coming to light, which, after six months in treatment was proving to be significantly less than the figure at which I had started Day Care.

Therefore, I was told I had to regain the weight that had been lost since leaving the ward and to do this before my next review, which was in about three weeks and if this was not achieved then it would be back to hospital for me.

Although absolutely livid, I agreed this was fair, given the rules of this program, and I could not argue with this. After all, I had found some of my old weights that I had managed to conceal in my clarinet reed boxes, hidden in my clarinet case, when I was in hospital and if I was to be spot weighed, I could always use these in times of desperation and then I would not be stupidly 'caught out' again.

As much as I *wanted* to get better, hospital remained my worst nightmare – especially being admitted at my current weight – being only 1kg from my highest weight ever! I felt cheated and like a fraud all over again, for being the only patient blatantly with enough courage to be truthful about their weight with the hospital staff.

Angel Just-Rights

Wednesday 26th May 2010 – In order to celebrate the looming changes in Day Care attendees and staff, namely the 'graduation' of two patients and the 'moving on' of one member of staff, it was decided that the group would meet today for 10am for snacks as usual, then pick up our packed lunches (we had all chosen from the canteen the day before and piled the food up in the fridge) and then make our way to the museum, where we would have our lunch together in the gardens before returning to the hospital for the remainder of the day, including afternoon snacks as usual.

From the time I left the confines of Day Care yesterday, I was dreading this outing and my head was screaming at me until I arrived at my sister's the very day next day.

So follows this day in the life of Me:

07:30 – Alarm goes off. Oh no, it's the outing today...*Lie in. Don't go. Have a few more minutes in bed. Go on. There is no way you can have all that lunch that you picked up yesterday, is there? You know you can't. How dare you take yourself off and enjoy yourself when you have so much else to do! Think of that big sandwich, all of which you will have to eat, you greedy thing and look at you! Imagine that thick milkshake you have never even tried before, it is more calories than the yogurt that all the others are having you imbecile why did you choose that you simple huge idiot! And that pasta salad, plus a cereal bar on top of it all too! There is no way you will manage it all. No way. Just imagine everyone else trying to make you eat it. In public! They can do it. You cannot and should not and do not in any way, shape or form need to! You will spoil the day out for everyone...!*

...Definitely shouldn't go. How can you look round the museum slowly, pretending you are interested, when I will be forcing you to walk and pace up and down the stairs, fidgeting at least, keep moving, don't you dare enjoy, don't you dare relax..!

...No! Forget that musical instrument section! You won't love it! Go another day! I won't let you enjoy it! You can't! How dare you! Even if you force yourself to have all that lunch, you'll then have to

454

saunter back on the bus smiling and laughing and return to Day Care to also have snacks on top of all your indulgences! You can't! You just can't!

How would I deal with walking out of the safe hospital gates? How would I deal with waiting for the bus? How would I deal with getting on the bus and chatting to everyone as I pretended to be OK and fine and not freaking out at all? How could I walk around a museum with no-one there to hold my hand? I am scared. I can't get out or run away if I need to. I can't go. I just can't.

It's not even the food. Everyone else is doing the food and I want to be able to eat a proper packed lunch like normal people, it will be so good for me to practice and with the support of the whole group and the staff – such a great opportunity to have a proper packed lunch out! I really cannot miss this and shoot myself in the foot. No, just carry it all out in baby steps: they are all going to be there doing the same thing together. This is such a good opportunity – must take it.

Too unsafe; too uncertain; too much change; need safety; need support; need comfort; need Day Care. OK, first step, get up as usual and get ready.

08:30 – Mum rings as usual, to make sure I am up and having breakfast and I am. I voice my concerns about the outing to my Mum, very briefly, and she tries to persuade me that the fresh air will do me good. I don't voice all my concerns at all, but I do voice my apprehensive feelings and my overall desires not to go.

09:30 – On the bus. Caught it a bit late as was really thinking I wouldn't go, but then I would have to ring up and speak to them and I WANT to go. I want to start joining in with social events and this is going to be the easiest one because it is with people i.e. the group and staff that I trust, have been honest with and have opened up to and have begun to speak to and we are all supportive together. It is now or never. Go on, at least go in for snack (and then it'll be impossible for you to leave and walk out). Go on, don't let the others down. Don't appear cowardly...

09:50 – Arrive at Day Care. Put about three spoons of coffee in my hot milk and try to put less hot milk in it too. Shaking. I couldn't help it. Sitting at the table with the others drinking my milk and eating my biscuit. REALLY trying my absolute best to stay focused and happy for everyone, all the while dreading going into the unknown, that is this whole outing. Tried to block out my tears so much but couldn't – I picked up my bag and left heading straight for the toilets where I sobbed uncontrollably.

Lilly had followed me. I was highly distressed and managed to say to her that I just couldn't go through with today, no matter how hard I tried, I just couldn't do any more. She was fantastic and agreed that she understood I had "a lot going on for you at the moment" and she suggested that I took my bag of lunch from the fridge and come back tomorrow. I did. I wasn't even dreading the lunch – we were all going to do that and I needed this chance to 'be normal' outside of Day Care, yet with the support there. I was livid with myself for giving up this opportunity to experience it.

10:30 – Hurriedly I walked as far home as I usually do. In a right state, just wanting to get as far away as possible from being made to do that which I felt too out of my control and I immersed myself in the routines that I knew and felt safe with. I was scared and needed safety.

After walking to my usual bus stop, I caught the bus straight to Kings Cross, during which I wrote a brief note to my sister and to my Mum, whom I knew was spending the day with Kerry and the children. I needed comfort. I needed to feel safe. I needed not to be compelled into starvation and exercise.

I arrived at the train station and bought a ticket to my sister's. On the train journey I remembered a quote that I had written down that morning during breakfast while watching an old favourite children's television programme:

"That which cannot be cured; must be endured"

I accepted that I could only muster the strength enough to continue making these baby steps through recovery if I was able to trust in, be honest with and to speak to my family and only if they could apply the same treatment to me.

I now knew that measurable steps were the only way to start to reclaim Rebecca and for this, I needed to feel certain that my family would always be there for me outside of the support I so gratefully received through the Day Care treatment that continued to keep me alive and well.

Today was meant to be a test.

12:30 – On arrival at my sister's front door, I greeted my family with a warm smile and with my note:

- Please don't be cross

- I went to Day Care

- During snacks I was distressed

- Lilly agreed I had "too much going on at the moment" and we agreed I should come back tomorrow

- I don't want to talk about it

- Please don't be cross

- I've got my lunch in my bag

My family spoke nothing of anything. They were unbelievably kind, supportive and showed they were unconditionally there for me.

I loved playing with my nephew all day long and my nephew appeared to love me too. I will always remember the feelings of comfort, safety and solace I experienced on this day as we were all one step further in the turning of my key. My family were listening to me and what's more, I allowed my nephews' absolute cuddles as we walked back to the train station, not firstly because I wanted to carry his heavy load (which is why my sister tried her best to have him walk) but I sensed he really wanted to by carried by me, his Auntie, and would not let his grip go from around my neck and nestling his head, safe and hidden, tightly under my chin. I know he was listening too, because I know how well he now understands conversations! Although he is unable to communicate through his own voice in speech, he understands everything that is spoken. Not only was he listening to my actions, he was now responding to my voice.

I know he was enjoying the cuddles as much as I was. He was hanging on to me as close as close could be. I will never forget the warm feeling of love this filled me with inside. I was wanted, I was needed, I was trusted, I was respected. I was there, unconditionally for this child. I was there to love him, I was there to protect him, I was there to make sure he was safe and always happy.

18:00 – Arrived home to my flat in London. Walked most of the way. I had managed my lunch (half) but it was a sandwich I was not used to. Ate usual dinner. Very thankful to my amazing family being there for me today and adhering to my very needs and wishes.

20:00 – Spen calls my mobile. I leave him to speak to my answer phone. I learn that in response to my email giving him the opportunity to contribute anything he wished to my Memoir of 1980 – 2010, he is requesting that I send in the post to him "the sections that relate to me so I can read them and comment on them." After immediately worrying and feeling overpowered and suddenly out of control yet again, I thought rationally and sensibly, for Rebecca. I sent him an email assertively yet politely stating that this book is *my reality and my truth* and anything he wishes to contribute I would certainly include, but in no way was it going in the post or over the internet! I received an email in return, stating that "I will be making no comment".

For the first time in many years – maybe since my rebound days in 2003 – I felt in control, I felt powerful, I felt **empty of fear and empty of dread, I felt unrestricted, unaffected, reconciled; I felt present.** I felt amity, almost happy, harmonious! I saw a life that I felt I could grab. I had just needed him to know that I was no longer keeping secrets and that he no longer had this utterly dark and suppressive holding power over me; it had been lifted.

Now he could live a life of uncertainty instead of OVERPOWERING ME!

I now could say, truthfully and honestly:

I FELT FREE

Angel Just-Rights

Friday 28th May 2010 – Monday 31st May 2010

(Spring Bank Holiday Weekend)

- I, Rebecca, kept to my meal plan the most I have ever done before.

- *My Dear Mum was able to support me righteously with this.*

- I, Rebecca, enjoyed helping Little Brother and Mum tidy the garden.

- *My Dear Mum was able to support me righteously with this.*

- I, Rebecca, was able to laugh with Mum, Little Brother and his wife, naturally without feeling a pressure to put on an act and fake smiles.

- *My Dear Mum was able to support me righteously with this.*

- I, Rebecca, was able to clomp and resist those ever ceaseless urges goading me to leave my poor Mum alone earlier and earlier in order to simply must now vigorously compensate through the night and also the next morning for the extent that my gluttony was reaching at home here in Grenada.

- *My Dear Mum was able to support me righteously with this.*

- I, Rebecca, actually asked "Can we have some Christening Cake...?" actually admitted to "Enjoying that chicken curry..." actually spoke of "Looking forward to that egg custard all weekend..."

- *My Dear Mum was able to support me righteously with this.*

- I, Rebecca, was able to discuss life memories with Mum.

- *My Dear Mum was able to support me righteously with this.*

- I, Rebecca was able to listen, to reflect and to express my thoughts on a newspaper article relating to a lady who had fled abroad from her partner, who was up for assault charges, while she sadly disappeared on holiday and finally took the lives of their two children, surrendering her own to a life in jail.

  Mum explained that while the lady appeared clever and sensible and was maintaining a good job, she was "obviously mentally unstable or something...it's all very sad...just shows that everything can be sorted out if only you speak about it and talk to people, then something can always be done to help...or it will just end in tragedy".

  I heard her message, loud and clear. At the same time I was able to put it to her that maybe, just maybe, the fear of having extreme judgments imposed upon her and her family – that of sheer shame, for example, total loss of respect, every ounce of pride and dignity suddenly being abolished by the

  public and by her own family and her own friends suddenly being ripped away from her, naked for all to see and judge – how this reaction could be deemed worse than losing her own freedom to a life trapped in a prison, just deserving punishment and restriction of freedom, a life bound for torture...

- *In her pause to think and react, thus to clearly really listen and to hear me, I am sure that my Dear Mum was able to support me righteously with taking on this perspective to some extent too.*

- I, Rebecca went shopping with Mum on the train to Paylark, which was also on the way back to London, for me. We were able to enjoy each other's company on the train and also whilst shopping, when suddenly I realised that the clock-face of my necklace (Book 3: The Bigger Picture, Part 2, Chapter 31) had come off in my hand and I exclaimed unto my Mother, who said to me that she never liked the clock-face on my necklace anyway and that it now looks so much better with just the small silver butterfly left hanging free around my neck. I listened and heard and I completely agreed. Time had run out. I was now getting my life back.

- *What was more; my Dear, Dear Mum had just confidently and openly spoken her invaluable accordance to me.*

II. AND FINALLY,

TO MY DEDICATED READER

I COULD NOW at least respect there is a difference between 'feeling fat' and 'being fat' and I know that with this new-found support of my family can continue in taking these small baby steps and 'to sit with' and to feel just about alright with "being fat" because I have learned and accepted that 'FAT' is not a feeling. So I when I am "feeling fat" I know I am definitely 'feeling' something and I try to work out exactly what that feeling is.

Thus, rather than impulsively focusing negatively upon my body – destroying the enemy – to which there is a simple answer i.e. to focus on losing weight in every which way I know how, I have learned to try and recognise there is an external problem, no matter how incredibly scary, or wrong, or tiny, or way out of my control it may seem to so definitely be. Do not distract from the real issue as things can be avoided or denied for some time, but nothing will ever be hidden.

While really thinking about, even if not always answering, those times of really 'feeling fat', times where there seems no other plausible answer but to give in and return to *Angel*, instead I will TRUST, BE HONEST AND SPEAK to those who I know are there for me. Only then could I continue to reclaim the life that is awaiting me away from this prison of eating disordered existence.

If my story, my truth, of *Angel Just-Rights* can flicker any light of hope inside of you, my Dear Reader, then all my lost years and hell on this earth would not have been wasted completely in vain. You too, can realise that all the colours in the world have always been there for you, yet you choose to keep sinking and sinking further into that black hole that made you feel so safe, yet will leave you really with nothing.

I do not deny it will be long and hard, I do not deny it will be immensely and unbelievably scary at times and feel so wrong that the wish to put an end to it all and to die instantly will overwhelm, I

463

do not deny the urge and the will to give up or to give in at times *will sometimes overpower*, I do not deny that the urges desperately seeking rigorous gym sessions, immersions of the soul in alcohol, night-life and promiscuity and the immense compulsion to somehow slash out that anger and energy right upon oneself...until instant release is felt in unhealthy ways of coping...will continue to scream out at me in such horridly believable thoughts inside. Strength to ignore those urges, the screams, the avoidance and be truly strong for ourselves, even speak out our thoughts and worries to those who have learned to support us in a way that we can contemplate receiving and listening properly to, as uncomfortable as it may be, try to accept that 'feelings' cannot injure us and instead 'sit with it' and believe it will always pass. Time never stands still.

Dear Reader, in three weeks' time I will be celebrating my 30th birthday. If I let *Angel* convince me to avoid change for any longer and convince me I am not motivated enough or ready enough yet to begin the process of 'recovery', I know I will be dead before I gain the motivation required to commit to such a step.

I know I will try for moderation, but will still strive for perfection. Maybe I won't feel able to have cake on my birthday and maybe I won't make my meal out to the restaurant I desired. Maybe I won't even make seeing my friends because of *Angel's* screams, once again. But now have understanding and freedom with a trust and support in the staff and patients I have made close friendships with at Day Care, in my Dear Mum, in my Dear Auntie and maybe also in my "friends" that I have avoided over the years. I have the determination to build up my health by, and thereafter I do so hope, the 2nd July 2010.

Angel Just-Rights

I Therefore Pledge To Measurably Mending Micci:

From All I Have Learned;

In All I Continue To Learn;

With All My Determination To Preserve;

My Inside Candle To Shine And To Burn:

Shadow *Angel*, I WILL DEFY!

Right In this World, For Me, I WILL LIVE;

To A Life, In Moderation, I WILL GIVE;

Sincerely, Honestly, Fully Whole-heartedly;

Openly, Willingly, All Secrets Out Finally;

A Life I Give ONE FINAL TRY

By 2nd July 2010

When Her Story May Well Be Out:-

Will Micci Maintain Strength To 'Live' Once Again?

Or To *Angel* Lapse Darting In Doubt?

Acknowledgments

For Auntie Ann

In no way could I have asked for a more supportive Auntie and Uncle during the whole of my illness. It all began from the day of my first hospital admission, which was the day I had given poor Mum – in the absence of my late Father – permission to inform her sister-in-law of the news; and specifically to share, only with her.

In your devoted consistency Dear Auntie I have found, and amazingly continue to find, a little extra encouragement and support for Rebecca throughout daily battles to beat the weaknesses out of my deceiving shadow, now entrenched into my being. Your ongoing subtle gestures push me to make that extra effort, to take that extra risk, to stretch those strict boundaries just a little further. I have learned there is such unconditional care and understanding in you, Dear Auntie, such that I continue to question the rules, the regimes and the torments of my own shadow, while allowing my trust in your honesty and understanding. Hearing the values and morals by which you live your life, have been of help to me beyond recognition.

Diligently writing weekly letters, where the overriding response from various others have been to actively disengage (my perception), thus communicating their feelings through rage, anger, avoidance, shame, disgust and embarrassment at my now open (since admission to hospital) "severely mentally ill thinking", you have been there supporting me throughout my struggles and I want you to know how my receiving each and every one of your letters has meant something special to me.

Angel Just-Rights

At first, I was unforthcoming in my abilities to even accept this post that kept appearing under my door, or that was consistently being handed to me by nursing staff in the hospital, as it meant somebody was thinking about me and that somebody was discreetly showing me they cared. Such a concept I initially found extremely difficult to comprehend, let alone appreciate, because it was a gesture of kindness that would sit uncomfortably provoking an ironically safe yet moreover disturbing and uncomfortable feeling inside of me. This feeling, I can describe as 'unsettling' mixed with immediate confusion, anger and fear; and I was totally unable to welcome this love with any warmth to the extent that I would berate myself if my heart would jump in a moment of joy upon receiving your next letter. I would leave 'the unknown' unopened for days, while coming to terms with these feelings until it would begin to feel 'okay' to open. That is, I suppose, until it felt 'okay' to let someone into the tiny private space I had created around myself.

Slowly overcoming these reactions, I would quietly look forward to receiving your next instalment (although I must state that never once was any form of communication ever simply 'expected' from you). But here was something I now allowed to make me feel a little bit special as, I concluded, these letters were not a threat or even an intrusion into my life, but nothing more than solely an option of something for me to accept, if and when I should choose.

Dear Auntie Ann, you were so prompt, so perfect, so reliable in the regularity and the content of your writings that, unbeknown to myself at the time, this true devotion and support was to be my inauguration in embarking upon the climb into reformation, healing and well-being and I am so thankful to this today and will continue to be thankful forevermore. Over the last three years, this gentle tenderness became my longstanding, true guardian: ultimately, I could control our level of contact whilst learning to 'ride' confusing and unwanted feelings of indecisiveness, hesitation or tentative thinking that would so negatively overwhelm me.

Now cherished is this tiny prick into my then timorous soul, as exactly the start I needed. You encourage me to venture from the chaotic everyday life I had retreated into, and in the thick uncertainty, insecurity, fear and dread you slowly infiltrated your love into my sinking, lonely bubble. In efforts to nurture an inspiration in me, your youngest niece, you have thoughtfully included newspaper cuttings and numerous creative distractions. As it became well-known to hospital staff and peers alike, rekindling forgotten skills became an absolute saviour in working to distract my body and mind, to channel intrusive thoughts, spurn away intense feelings and compelling behaviours that I found impossible to deal with. Instead, concentrating on creating a plethora of knitted scarves – be it day or night, height of summer or depths of winter – grounded my being and warmed my own heart, particularly upon suddenly realising the set of gifts I had made and could offer to those I had so selfishly angered and worried throughout my illness until that time, Christmas 2009.

On your surprise visit to the hospital, Dear Auntie, you brought for me a stunningly beautiful 1,000 piece jigsaw, which we began together while chatting. I want you to know this jigsaw has helped me, in particular upon discharge and having now completed it (minus the complete border, as you are aware) while forcing myself to sit with my thoughts and feelings at the weekends at home in the company and support of Dear Mum. My Mum and I would sit together in the evenings after dinner, replicating 'rest period' as learned in hospital, enjoying spending time together. Yet finding myself without the faithful support of hospital staff and fellow patients, this was not an easy task without the distraction of your jigsaw to focus on. You also sent post cards and photographs and never missed a week in your communications, even when you had travelled away or if a week had been particularly busy and chaotic in your own life, Dear Auntie, and for this I am extremely heartened.

You always manage to say the right things, even when we meet in person; never too much and not too little. You demonstrate consideration and clarity when assuring your ongoing support for me. For all the above, I thank you from the bottom of my heart.

In contrast, so insolent and selfish was my own behaviour. I never felt able to contact you or even reply to you fully, as I could never match your kindness or your exciting news. Me, I would pathetically send the odd email now and then in order to thank you

Angel Just-Rights

for your thoughts. Subsequent to 'The Auntie Ann Event' however, I knew that I just had to apologise to you, to my only Dear Auntie, and that this meant forcing myself to do something that I had never done before: to open myself up into being honest and truthful and to trust in the response of another; to trust further in YOU. I had to turn around the aftermath of this (and I quote your own words) "rude", "cunning", "deceitful" act I had impulsively, so strongly, expressed...*So superbly and selfishly had those ceaseless sequesting shadows of Angel delighted as she ran thick and fast from her very worst fears,* as Micci, shrivelling away once again and smothered under the trusted wings of *ever faithful Angel Just-Rights.* But I, Rebecca, realised I had to take responsibility for this event by way of confronting my one and only famous safe seraph, turned eternal oppressor that had invigorated my fleeing back into isolation and far from those who truly really cared. Once again, I had abandoned real help, defaulting to follow that with which I felt safe: *Angel.*

...Infested with ferocious unfairness, terrifying and helplessly insidious insecurities invading her world – unbearable was this overwhelming uncertainty, like that perilous plane and those malfunctioning brakes – Rebecca now recognised it was time, somehow, to find strength to trust flight of my own through using baby steps in allowing / testing / experimenting, with true help offered from my family.

I have now learned and understood how *Angel Just-Rights* gradually manifested: formerly a life of seeming success and flawless finesse, now fully entrenched in tedious, compelling and unflinching shape-shifting conceit, subsisting ambiguously on indelicate and distant ironic delight, with aims solely to steadfastly devastate everyone and everything in my life, until all is lost, including all signs of hope, future and especially recovery. No more.

Dear Auntie, I thank you for your kindness and your devotion, for your truthful manner and your nurturing support. I thank you for your unfaltering friendship and for your unassuming honesty. I thank you for always listening, always hearing, never judging, and well-advising.

Thank you, so very much.

APPENDIX 1 – LETTER TO REBECCA

Dear Rebecca,

In three years' time, you will be 31 years old. Where did your 20's go? Gradually they slipped away in solitude, isolation, deceit, and anger and time stood still – or so it seemed. You need to face the world, give up your secrets, be open and trust your family and true friends who are trying to help you. Only then can you stop living a lie and begin to start living a full and happy life in the real world. This will make others around you happy too.

The last few years have made you miserable, lonely, lose friends, make family terribly worried, destroy your health, feel depressed, and live a reckless, lonely, fake lifestyle. This HAS to stop! You will never achieve a house in a nice area with a boyfriend, a family, close female friends that you can enjoy spending time with (more than going out drinking with), a natural happy feeling from inside rather than scared, secretive, always thinking about something else kind of feeling, if you don't give up these ways.

You will never be able to move jobs into a career / area of work that is suitable for you rather than staying in a single job that is so flexible you can keep your old ways.

You will never take the step to belong to an orchestra or to set up your chamber group, or to teach again.

You will never meet somebody to have a relationship with, or be contented enough in your mind to continue with anybody... You will never marry, kids...

You will never be able to travel and visit even your friends in the UK, or go abroad with family or friends; never visit India. You will never go anywhere with others.

You will have to make your Mum happy again. Go away with her and be normal. Be able to do this as soon as possible, especially by 31.

Angel Just-Rights

You have a responsibility to you Nephew – don't let him grow up knowing his Auntie was ill. You need to be there for him – he'll be 3 years old in 3 years' time.

APPENDIX 2 – REBECCA'S CLARITY FLOWCHART

SITUATION
- Be strong / assertive / self-confident / fight for yourself / self-worth / dignity. INNER STRENGTH: USE IT. Know what's right and FIGHT FIGHT FIGHT.
- Blame self for being in the situation / for not thinking / for not planning. Predicament could have been avoided.

EVENT
- FREEZE FREEZE. Close eyes / remove from situation / will be over, then think about it / alone / lose voice / lose strength.
- Thinking...will be over...idiot / more planning to avoid PUT SELF IN SITUATION! BLAME! Failed again.

THOUGHTS
- Upset with self / blame self again, again, again, why, why, why. Idiot, stupid, silly, naive. Be strong / do different next time / never again / still alive. FORGET FORGET FORGET. Disgust and shame.
- Disgust / shock / surprise. WEAK WEAK WEAK WEAK WEAK failure, why so weak, why why why. Ashamed / want to die or BE BUSY. Failure and weak.

BEHAVIOURS
- Carry on with life. FORGET FORGET FORGET. You are STRONG STRONG STRONG and can deal with anything. Be with family / seek support / happy environment to forget buried secret. Fake smile / Fake life.
- Depressed / hide / no way out / no answers to a happy life. Blame self. WEAK WEAK WEAK FAILURE FAILURE FAILURE. Need to PUNISH PUNISH PUNISH and HURT HURT HURT to numb pain and blame.

EFFECTS
- RESTRICT SEVERELY / FEEL EMPTY. FAKE LIFE. Seek support / care / safety with family / see friends / go to the gym. EXERCISE. MORE MORE MORE to FORGET FORGET FORGET. KEEP BUSY and set goals to ACHIEVE ACHIEVE...Courses: music, work, friends, part-time job. MORE MORE MORE. BUSY BUSY BUSY.
- PUNISH / BINGE / FEEL RELIEF / ABSOLUTE NUMB. Tired / abuse body / sleep / depressed. WRECKLESS LIFE. Turn to friends / go out / drink / dance / clubbing. Want to FORGET, be HURT, treated badly, wreckless. PUNISH. Remember "You're strong and can deal with anything. Unhealthy ways of making money / better life / family proud. ACHIEVE ACHIEVE ACHIEVE

RESULT
- Tired / depressed / stay indoors / avoid family and friends. Not even fake life anymore. Why try. No way out.

OUTCOME
- INNER STRENGTH - To recover / positive / situations able to deal with / support there / ambitions / strength / fight. FACE EMOTIONS = OVERWHELMING = LIFE
- WEAKEST OF THE WEAK (always wins) - Give up the feelings / run away / stop fighting / go back to what feels safe and numb. No feeling of disgust / shame / failing / stupid / blame. HIDE = CONSUMED = FAKE LIFE / NO LIFE. DEATH.

CONTRIBUTIONS

Hi Micci

Here are a few personal motivators for you:

Watching your little nephew and niece growing, developing and changing throughout their lives and having you to help and see who they will become. Your Nephew loves being with you so much – he has so much fun and misses you a lot when you leave. He talks about you a lot and I know your Niece will be the same. You are amazing and so natural with them both. They love you so much and want their auntie to get better quickly.

You are my sister - I love you very very much and really want you to get well so that you feel happy and at ease. I love spending time with you and it would be nice to spend more time together. I have always felt close to you ever since we were growing up. You know you are welcome anytime and I know Kyle feels the same.

I know that I can be interfering and that I nag but I do it because I love you and care for you so deeply. Here are a few photos – I also have more for you.

Lots and lots of love, from Kerry and family x

Hey Micci,

This is a photo I found of Happy Micci who looks very content in the Jacuzzi on holiday with Dad and Little Brother! I would like Micci to be happy, healthy, grown up, content and worry free now like in this photo :-)

Little Bro x

Angel Just-Rights

Hey Micci,

Dead happy for you Micci, really really am.

I love you to pieces, I see you as the big sister that I never had and just want you to be happy and see the gorgeous girl that you are - I have attached a picture that to me sums up some of these feelings. Sending a big huge massive hug your way,

Little Sis x

Rebecca,

A beautiful intelligent girl, lost to a terrible illness, hopefully making a comeback.

Mum x

Hopefully the contents of this book will help sufferers and carers to understand more the complex and destructive nature of this illness.

Auntie Ann

To Micci

My dear friend you are a star

Don't let no-one tell you otherwise near or a far

Good times and laughs we have shared

The moments we have dared

Going around London here and there

Fear not for you shall always have a friend here

Luv Lucy

Many Shades

Angel Just-Rights

"With time I find what once was stray,

age will light and path the way,

as the sun descends and shadow grows,

the sands slip through just like water flows,

I dream a dream, it's not too late,

I dream a dream, I must not forsake,

for once there was a bird that sang,

a song that spoke of a distant land,

the heart would light up to hear of this place,

she was full of hope, beauty and grace,

her eyes were wide and full of light,

and sparkled like stars in the darkest night,

as the song went on, it would keep you gazed,

the mind would wonder and be amazed,

words are magic, I can't pretend,

with broken wings this story ends,

the sun slowly fades as time has passed,

this pictured dream was not to last,

age will light and path the way,

with time I find what once was stray..."

Rav

Dear Micci,

Friendship is about listening but not judging. Being there at the right time. A smile and a friendly face, a text that says just what you want to hear! Someone that doesn't mind if you repeat yourself and keep making the same mistakes. Gives you advice, but doesn't turn against you when you don't take it. You can be yourself, show your strengths and your weaknesses. You can be crazy, silly, sensible and sad, anything you want to be...

Micci has been a true friend.

Love Sarah x

No comments forthcoming from Spen

No comments forthcoming from Amir

Rebecca,

You have come so far and worked so hard to get where you are. All our wishes are for you to carry on towards good health.

Nursing Staff

ALMANAC

PREFACE: LISTEN AND LEARN (03/03/10 – 23/03/10)

i-EVOLUTION OF THE MEMOIR (03/03/10)

1-FORCED TO BE OPEN AND HONEST WITH MY DEAR MUM

-AND TO APOLOGISE

2-FORCED TO BE OPEN AND HONEST WITH MY DEAR AUNTIE ANN

-AND TO APOLOGISE

3-FORCED TO PICK UP THE KEY

-AND TO THANK

4-FORCED ONTO THE SAFE ROUTE

-AND GUIDED EVERY STEP OF THE WAY

5-FORCED TO SPEND 'A PERIOD OF TIME ON REFLECTION' EXACTLY AS

-'A PERIOD OF TIME ON REFLECTION'

ii-SIGNIFICANCE OF THE COMPLETION OF 'SECRETS OUT' (23/03/10)

PREAMBLE: A NOTE TO MY DEAR FAMILY (1980 – 2010)

TRUTH OF MY PAST DOUBLE LIFE-INTRODUCTION. PURPOSE AND WISH

Angel Just-Rights

~

~

~

PART 3: THE FIRST LESSON LEARNED: HONESTY BEGINS WITH YOURSELF (19/04/10...CONT.)

CHAPTER 32-DIARY ENTRIES – HONESTY-ADMIT DENIAL!

~

INTERLUDE IX ~ DREAMS ~ HOW BAD CAN THINGS GET?

...A 1 & 2-WEDNESDAY 21ST April 2010...

~

CHAPTER 32i-DIARY ENTRIES – HONESTY, CONTINUED

-BE HONEST WITH YOURSELF FIRST!

PART 4: TWO FINAL POINTS ~ THOUGHTS FOR LIFE – MUMMY AND DADDY ~ CONCLUSION (25/04/10 – CONT.)

CHAPTER 33-FINAL DIARY ENTRY: TWO FINAL POINTS

-BELIEVE IN YOURSELF, BEFORE YOU CAN TRUST IN OTHERS!

CHAPTER 34-THOUGHTS FOR LIFE – MUMMY AND DADDY ~ CONCLUSION

-MY FIRST MEMORY WITH DAD

-MY FIRST MEMORY WITH MUM

-CONCLUSION

POSTSCRIPT: A NOTE TO MY DEAR FAMILY (1980 – 2010)

Angel Just-Rights

LIVING IN REALITY... AND THE FUTURE

APPENDIX B: HOSPITAL HEADSPACE: REBECCA'S
CLARITY FLOWCHART

CONTRIBUTIONS

ALMANAC

AFTERWORD AND FURTHER INFORMATION

The following information has kindly been permitted by professors and established charities working to raise awareness and to support the affected, relating to some of the key issues touched on in this book.

This information has been included with the hope to encourage an understanding in my reader over some of the struggles that – and only now can I admit, and still only on occasion – were whole-heartedly buried / forgotten / denied strictly from myself and throughout my past life.

Dear Reader, over the last three years and with the care and support of all the amazing hospital staff and especially those at the Day Care service, I know and feel that now I am armed with a deep understanding into the illness that has stolen my life for so long and now I am at my strongest. I am now Rebecca, who wishes for health, contentedness, family, children, friends, love, peace, and am determined to fight for a life in this world, one last time.

My goal, only spoken right here: to gain back my period by my 30th birthday on 2nd July 2010 by listening to those I have learned to trust and who now I know only want the best for me and to seek comfort and security in healthy ways of coping and living, through trust and through speech rather than listening to and believing, above all others, in Angel, whose words will only destroy us.

This book is my story. *Angel* is to delight no longer.

Dear Family, I include this section most importantly for you, in-so-far as for us all to be able to keep loving one another and to move on and in times of my struggle, each of you may (I can only hope after reading my story) become willing and apt to supporting me healthily and positively, as you have all (with me) been learning to do.

It is NOT included with intentions of erupting blame or anger. I, as yourselves, only wish for us all to be happy and to live each second of our lives as fully as we are lucky enough to be able. Life is too short to busy it with anger, blame or frustration.

Angel Just-Rights

Please, I am SO SORRY for all the pain that I have selfishly put you all through. In particular, I am so sorry – Dear Mum – who, over the past three years has soulfully borne the brunt of my utterly disrespectful, bitter, cruel, callous tongue.

Please, please, please do not be angry with me, Dear, Dear Mum.

Please, please, please do not be furious with me or disown me.

I do not know how it all ended like this. I still just want to forget.

But I now understand myself more than ever and see that silence will always manifest and explode in my life in this way. I have successfully built a trusted support network around me in Day Care staff and patients that is slowly growing to involve my housemates, my immediate family and maybe even spread to my friends and colleagues, even significant others.

So as the life of Micci grows stronger still any concept of a future or reaching any dreams remain so far away, if not purely impossible. The journey is so long and scary, yet maybe I can reach it with both my own determination to succeed in sailing against everything I have previously known to be right and to have kept me feeling safe in the world always assuring me 'your only loyal protector', and also now with your understanding, support and comfort in knowing that I can trust and feel safe in listening to YOU, over the threateningly ferocious screams of Angel that constantly fight for my soul.

This is all I need and this is all I ask: please help my fight to overpower this shadow. Please be truthful and shed no blame or looks of hate, detest or scorn because I love you all so much. In times of fear and struggle I only wish to be by Dear Dad, yet I remain persevering in this world for you: Dear Mum, Dear Brother, Sister, Nephew...

Further information on eating disorders, "hurts"; other issues touched on in this book:

www.something-fishy.org

www.lanternproject.org.uk

www.womens-health.co.uk

www.nhs.co.uk

www.rcpsych.ac.uk

www.wikipedia.org

www.teethgrindingcure.com

www.analysedreams.co.uk

www.dreammoods.com

www.wix.com/RebeccaAngelParker/RebeccaAngelParker

Speaking Out for Self Discovery: A Psychotherapist's Approach to Helping People with Eating Disorders by Joanna Poppink, M. F. T, Los Angeles Psychotherapist, author of Healing Your Hungry Heart through Conari Press; http://www.eatingdisorderrecovery.com.

MICCI JUST ALRIGHT?

A: Rebecca's Rewards

Or More Hospital Wards...

July 2010

Dear Auntie Ann,

I am pleased, yet somewhat dismayed to inform you that your beautiful jigsaw now finally stands complete with decorative border but there is, however, *one final piece missing...*

...to be continued

Lightning Source UK Ltd.
Milton Keynes UK
UKOW050937250911

179263UK00001B/2/P